BUTTERFLIES
THROUGH
BINOCULARS

THE EAST

BUTTERFLIES
THROUGH
BINOCULARS

THE EAST

Jeffrey Glassberg

New York   Oxford
OXFORD UNIVERSITY PRESS

OXFORD UNIVERSITY PRESS

Oxford New York

Athens Auckland Bangkok Bogotá Bombay
Buenos Aires Calcutta Cape Town Dar es Salaam
Delhi Florence Hong Kong Istanbul Karachi
Kuala Lumpur Madras Madrid Melbourne
Mexico City Nairobi Paris Singapore
Taipai Tokyo Toronto Warsaw

and associated companies in
Berlin Ibadan

Published by Oxford University Press, Inc.
198 Madison Avenue, New York, New York 10016

Oxford is a registered trademark of Oxford University Press

Library of Congress Cataloging-in-Publication Data
Glassberg, Jeffrey.
Butterflies through binoculars: the east/
by Jeffrey Glassberg.
p. cm. Includes bibliographical references and index.
ISBN 0-19-510668-7 (pbk.)
1. Butterflies—East (U.S.)
2. Butterflies—East (U.S.)—Identification.
3. Butterfly watching—East (U.S.)
I. Title.
QL551.E16G58 1998 585.78'9'0974—dc21 97-26499

3 5 7 9 8 6 4
Printed in Hong Kong
on acid-free paper

Contents

Acknowledgments

N THE ACKNOWLEDGMENTS to the first book in this series, I said that without the active encouragement and support of my wife, Jane Vicroy
Scott, I would not have embarked on that project at all. That statement
is just as true for this guide. In addition, Jane has not only tolerated the
frequent and extensive trips afield required to produce this book, she
has actually encouraged me to take the financially nonremunerative
life pathway I now travel. I can only hope that this work leads to
increasing public joy in butterflies, and that this enjoyment leads to an
ethic, and a movement, to save our butterflies before it is too late, so
that Jane's support, her confidence, and her love, are repaid by causing
the world to be just a little bit better than it would have been otherwise.

Without the help of my son, Matt Scott, this book would probably
have never been completed. In addition to setting up computer hard-
ware, he quickly learned how to use the software required to do the
plate layouts and create the maps, and then patiently taught me how
to use them. At the next-to-last moment, some changes were made to
the design program for the maps and phenograms; Jim Springer provided tremendous help in accomplishing these changes.

Because almost all of the information contained within the first
field guide of this series, *Butterflies through Binoculars: Boston-New York-
Washington*, was useful in creating the present guide, all of those who
helped in the creation of that work are owed thanks here as well. I
hereby incorporate the acknowledgments section of that guide in this
work by referring the reader to that guide. I would also like to thank
Kirk Jensen for his help with that first book.

Many people have contributed to the creation of this field guide. In
fact, so many people have helped that I fear I may have omitted some
contributors. If I have, please accept my apologies. Contributing

butterfly reports and locality information that helped me find butter
flies for photography were: Dave Norris and Dave Wagner for
Connecticut; Dave Bagget, John Calhoun, Rick Cech, Harry Darrow,
Tom Emmel, Kathy Malone, Marc Minno, and Charles Sekerman for
Florida; Tim Orwig and Dennis Schlicht for Iowa; Jeff Ingraham and
Harry Zirlin for Maryland and Virginia; Brian Cassie and Dick Hildreth
for Massachusetts; Dave Ahrenholz, Robert Dana, Tim Orwig, and
Dennis Schlicht for Minnesota (you betcha); Bob Moritz for Nebraska;
Dale Schweitzer and Wade and Sharon Wander for New Jersey; Bob
Dirig and Kathy Schneider for New York; Harry LeGrand, Steven Hall,
and Bo Sullivan for North Carolina; David Parshall for Ohio; Nora
Jones for Oklahoma; Francois Lessard for Quebec; Hoe Chuah, H.A.
Freeman, Joann Karges, and Ken Steigman for Texas; Tom Allen for
West Virginia; and Sue Borkin, Mike Grimm (how was he to know that
I would fall into Kangaroo Lake?), and Ann Swengel for Wisconsin.

Sue Borkin accompanied me on a successful trip to find Swamp
Metalmarks in Wisconsin. Brian Cassie set up a rendezvous at Wilsons
Mills that resulted in a Bog Fritillary and Jutta Arctics. Chuck
Conaway and Nora Jones took me to Pontotoc Ridge Preserve in
Oklahoma; I was rewarded with beautiful fields of flowers and some
great butterflies. I followed Edna Dunbar's streaking path up Mt
Greylock to Early Hairstreaks. With the able field help of Valerie Giles
and Dave Wagner I found some of the last remaining Persius
Duskywings in the Northeast. Without the presence of Eric Hoffman,
I never would have found Mitchell's Satyrs at Fort Bragg. Francois
Lessard and I spent an exciting day at Lanoraie, Quebec, reveling in an
abundance of Bog Elfins. Bob Moritz joined me for forays into
Nebraska and South Dakota while Jerry Nagel showed me northeastern Tennessee and Diana Fritillaries. Tim Orwig and Dennis Schlicht
met me at a prairie remnant in Minnesota where we thrilled to one of
the few remaining populations of Dakota Skippers and Poweshiek
Skipperlings. My heartfelt thanks to all of you for giving your time and
efforts to help this project.

In preparing this work, there were many occasions when I exam-
ined museum specimens for identification features and for geographical and temporal distributions. I thank Jim Miller, Fred Rindge, and

Cal Snyder at the American Museum of Natural History, NY and John Burns and Bob Robbins at the United States National Museum, Smithsonian Institution, Washington, D.C. for allowing me to examine specimens under their care.

A critical feature of this book is the photographs. After I laid out the plates, Guy Tudor made several useful suggestions that improved that layout. Although I have traveled extensively in the East for years, searching for and photographing butterflies, still, in the end, there were some 38 of the 629 photographs needed for this book that I did not have. The following individuals generously provided their own photographs to fill the gaps (see photo credits appendix for specific list of photos): John Acorn, Chris Adams, Dave Ahrenholz, Ron Boender, Derb Carter, Steve Cary, Rick Cech, Charlie Covell, Robert Dana, Larry Darrow, Tom Emmel, Stephen Hall, Jeff Ingraham, Bernard Jackson, Rich Kelly, Jack Levy, Jim Nation, Philip Nordin, Peter W. Post, Don Riepe, Joe Spano, Pat Sutton, and Harry Zirlin.

An important feature of this guide are the range maps. After constructing a preliminary set of about 275 maps, using all published, and much unpublished, information, I sent these maps to active field workers throughout the East for review. The following reviewers, arranged by state, or province, of residence greatly increased the accuracy of the maps. Many of the reviewers were knowledgeable about whole regions. I am indebted to them for taking the considerable time required to closely inspect these maps and suggest changes, based upon their first-hand knowledge: **Connecticut,** Larry Gall; **Florida,** John Calhoun, Marc Minno, Jeff Slotten; **Georgia,** James K. Adams; **Illinois,** George Burger, David Hess; **Indiana,** John Shuey; **Iowa,** Ronald Harms, Tim Orwig, Dennis Schlicht; **Kansas,** Marvin D. Schwilling; **Louisiana,** Gary Noel Ross; **Maryland,** Richard Smith; **Massachusetts,** Brian Cassie; **Michigan,** Steven J. Mueller, Mogens C. Nielsen; **Minnesota,** David Patterson, John Weber; **Mississippi,** Leroy C. Koehn; Bryant Mather; **Missouri,** Richard Heitzman; **Nebraska,** Neil Dankert; Jim Reiser, Steve Spomer; **New Jersey,** Pat Sutton, Dale Schweitzer; **New York,** Robert Dirig; Mark Gretch, Tim McCabe, Guy Tudor; **North Carolina,** Harry LeGrand; **North Dakota,** Ronald Royer; **Ohio,** David Parshall; **Oklahoma,** Chuck Conaway,

John Nelson; **Ontario,** Alan Hanks, Don LaFontaine, Kirk Zufelt
Pennsylvania, Curtis Lehman, David Wright; **Quebec,** Victor Hellebuyck
Francois Lessard; **South Dakota,** Gary Marrone; **Tennessee,** Jerry Nagle
Texas, Charles Bordelon, Jr., Hoe-Hin Chuah; H.A. Freeman, Joann
Karges, Stephen Williams; **Vermont,** Don Miller; **Virginia,** William T. Hark
Harry Pavulaan; **West Virginia,** Tom Allen; **Wisconsin,** Ann Swengel.

In addition, most of these correspondents provided information
about nectar sources in their areas that was used to compile the list of
important nectar sources that appears on page 9.

I hope that the phenograms shown in many species accounts, dis-
playing average flight times and abundances at four locations in the
East, will allow most readers to "quadrangulate" local flight times in
most parts of the East. Many thanks are due to Rick Cech, Harry
LeGrand, Jr., Gary Noel Ross, Ann B. Swengel, and Jim Springer, for
the considerable time and effort required to provide the information
used to create and compile these phenograms.

A draft of this manuscript was reviewed by Harry LeGrand, Bob
Robbins, Jane V. Scott, and Ann Swengel, each of whom made many
corrections and provided many suggestions that greatly improved the
final product. Thank you all for for your tremendous help with this.
Inevitably errors remain. Please let me know of the ones you locate,
especially if they are substantive errors.

Lastly, I would like to thank you, the reader, for using this book, a
step that links you to the growing butterflying community. Join with
us on an exciting lifetime adventure that is earth-friendly and good for
you—butterflying is fat-free and yet still full of flavor!

INTRODUCTION

WHO DOESN'T LOVE BUTTERFLIES? Beautiful and graceful, varied and enchanting, small but approachable, butterflies lead you to the sunny side of life. And everyone deserves a little sunshine. For centuries, peoples throughout the world have associated butterflies with freedom and the human soul. In today's complicated era, ever more people have a reawakened sense of connection to nature and a desire to participate in the natural world. Helping to make this connection, butterflies are the wildlife for the 21st century. Why? No matter where you live, there are sure to be butterflies near you—if only you will look! Unlike grizzly bears, butterflies do not need miles of wilderness to survive. They can thrive even within our urban and suburban areas—the parts of the continent where most people actually live. Surveys show that butterflies—which do not bite, sting, or carry diseases—are the type of wildlife that people most want to see near their homes. Grizzlies, as magnificent as they are, don't make the list. Butterflies aren't perfect, it's true—they don't sing very well for example (actually not at all). The silver lining (for humans) is that butterflies also don't hear very well! So, if, like me, you tend to chatter a lot with your companions and do not know the meaning of the word pianissimo, you needn't worry. You won't scare the butterflies away (other humans are a different story).

Besides being just plain fun, butterflying is rewarding in many ways. It serves as a stimulus to go outdoors, and engage in healthy physical activity. It is a challenging and gratifying experience to learn to identify butterflies, especially skippers. Since so much remains to be learned about these wonderful insects, your knowledge of the butterflies of your area may make a contribution to science. Lastly, butterflying allows one to monitor the local environment. Knowledge of the stability, or decline, of local butterfly populations is an important tool in environmental protection.

The purpose of this book is to enable you to identify adult butterflies in the eastern United States and southeastern Canada. The area covered by this guide is the eastern United States and the southern part of Canada west to a line running diagonally from just south of Houston, Texas northwest to the western edge of Manitoba, as shown in the figure on page 215. This book treats all species regularly found within this area. The world of butterflies is multifaceted, and as you learn to identify butterflies you will almost certainly become interested in many other aspects of their world. In this guide, however, many interesting topics related to butterfly study are either not included, or are treated in a cursory fashion, because inclusion of this material would create a bulkier, less portable book—a book that would work less well as a field guide. If you are interested in learning more about butterfly natural history, systematics, ecology, or gardening, please refer to the bibliography where many fine books covering these, and related subjects, are listed.

Binoculars

I strongly urge you to get a pair of close-focusing binoculars. Butterflies are generally small making them difficult to see well with the naked eye. Good, close-focusing, binoculars, will present a sharp image when the butterfly you are viewing is less than 6 ft. away. The butterfly will fill your field of vision, giving you a new view of the world. Although you'll be able to identify many butterflies without binoculars, you won't see much of the incredible detail, and shimmering colors, that makes butterflying so rewarding. Without close-focusing binoculars, identifying skippers and hairstreaks may well be hopeless. If you use standard-issue binoculars, you will be backing up constantly, making the butterfly appear smaller and defeating the purpose for which you brought along the binoculars in the first place.

Other factors to consider in buying a pair of binoculars are power, size, weight, field of view, clarity, and brightness. Two numbers (for example 8x42) describe some basic features of binoculars. The first number indicates the power of magnification. Eight-power binoculars will make an object eight feet away appear as large as if it were one foot away. The second number is the diameter of the objective lens (in millimeters). In general, the larger this number the brighter the image will be.

As of this writing, binoculars that have the requisite close-focusing eature for butterflying are: Bausch & Lomb 8x42 and 10x42 Elites; Cabela 8x and 10x; Celestron 8x42 Regals; Minolta 8x22 and 10x25 Pocket binoculars and 6x and 8x UC binoculars; and Swift 8x Trilytes. I am sure that others will soon appear. Ask your butterflying friends what binoculars they are using, or visit the North American Butterfly Association's website (the address is on page 215) for the latest information. Test the binoculars you intend to buy for close-focusing, and to ensure that they feel comfortable for you. Which pair is best is a matter of personal preference. I use 10x pocket binoculars but many people find these difficult to use and prefer one of the other binoculars listed above.

How to Identify Butterflies

If you are just beginning to butterfly, the first step is to learn to recognize the six families of butterflies found in our area—swallowtails, whites & yellows, gossamer-wings, metalmarks, brushfoots, and skippers. This shouldn't be too difficult because, in general, butterflies belonging to these different families have different wing shapes, sizes, colors, and behaviors. Certain subfamilies are also easy to recognize, for example, coppers, hairstreaks, and blues among the gossamer-wings, and spreading skippers and grass-skippers among the skippers. Refer to the short discussion of each butterfly family and subfamily directly preceding the species accounts for that family or subfamily. Once you know what family or subfamily the butterfly belongs to, go to the appropriate plate(s) and see if you recognize the butterfly you have found. Many species, such as the Zebra Swallowtail on plate 1, are so distinctive that you will probably immediately recognize the illustration.

With butterflies, you can make identification much simpler by asking yourself: Where am I? What time of the year is it? What habitat is this? Is this butterfly closely associating with a particular plant? Many species are found only in certain areas. Some fly only in the early spring, others only in mid-summer. Most species are found in some types of habitats and not others, and related species often are associated with different caterpillar foodplants.

For example, if you are looking at a green-colored hairstreak, you will see on plate 19 that there are five possible species. Look at the plate and read the notes on the facing page. Most species can be identified by observing certain "field marks" that distinguish that species from sim ilar species. On the facing page you will also learn that Junipe Hairstreaks are found amidst stands of red cedars while similar Hessel' Hairstreaks are found in white cedar swamps. If you are standing in dry field with red cedars, it is extremely unlikely that you are observ ing a Hessel's Hairstreak. *Probable* (but not certain) identification b habitat works well for butterflies, much better than it does for birds, fo example. Also, look carefully at the range maps. Silver-bande Hairstreaks are found only in southern Florida, while Early Hairstreak live only in the northeast and in the Appalachians, and are rare. So although strays are not impossible, over most of the East, if you see green-colored hairstreak, it is almost certainly a Juniper Hairstreak!

Here's another example. I was in Gainesville, Florida looking at rather small, dark duskywing with some small white spots at th forewing subapex but lacking a forewing cell spot. Its small size and th absence of a forewing cell spot ruled out Juvenal's and Horace' Duskywings while the white forewing subapical spots ruled ou Sleepy and Dreamy Duskywings. It lacked the prominent mottling o Mottled Duskywings (which have not been seen in the area anyway) leaving Persius, Columbine, Wild Indigo, and Zarucco Duskywing a the remaining possibilities. Looking at the range maps, you can see tha Persius and Columbine Duskywings do not occur anywhere nea Gainesville. This left Wild Indigo and Zarucco duskywings, two specie whose females can be exceptionally difficult to separate—and this wa a female. Zaruccos are usually larger than Wild Indigos, and this indi vidual was smaller than any Zarucco I had seen. Although Wild Indig Duskywings have not been found yet in northern Florida, they hav been found just north of there and their range is expanding. So thought, "Is this a Wild Indigo?" The butterfly answered the questio for me when she flew to a very small black locust and laid an egg! Blac locust is the caterpillar foodplant for Zarucco Duskywings, but not fo Wild Indigo Duskywings.

If you are seriously motivated to learn butterfly identification, prob ably the best approach is to look at the plates in this book wheneve possible. This way you can burn the images of the different specie into your brain so that when you encounter a species in the field tha you have never seen before, it will look familiar to you. You should als ead the full species accounts, these often include more identification information than is included on the pages facing the plates.

Remember that the appearance of a species of butterfly can vary greatly from individual to individual and that the appearance of the same individual can vary with the quality and quantity of light. Often when a species undergoes a population explosion the range of variation increases even more. Additionally, the appearance of the same individual butterfly will change over time. When it first emerges from its chrysalis it will be very bright and in pristine condition. Often its wings will have a beautiful sheen. As the adult butterfly ages, scales will be lost and wings will become frayed and torn. Its color may fade. Identifying the last Northern Broken-Dash of the season can be a real challenge! Sometimes identifying an individual butterfly is too great a challenge for anyone and it should be left as "unidentified." This might be because the butterfly was too worn, not seen well enough, or was too easy to confuse with similar species. As you gain experience, you will begin to identify an ever greater percentage of the butterflies you encounter. I strongly recommend that you **use more than one field mark to identify a butterfly that is unusual for the location, habitat, or season in which you find it.** It is possible to find aberrant individuals that lack a certain spot, or have an extra line, or have a different color. For real rarities, it is best to rely on a combination of marks.

How to Find Butterflies

Location, location, location. Butterflies can be seen almost everywhere, from the skyscraper canyons of Manhattan, to the verdant meadows of the Ozarks, from the great swamps of the southeastern United States to the dry prairies of Manitoba. Some areas, however, are a tad more productive than others. The most productive habitats for butterflies, those that have the greatest diversity of species and the largest numbers of individuals, are open areas with natural vegetation. Butterflies are more common in open areas because, as with people, most butterflies like sunshine. They are more common in areas with native plants because, for the most part, these are the plants that caterpillars require as foodplants. So, for example, you will find very few species of butterflies on large manicured lawns—these are essentially biological deserts.

Some of the best habitats for butterflies are wet meadows, brush fields, oak savannas, and prairies. Look for areas with a great variety of vegetation—butterfly diversity is usually correlated with the complexity of the landscape. Some specialized and geographically limited habitats harbor special butterfly species. Boundaries between two different types of habitats will usually have more butterflies than either habitat by itself. Thus butterflying an open meadow adjacent to a woodland will be more productive than searching either in a woodland or in a meadow distant from a woodland.

How do you find butterfly habitats? One way is by looking at a map for, and then visiting, the local, county, state, or national parks near where you live. These parks will often have good habitats for butterflies. Check out the nature preserves in your area—The Nature Conservancy, for example, has important preserves in many parts of our region (see page 216 for the address)—as these may harbor rare species. A second method is to search for power line cuts or railroad right-of-ways and walk along these corridors. These narrow corridors often slice through a variety of habitats and may provide an excellent habitat themselves. Another approach is to randomly drive along roads, looking for abandoned fields and other likely habitats. If you drive along dirt roads, a bonus is that the dirt roads themselves are often a good place to find butterflies.

For finding species outside your area, check the range maps and habitat section for the species. In addition, for many species, the location at which the photograph of that butterfly was taken may be a good area to find the butterfly (this information is given on the page facing the plates).

Timing is important. To see all the species in your area you will have to be in the field periodically throughout the warmer months. The elfins only fly in the early spring and Leonard's Skipper only flies in the fall. In between these extremes, many species fly for perhaps only a month in the summer. Because behavioral patterns differ among species, you will find the most butterflies by searching at different times of day. Some butterflies become active at dawn. However, luckily for people like me—who prefer a leisurely breakfast—the peak of butterfly activity is probably from around 10:30 A.M. to about 3:00 P.M., rather than at dawn.

Friends are important too. Unless you teach third grade you don't have eyes in the back of your head. Butterflying with a small group of friends allows each of you to spot some butterflies that the others would have missed.

Butterfly Concentrators

Having found a likely looking habitat for butterflies, you now will want to search for the butterflies themselves. Sometimes butterflies are everywhere, by the thousands. But many times, the numbers of butterflies are much smaller. When this is the case, your search for butterflies can be helped by locating certain environmental features that concentrate butterflies.

Flowers. The great majority of adult butterflies feed by nectaring at flowers. Almost all flowers are used at some time by some butterflies, but some flowers are much more attractive to butterflies than others. Some of the best, widespread, wild nectar sources for spring, summer, and fall are listed on page 9. Other plants may be important in your area. Locating stands of attractive flowers is the easiest way to find many butterfly species. If you are not familiar with these plants, you will probably want to consult a wildflower guide.

It has become popular for authors of butterfly books to list all the flowers at which they have seen a butterfly species nectaring. This is rather like listing all the trees on which one has seen a bird perched. It is information—but fairly meaningless information. Although flowers differ greatly in their attractiveness to butterflies, within broad groups of related butterflies there is little variation from butterfly species to butterfly species in the flowers they find attractive. Yes, larger butterflies with longer tongues will be able to nectar at flowers with longer floral tubes, and yes there is variation from butterfly family to family in flower preference, but, with a few exceptions, one grass-skippers' preference will be the same as another's.

Hilltops. Many butterflies will congregate on the tops of hills. See the behavior section, below, for more about hilltopping.

Mud puddles. A wide variety of species will congregate at damp sand or gravel.

Trails and dirt roads. Not only are butterflies easier to see along a trail but the trail itself serves to concentrate some of them. Believe it or not,

many butterflies, such as buckeyes, prefer trails to undisturbed vege
tation. If the trail is through a woodland, it needs to be wide enough t
allow in sunshine to be a useful butterfly concentrator.

Caterpillar foodplants. Many species of butterflies have caterpilla
that will use only a few, or even just one, plant species as a foodplan
These special plants act to concentrate the adult butterflies as wel
since females will come to these plants to lay their eggs. So, look fc
hackberry trees to find Hackberry Emperors, and for yuccas to fin
Yucca Giant-Skippers. Each species account includes a section o
caterpillar foodplants.

What is a Butterfly?

Butterflies are a group of evolutionarily related animals. They ar
grouped as part of the class Insecta, and together with the moths cor
stitute the order Lepidoptera. This word derives from the Greek word
for scale (*lepid*) and wing (*ptera*). True butterflies (superfamil
Papilionoidea) and skippers (superfamily Hesperioidea) are usuall
considered together as butterflies, and separately from moths. It
generally easy to distinguish between butterflies and moths.

Almost all of our butterflies are active exclusively during the da
while the great majority of moths are active only at night. Som
moths are active during the day, but these can usually be identified b
their flight which is characteristically stiff and very erratic. This
because most moths have structures, called a frenulum and a retinac
ulum, that hook the forewing to the hindwing. Butterflies lack thes
structures and thus, in general, fly much more gracefully than moth
When seen clearly, our butterflies are distinguished from moths by th
shape of their antennas. Butterflies and skippers have a club (
swelling) at the end of their antennas while almost all moths do nc
(see page 41).

Butterfly Biology
Life Cycle

Each butterfly goes through four distinct stages in its life: egg, cate
pillar, pupa (chrysalis) and adult. The change from caterpillar to pup
to adult butterfly involves major changes in appearance. This proces
of great physical change, called "metamorphosis," has captured th

Some Important Natural Nectar Sources

SPRING
Dandelion *Taraxacum officinale*
Blueberries *Vaccinium* spp.
Blackberries/dewberries *Rubus* spp.
Wild plums/wild cherries *Prunus* spp.
Red clover *Trifolium pratense*
Redbud *Cercis canadensis*
Blue flag *Iris versicolor* (north)
Wild strawberry *Fragaria virginiana* (north)
Lantana *Lantana* (Texas)

SUMMER
Common milkweed *Asclepias syriaca*
Orange milkweed *Asclepias tuberosa*
Swamp milkweed *Asclepias incarnata*
Dogbanes *Apocynum* spp.
Sumacs *Rhus* spp.
Coneflowers *Echinacea* spp.
Thistles *Cirsium* spp.
Vervains *Verbena* spp.
Bergamots *Monarda* spp.
New Jersey tea *Ceanothus americanus*
Pickerelweed *Pontederia cordata* (south)
Cow vetch/purple vetch *Vicia cracca/americana* (northeast)
Spanish needles *Bidens alba* (Florida)
Lantanas *Lantana* spp. (Florida & Texas)

FALL
Asters *Aster* spp.
Joe-pye weeds *Eupatorium* spp.
Goldenrods *Solidago* spp.
Blazing-stars *Liatris* spp.
Ironweeds *Vernonia* spp.
Pickerelweed *Pontederia cordata* (south)
Purple loosestrife *Lythrum salicaria* (northeast)
Spanish needles *Bidens alba* (Florida)

imagination of peoples throughout the world. Many native peoples in the Americas, including the Papagos and the Aztecs, have myths and gods based upon butterfly transformations.

EGG

An adult female that has mated has the capacity to lay fertilized eggs. A considerable part of her day is spent searching for appropriate plant on which to lay her eggs. A butterfly usually recognizes the right plant by a combination of sight and smell. Butterflies have a very acute sense of smell. They have chemoreceptors (cells that respond to "tastes" and "smells") on their antennas and the bottom ends of their legs. Most species lay their eggs on a plant that the newly hatched caterpillar will eat. Some species lay only one egg per plant. Others place a mass of eggs together. Some species lay their eggs mainly on flower buds; others place them on the undersides of leaves; still others lay their eggs at the base of a tree. How many eggs a particular female lays varies greatly from species to species. Over the course of their lives some butterflies will lay only a few dozen eggs. Most probably lay a few hundred, while some, such as Regal Fritillaries, lay a few thousand. The eggs themselves are quite interesting; each butterfly family has a different egg architecture.

CATERPILLAR

When the egg hatches, usually after less than a week, a tiny caterpillar emerges. This voracious eating machine spends almost all of its time eating and growing. As it rapidly increases in size, it outgrows its outer skin (called an exoskeleton). The old skin splits and is shed, revealing a new, larger, and baggier skin below. This process happens a number of times (usually three or four) over the course of about two or three weeks. The great majority of caterpillars do not successfully become butterflies. Most are either eaten by predators, especially wasps and birds, or they are parasitized, usually by one of many species of parasitic wasps or flies, or they become infected by fungal or viral pathogens. The world of caterpillars is a fascinating one, with varied shapes and colors, full of interesting behavior—much of which is used to avoid predators. Identifying caterpillars is a vast subject—one requiring its own book.

When a caterpillar has grown to full size, it attaches itself to a support and becomes a pupa. Sometimes this happens on the caterpillar food-plant itself, but more often the caterpillar wanders away from the food-plant and attaches itself to a twig or a blade of grass. The moulted caterpillar, now encased in a hard outer shell (chrysalis), becomes a pupa—seemingly lifeless and inert. But inside this shell, an amazing transformation is taking place. The tissues and structures of the cater-pillar are being broken down and replaced with the tissues and struc-tures of the adult butterfly. If development proceeds without impediment, within a week or two an adult butterfly will emerge. If not, the pupa may enter a resting state for a few months, or overwinter.

ADULT

Eventually, when the adult inside the chrysalis is fully formed, the chrysalis splits open, and the adult butterfly emerges. Often this hap-pens very early in the morning. In the chrysalis, the wings are wrapped tightly around the butterfly's body. After the adult emerges, its wings unfurl as fluid pumps through the wing veins. This is a very vulnerable time in a butterfly's life, as it basks in the sunshine to warm itself and to harden and set its wings. Once the adult butterfly emerges from the chrysalis it grows no larger. So if you see a small butterfly, it is not a baby butterfly—it is a fully formed adult.

Lifespan

Most adult butterflies live for a relatively brief time. Some small blues may live only a few weeks, while large brush-footed butterflies, such as Mourning Cloaks and Monarchs, may live up to about eight months. Most adult butterflies can live about two to four weeks, if they are not eaten by predators, such as crab spiders, dragonflies, birds, and lizards.

Broods

The adults of some species of butterflies fly only at a particular time of the year. Adults of single-brooded species all emerge from their chrysalids at roughly the same time, i.e., over a period of a few weeks or, less commonly, a few months. For example, Brown Elfins fly only in the early spring, then the adults mate and the females lay eggs. The

caterpillars that soon hatch feed on flowers and young fruit for abou
three weeks and then pupate. The pupas enter a resting period (dia
pause) during the summer, fall, and winter and new adults emerge the
following spring. So, Brown Elfins are single-brooded.

Some species have two or more broods each year. Adult Junipe
Hairstreaks, closely related to Brown Elfins, also fly in the spring. Bu
when the caterpillars grow up, many of the resulting pupas, rathe
than overwintering as the Brown Elfins do, quickly develop into adul
butterflies and this second brood flies in the mid- to late-summer. The
offspring of this second brood then overwinter as pupas and the result
ing adults fly the next spring. Usually, the adults of an early brood wil
have subtle differences in appearance from those of a later brood.

In general, the farther north one goes, the summer is shorter and so
the more likely it becomes that butterflies have time for only a single
generation per year. In the warm South, most species have more than
one brood each year.

Let's go back to the basic concept of broods. When we say that
Brown Elfins fly only in the early spring, is this absolutely true?
Probably not. Although I know of no reports of Brown Elfins flying in
the summer or fall (notwithstanding mountain populations where
it's springtime in July), I am sure that, occasionally, a Brown Elfin
adult will emerge from its chrysalis at an "inappropriate" time of the
year. Nature is not absolute. Variation and flexibility lead to new
avenues for a species to explore. Sometime, somewhere, a Brown
Elfin will either be subjected to unusual environmental conditions, or
it will carry a mutation, that will cause it to emerge in July, or August,
or September! But, these events are certainly very rare, and if they
have occurred they have probably gone unnoticed because there
have been so few butterfliers. I predict that eventually, many species
of butterflies will be found to fly (very, very rarely) way outside their
usual flight times.

In a similar vein, we know that most single-brooded butterflies take
one year to complete their life cycle and that some butterflies, mainly
those that occur in the far north, may require two years to complete
theirs. We are now discovering that even in the temperate zone, especially in arid areas, some individual pupas of certain species may
remain dormant for two, three, or even four years! Because a loca

population may be wiped out by drought, or flood, or disease, it makes sense to have a small percentage of a population remain dormant for a number of years. It may be that most butterfly species have this capability.

In addition to helping you know when to search for a butterfly, knowledge of broods is helpful in understanding butterfly ecology and evolution. Often, where a species is single-brooded, the farther south one goes the larger will be the individuals of that species. Then, when one reaches the area where the species becomes two-brooded, individuals are often smaller. This transition zone between single and double-brooded populations of the same species is one of tension. The shift from one to two broods may create something of a barrier to the free flow of genetic material between the populations, because the adults may not fly at the same time of year. Because different plants may be available south or north of the transition zone, the two populations may become ecologically segregated as well. It may be that this one-brood/two-brood shift sometimes plays a role in speciation events.

Distribution

Why is a butterfly species found in one place and not another? Part of the answer is straightforward. Temperature extremes may limit the range of a butterfly. For example, if none of the life stages of a species can survive freezing temperatures, then a species will not be resident in areas that have occasional winter freezes. Some species may be sensitive to extreme summer heat. Others may be particularly sensitive to fungal diseases encouraged by high humidity. If a butterfly depends upon a particular caterpillar foodplant, then you will not normally find that butterfly in areas without that plant. But some caterpillar foodplants are abundant and widespread while the butterfly that depends upon that plant is scarce and very locally distributed. In these cases, obviously other factors are at work. For many species, it may be that availability of adult nectar sources is a more important limiting factor than the availability of caterpillar foodplants. Or perhaps other features of the environment are critical. For species whose males set up territories, the number of available perches that are "just right" may be important. Some butterfly species appear to depend upon certain species of ants to properly tend the caterpillars. With most species, we really do not know, and a lot of work remains to be done.

At least some butterfly distributions may be accidental, a result of a history during which the species found its way to some suitable areas but not others. Or a previously widespread butterfly may now exist mainly in small relict populations over part of its range, like Melissa Arctic and probably Mitchell's Satyr. And, butterfly distributions change over time. So, over the past 20 years, Regal Fritillaries have withdrawn from almost all of the northeastern United States, while Common Ringlets and the northern race of Silvery Blues have greatly expanded southward. If global warming becomes a reality, we may see major changes in the ranges of many butterfly species.

Behavior

Because so little is known about much of butterfly behavior, this is an area where patient observation can increase our knowledge. Here are a few types of behaviors to look for when you are watching butterflies.

BASKING

Butterflies are cold-blooded—their body temperature largely depends on the ambient temperature. When it is cold outside, butterflies want to warm up and employ two different basking strategies to do so. Some butterflies sit in the sunshine in an exposed spot (or even better, on a warm rock) and open their wings. This allows the sun's rays to warm them. Some spring and cold-climate flying white butterflies are especially adapted to this type of dorsal basking. They open their white wings part way and sit in the sunshine. The sun's rays bounce off the angled white wings and are directed to the black body, where the warmth does the most good.

Other butterflies engage in lateral basking. These butterflies, including many of our spring hairstreaks, sit in the sunshine with their wings closed. Then they tilt their bodies so that the plane of their wings is perpendicular to the sun's rays, the most efficient way to capture the warming energy of the sun.

HILLTOPPING

Many humans go to singles bars because prospective mates may be concentrated at these locations. Hilltops are the butterfly equivalent of ingles bars. The males of many butterfly species may be most easily found by climbing to the top of the highest hill in the vicinity, especially if the top of the hill is open and if at least some of the slopes are quite steep. Here, the males patrol the area looking for females or they select a favored perch and wait. Unmated females also fly up here (otherwise the system wouldn't work), but already mated females spend more time elsewhere, looking for hostplants and nectar.

MUDPUDDLING

Many butterflies, especially males, congregate at damp sand. Here they imbibe salts along with the water. Seeing a large mud puddle party with many species of swallowtails and other butterflies is a thrilling experience.

COURTSHIP

We have little detailed knowledge about most butterflies' courtship patterns. Males of many species stake out territories. They then police these, either by flying back and forth, or by occasionally sallying forth from a favored perch, making sure that they're the only male around when a female saunters into the territory. Although the main objective would seem to be to drive away other males of the same species, some aggressive males try to drive off everything that moves, including birds and sometimes humans! Some butterflies have almost no courtship displays. The males simply fly up to a landed female, and if she is receptive, mate immediately.

Other butterflies behave differently. Most male hairstreaks set up territories, then fly up to greet a female flying through their territory. He flies with her until she lands, then lands next to her, usually facing her, and fans his wings. This disperses the "mating perfume" (a pheromone) that most male hairstreaks have in special patches of scales on the upper side of their forewings. Many other butterflies are also territorial, while another group of males, taking the initiative, uses patrolling behavior to locate females—they just keep flying till they find them. Male Barred Yellows land alongside a female and flick open their forewing closest to the female. They place their forewing right in front of the female, touching her antennas, presumably to dazzle her with their great bar! Most males of a given species will gen-

erally engage in either patrolling or territorial behavior, but not both
But males can sometimes switch between perching and patrolling and
this is sometimes related to population density.

Migration

Perhaps surprisingly, many butterfly species undertake migrations
We know very little about these movements. Here again is an area
where careful observation by an increasing number of butterfliers will
provide real new information.

While all butterflies move around, most don't migrate in the traditional sense. What they do is to disperse in a random direction from the
site where they emerged from the chrysalis. Some adults immediately
fly away from their emergence site, others stay around for most of their
life, then wander off as they get older, while some never leave. If none
of the population ever left the original site, butterflies would never be
able to colonize new, suitable, sites. Since a high proportion of butterfly
species live in habitats that disappear over time (meadows being
replaced by woodlands, etc.), this dispersal is critical to the survival of
butterfly species. So, a stray butterfly can appear almost anywhere.

Many butterflies that spend the summer in the northern United
States and in Canada cannot survive northern winters. Each year, as
the weather becomes warmer, butterflies from the southern United
States, or from Mexico, fly north to repopulate these regions. Species
that move northward each year include Cloudless Sulphur, Little
Yellow, Painted Lady, Red Admiral, Clouded Skipper, Sachem, and
Fiery Skipper. For some species these northward dispersals are gradual,
but, in especially good years, one can see Painted Ladies and Cloudless
Sulphurs streaming out of northern Mexico.

For most species the reverse migration, south in the fall, is usually less
obvious, but occasionally spectacular. On one September day I observed
about 6000 Monarchs, 4000 Red Admirals, 4000 Question Marks, and
2000 Mourning Cloaks flying south through a 10-foot wide path adjacent to a beach in New York City. Each year in southern Texas, as thousands of Queens and *Phoebis* fly southward, many are killed by cars on
the East-West crossroads. The exact nature of these migrations is still not
well understood. With many of these species we are not sure where
they spend the winter. With tortoiseshells and anglewings in particular,

may be that the same individual who migrates south in the fall returns its more northern home early in the spring. But, no one has yet been ble to follow a butterfly to know for sure!

However, we do know that most Monarchs east of the Rockies pend the winter in roosts in the mountains of central Mexico. lthough we are beginning to understand something about how Monarchs orient their migratory flight, how they manage to find and recognize these highly localized sites is a complete mystery. There is a new population of Monarchs each year and so none of the Monarchs have ever been to these Mexican overwintering sites before!

Butterfly Gardening

If you have a garden, even a small one, the chances are good that you can enjoy butterflies right at home. Many common garden flowers, such as zinnias and marigolds, are attractive to butterflies. If you plant special plants such as butterfly bush (*Buddleia*) and orange milkweed *Asclepias tuberosa*)(called butterflyweed in the horticultural trade) you will attract many of the butterflies in your neighborhood to your garden while these plants are in bloom. Although somewhat more difficult to obtain and maintain than common garden flowers, I encourage you to try some of the native wildflowers that are excellent nectar sources for butterflies (see the list on page 9). One advantage of this approach is that the butterflies in your neighborhood may already be familiar with these plants, and thus have learned to come to them for nectar. Of course, the species of butterflies that you attract will depend on the species that are present in your vicinity. If you live close to woodlands and meadows, you will attract many more species than if you live in a suburban development. But even flower gardens in Manhattan can attract a fair number of species.

An important point to keep in mind when planning a butterfly garden is that you must have caterpillars before you can have adult butterflies. The best butterfly gardens include many caterpillar foodplants (see Table 1) so the butterfly garden will "grow" butterflies, not just waylay some of the adults that happen to be in the neighborhood. If you are interested in a specific butterfly species, look up the account for that species and note its caterpillar foodplant. If you live within the range of the butterfly, and if there are natural populations close by,

Table 1 Some Caterpillar Foodplants (Suitable for the Garden) of Widespread Butterflies

PLANT NAME	FOODPLANT FOR THESE CATERPILLAR SPECIES
Asters (*Aster*)	Pearl Crescent
Cassias (*Cassia*)	Little Yellow, Sleepy Orange, Cloudless Sulphur, Orange-barred Sulphur
Citrus (*Citrus*)	Giant Swallowtail
False Nettle (*Boehmeria cylindrica*)	Red Admiral
Fennel (*Foeniculum vulgare*)	Black Swallowtail
Hackberries (*Celtis*)	American Snout, Hackberry Emperor, Tawny Emperor, Question Mark
Mallows/Hollyhocks	Gray Hairstreak, Common Checkered-Skipper
Milkweeds (*Asclepias*)	Monarch, Queen
Parsley (*Petroselinum*)	Black Swallowtail
Passion-vines (*Passiflora*)	Gulf Fritillary, Zebra (Heliconian), Variegated Fritillary
Pawpaw (*Asimina triloba*)	Zebra Swallowtail
Pearly-everlastings (*Anaphalis*)	American Lady
Pipevines (*Aristolochia*)	Pipevine Swallowtail, Polydamas Swallowtail
Rock-cresses (*Arabis*)	Orangetips and marbles
Purpletop grass (*Tridens flavus*)	Common Wood-Nymph, Little Glassywing, Zabulon Skipper
Sassafras (*Sassafras albidum*)	Spicebush Swallowtail
Snapdragon (*Antirrhinum major*)	Common Buckeye
Sunflowers (*Helianthus*)	Silvery Checkerspot, Gorgone Checkerspot
Turtlehead (*Chelone glabra*)	Baltimore Checkerspot
Violets (*Viola*)	Greater and lesser fritillaries, Variegated Fritillary

lanting the indicated foodplant will give you a chance to enjoy this utterfly in your garden. Unlike many moth caterpillars, most butter-y caterpillars will not destroy the plants they are eating (well, some-mes they do become overexuberant). In addition, because they eat nly very specific plants, you do not need to worry about them spread-ig to your roses or your rhododendrons. They will not eat these lants, or the vast majority of others that happen to be in your garden.

The more complex your garden becomes, the more attractive it is kely to be to butterflies. Try using many kinds of caterpillar foodplants nd different nectar sources. Because butterflies fly from early spring to ite fall, your garden should contain a procession of flowers that bloom hrough the seasons. In addition, many butterfly species feed on small, iconspicuous plants that most gardeners would regard as weeds. If ossible, allow a few areas of your garden, perhaps areas that are not asily seen, to become weedy. You'll be amazed by the beautiful but-erflies that these areas will export to your more formal garden!

Besides plants, you should consider a few other features for your but-erfly garden. As we saw in the behavior section, butterflies like to bask n the sun, and they like to sip moisture at damp sand or gravel. You can rovide a basking area by placing some flat stones in a sheltered, but unny, location. If you do not have an area that is naturally damp, try urying a bucket or container filled with sand, adding water as necessary.

Butterfly Photography for Nonphotographers

3utterflies are often very approachable. This approachability makes utterflies easy to photograph. With a little patience, a little experience, ind most important of all, the right equipment, anybody, even the ohotographically inept, like me, can take great photographs of butter-lies *while still enjoying the butterflies themselves.*

In contrast, birds and flowers, for different reasons, are difficult to ohotograph. To photograph birds, for example, the photographer leeds to focus single-mindedly on photography at the expense of see-ng many birds. While a professional photographer may also take this ipproach with butterflies—spending the whole day hoping for one great picture—you needn't.

Before I make my suggestions, I must confess that I know very little ibout cameras and the technical aspects of photography. Before I began taking photographs of butterflies about 10 years ago, I hadn' even taken snapshots with a brownie! So, if you are the sort of perso who hungers for detailed technical information, you will need to loo elsewhere—the magazine *American Butterflies* is a good place to start.

Why Take Photographs?

You can certainly enjoy butterflies without photographing them, an photography does take some time away from observation and can co quite a bit. Why do it? Well, for one thing it's the easiest way to shar your butterflying experiences with others. You can describe you experiences to others with words, but you need to be a talented speak er or author to do justice to the beauty of butterflies and the thrills butterflying. But, with modern photographic equipment, you do n need to be a talented photographer to let people see the actual butter fly that you saw—or the field of flowers in which it flew—you ju need to push the button.

Another reason to take photographs is that you can document th species that you see. You know, when you see some strange specie and describe it to others, they may say "that can't occur around her you must have misidentified it." When a European butterfly, th Small Tortoiseshell, appeared in New York City, photographers wer able to document its occurrence so that there was no question of th validity of the report.

Photographs also allow you to hone your identification skills. B looking carefully at a series of photographs that you have taken, you wi be able to notice small identification points not mentioned elsewhere.

Equipment

CAMERA BODY

Most people will find that a 35 mm single-lens reflex camera give them the best results. I strongly recommend using a model that ha autofocusing and automatic shutter speed and aperture setting pro grams. Minolta autofocusing has always worked well for butterflie Although the older Canon and Nikon autofocusing models did no work well for butterflies, the newer models are greatly improved. Tw advantages of the autofocusing are that, it's probably more accurat than most people, and it frees up one of your hands to do other things

I want to get close to the ground to approach a butterfly, I can put my left hand down to help balance myself, then lean forward and shoot the scene with just my right hand. Or, if there's a butterfly over my head, I can lift the camera over my head and just point it, the camera will do the rest. I also think that having your hand turning the barrel of the camera to focus it increases the chances of the butterfly detecting this movement and flying off.

LENS

Although it is possible to obtain passable photographs using a standard 50 mm lens, to take consistently good shots you should use a 100 mm macro lens. Make sure that you are getting a true macro lens, one that at closest focus results in a life-size image on the film. Many lenses listed as "macro" lenses, including all (I think) of those that are also zoom lenses do not have this feature. Without the 100 mm macro lens the butterflies will generally look small in your pictures; with such a lens, the butterflies will fill the frame.

FLASH

Some photographers like to shoot all their pictures using natural light. They feel that the resulting photos look more natural. While one can certainly obtain some great photographs using natural light, my own experience is that, for the type of pictures most people take, photographs taken using natural light often look highly unnatural! In addition, the less available light one has, the longer one must expose the film to obtain the same brightness. Since butterflies often move, using slow shutter speeds is not often an option—unless you've stuck a frozen butterfly on a flower (see below). In addition, a 100 mm macro lens, at closest focus, has a very shallow depth of field, so with available light one is not likely to get the entire butterfly in focus, let alone parts of the foreground and background. All of this argues for the use of a flash to provide extra light.

For the nonphotographer photographer there are really two choices for flash arrangements. The first is the standard flash mounted on the top of the camera. This can work fairly well. An advantage to these flashes over ring flashes is that they have much more power, creating good illumination of butterflies that are quite distant. One drawback, however, is that the angle of the flash may not be entirely suitable for illuminating butterflies at the closest focusing distance, leading to unwanted shadow. Also, using a flash mounted on the camera body, you will have only fixed, point source of light and sometimes it is advantageous to illuminat the butterfly from an angle, or with light from more than one angle.

The second type of flash is a ring flash. Rather than sit on the top of the camera body, the ring flash fits around the end of the macro len. An advantage of this system is that the flash is always aimed properly yielding a very high percentage of eminently usable photos. Another advantage is that with four lights in the ring, you can vary the angle of light if you want to. A disadvantage of this system is that ring flashe are underpowered (they are intended for very close macro photogra phy) making it difficult to properly illuminate targets at a distance such as swallowtails. Another disadvantage, for some purposes, is tha although the butterfly will be sharp and well-illuminated, this system tends to produce a higher percentage of photographs in which the background is black than does a camera-mounted flash. Black back grounds result when the available light on the butterfly is muc. greater than the available light on the background. On many camer settings, the flash light will overpower any natural light and becaus the light from the flash drops off as the square of the distance from the flash, only objects very close to the focal plane of the butterfly will b properly illuminated. (The same effect happens with all flashes, bu because the ring flash is closer to the butterfly the effect is accentuat ed with a ring flash.) For the purposes of showing other people jus how the butterfly looks, black backgrounds may be a plus, becaus one's attention is focused on the butterfly. But, in terms of a beautifu photograph, some people find a black background objectionable Since most of my photographs in this book were taken using the rin flash system, you can judge for yourself if this system might be suitabl for you.

FILM

In a few years time, the performance of digital cameras will equal o surpass that of traditional cameras. But, for now, film is still superio and the basic choice is between print and slide film. An advantage t prints is that you can easily view them yourself or with a small grou of people. However, compared to slide film, there are many disadvan

ges—you can't use them for talks to groups of people, they are bulki-
- to store, and their resolution is not as good. Since I use slide film
xclusively, I can't really make a recommendation about which print
lm is best. Sharper pictures are possible when you use film with
wer ASA numbers. ASA 25 film will yield much sharper pictures,
at can be greatly enlarged, than will ASA 200 film. But, the ASA 200
lm can be used under much lower light conditions. If you are pho-
graphing without a flash, you will want to use ASA 200 film, or
igher. With a flash, you can use ASA 25 or 64 film. I use Kodachrome
4 film, believing that, overall, its color veracity is the best. This film
lso has a reputation for long-term color stability.

CCESSORIES

or most butterfly photographs it is a good idea to keep an ultraviolet
lter over your lens. You'll want a strap for your camera. A good wide
ne will do less damage to your shoulder than a narrow one. You'll
robably also want to take extra batteries and film with you on hikes.
use a pouch that fits around my waist. It is small, but still large
nough to carry four rolls of film, extra sets of AA batteries for my
ash, and a lithium battery for the camera itself.

Taking the Photo

PPROACHING THE BUTTERFLY

Vhen you see a butterfly you want to photograph, you naturally
vant to rush right up to it and grab its picture. Unfortunately, butter-
lies are pretty good motion detectors. So, you need to slow down.
nd be more graceful. The more slowly and gracefully you move, the
ess likely you will frighten the butterfly. But, let's get real. If you
nove slowly enough the butterfly is guaranteed to have flown before
ou get in place for your photograph. So, you need to strike a balance.
ust where that balance lies is best learned by experience. It will also
ary from butterfly species to species, and from butterfly individual to
ndividual. Some butterflies that are nectaring, or, that are mud pud-
lling, will sit still forever. Others almost never stop. If you have a
hoice, find one that stops. If you are trying to photograph a Georgia
atyr and there are a number of individuals present, watch for an
ndividual who is landing more frequently and for longer periods of

time than others. It will probably continue to do so as you try to photograph it. The same type of advice applies to those times when you especially want the upperside of the butterfly, or alternatively, the underside. Whatever you want, the butterflies will be doing the opposite. The few individuals who occasionally open their wings may well continue to do so. Focus on them.

If you have a choice, it is best to approach the butterfly from a low position, rather than from over its head. This way you'll be less likely to startle it. You'll also be less likely to startle it if you avoid having your shadow pass over the butterfly.

FRAMING THE BUTTERFLY

Proper framing is important for both aesthetically desirable results and easy identification of the butterflies in your photos. To clearly see your butterfly you should strive to have the butterfly's wings parallel to the plane of the film in your camera. Many times you will need to be on one knee, or on your belly, and/or with your body contorted into ludicrous positions to effectively accomplish proper framing. If the angle of the butterfly is off just a little, this will distort the perspective and make it more difficult to examine spot shapes and patterns that are important for identification. Of course, if you just want an interesting angle, that is a different story. Another decision you will make is what to include in the frame along with the butterfly. This is an aesthetic decision that depends upon your "eye"—what looks good to you. Like anything else in this world, some people are better than others in creating pleasing photographic compositions. But unless you want to sell your photos to mass circulation magazines, this may not matter to you.

Another important point of this section is that late breaking research shows that Mourning Cloaks and Ruddy Daggerwings, playing a dark butterfly version of the old cat and mouse game, are often responsible for the missing fig newtons. Photos show them, fig-legged, skulking around fruit! Then again, maybe they were framed.

Photo Etiquette

Photo etiquette requires consideration for other people, for the butterfly, and for the environment. As more and more people take up

utterflying and butterfly photography, this will become more
nportant.

If you are with other people, you should consider their needs. A
record shot from a distance, without a flash, is okay, but going right up
to a butterfly to photograph it, or using a flash, carries the risk with it
of frightening the butterfly away. When I lead groups of people on
butterflying trips I ask photographers to wait until everyone has had
a careful look at the butterfly. (Of course, some people probably think
that I'm not so good at policing myself!) If there is more than one photographer present, you might try a system of alternating who photographs first, although some butterflies are very cooperative and
allow more than one person to photograph them at the same time. If
a butterfly is sitting on the ground with its wings closed, but occasionally opening them, there can be a photographer on each side of
the butterfly, each photographing its underside, while another photographer is behind the butterfly, waiting for its wings to open to
photograph its upperside. Believe it or not, this has worked on a surprising number of occasions.

You should also consider the butterfly. Some photographers will do
almost anything to obtain a photograph. They will capture a butterfly,
place it in an ice chest to cool it, then pose the almost frozen butterfly
on some colorful flower or background so they can photograph it to
their heart's content. Putting aside the fact that there are times when
butterflies are injured just by capturing them (and any injury to a butterfly is probably fatal), my opinion is that while photographers may
believe that photographs obtained in this way are okay, if they don't
inform readers that this is how the photographs were obtained then
they are inadvertently deceiving the public. People looking at these
photographs will believe that these artificial poses and situations can
normally be found in nature. They cannot.

Last, but not least, you should consider the environment. When you
walk up to butterflies for your photograph, do not trample flowers and
other plants along the way. Any human action can cause environmental problems, especially when repeated by large numbers of people. Although it's impossible to avoid accidents, you can minimize the
damage your activities cause by being aware of potential trampling
problems and exercising care when you photograph.

RECORD KEEPING

More than just being pretty pictures, your photographs can be importa
records of what kinds of butterflies were in what locations at wh
times. I urge you to label your photographs. Not with some type
arcane code, but with the date the photograph was taken and the loca
ity where it was taken written directly on the slide holder, or on the bac
of the print. A code is close to useless. Sure *you* know the code, you'
even written it down in a notebook. But, as the years go by you'll forg
the code or lose the notebook. And, I won't be the first to tell you, yc
will die. Invariably, eventually, your photographs will become separa
ed from your code. Ask any museum curator, and they will tell you th
butterfly specimens that do not have date and locality data, written c
a label that is on the same pin as the specimen, have almost no value.

In order to write this information on your photographs, you w
need to record it when you take the pictures. Relying on your mem
ry is a bad idea and will eventually lead to mistakes that are mislea
ing to others and embarrassing to yourself. Carry a small noteboc
with you. I number each roll of film I shoot, by year and sequence, e.g
97-11 would be the eleventh roll of film in 1997. Then in my fie
notebook, after the heading 97-11, the first hand-written entry mig
read "1. Great Southern White, Homestead, Dade Co., FL 3/25
When my slides from roll 11 come back developed, I refer to my fie
notebook and write the information on the slide. If I have taken mo
than one photograph of what *I am sure* is the same individual butterf
(the butterfly has never left my sight), then I indicate that in my not
book, and cross-label all the slides of the same individual by sayir
something like, see 1-5T, writing that same instruction on all fiv
slides of the Great Southern White. This is especially important whe
you want to study the upperside and underside of the same butterfl
either for ID, or to see if certain upperside characteristics are associa
ed with certain underside characteristics.

STORAGE AND PHOTOGRAPH RETRIEVAL

You should protect your photographs from excessive heat, hig
humidity, dust, and light. Prints can be stored in photo albums, or ju
in envelopes. Some people store their slides in carousels, others stor

em in the boxes in which the developed slides are returned, while
hers use special enamel slide cabinets. I store my slides in clear plas-
c pages with compartments for individual slides. Use only plastic
ages that are labelled as archival for slides, others contain polyvinyl
iloride which can destroy your photos over time. These clear plastic
ages, generally of polyethylene or of polyester polypropylene, then fit
ito three-ring binders

Some photographers store their photographs by trip, or by time
eriod. I store my butterfly slides in taxonomic sequence. This makes
very easy to find slides of particular butterfly species to illustrate
ticles or talks.

EWING YOUR PHOTOGRAPHS

you want to share your photos with groups of people, you need to pro-
ct them onto a screen or a white wall using a slide projector. For view-
ig yourself, it is best to use a loupe, a type of magnifying glass especially
iade for viewing slides. Although I just hold the slides up to a light and
ok through the loupe, many people prefer placing the slides on a light
ox. Loupes and light boxes are available from camera supply stores.

Conservation

his is the raison d'être of this book. I want to show you the beauty and
irills to be found in the world of butterflies so that you become pas-
onate about butterflies; so that butterflies become an important part
f your life; so that when a government agency sprays the last home of
chaus' Swallowtails with butterfly-killing mosquito spray you will
el their pain; so that when the military proposes to run tanks over the
ist home of Regal Fritillaries east of the Mississippi River you will
rotest; and so that when the habitat for the last colony in your area of
ronze Coppers, or Dakota Skippers, or scores of other species that
epend upon us for survival, is about to be made into a shopping cen-
er, you will stop the development.

As you study the range maps that accompany the photographic
lates, you will notice that quite a few species have part of their range
olored bright red (also see Table 2). This indicates that the species has
isappeared from a large area it formerly inhabited. The red color real-
y understates the loss of butterflies in our region becauses it does not

include all those areas where species that were formerly common have become rare, or areas where there now exist only a few colonies while previously there were many. While in some cases the reasons for a species' loss are mysterious, the decline of most species has been due to human activities.

The main reason we are losing so many butterflies is that humans continue to expand their realm and destroy the habitats that butterflies need to survive. Wetlands are drained, woodlots are cut, fields are converted to parking lots or lawns. Of course, habitat loss affects almost all wildlife, but butterflies carry an added double-burden. The first burden is that most of our butterflies require habitats that are ephemeral, i.e., these habitats will disappear in a relatively short period of time due to natural succession. Most open areas, left to their own devices, will become woodlands. In earlier times, the loss of these open areas was offset by the generation of areas newly opened by grazing animals and especially by fire. Now, humans suppress fire except as an often misguided conservation tool as discussed below. Previously, rivers and streams meandered, creating new wetlands as older ones disappeared. Now, rivers are channelized and few new wetlands are created.

In much of the East, especially the megatropolis areas where most of the population lives, there are really only two types of habitat. There are large swaths of artificial lawns, and there are areas that are allowed to be "natural" and become woodlands. The lawns are biological deserts that support almost no butterflies. They do however support enormous populations of Canada Geese which people then desperately try to remove. They also cost money to maintain by frequent mowing, waste water, and pollute streams with fertilizers. Many areas, especially parks and large corporate grounds, could easily convert a substantial portion of these useless (and ugly—once you see how destructive they are) lawns into native grassland meadows, teeming with life, beautiful throughout the year, and without Canada Geese (which don't like those tall grasses on their bellies). Woodland, the other type of habitat, does support some butterflies, but very many fewer than open areas, especially when the woodland is "pure," without open disturbed areas either within it or adjacent to it.

So, in order to see fields filled with butterflies, we need to either create

e preserves that are very, very large, so that open areas are generat-
d naturally, or we need to manage land in a way that generates and
aintains open areas. This can be done. Ward Pound Ridge
eservation in Westchester County, New York, has been a county park
nce 1925, when the fields and woodlots of 32 farms were acquired
d combined. The park now contains about 4700 acres and most of
e fields have grown back to mature woodlands. But large areas of the
ark are maintained as open grassland by a program of annual early
ring, or late fall, mowing. These fields literally swarm with thousands
f individuals of 85 species of butterflies, making Ward Pound Ridge
eservation one of the premier butterflying localities in the north-
astern United States.

On a larger scale, where mowing is impractical, fire can be used to
aintain open areas. Unfortunately, some of the conservation com-
unity and groups charged with the management of our natural
reas have made a devil's embrace of fire—"fire is good at keeping
reas open, let's burn like crazy." Yes, fire can be an effective tool in
aintaining open habitats, but one needs to carefully control burns so
at only *portions* of the habitat are burned every few years, always
aving refuges for species so that they can then re-colonize the
urned areas. Burning large areas without leaving refuges for the res-
dent butterflies destroys the butterfly populations present (along with
yriad other species of insects and plants). For example, one of the
w places east of the Mississippi where Arogos Skippers could still be
und until recently was in Ocala National Forest in Florida. Although
e Forest Service was alerted to the presence of this rare species and
f the danger of fire, in June of 1996 the Forest Service burned the
orthern section of the colony and then, in July, burned the southern
ortion. Arogos Skippers have not been seen since.

The second special burden of butterfly conservation is that surpris-
gly often, important butterfly habitats—even crucial ones— are dis-
urbed habitats that conservation professionals dismiss as "trash."
emember that most butterfly species require nectar flowers for
dults and that the availability of these energy sources may be a limit-
g factor for a species. In many pristine habitats, e.g., woodlands or
ine barrens in summer, there is a dearth of good nectar flowers. So,
utterflies, whose caterpillar foodplant may be a woodlands or pine

barrens plant, depend upon flowers that bloom along the edges of these habitats, often in disturbed fields. But a conservation professional, trained to look for "pure" examples of native habitats, may take one look at these weedy fields and turn up her/his nose. They may save the woodland, but not the weedy field. So, while conservation organizations save many pristine locations, we continue to lose the butterflies that we need to enrich our lives.

The good news is that, with proper planning, human and butterfly habitations are compatible. Because most butterfly populations do not need very large expanses of habitat, preservation of most species is feasible by creating an interconnecting network of small protected habitat units along with a few larger units. Small habitat units, perhaps as small as the yards of a few concerned neighbors, are sufficient to support small populations of many species, especially if these small units are loosely connected to other small units. But, butterfly populations are commonly subject to very large fluctuations in numbers. In particularly bad years for a particular species of butterfly, perhaps due to drought, or to a disease epidemic, the small units, with their small populations, will probably not survive. However, larger preserves probably will have large and varied populations and habitats that will ensure that some individuals survive a calamity. Then, when the population rebounds, the larger preserves will serve as reservoirs and overflow individuals will re-populate the small units.

A second factor reducing butterfly populations is pollution of the environment, especially pollution with pesticides. The past use of DDT greatly reduced many of our native butterfly populations. Although DDT is now banned, the use of other pesticides is widespread. These pesticides are especially employed for mass sprayings against gypsy moth infestations, for mosquito control, for agricultural use, and also by private homeowners. In most cases, the harm caused by these pesticides outweighs any possible usefulness (see "Must Butterflies Die for the Gypsy Moths' Sins?" in *American Butterflies*, Fall 1995, Vol. 3, no. 3).

A third activity capable of harming butterfly populations is the continued killing of rare and local butterfly species by some immoral collectors. A particularly tragic case is Mitchell's Satyr. In the northeast this butterfly was limited to a few fens in northern New Jersey, but the butterfly has now been extirpated by relentless collection pressure.

Table 2 Twenty-seven butterfly species that have declined over at least part of their range in the past 25 years.

SPECIES	REASONS FOR DECLINE
Schaus' Swallowtail	Habitat destruction; anti-mosquito spraying
Bronze Copper	Habitat destruction, draining wetlands, watercourse channels
Purplish Copper	Habitat destruction
Frosted Elfin	Habitat destruction
Hessel's Hairstreak	Habitat destruction
Bartram's Scrub-Hairstreak	Habitat destruction
Miami Blue	Habitat destruction and perhaps other unknown factors
Dusky Azure	Unknown
Silvery Blue	Unknown
'Karner' Melissa Blue	Habitat destruction
Swamp Metalmark	Habitat destruction and other unknown factors
Diana Fritillary	Habitat destruction
Regal Fritillary	Loss of large-scale open habitats; perhaps other unknown factors
Silver-bordered Fritillary	Habitat destruction; possibly competition with Meadow Fritillary
Tawny Crescent	Unknown
Mitchell's Satyr	Habitat destruction; killing by collectors
Zestos Skipper	Habitat destruction
Golden-banded Skipper	Unknown
Mottled Duskywing	Habitat destruction
Persius Duskywing	Unknown
'Appalachian' Grizzled Skipper	Unknown; possibly anti-gypsy moth spraying
Poweshiek Skipperling	Destruction of prairie habitats
Ottoe Skipper	Destruction of prairie habitats
'Pawnee' Leonard's Skipper	Habitat destruction
Dakota Skipper	Destruction of prairie habitats
Arogos Skipper	Habitat destruction
Two-spotted Skipper	Habitat destruction, draining wetands

One major colony was wiped out almost singlehandedly in the late 1970's by an individual who returned to the fen daily during successive seasons and each day killed every Mitchell's Satyr he saw. Even when collection pressure doesn't result outright in the demise of a rare colonial butterfly, each individual killed results in the depletion of the gene pool, and this loss of genetic diversity becomes more important as the colony becomes smaller. Each individual killed might have been the individual that contained a mutation that would have allowed the colony to survive the inevitable drought or epidemic that it will face.

Some people might ask: Why save butterfly species? Are they of any value? An extensive consideration of this question is outside the scope of this book but I would like to put forward a few short answers. (See *Why Preserve Natural Variety?* by B.G. Norton for a recent comprehensive discussion.) Each species, being unique, may possess unique properties useful to humans that will be irretrievably lost should a species become extinct. The recent discovery of a potent anticancer drug, taxol, in a species of yew that had been considered a "trash species" highlights this possibility. Because ecological systems are interrelated in complicated ways, the removal of a single species can have a much greater adverse effect than might have been anticipated. In many cases, the extinction of but a single species will result in the removal of a number of other species that are, in some way, dependent on the first species. Often, the fact that a species of butterfly is close to extinction can be seen as a symptom that an entire unique habitat is about to be destroyed. The collapse of many of the earth's ecosystems may result in a world hostile, at best, to humans.

In addition to these practical arguments for the preservation of butterflies, there are clearly aesthetic and moral reasons to insist that butterflies survive. Only recently have human beings seen peoples from other tribes as similar to themselves and thus "real human beings" worthy of protection. As people become ever more conscious of their environment, they may come to see that all biological entities have intrinsic value and are worthy of protection. Many years ago, the Greeks equated butterflies with the souls of people, using the Greek word *psyche* for both. One does not have to believe in Greek mythology to know that in a world without butterflies, the souls of all people would be greatly diminished.

Name

nglish and scientific names in this guide follow the North American
utterfly Association's (NABA) *Checklist and English Names of North
merican Butterflies.* Before the NABA checklist was published in
995, each author of a book about butterflies used whatever set of
ames struck his or her fancy. The result has been a confusing pletho-
a of names that has bewildered the uninitiated and made it more dif-
cult for the public to become involved with butterflies. We are now
n the road toward standardization, although this process will take
ears to be completed. If a widespread, currently in-print field guide
as used an English name different from the one used here, that
ame is also included in the index.

Although the scientific names used in this work follow the NABA
st, in those cases where I disagree with the species status given in that
st I say so.

Some people object to the use of the word "common" in many butter-
y (and other species') names, pointing out that many of these species are
ot common at all in much of their range. This is correct, but in species'
ames, the word "common" should be read to mean "widespread."

Size

he size of a butterfly can be difficult to determine in the field. Is the
ength of the forewing (FW) 9/16 inch or is it 11/16 inch? Because of
his difficulty, I have opted for expressing the size of each species rel-
tive to other standard species. Most of these standard species are
ommon and widespread, and thus you should rapidly become famil-
ar with them. The sizes of the standard species themselves are given
n Table 3 and in the species accounts for these species. **Perhaps the
asiest way to visualize the size of the standard species is to look at the
ilhouettes at the end of the book. All of the size standard species are
hown there at life size.** Because different groups of butterflies and
kippers typically are seen with their wings in different positions, I
ave chosen to use the length of the front margin of one FW, which
hould be visible in all cases, as the measure of size. The size given is
he average size in inches. Symbols used in this section are: "=",

meaning that the size of the species being discussed is equal to the siz
standard species, "<" meaning that the size of the species being dis
cussed is less than the size standard species, "<<" meaning much les
than, ">" meaning greater than, ">>" meaning much greater than
"≤" meaning less than or equal to, and "≥" meaning greater than o
equal to.

In addition to using these size standards you can determine th
actual size of a species by looking at the photographic plates. Eacl
plate has the species on that plate in the correct size relationship t
each other, and at the top left of the plate you are told whether th
actual size of the butterflies is smaller or larger than shown. For exam
ple the hairstreaks on plates 16–21 are shown at 2 1/2 x life size, i.e.
the size of each butterfly in the photographs is about 2 1/2 times larg
er than the actual size of the butterfly.

When considering size, remember that the size of different individ
uals of the same species can vary dramatically. Occasionally a run
individual will be drastically smaller than is normal for the species
And, although in many species both sexes are a similar size, as a gen
eral rule, females are larger than males.

Similar Species

Here, I try to alert you to the possibility of confusion with anothe
species. Generally, if one of a pair of similar species is common while th
other is rare, I mention only the similar species in the account of th
rare species to direct your attention to the more common look-alike.

Range

I describe, in very general terms, each species range **outside our region**
Ranges within our region are shown on the maps on the facing page
to the plates.

Abundance

I try to give information that will allow you to know when to search fo
a particular species and how likely you might be to find it. **I canno
emphasize enough that this section is intended as a rough guide**
Butterfly abundance can, and usually does, vary dramatically from yea
to year and from locality to locality. One of the pleasures of butterflyin;

Table 3 Length of 1 Forewing

SIZE STANDARD SPECIES	COSTAL MARGIN (IN INCHES)
Black Swallowtail	1 12/16
Eastern Tiger Swallowtail	2 3/16
Little Yellow	11/16
Cabbage White	15/16
Cloudless Sulphur	1 5/16
Eastern Tailed-Blue	8/16
Banded Hairstreak	10/16
Pearl Crescent	11/16
American Lady	1 2/16
Mourning Cloak	1 10/16
Great Spangled Fritillary	1 11/16
Little Wood-Satyr	13/16
Common Wood-Nymph	1 4/16
Monarch	2
Common Sootywing	9/16
Wild Indigo Duskywing	11/16
Northern Cloudywing	12/16
Silver-spotted Skipper	1 2/16
Least Skipper	8/16
Tawny-edged Skipper	9/16
Hobomok/Zabulon Skipper	10/16

is that each year is certain to bring its quota of surprises. Flight dates can also vary tremendously depending upon the weather pattern of the year. When I list a species as flying "All year," this does not usually mean that you will see this species whenever you visit the region where it is found. For example, I list the flight period of Eastern Pygmy-Blue in South Florida as "all year." This is because it has been found there in each month of the year. Yet, in October 1995 I searched many areas where I had found this species previously, but did not find any. So although a species may have been found in each month of the year over a many-year period, finding that species at a particular time in a particular year may depend upon the vagaries of that year's brood sequence and abundance level. Also, for more flight period and abundance information, see the phenograms at the end of many of the species accounts.

Major Foodplant

Listed as an aid to finding the adult butterflies are the major plant(s) or group of plants that are eaten by the caterpillars. For many uncommon butterflies the easiest way to locate colonies is to search for sites where the foodplant is common.

Comments

Here I include assorted information and/or thoughts that didn't fit easily into one of the above-listed categories.

Phenograms

For many species occurring in the Baraboo (and nearby Dexterville) Wisconsin area (WI); the New York City, New York area (NY); the Raleigh (and nearby sandhills region), North Carolina area (NC); and the Baton Rouge, Louisiana area (LA), phenograms, showing average flight periods, are provided at the end of the Species Account. The data for these phenograms was provided by Ann Swengel, Rick Cech (based on the copyrighted *Checklist of NYC Butterflies of the New York City Butterfly Club*—used by permission), Harry LeGrand, Jr., and Gary Noel Ross, respectively. Data compilation and computer layout was by Jim Springer. For those of you outside these regions, "quadrangulation" of the times should give you a rough idea of flight periods in your area.

he flight period and abundance presented is the *averaged* flight peri-
d and abundance broken into five-day blocks. Within these blocks,
bundance is depicted as:

RARE   UNCOMMON   COMMON   ABUNDANT

ctual flight period may vary by weeks in any given year and abun-
ance can vary dramatically. The phenogram for Pipevine Swallowtail
1ows that they are not normally found in the Baraboo region, while
1 Louisiana they are rare in April, become uncommon by June, and
ommon in August. The phenogram for Black Swallowtail shows that
1ey are often abundant in the New York City area in mid-July.

In some cases, information for a region in the phenogram doesn't
ompletely agree with information for that same region in the abun-
ance section. Such cases indicate a lack of uniformity of opinion
mong butterfliers.

About the Plates
Photographs

he 629 photographs (591 by the author) on the 71 color plates rep-
esent a first. The *Through Binoculars* books are the first field guides to
ny group of organisms that use photographs in a true field guide for-
1at. Unlike other books that use photographs, the species in the pho-
)graphs in this book are presented in the **correct size relationships** to
1e other species on the plate—the photographs having been careful-
/ enlarged or reduced to provide this relationship. On the top left of
ach plate, you learn the magnification or reduction from life size of
1at plate.

When males and females differ greatly in their appearance, both
exes are shown. In general, if the illustration is unlabeled as to sex, it
an be assumed that both sexes are quite similar (although experi-
nced butterfliers can probably discern the sex of most individuals by
ubtle differences).

Photographs were chosen and arranged so that similar species are
hown in similar poses, making comparisons for identification easier.
lmost all of the photographs were taken using the same camera
quipment and film, so in general there is a visual consistency to the
hotographs, making them easy to compare to each other. Other fac-

tors influencing the choice of photograph to illustrate each specie were the quality of the photograph, the condition of the butterfl illustrated, the typicality of the butterfly illustrated, and a desire fo geographical distribution. Of course, in some cases I had little choice For example, the photographs of Outis Skipper and Cofaqui Gian Skipper show the only individuals of these species I have ever seen.

Unless otherwise indicated, all photographs by the author wer taken in the wild, of unrestrained, unmanipulated butterflies. Tw photographs, of species for which no photographs of wild butterflic were available, are of museum specimens.

The black and white lines that appear on some of the photograph have been placed over the photographs to draw your eye to fiel marks whose positions are difficult to explain in words.

Facing Page Notes

The notes on the pages facing the plates are intended to serve as a quic reference to the most important identification features. In addition, th notes on these pages tell you where and when each of the photograph was taken, when known. Dates are shown as month/day/year. Th information can be useful in locating the species.

Maps

The range maps tell you where a species is normally found. If an are is colored on a particular map, this means that I believe there are **res dent populations** of the species in this area, or, if the species is an imm grant, that an **active field observer is likely to see the species in this are at least once every two to three years.** Because whether a species is resident or an immigrant often depends upon the severity of the win ter, I have not distinguished between resident and immigrant specie Occurrences of immigrant species vary tremendously from year t year and this makes it difficult to draw a line that demarcates a specie normal range expansion. For example, prior to about 1950, Long tailed Skippers occurred fairly often in northeastern United State Then, from 1950 to 1990, none were seen. Since 1990, good numbe of this species have been seen each year in the northeastern Unite States. Do I show the Northeast as part of the species range? Mayb they will not occur there for another 40 years! So, while the maps c ιe pages facing the plates are there to help you make a quick decision regarding the likelihood that your tentative identification is correct, ou should also read the abundance section of the species accounts to ·arn about immigrant butterflies.

Because the scale of the maps had to be quite small to fit them on ιe pages facing the plates, it was not possible to show local details of ιecies occurrences. So, even if you live within the range shown for a articular species, it may be that it does not occur in the county in ·hich you live, probably because the right habitat is absent. A purple ιot indicates that the species' range in this area is much smaller than ιe actual area covered by the purple dot.

It is important to remember that butterflies have wings and will ·ander outside their normal range, occasionally for a great distance. ust because your location is not included in the normal range of a ιecies does not mean that it is impossible to see that species where ιou live, just that it becomes increasingly unlikely the farther from the ιormal range you go.

In addition to showing the ranges of butterflies, to my knowledge, ιese maps are the first to provide information about butterfly broods see the discussion of broods on page 11). The different colors on the ιap indicate the number of broods a species normally has in each ιortion of its range. Yellow indicates one brood, green indicates two ·roods, and blue indicates three or more broods. In general, you will eed to search for a single-brooded species at a particular time of the ·ear, while three brooded species may be present during most of the ·arm season. Because there is so little information about brood ιequences in most localities, many of the lines dividing numbers of ·roods are only my best guess. One of the purposes of this part of the ιaps is to stimulate you to find where they are wrong. Hopefully this ·ill lead to greater knowledge for the entire butterflying community. ·s I briefly discuss in the butterfly biology section dealing with broods, ιnowledge of brood transitions may be important to our understand-ιg of butterfly ecology and evolution.

A fifth color, red, is used in the range maps to indicate that portion ·f a species' former range, from which it has been extirpated, i.e., it no ·nger is found there. Red is used only if the best available information ιggests that there are no longer any resident populations within that

portion of its historic range. I'm sure that I will be criticized whe
almost certainly, a species is found within the area in which I show
as extirpated. But, I have decided to risk that criticism in order to avo
misleading butterfliers into thinking that they have a reasonab
chance of seeing some species that hasn't been seen in their area for 2
years. In addition, I hope that highlighting the substantial number
butterfly species that are in trouble will encourage actions to sav
those that remain.

Near the western edge of the maps you will see a diagonal lin
running from just south of Houston, Texas north to the Nor
Dakota/Canadian border. This line represents the western limit of the ar
covered by this field guide. The entire outlines of the states along th
western edge are shown to make it easier for you to quickly grasp a loca
tion on the map. In addition, species ranges west of the limit line are als
shown, if a species treated in this work is found west of the limit line. We
of the limit line there are other species that are not treated in this guide

I consulted all the published (and many unpublished) region
works about butterflies, and then constructed preliminary maps. Thes
were then sent to active field workers throughout the area covered s
that the most current information could be incorporated into the map
Errors in the final maps should not be ascribed to area reviewer
because I did not always follow their recommendations. For one thin
opinions from area reviewers were sometimes contradictory! Th
acknowledgments section lists those individuals who helped mak
these maps the most accurate representation of current butterfly range
yet produced. Ultimately, because our knowledge of butterfly range
and brood sequences is still very incomplete, I made many assumption
and guesses in the range maps. Some of these will prove to be correc
many will be wrong. Until the last three years, there have been (at an
one time) perhaps only a few hundred active field workers trying t
cover all of North America! These field workers, overwhelmingly co
lectors (almost no one used binoculars for butterflying prior to the pul
lication of the first *Butterflies through Binoculars*), have provided th
framework of information that now allows us to move forward. A
thousands of butterfliers begin to provide comprehensive informatior
revisions of these maps will provide more accuracy and detail.

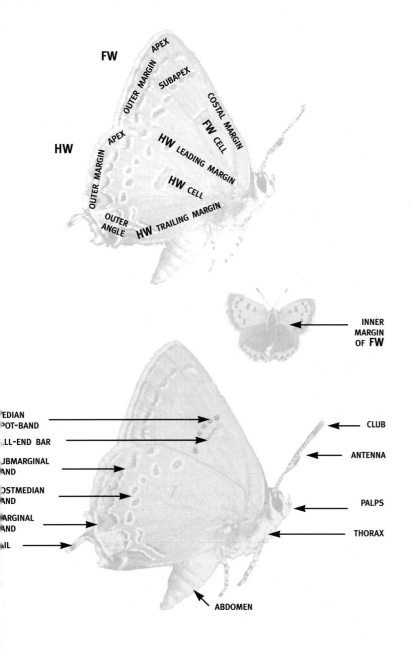

FW

APEX

SUBAPEX

OUTER MARGIN

COSTAL MARGIN

FW CELL

HW

APEX

OUTER MARGIN

HW LEADING MARGIN

HW CELL

OUTER ANGLE

HW TRAILING MARGIN

INNER MARGIN OF FW

EDIAN POT-BAND

LL-END BAR

UBMARGINAL AND

OSTMEDIAN AND

ARGINAL AND

IL

CLUB

ANTENNA

PALPS

THORAX

ABDOMEN

ABBREVIATIONS

A	abundant, you are likely to encounter more than 20 individuals per field trip to the right locality at the right time
C	common, you are likely to encounter between 4 and 20 individuals per field trip to the right locality at the right time.
FW	forewing
HW	hindwing
L	local, not generally distributed, even within the range shown, absent from many areas with seemingly suitable habitat
NF	national forest
NP	national park
NWR	national wildlife refuge
R	rare, rarely seen even at the right place at the right time
S	stray, not part of the region's normal fauna and not seen most years
SF	state forest
SP	state park
U	uncommon, you are likely to see 0–3 individuals per field trip to the right place at the right time
WMA	wildlife management area
WPR	Ward Pound Ridge Reservation, Westchester County, NY
♂	male
♀	female

STATE ABBREVIATIONS

AL Alabama	**MA** Massachusetts	**OK** Oklahoma
AR Arkansas	**MD** Maryland	**PA** Pennsylvania
AZ Arizona	**ME** Maine	**SC** South Carolina
CA California	**MN** Minnesota	**SD** South Dakota
CO Colorado	**MO** Missouri	**TX** Texas
CT Connecticut	**NC** North Carolina	**TN** Tennessee
DE Delaware	**NE** Nebraska	**VA** Virginia
FL Florida	**NH** New Hampshire	**VT** Vermont
GA Georgia	**NJ** New Jersey	**WI** Wisconsin
IA Iowa	**NM** New Mexico	**WV** West Virginia
LA Louisiana	**NY** New York	**WY** Wyoming
	OH Ohio	

SPECIES ACCOUNTS

Swallowtails
(family Papilionidae)

vallowtails are our largest butterflies. Their long tails and often slow flight
ake them among our most graceful.

Pipevine Swallowtail *Battus philenor* **Plate 1**

SIZE	Black Swallowtail
SIMILAR SPECIES	Spicebush Swallowtail, Black Swallowtail, Red-spotted Purple.
IDENTIFICATION	A very dark swallowtail above with strongly iridescent blue HW. Below, note the large **single** orange spot-band on **iridescent blue**. Spicebush and Black swallowtails have blue that is not iridescent and **two** orange spot-bands. Red-spotted Purple lacks tails.
HABITAT	Wide-ranging, this swallowtail can be encountered almost anywhere, but is found primarily in open situations near deciduous woodlands, including gardens and beach areas.
RANGE	Also west to California, south to southern Mexico.
ABUNDANCE	LC but R-U over much of the East. RS north to Maine, South Dakota and Manitoba (1 record). Flies Feb.–Oct. in Florida and Deep South, Apr.–Sept./Oct. (2 broods, mainly May and July/Aug.) farther north.
MAJOR FOODPLANT	Pipevines (*Aristolochia*) including ornamental vines and the native hosts *A. durior*, *A. reticulata*, and *A. serpentaria*.
COMMENTS	In earlier times this species seems to have been more common in the Northeast, perhaps because ornamental pipevines were common garden plants in Victorian times. The growth of butterfly gardening may bring them back!

	MAR	APR	MAY	JUN	JUL	AUG	SEP	OCT
WI								
NY								
NC								
LA								

Polydamas Swallowtail *Battus polydamas* **Plate 1**

SIZE	≥ Black Swallowtail.
SIMILAR SPECIES	Black Swallowtail.
IDENTIFICATION	The rapidly flying Polydamas Swallowtail is easy enough to ide tify when one gets a good look at it–something that is not so ea to do! It is generally a fast flyer, more powerful than Bla Swallowtail, and when nectaring it continues to rapidly beat wings. This species lacks tails (but, of course, Black Swallowta sometimes lose theirs) and has a wide dirty **yellow postmedia band above**. Male Black Swallowtails have narrower, bright ye low median bands and yellow marginal spots above. Belo Polydamas Swallowtails are dark with **dull red marginal spo** on the HW and **red spots on the body**.
HABITAT	Gardens and vacant lots, edges of woodlands.
RANGE	Also, the West Indies and south Texas south through tropi Americas.
ABUNDANCE	U in south Florida—Apr.–Nov. RS north to Gainesville, Flori and Houston, Texas.
MAJOR FOODPLANT	Pipevines (*Aristolochia*).
COMMENTS	Perhaps easiest to find at gardens with planted pipevines, such outside of Butterfly World in Fort Lauderdale, Florida or Fairchild Gardens south of Miami. Even though it lacks tails, t Polydamas Swallowtail is closely related to Pipevine Swallowta

Zebra Swallowtail *Eurytides marcellus* **Plate 1**

SIZE	≤ Black Swallowtail.
IDENTIFICATION	The aptly named Zebra Swallowtail can be confused with none our other butterflies. The black-striped white triangular win with graceful tails are distinctive. Also note the bright-red medi HW stripe below.
HABITAT	Open brushy fields and woodlands, especially along watercours
ABUNDANCE	LC. 3 broods, Feb.–Sept. in Florida and the Deep South, probably broods farther north—Apr.–Aug./Sept. (the first brood is usua the most common). RS to Nebraska and South Dakota (1 record
MAJOR FOODPLANT	Pawpaws (*Asimina triloba* and *Asimina parviflora*).
COMMENTS	Summer individuals are larger with broader black bands and long tails than spring individuals. Flight is usually lower to the grou than our other swallowtails and is very direct with rapid wingbea

	MAR	APR	MAY	JUN	JUL	AUG	SEP	OCT
WI								
NY								
NC								
LA								

Black Swallowtail *Papilio polyxenes* **Plate 2**

SIZE 1 12/16 inch.

SIMILAR SPECIES Spicebush Swallowtail, Pipevine Swallowtail, Eastern Tiger Swallowtail (black females).

IDENTIFICATION Throughout much of the East, there are 4 species of "black" swallowtails: Black Swallowtail, Spicebush Swallowtail, Pipevine Swallowtail, and the black form of the female Eastern Tiger Swallowtail (Polydamas, Ozark, and Short-tailed Swallowtails are very restricted geographically—see those species for discussion). Below, Black and Spicebush Swallowtails have 2 rows of orange spots; the Pipevine and black female Eastern Tiger Swallowtails, only one; Polydamas Swallowtail, none. Below, the **yellow orange HW cell spot** or the FW subapical yellow spot distinguish this species from all others. Also note that the **FW postmedian and marginal yellow spots go all the way to the costal margin** while in Spicebush Swallowtail, they stop short. Also below, the HW median orange spot-band is complete (Spicebush Swallowtails lack one of the orange spots). Above, males, with their bright yellow spot-bands across both wings are obvious. Some females can appear surprisingly similar to some female Spicebush Swallowtails but can be separated from this and other species by the presence of a yellow FW subapical spot. Black Swallowtails usually have a less powerful flight than Spicebush Swallowtails.

HABITAT A swallowtail of open areas, especially of disturbed habitats; fields, meadows, tidal marshes, and suburban lawns.

RANGE Also, south in the mountains to Peru.

ABUNDANCE Generally U-C. Flies all year in Florida; 2–3 broods, Apr./May–Sept. farther north.

MAJOR FOODPLANT Parsley, fennel, carrot (wild or not), and other umbellifera.

COMMENTS The beautiful Black Swallowtail has adapted well to suburban and urban environments. Sometimes, eggs are laid even on parsley growing on the terraces of Manhattan's high-rise apartments. This hilltopping species is quite fond of clovers as nectar sources and tends to stay closer to the ground than our other swallowtails. In northern North Dakota and southern Manitoba there are various "black" swallowtails that appear intermediate between Black and Old World swallowtails. These are probably hybrid populations and have been called "Kahli" Swallowtails.

	MAR	APR	MAY	JUN	JUL	AUG	SEP	OCT
WI								
NY								
NC								
LA								

Ozark Swallowtail *Papilio joanae* Not Illustrated, see plate 2 for map.

SIZE = Black Swallowtail.

SIMILAR SPECIES Black Swallowtail.

IDENTIFICATION Probably not safely identified except by range, habitat, and food-plant preference. Closely resemble Black Swallowtails, especially in the spring, and, because the woodlands are open in springtime, the 2 species often occur together. In summer, look for Ozark Swallowtail in deep forest where Black Swallowtail is not found. If possible, look at the orange eyespot at the outer angle of the HW above. Ozark Swallowtail usually has the black pupil within this spot touching the trailing margin while Black Swallowtail has the black pupil centered. Richard Heitzman, who described the species, suggests looking at the orange spots below. Ozarks have little or no yellow, while Blacks usually have a fair amount of yellow in these spots.

HABITAT Cedar glades and woodlands.

RANGE See map on plate 2.

ABUNDANCE R-U. 2 broods, Apr.–Sept.

MAJOR FOODPLANT Meadow parsnip (*Thaspium barbinode*), yellow pimpernel (*Taenidia integerrima*) and other Apiaceae.

COMMENTS Although this species looks for all the world like a Black Swallowtail, an analysis of its mitochondrial DNA by Felix Sperling suggests that it is more closely related to the Old World Swallowtail.

Short-tailed Swallowtail *Papilio brevicauda* Plate 2

SIZE < Black Swallowtail.

SIMILAR SPECIES Black Swallowtail.

IDENTIFICATION Very little range overlap with Black Swallowtail. Above, note some **orange in yellow median HW band**. Also note **very short tails**.

HABITAT Heathland, grassy sea cliffs, gardens, and glades.

ABUNDANCE U. 1 brood. June–July, occasionally with a partial second in early Aug.

MAJOR FOODPLANT Umbellifers, especially Scotchman's lovage (*Ligusticum scothicum*) and cow parsnip (*Heracleum lanatum*).

Giant Swallowtail *Papilio cresphontes* Plate 3

SIZE ≥ Eastern Tiger Swallowtail.

SIMILAR SPECIES Palamedes Swallowtail.

IDENTIFICATION At a distance, note the contrast between the dark wings above an the pale wings below. Above, the wings are dark brown (almost black) with prominent yellow bands. Note the "Xs" these bands form near the apexes of the FW's and the yellow spot in the HW tails. Below, note the striking cream-colored body and cream-colored wings with HW blue median spot-band.

HABITAT	Open woodlands and fields, gardens, and hillsides near woolands.
RANGE	Also south to West Indies and northern South America.
ABUNDANCE	C in Florida where it flies all year, U-C Deep South, generally LR-U farther north. 2 broods, mainly May–Sept., the second usually more common. RS to North Dakota and Manitoba (2 reports), Minnesota, New Jersey, New York, and Connecticut. Occasionally forms small transient colonies north of the range shown.
MAJOR FOODPLANT	Rutaceae: prickly ash (*Xanthaxylum americanum*) and hoptree (*Ptelea trifoliata*) through most of the range, citrus and wild lime in the Deep South.
COMMENTS	More widespread northward in the late 1800's.

	MAR	APR	MAY	JUN	JUL	AUG	SEP	OCT
WI								
NY								
NC								
LA								

Schaus' Swallowtail *Papilio aristodemus* **Plate 3**

SIZE	≤ Eastern Tiger Swallowtail.
SIMILAR SPECIES	Giant Swallowtail, Palamedes Swallowtail, Bahamian Swallowtail.
IDENTIFICATION	Above, yellow bands are narrower and duller than on Giant Swallowtails or Palamedes Swallowtails, and unlike Giant Swallowtail, bands do not form an "X" near the FW subapex. **Note the bright yellow antennal clubs (of males) and lack of yellow spots in tails.** Below, there is an extensive, **rusty-colored patch in the HW median**. Flight is usually lower than Giant Swallowtail (within 3–4 ft. off ground). Ground color above is paler brown and bands are paler, duller yellow, so there is less contrast than in Giant Swallowtail. Overall shape is much squarer than elongated Giant Swallowtail.
HABITAT	Tropical hardwood hammocks.
RANGE	South Florida and the West Indies.
ABUNDANCE	LR, late April/May–early June.
MAJOR FOODPLANT	Wild lime and torchwood (*Amyris elemifera*).
COMMENTS	This species, listed as a federally endangered species, is the subject of recovery and reintroduction efforts on the Florida Keys, where it came close to extinction, due mainly to habitat loss and mosquito control programs.

Bahamian Swallowtail *Papilio andraemon* **Plate 3**

SIZE
: ≤ Black Swallowtail.

SIMILAR SPECIES
: Giant Swallowtail, Schaus' Swallowtail, Palamedes Swallowtail

IDENTIFICATION
: Remember, Bahamians have bars and bricks (not the Bahamia people who are, in my experience, warm and hospitable, b rather the swallowtails). Above, the **yellow bar** in the FW ce separates this species from either Giant or Schaus' Swallowta but be careful—the larger Palamedes Swallowtail also has a ye low bar in the cell. Male antennal clubs have yellow. Below, no the **"brick"** — a squared off rusty-colored patch jutting into th postmedian band.

HABITAT
: Tropical hardwood hammocks.

RANGE
: Florida Keys and West Indies.

ABUNDANCE
: LR. Recorded May–Oct. on the upper Florida keys.

MAJOR FOODPLANT
: Torchwood (*Amyris elemifera*) and other Rutaceae.

COMMENTS
: Currently, found on Elliott Key and vicinity, making this one of th most (the most?) geographically restricted, resident U.S. butterflie

Eastern Tiger Swallowtail *Papilio glaucus* **Plate 4**

SIZE
: 2 3/16 in.

SIMILAR SPECIES
: Canadian Tiger Swallowtail, Spicebush Swallowtail (blac form females).

IDENTIFICATION
: This boldly colored swallowtail is one of our most spectacular an familiar butterflies. Bright yellow wings with black stripes mak this usually very large swallowtail immediately identifiabl Females are dimorphic (have two forms) with some having blac wings. The percentage of black form females increases as on moves southward. Below, these are easy to differentiate fro other "black" swallowtails because they lack the HW media orange spot-band of Black and Spicebush swallowtails and th iridescent blue of Pipevine Swallowtails. They also usually retai a shadow of the "tiger" pattern. See also, Canadian Tig Swallowtail.

HABITAT
: Deciduous woodlands, especially woodland edges and wooded wate courses. Often seen soaring high among the trees in suburban yards

RANGE
: Also south through Mexico.

ABUNDANCE
: Generally C-A, 2 broods, March/April–Sept./Oct. Uncommon i south Florida.

MAJOR FOODPLANT
: Wild black cherry (*Prunus serotina*) and tulip tree (*Liriodendron tulipifera*

COMMENTS
: Inordinately fond of aromatic Oriental lilies (*Lilium rubrum*). Th tiger swallowtails and the lilies are each wonderful by themselve Together, they induce a state of bliss.

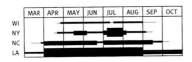

	MAR	APR	MAY	JUN	JUL	AUG	SEP	OCT
WI								
NY								
NC								
LA								

Canadian Tiger Swallowtail *Papilio canadensis* **Plate 4**

SIZE ≤ Black Swallowtail.

SIMILAR SPECIES Eastern Tiger Swallowtail.

IDENTIFICATION Below, look for the continuous yellow marginal band on the FW (Eastern Tiger Swallowtail tends to have this band broken into spots) and the broad black stripe along the trailing margin of the HW taking up more than 1/2 the width of the distance to the first vein (Eastern Tiger Swallowtail has this line narrower). Although this species is smaller than average-sized Eastern Tiger Swallowtails, this is not a very useful characteristic in areas where both occur.

HABITAT General in northern deciduous and deciduous-coniferous woodlands and edges.

RANGE Also western Canada and Alaska.

ABUNDANCE C-A. 1 brood, mainly late May–mid July.

MAJOR FOODPLANT Birches and aspens.

COMMENTS Eastern/Canadian Tiger Swallowtails are a borderline species/subspecies pair. Although populations in the far north are clearly different from populations to the south, there appears to be a broad blend zone in much of New England and North Dakota. The status of this species in the Appalachians is uncertain. Intermediate forms may be seen anywhere near, and extending from, areas along the southern edge of the range map for this species. Unlike Eastern Tiger Swallowtails, females of this species are almost never black.

Spicebush Swallowtail *Papilio troilus* **Plate 2**

SIZE ≥ Black Swallowtail.

SIMILAR SPECIES Black Swallowtail, Pipevine Swallowtail, black-form female Eastern Tiger Swallowtail.

IDENTIFICATION Below, note **2 orange spot-bands (marginal and postmedian) on the HW**, the absence of a yellow spot in the HW cell, and 1 **missing orange spot in the HW median spot-band**. Pipevine and black form female Tiger Swallowtails have only 1 orange spot-band while Black Swallowtails have a yellow spot in the cell and a complete orange median spot-band. Above, males are easily recognized by the beautiful cloud of bluish-green on the HW.

HABITAT | Open woodlands and their borders. Confined more closely woodlands than our other swallowtails.

ABUNDANCE | U-A. Florida & south Georgia west to east Texas—Feb.–Oct; els where, 2 broods mainly Apr.–Sept. RS to eastern Nebraska, Sou and North Dakota.

MAJOR FOODPLANT | Sassafras (*Sassafras albidum*) and spicebush (*Lindera benzoin*).

COMMENTS | Look on sassafras for the late instar caterpillars. Penultima instar caterpillars are adorable, while last instar individuals a flamboyant mini-dragons.

Palamedes Swallowtail *Papilio palamedes* Plate 3

SIZE | = Eastern Tiger Swallowtail.

SIMILAR SPECIES | Giant Swallowtail.

IDENTIFICATION | A large, very dark-brown and yellow swallowtail of souther swamps. Below, note the **yellow stripe along the base o the wings.** Above, note the **wide yellow HW postmedia band.** In flight the yellow "flash" on the HWs distinguish Palamedes from Giant Swallowtail. The dark brown/black fad to brown.

HABITAT | Southern swamps and adjacent open areas.

RANGE | Also northeastern Mexico.

ABUNDANCE | LC-A. 2 broods (possible 3 in Florida)—March–Oct./Nov.

MAJOR FOODPLANT | Red bay (*Persea borbonica*).

COMMENTS | Bob Pyle aptly described this species as "the signature swallowta of the great [southeastern] swamps." Despite their color and pa tern differences, Palamedes and Spicebush swallowtails a closely related. Both have similar courtship flights, with a fema flying a foot or two above the ground and a male flying slow about 2 feet above her. Sometimes the two species will cou each other!

Pierids, or Whites and Yellows
(family Pieridae)

Pierids are white and yellow butterflies that range in size from small to large. The whites' and yellows' colors are due to the presence of pteridines, pigments that are characteristic of pierids and that are rarely found in other families of butterflies. Their fairly rapid and low flight, usually with only short stops for nectar, draws one's eye to them as they nervously course about open fields. They often will not sit still to allow you a leisurely study of their appearance. So ubiquitous are they that many people believe that the word "butterfly" derives from a common European yellow. Unlike most of our other butterflies that tend to have definite broods and appear only at specific times of the year, many white and yellows are continuously brooded and thus fly essentially all season long.

Florida White *Appias drusilla* Plate 5

SIZE	≥ Cabbage White.
SIMILAR SPECIES	Great Southern White.
IDENTIFICATION	Very difficult to distinguish from the much more common Great Southern Whites on the wing. At rest, unlike Great Southern Whites, the **antennal clubs are white**, not phosphorescent blue. Above, the black margin on the FW doesn't extend inward along the veins as it does in Great Southern White. Below, Florida Whites have **orange at the base of HW leading margin** that Great Southern Whites lack.
HABITAT	Tropical hardwood hammocks.
RANGE	Also south through West Indies and tropical Americas.
ABUNDANCE	LU-LC. All year in southern Florida, irregularly straying north to Gainesville. Rare stray east to Houston and north to Kansas and Nebraska (1 record).
MAJOR FOODPLANT	Jamaican caper (*Drypetes lateriflora*).
COMMENTS	A good place to find this butterfly is Matheson Hammock County Park, Dade Co., Florida, where it flies in the shade and dappled light along narrow trails through the hammock.

Checkered White *Pontia protodice* Plate 5

SIZE	= Cabbage White.
SIMILAR SPECIES	Cabbage White, Falcate Orangetip.
IDENTIFICATION	When well seen, the extensive black or dark brown wing markings are distinctive. Females have more extensive markings than

males. In flight, this species is similar to Cabbage White but the white ground color appears chalky with a slight bluish tinge. Its flight tends to use deeper wingbeats and to be more direct than the swerving flight of Cabbage Whites.

HABITAT Disturbed open areas, especially beach areas, abandoned railroad tracks along the coast, and other sandy areas.

RANGE Also western U.S. and northern Mexico.

ABUNDANCE Usually most common in Florida and the southern Midwest, the abundance of this species greatly fluctuates. In the East, it is generally rare and its presence is usually unpredictable. Flies March to Nov. in Florida, Georgia, and Mississippi.

MAJOR FOODPLANT Crucifers, especially peppergrass (*Lepidium*).

COMMENTS The Checkered White has been described as "formerly much more abundant" by about every author for the past 100 years! It seems likely that this primarily western, southern, and midwestern species sporadically became abundant in the northeast on agricultural lands, the acreage of which is now greatly reduced.

	MAR	APR	MAY	JUN	JUL	AUG	SEP	OCT
WI								
NY								
NC								
LA								

Western White *Pontia occidentalis* Not Illustrated, see Plate 5 for map.

SIZE = Cabbage White.

SIMILAR SPECIES Checkered White.

IDENTIFICATION Very difficult to distinguish from Checkered Whites. Males are easier than females and summer individuals are easier than the spring broods. In general, Western Whites have more dark spots than Checkered Whites and are a little larger. On the FW marginal black spot-band, Western White males have a set of 5 or 6 spots while Checkered White males almost always lack spots 3 and (counting down from the FW apex). Western White females generally have gray dark markings, while Checkered White females tend toward brown. Western Whites usually have solid black abdomens, with little or no white "powdering," while Checkered Whites generally have abdomens with extensive white.

HABITAT Mainly montane open situations.

RANGE Western North America.

ABUNDANCE LR-LC (Manitoba). 2 broods. May–mid July, Aug.–mid Sept.

MAJOR FOODPLANT Crucifers.

COMMENTS In theory, Checkered Whites are a lowland species while Western

Whites are at high elevations. Unfortunately for easy identification, Checkered Whites can be found above 10,000 ft. while Western Whites fly in the lowlands of the northwest portion of our region.

Mustard White *Pieris napi* **Plate 6**

SIZE	≤ Cabbage White.
SIMILAR SPECIES	Cabbage White, West Virginia White.
IDENTIFICATION	Spring-flying individuals usually have wing veins below edged with dark greenish-black. West Virginia Whites have veins edged with paler, more diffused gray. Summer-flying individuals are often immaculate both above and below.
HABITAT	Northern deciduous forest.
ABUNDANCE	LR-U through much of its range. RS to South Dakota. Mainly 2 broods, late April–mid June; early July–Aug. 1 brood in far north.
MAJOR FOODPLANT	Crucifers.
COMMENTS	There is some recent evidence that the Mustard White complex may consist of a number of different species and a number of books have appeared that jump on this bandwagon. This is a mistake. Stable names are important, especially for those people who are not experts (that is, just about everyone). Changes to well established names should be made in works intended for the public only if the **published evidence is overwhelming** that the change is correct. While the Mustard White complex may eventually be shown conclusively to consist of more than one species, the evidence published to date is not overwhelming.

West Virginia White *Pieris virginiensis* **Plate 6**

SIZE	≤ Cabbage White.
SIMILAR SPECIES	Mustard White, Cabbage White.
IDENTIFICATION	Below, note the **wing veins edged in pale gray**. Spring-flying Mustard Whites have veins edged with much darker greenish-black. Above it is immaculate white but early spring Cabbage Whites often have reduced black spots above and are sometimes immaculate. Check below. In flight, West Virginia Whites appear grayer than Cabbage Whites with a weaker flight that keeps them closer to the ground. But, check below.
HABITAT	Rich transition-zone deciduous woodlands with good stands of the foodplant (this is usually near streams).
ABUNDANCE	LC in the southern and mid-Appalachians, otherwise LR-LU, 1 brood, mainly April–May.
MAJOR FOODPLANT	Toothworts (*Dentaria diphylla* and *D. laciniata*).
COMMENTS	This species is very closely related to Mustard White.

Cabbage White *Pieris rapae* Plate 6

SIZE	15/16 in.
SIMILAR SPECIES	Clouded/Orange Sulphur (white females).
IDENTIFICATION	This common to abundant European introduction is an often high-flying white with a fairly strong but erratic (swerving) flight. Seen well, Cabbage Whites have either **1 (males) or 2 (females) black spots and a dark subapex on the FW above** but early spring individuals sometimes have these markings greatly diminished. Below, there is usually a strong yellowish cast to the HW.
HABITAT	Any type of open or lightly wooded terrain, especially gardens, roadsides, and agricultural lands. Also present in urban areas.
RANGE	Holarctic.
ABUNDANCE	Generally, C-A, but R-U at southern edge of range. Flies early spring to frost.
MAJOR FOODPLANT	Crucifers.
COMMENTS	Probably our most ubiquitous butterfly. The Cabbage White is one of only two non-native butterfly species that are now widespread in eastern North America (European Skipper is the other). In the middle of summer, the vision of hundreds of these whites dancing around the blooming purple loosestrife plants (another introduced species that is generally considered a pest) creates the impression that one has been transported into a Walt Disney fairyland. Although many people disparage this species, because it is so common and non native, close observation reveals it to be one of the most graceful inhabitants of the air.

	MAR	APR	MAY	JUN	JUL	AUG	SEP	OCT
WI								
NY								
NC								
LA								

Great Southern White *Ascia monuste* Plate 5

SIZE	≤ Cloudless Sulphur.
SIMILAR SPECIES	Cabbage White, in south Florida see Florida White.
IDENTIFICATION	The **phosphorescent blue antennal clubs** are distinctive. Female can be either white, or smoky brown, largely depending upon season
HABITAT	Open situations, especially along the coast, including dunes, salt marshes, fields, and gardens.
RANGE	Also south through tropical Americas.
ABUNDANCE	C-A south Florida where it flies all year, decreasing north Georgia (mainly fall). R, east Texas coast. RS to coastal Mississippi and central Florida.

JOR FOODPLANT Saltwort (*Batis maritima*), many crucifers, and capers.

COMMENTS This species will very rarely undergo a real population explosion—sending emigrants out through the continent, with records extending north to North Dakota! Under such circumstances it might be found anywhere.

Large Marble *Euchloe ausonides* **Plate 7**

SIZE ≤ Cabbage White.

IMILAR SPECIES Olympia Marble, Falcate Orangetip (female).

IDENTIFICATION Distinguish from Olympia Marble (ranges probably don't overlap in our area) by **antenna checked with black** (Olympia Marble has white antenna) and below, by middle green band having two prongs near leading edge of HW. Female Falcate Orangetip has HW below with much more mottling and has falcate FW wingtips.

HABITAT A wide variety of open situations in the mountains or the north.

RANGE Western North America.

ABUNDANCE LR-LU. Southern Ontario and Manitoba. 1 brood. Mid May–early July.

AJOR FOODPLANT Crucifers, mainly rock cresses (*Arabis*).

Olympia Marble *Euchloe olympia* **Plate 7**

SIZE ≤ Cabbage White.

IMILAR SPECIES Falcate Orangetip, Cabbage White.

IDENTIFICATION Small size and more angled wings allow one to distinguish this species from Cabbage White in flight. Below, the beautiful green marbling is distinctive. Female Falcate Orangetips have more extensive, more fractured marbling, and have falcate FWs. Cabbage Whites lack marbling below.

HABITAT Poor soil areas such as limestone and sand or shale barrens, grasslands, dunes, and open cedar glades.

ABUNDANCE LR (Appalachians)-LU (Midwest). 1 brood, mainly mid April–mid May.

AJOR FOODPLANT Rock cresses (*Arabis*).

COMMENTS Below, fresh individuals have a beautiful rosy flush on the base of their HWs and along the costal margin of their FWs. Flight is quite rapid and far-ranging, making observation difficult.

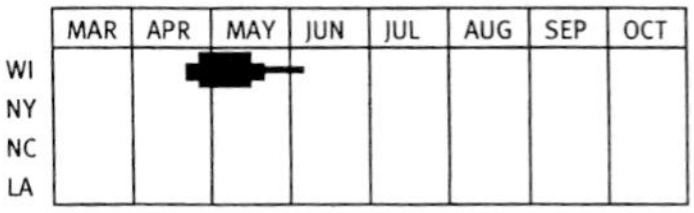
MAR
APR
MAY
JUN
JUL
AUG
SEP
OCT
WI
NY
NC
LA

Falcate Orangetip *Anthocharis midea* **Plate 7**

SIZE   < Cabbage White.

SIMILAR SPECIES   Checkered White.

IDENTIFICATION   This is a small, early spring white. Males, with their bright ora█ wingtips contrasting with otherwise white wings, gladden █ heart and are unmistakable. Females have blunt (falcate) F█ and are heavily marbled below. Flight is fairly weak and v█ close to the ground, rarely rising more than a couple of feet hi█

HABITAT   Open woodlands with small crucifers.

ABUNDANCE   LU-LC. 1 brood, March–April north Florida-east Texas, north█ West Virginia-Oklahoma; April–May farther north. RS to Nebra█ (1 record).

MAJOR FOODPLANT   Crucifers, mainly rock cresses (*Arabis*) and bitter-cresses (*Cardami*█

COMMENTS   Females appear a week or so later than the males.

	MAR	APR	MAY	JUN	JUL	AUG	SEP	OCT
WI								
NY								
NC								
LA								

Clouded Sulphur *Colias philodice* **Plates 6 & 8**

SIZE   = Cabbage White.

SIMILAR SPECIES   Orange Sulphur.

IDENTIFICATION   A strong-flying medium-sized sulphur of open fields. Since s█ phurs almost always land with their wings closed, it is difficult█ get a good view of their upper wing surfaces. Above, which c█ be seen in flight, is clear lemon-yellow with **no orange patch**█ Both sexes have black FW borders above but females have yell█ spots within the border. Orange Sulphur has at least so█ orange above. Some female Clouded and Orange sulphurs la█ the yellów and/or orange pigments and are off-white with t█ usual black pattern. They can be distinguished from Cabba█ Whites by their less swerving flight patterns, their off-wh█ appearance, and their black markings. Although Cloud█ Sulphur females generally have a narrower black FW bor█ than Orange Sulphur females, distinguishing the white female█ the field may not be possible.

HABITAT   Open fields, roadsides, suburban areas, etc.

RANGE   Also western North America.

ABUNDANCE   C-A, becoming U-R southward. RS south to Gulf of Mexi█ Many broods, March/April – frost; Maine, May–Oct.

MAJOR FOODPLANT   White clover (*Trifolium repens*).

COMMENTS   Many reports of this species from the Deep South are really█

Orange Sulphurs with very little orange.

	MAR	APR	MAY	JUN	JUL	AUG	SEP	OCT
WI								
NY								
NC								
LA								

Orange Sulphur *Colias eurytheme* **Plates 6 & 8**

SIZE	= Cabbage White.
SIMILAR SPECIES	Clouded Sulphur.
IDENTIFICATION	A strong-flying medium-sized sulphur of open fields. Above with at least some orange (this can be seen in flight). Because this species sometimes hybridizes with Clouded Sulphur, calling *all* individuals with any orange above Orange Sulphurs is only an operational definition. See Clouded Sulphur for a discussion of white females.
HABITAT	Open fields, roadsides, suburban areas, etc.
RANGE	Also western North America and south to central Mexico.
ABUNDANCE	C-A, but R-U near southeastern and northern edges of range, early spring (temperatures over 55°F) – frost.
MAJOR FOODPLANT	Alfalfa (*Medicago sativa*) and other Fabaceae.
COMMENTS	A southern species, not established in the Northeast until around 1930 but now one of the most abundant butterflies, especially around cultivated fields.

	MAR	APR	MAY	JUN	JUL	AUG	SEP	OCT
WI								
NY								
NC								
LA								

Pink-edged Sulphur *Colias interior* **Plate 8**

SIZE	= Cabbage White.
SIMILAR SPECIES	Clouded Sulphur.
IDENTIFICATION	This denizen of northern blueberry barrens is distinguished from Clouded Sulphur by the **single HW central spot** (Clouded Sulphur has a doubled HW central spot) and by the more prominent pink wing edgings (although Clouded Sulphur can have a significant amount of pink). Females have greatly reduced black borders above and this can sometimes be seen through the wings. In addition, Clouded Sulphurs almost always have postmedian spots (sometimes faint) on the HW below. Pink-edged Sulphurs lack these and have a cleaner, more uniform ground color below.
HABITAT	Northern heath barrens.
RANGE	Also west through northern U.S. and Canada.

ABUNDANCE   R-U; 1 brood—mid June–mid August.

MAJOR FOODPLANT   Blueberries.

COMMENTS   This species can sometimes be common around cultivated blue-berry patches.

	MAR	APR	MAY	JUN	JUL	AUG	SEP	OCT
WI								
NY								
NC								
LA								

Southern Dogface *Colias cesonia* Plates 8 & 12

SIZE   > Cabbage White.

SIMILAR SPECIES   Clouded Sulphur.

IDENTIFICATION   A bright yellow sulphur, slightly larger than Clouded Sulphur, with a bold black outline of a dog's head above. Below, note pointed FWs and the outline of dog's head pattern through the FW. The fall form has the HW below suffused with pink.

HABITAT   Dry roadsides and fields, usually near open woodlands.

RANGE   Also south through the Americas.

ABUNDANCE   U-C north Florida, south Georgia, west to Texas—March–Oct East of Appalachians, a rare and erratic immigrant north to Virginia. More common west of Appalachians, mainly Aug.–Oct. RS north to Ontario (1 record), North Dakota, and Manitob. (old records).

MAJOR FOODPLANT   Pea family.

COMMENTS   Although I have seen swarms of thousands of these butterflies in the Rio Grande Valley of Texas, this butterfly is never this abun-dant farther north.

	MAR	APR	MAY	JUN	JUL	AUG	SEP	OCT
WI								
NY								
NC								
LA								

Cloudless Sulphur *Phoebis sennae* Plates 11 & 12

SIZE   1 5/16 in.

SIMILAR SPECIES   Orange-barred Sulphur.

IDENTIFICATION   Size alone will usually suffice to distinguish phoebis from yellow or other sulphurs. This is by far the most common and widespread phoebis and the only one likely to be seen north of central Florida or southern Texas. It has a high, directional, sailing flight with characteristic deep, powerful wingbeats. This species can usually separated on the wing from its congeners by its yellow upper wings. Males are pale yellow; females vary from orange-yellow off-white (although white females are scarce in the east). Green-yellow below, males have few markings while females' more extensive markings include a broken FW postmedian line. Large Orange Sulphurs are bright orange above. Orange-barred Sulphurs are usually larger and have deep orange markings above, but these can sometimes be difficult to see in flight.

HABITAT	A wide variety of open situations.
RANGE	Also south through tropical Americas.
ABUNDANCE	C-A all-year resident in the Deep South; as the season progresses Cloudless Sulphurs move northward in large numbers, usually reaching North Carolina and Oklahoma by mid April, West Virginia by May, Missouri and Indiana by June. Late summer/fall brood moves rapidly up the Atlantic coast, usually reaching New York (where it is R) by Sept. and occasionally reaching Maine and probably adjacent Canada. Much less common away from the immediate coast. Similar behavior west of the Appalachians brings rare strays north to Ontario, Minnesota, and South Dakota, tending to follow river valleys.
MAJOR FOODPLANT	Cassias.
COMMENTS	Numbers fluctuate markedly from year to year.

	MAR	APR	MAY	JUN	JUL	AUG	SEP	OCT
WI								
NY								
NC								
LA								

Orange-barred Sulphur *Phoebis philea* Plates 11 & 12

SIZE	≥ Cloudless Sulphur.
SIMILAR SPECIES	Cloudless Sulphur, Large Orange Sulphur.
IDENTIFICATION	Above, males are **yellow with orange patches** on both the FWs and HWs. Females range from yellow to white above, lack the FW orange patches, usually have rich reddish HW borders above and often have rich reddish suffusions below. Below, FW postmedian line is broken as in Cloudless Sulphur. Cloudless Sulphurs are all yellow, Large Orange Sulphurs are all orange and have a straight FW postmedian line below.
HABITAT	Gardens and open woodlands in subtropical areas.
RANGE	Also south through tropical Americas.
ABUNDANCE	C all year southern Florida; rare stray to Georgia coast, Sept.-Nov. Reports of strays northward (e.g., Maine, Wisconsin, Kansas, Nebraska) mainly date to more than 60 years ago, but there is a June 1987 record from Ontario.
MAJOR FOODPLANT	Cassias.

COMMENTS Bouncing as it flies, this large, bright yellow and orange dream-come-true is the apotheosis of "butterflyness." A wide-ranging butterfly, this species colonized south Florida (presumably from Mexico) in the 1920's.

Large Orange Sulphur *Phoebis agarithe* Plates 11 & 12

SIZE = Cloudless Sulphur.

SIMILAR SPECIES Orange-barred Sulphur.

IDENTIFICATION A very large sulphur that is **bright orange above**. Below, note the **diagonal, straight line on the FW**. Orange-barred Sulphurs are yellow with orange patches above and have a broken post-median line on the FW below.

HABITAT General in open tropical and subtropical situations, including gardens and woodland edges.

RANGE Also south through tropical Americas.

ABUNDANCE C all year southern Florida; 1 record June 1995 western NY. Regular but rare immigrant north to Houston. Rare stray to New York, Missouri, Kansas, Nebraska, and South Dakota (twice).

MAJOR FOODPLANT Many Fabaceae.

COMMENTS Most records are old but the western New York record is from June 1995. Then again, with the proliferation of "butterfly houses" maybe this was an artificial occurrence.

Statira Sulphur *Phoebis statira* Plate 12

SIZE = Cloudless Sulphur.

SIMILAR SPECIES Cloudless Sulphur, Lyside Sulphur.

IDENTIFICATION Above, similar to Cloudless Sulphur. Below, females are either marked as shown on plate 12 or are immaculate ivory white, but with **some yellow at the base of the FW costal margin and along the FW disc**. Males are similar but are tinged yellow-green. In Florida, most, if not all, females resemble the individual shown on plate 12. The FW cell-end markings below are dark pink, usually pretty much "filled in", and have a smaller projection toward the costal margin. There are no markings on the basal 1/ of the HW. Other phoebis have FW cell-end markings that are larger, of nearly equal size, and that are not so filled in. Usually has a pinkish patch at the apex of the FW. Note the **puckered appearance of the outer 1/3 of the wings**. Lyside Sulphur smaller, greener, usually with a characteristic whitened HW vein.

HABITAT In Florida, open areas near salt marshes or mangroves—near stands of *Dalbergia*. More general elsewhere in range.

RANGE Also south through tropical Americas.

ABUNDANCE	LR-LU, Feb.–Nov., south Florida rarely straying north to Gainesville, with 1 Georgia record.
MAJOR FOODPLANT	*Dalbergia* and *Cassia.*
COMMENTS	A very easy species to overlook amidst the much more common Cloudless and Lyside sulphurs.

Lyside Sulphur *Kricogonia lyside* **Plate 12**

SIZE	= Cabbage White.
SIMILAR SPECIES	Statira Sulphur, White Angled-Sulphur.
IDENTIFICATION	Extremely variable. Above, varies from yellow to white with yellow patches, to white. Below, often distinctively green with a prominently whitened vein running through the HW and a yellow flush to the FW disc, but can be pale yellowish to almost white without the whitened vein.
HABITAT	Tropical and subtropical scrub.
RANGE	West Indies and southern Texas south to Venezuela.
ABUNDANCE	LR-LU, south Florida, July–Sept. Midwest, RS north to Missouri and Kansas.
MAJOR FOODPLANT	Probably lignum vitae (*Guaicacum sanctum*) in Florida.
COMMENTS	Common to abundant in the Rio Grande Valley of Texas, it may be only a temporary colonist in the Florida Keys.

Barred Yellow *Eurema daira* **Plate 9**

SIZE	≤ Little Yellow.
SIMILAR SPECIES	Little Yellow, Dainty Sulphur.
IDENTIFICATION	A very small, weak-flying yellow. Above, yellow, or white, or with FW yellow and HW white. Males have a black bar along the FW lower margin that can sometimes be seen either in flight or through the wings when landed. Below, HW with weak pattern, winter individuals suffused with rusty-brown. The HW apex is usually vaguely darker with an inwardly directed line. Base of FW at costal margin is white or tan with darker flecking, Little Yellow is pure yellow here.
HABITAT	Disturbed open situations—roadsides, vacant fields, gardens, etc.
RANGE	South through tropical Americas.
ABUNDANCE	C-A Florida—all year; north to Georgia, Mississippi—Feb.–Dec. RS north to North Carolina, Missouri, Wisconsin, and South Dakota (1 report).
MAJOR FOODPLANT	Pencil flower (*Stylosanthes hamata*) and other legumes.
COMMENTS	Migrates southward from north to south Florida in the fall.

	MAR	APR	MAY	JUN	JUL	AUG	SEP	OCT
WI								
NY								
NC								
LA								

Mexican Yellow *Eurema mexicana* **Plate 10**

SIZE   = Cabbage White.

SIMILAR SPECIES   Clouded Sulphur, Little Yellow.

IDENTIFICATION   Note the **tailed HW. Above the ground color is pale yellow to white** with a dramatic "dog's face" pattern. Clouded Sulphur and Little Yellow lack tails. Other tailed yellows are orange above.

HABITAT   In our area, most likely in arid areas, but it could occur most anywhere.

RANGE   Mexico south to Colombia.

ABUNDANCE   R immigrant north from Mexico, more or less regularly reaching Kansas—July–Nov.; very rarely reaching Mississippi, Ohio, Indiana, Wisconsin, North Dakota, and Manitoba.

MAJOR FOODPLANT   Legumes, including *Acacia*.

Tailed Orange *Eurema proterpia* **Plate 10**

SIZE   = Cabbage White.

SIMILAR SPECIES   Sleepy Orange.

IDENTIFICATION   Stray only. Very deep orange above. Two forms, one tailed and highly striated with brown below (winter-dry season); the other HW sharply angled, but not tailed, and unmarked orange below (summer-wet season). Both lack a FW cell-end bar. Sleepy Orange is untailed and has a black spot at the end of the FW cell.

HABITAT   Tropical woodlands.

RANGE   West Indies and Mexico south to Peru.

ABUNDANCE   RS to Kansas and southeastern Nebraska (1 record).

MAJOR FOODPLANT   *Cassia*.

COMMENTS   At some times of the year, one can encounter both forms on the same day.

Little Yellow *Eurema lisa* **Plates 9 & 10**

SIZE   1 1/16 in.

SIMILAR SPECIES   Clouded Sulphur.

IDENTIFICATION   A small yellow, very bright yellow above, with a rapid, low, and straight flight path, is likely to be this species. It is much smaller and brighter than Clouded Sulphur. If seen landed, note the scattered smudged dark markings on the HW below and the **black** (not dull pink) antennas. The extent of markings below quite variable. Most individuals have a pink spot at the HW apex, although this spot is often diminished or absent in males.

HABITAT   Most common in disturbed open areas, especially in dry, sandy grassy fields.

RANGE   Also West Indies and south to Costa Rica.

ABUNDANCE	C-A all year resident in deep south, becoming progressively rarer far-ther north, irregularly immigrating to Massachusetts, Maine, Ontario, Wisconsin, and South Dakota, mainly late July–early Sept. in the north.
MAJOR FOODPLANT	*Cassia.*
COMMENTS	By far our most widespread and common yellow (*Eurema*).

	MAR	APR	MAY	JUN	JUL	AUG	SEP	OCT
WI								
NY								
NC								
LA								

Mimosa Yellow *Eurema nise* Plate 9

SIZE	≤ Little Yellow.
SIMILAR SPECIES	Little Yellow.
IDENTIFICATION	Mimosa Yellows fly at the edges of woodlands. Unlike similar Little Yellows, they rarely venture into the open adjacent areas, and if they do they usually do not remain for long. Beside behavior, note two marks to distinguish this rare species from Little Yellow. First, look carefully at the black border at the FW apex (this can usually be seen from below, looking through the wing). Mimosa Yellow has a much narrower border than does Little Yellow. Second, Mimosa Yellow lacks a black spot near the base of the HW below that Little Yellow has (see photo).
HABITAT	In U.S., edges of tropical hardwood hammocks.
RANGE	Also West Indies and southern Texas south through tropical Americas.
ABUNDANCE	LU-LR, May–Dec. RS north to Kansas, Nebraska (1 record).
MAJOR FOODPLANT	*Mimosa.*

Dina Yellow *Eurema dina* Plate 9

SIZE	≥ Little Yellow.
SIMILAR SPECIES	Little Yellow.
IDENTIFICATION	Yet another denizen of tropical hardwood hammocks (and especially their brushy edges), Dina Yellow is larger and more orange-flushed than Little Yellow. Males are bright orange-yel-low with a very narrow black FW border. Females are yellow with an orange flush. Below, note the **pinkish-brown apex-es of both FW and HW**. Little Yellow lacks a pinkish patch on the FW apex.
HABITAT	Tropical woodlands.
RANGE	Also, West Indies, Mexico to Panama.
ABUNDANCE	LU-LC, all year.

MAJOR FOODPLANT Mexican alvaradoa tree (*Alvaradoa amorphoides*).

COMMENTS Established in south Florida in 1962. Now **extremely local** in the Homestead area with a few reports from Key Largo.

Sleepy Orange *Eurema nicippe* Plate 10

SIZE = Cabbage White.

SIMILAR SPECIES Orange Sulphur.

IDENTIFICATION This butterfly is bright orange above with black borders. It flies closer to the ground than Orange Sulphur, with weaker wing-beats and is a darker orange above. Seen well, note the black antennas (Orange Sulphur—dull pink) and the characteristic **diagonal brown markings** on the HW below. This species has 2 color forms and the HW ground color below can be either yellow or a dull reddish color.

HABITAT Roadsides, open fields, and open pine woodlands.

RANGE Also, west to southern California, West Indies, and Mexico south to Costa Rica.

ABUNDANCE U-C all year resident in Deep South (but even here, most common Aug.–Oct.). Moves northward in summer, fairly regularly to Kansas, Ohio, and West Virginia (R-U, May–Oct.) and irregularly to South Dakota (2 records), Wisconsin, Ontario, and southern New Jersey.

MAJOR FOODPLANT *Cassia.*

COMMENTS The name "sleepy" does not refer to this species' flight—which is quite perky. Rather, there are no "eye-spots" on the wings (unlike Clouded and Orange sulphurs) and thus *Eurema nicippe* has its eyes closed and is sleepy! See also, Sleepy and Dreamy duskywings.

	MAR	APR	MAY	JUN	JUL	AUG	SEP	OCT
WI								
NY								
NC								
LA								

Dainty Sulphur *Nathalis iole* Plate 8

SIZE ≤ Little Yellow.

SIMILAR SPECIES Barred Yellow, Little Yellow.

IDENTIFICATION A tiny sulphur, more greenish yellow above than Little Yellow. Flight, even lower to the ground than Barred Yellow. Below, note the dark greenish HW and the **black spots on the FW submarginal area**.

HABITAT Fields, roadsides, and other disturbed habitats.

RANGE Also, west to southern California and south to West Indies and Guatemala.

ABUNDANCE C-A all year resident South Florida. LC north Florida/south Georgia west to east Texas—May/June–November (most common Aug.–Sept.). Regularly north to Kansas (R-U June–Oct.), irregularly north to South Dakota (June–Oct.), Manitoba, Missouri, Wisconsin (R-U Aug.–Oct), Michigan. RS to Ohio, Ontario (2 records), North Carolina (1 record), Virginia, and Pennsylvania.

MAJOR FOODPLANT Spanish needles (*Bidens pilosa*) in Florida, fetid marigold (*Dyssodia papposa*) and other daisy family plants in Midwest.

COMMENTS Quite variable in detail, this butterfly is still distinctive.

	MAR	APR	MAY	JUN	JUL	AUG	SEP	OCT
WI								
NY								
NC								
LA								

Lycaenids or Gossamer-wings (family Lycaenidae)

This is a very large worldwide family of butterflies consisting, in our area, of coppers, hairstreaks, blues, and harvester. Most species are quite small, although a few tropical hairstreaks are larger than an American Lady. Many gossamer-wings are myrmecophilous (ant-loving). The caterpillars secrete a "honey-dew" from special glands that attracts certain species of ants. These ants then "tend" the caterpillars helping to protect them from predator species. The caterpillars of many gossamer-wings (including some of ours) feed on flower parts.

Harvester *Feniseca tarquinius* **Plate 15**

SIZE = Banded Hairstreak.

SIMILAR SPECIES American Copper.

IDENTIFICATION A medium-sized lycaenid, bright orange above with bold black markings. Below, note the orange disc of the FW and dull reddish-brown HW with **delicate white markings**. Unlike American Copper, this butterfly is often seen on tree leaves.

HABITAT Woodlands, especially near watercourses or wet areas with alders.

ABUNDANCE R-U. 2 or 3 broods. North to Washington, DC, Missouri, Kansas—April–Oct. Northward—May–Sept.

MAJOR FOODPLANT Woolly aphids, usually on alders or beech.

COMMENTS   Harvesters are our only butterflies with carnivorous caterpillars. The caterpillars feed on other insects (woolly aphids) rather than on plants. Adults can sometimes be found sunning themselves in woodland glades in the late afternoon. Usually quite rare and a good find, this species occasionally undergoes population irruptions. Its closest relatives live in Africa.

	MAR	APR	MAY	JUN	JUL	AUG	SEP	OCT
WI			–	–	–	■	– –	
NY			–					
NC		—		—				
LA								

American Copper *Lycaena phlaeas* **Plate 13**

SIZE   = Banded Hairstreak.

SIMILAR SPECIES   Bronze Copper, Harvester.

IDENTIFICATION   A tiny flash of orange announces this whirling dervish. Above, the FWs are lustrous orange with black spots while the HWs are dark brownish-gray with a brownish-orange submarginal band. Below, note the orange FW disc and grayish HW with narrow orange marginal band.

HABITAT   Disturbed open areas, fields, sandy prairies, power-line cuts, etc.

RANGE   Also, Holarctic and some East African mountains.

ABUNDANCE   Mainly C-A in the northeast, LR in the southern Appalachians, U-C Midwest. 3 broods—mainly late April–mid Oct.; Maine/New Brunswick—perhaps only 2 broods, June–Sept. RS west to South and North Dakota.

MAJOR FOODPLANT   Various docks (*Rumex*) including sheep sorrel (*Rumex acetosella*).

COMMENTS   Some authors state that the population of this species in eastern North America is not native, but rather was introduced from Europe during colonial times. The evidence to support this assertion is meager. The main argument is that the major caterpillar foodplant in eastern North America is sheep sorrel, a native of Eurasia. But the main caterpillar foodplant for Hayhurst's Scallopwing and Common Sootywing is now the alien lamb's squarters, while caterpillars of Wild Indigo Duskywing now overwhelmingly feed on the introduced crown vetch. The most often cited caterpillar foodplant for Gray Copper is the alien broad dock. If these species have switched to alien plants, why couldn't American Coppers? The additional argument, that the eastern population seems to more closely resemble the Scandinavian population than the populations in the American far north, has not been established and would be far from compelling even if true.

	MAR	APR	MAY	JUN	JUL	AUG	SEP	OCT
WI								
NY								
NC								
LA								

Gray Copper *Lycaena dione* **Plate 13**

SIZE	≥ Pearl Crescent.
SIMILAR SPECIES	Bronze Copper, Acadian Hairstreak.
IDENTIFICATION	A very large copper. Below, grayish-white; HW with orange marginal band. FW disc is gray, not orange as in Bronze Copper. HW with many black spots (Acadian Hairstreak lacks black spots on HW base and is much smaller). **Above, gray.**
HABITAT	Moist meadows, roadside ditches, and other wet, open situations in the prairie province.
RANGE	Also, west to Montana and Alberta.
ABUNDANCE	R-LC; 1 brood June–late July/early Aug.
MAJOR FOODPLANT	Broad dock (*Rumex obtusifolius*) and other docks.
COMMENTS	Rarely encountered in numbers.

	MAR	APR	MAY	JUN	JUL	AUG	SEP	OCT
WI								
NY								
NC								
LA								

Bronze Copper *Lycaena hyllus* **Plate 13**

SIZE	≥ Pearl Crescent.
SIMILAR SPECIES	American Copper, Gray Copper.
IDENTIFICATION	A very large, floppy-flying copper. Although in a picture it closely resembles American Copper, when encountered in the field there is no doubt about its identity. The logical flip side of this is that if you are in doubt of a butterfly's identity, it is not this species. Above, males are purple with orange tints, while females have their ground color paler yellowish-orange. Below, note the pale, almost white ground color, the orange FW disc, and the broad marginal HW orange band. Gray Coppers are gray above and lack the orange FW disc below.
HABITAT	Low wet meadows/marshes, especially in river flood plains.
RANGE	Also west to northeastern New Mexico, Idaho, and Alberta.
ABUNDANCE	Mainly LR-LU. 3 broods south—May–Oct. 2 broods northward—mainly June and August.
MAJOR FOODPLANT	Water dock (*Rumex orbiculatus*) and curled dock (*R. crispus*).
COMMENTS	Man's penchant for draining wetlands and channeling rivers has caused this species to decline in many areas.

	MAR	APR	MAY	JUN	JUL	AUG	SEP	OCT
WI				—	—		—	—
NY								
NC								
LA								

Bog Copper *Lycaena epixanthe* **Plate 14**

SIZE = Eastern Tailed-Blue.

SIMILAR SPECIES Purplish Copper, Dorcas Copper.

IDENTIFICATION A very small, weak-flying copper that somehow manages to elude you as you follow it in a bog. Below, note the **very pale HW**. Purplish and Dorcas coppers are darker, more copper-colored. Above, females are evenly brown-gray with a slight purplish sheen. Female Purplish and Dorcas Coppers have a pale, orangish area outside the FW postmedian band. Males are more intensely purple, but have fewer black spots than Purplish and Dorcas coppers.

HABITAT Acid bogs with cranberries.

ABUNDANCE Generally LR but LC on Cape Cod and northwestern Wisconsin. 1 brood mainly mid June/early July–late July/mid Aug., occasionally into early Sept. in Maine, New Brunswick, and Manitoba.

MAJOR FOODPLANT Cranberries (*Vaccinium macrocarpum* and *V. palustris*).

COMMENTS Not usually found in commercial cranberry bogs due to the use of pesticides.

	MAR	APR	MAY	JUN	JUL	AUG	SEP	OCT
WI								
NY				—	—			
NC								
LA								

Dorcas Copper *Lycaena dorcas* **Plate 14**

SIZE ≥ Eastern Tailed-Blue.

SIMILAR SPECIES Purplish Copper, Bog Copper.

IDENTIFICATION Generally larger than Bog Copper and smaller than Purplish Copper, but this may be difficult to determine in the field. Both males and females have the **orange submarginal line only weakly developed**. This line is usually much more developed in Purplish Copper. Below, on the HW look for a weak orange submarginal line. Bog Copper is paler below. In our area female Dorcas Coppers lack the bright orange of female Purplish Coppers. Perhaps best bet is close association with the hostplant (although Purplish Coppers have been reported to occasionally use cinquefoils).

HABITAT	Northern bogs and marshes in association with its caterpillar foodplants.
RANGE	Also west in Canada to Alberta.
ABUNDANCE	LR. 1 brood. Indiana, Ontario, Wisconsin, late June–Aug.; Maine, late July–late Aug.
MAJOR FOODPLANT	Shrubby cinquefoil (*Potentilla fruticosa*) and probably marsh cinquefoil (*P. palustris*).
COMMENTS	The isolated Maine-New Brunswick subspecies (*claytoni*) is threatened. On the Gaspe peninsula, 'Salt Marsh' Dorcas Copper (subspecies *dospassosi*), flies in late July and early August, uses silverweed (*Potentilla anserina*) in salt marshes as its hostplant, and may be a separate species.

Purplish Copper *Lycaena helloides* Plate 14

SIZE	= Banded Hairstreak.
SIMILAR SPECIES	Dorcas Copper, Bog Copper.
IDENTIFICATION	See discussions under Bog and Dorcas coppers.
HABITAT	Open moist situations, often disturbed.
RANGE	Also west to California and Alaska.
ABUNDANCE	LR-U. 2 or 3 broods. Late May–Sept.
MAJOR FOODPLANT	Docks (*Rumex*) and knotweeds (*Polygonum*).

	MAR	APR	MAY	JUN	JUL	AUG	SEP	OCT
WI			—		—	—	—	
NY								
NC								
LA								

Hairstreaks

The name of these small but intricately patterned butterflies is thought to be derived either from the many lines or streaks that tend to appear on the HW below or from the usual presence of fine, hair-like tails. 33 species occur in our region while about 1000 species of hairstreaks inhabit Central and South America. Many species have an eye-spot near the outer angle of the HW below that tends to attract the attention of predators to the wrong end of the butterfly. The subterfuge is usually enhanced by tails that resemble antennas. When the hairstreak lands with its head facing downward and its tails move in the air as it "saws" its HWs back and forth, the effect is complete. Many tropical species have this eye-spot pattern greatly developed and it is not unusual to find individuals who have sacrificed the missing portions of their HWs to birds.

Atala *Eumaeus atala* Plate 16

SIZE	>> Banded Hairstreak.
SIMILAR SPECIES	Great Purple Hairstreak.
IDENTIFICATION	This sensational animal is difficult to misidentify, except in flig when it looks remarkably mothlike. The bright orange abdom and red on the base of the HW can remind one of a Great Purp Hairstreak but the triple spot-band of phosphorescent aquam rine spots on the HW below is unique.
HABITAT	Anyplace its foodplants want to be, including urban and subu ban plantings. Occasionally even found in natural habitats!
RANGE	Also, West Indies.
ABUNDANCE	LC. All year.
MAJOR FOODPLANT	Coontie (*Zamia pumila*) and other introduced ornamental cyca
COMMENTS	Not too long ago, this species was thought to be gone from t U.S., a victim of the rapid development of South Florida. B since 1970, landscape gardeners and butterfly gardeners ha planted increasing numbers of coontie and other cycads and t population of this butterfly, one of the more sensationally cc ored, is now booming.

Great Purple Hairstreak *Atlides halesus* Plate 16

SIZE	>> Banded Hairstreak.
SIMILAR SPECIES	Atala.
IDENTIFICATION	A very large, dramatically marked hairstreak. When it flies, o can see the flash from the shining iridescent blue (not purp scales covering the entire wings above. Females have mo restricted, non-iridescent, blue above. Below, the FW has an i descent turquoise patch, while both the FW and the HW ha large red spots near their bases. Note the striking oran abdomen.
HABITAT	Edges of moist woodlands.
RANGE	Also, west to California and south to Guatemala.
ABUNDANCE	U-LC. Feb.–Nov. Florida, southern Georgia, and southe Mississippi. U, Atlantic coastal plain north to southeaste Virginia and Delaware. LR north to Oklahoma, southe Missouri, southern West Virginia and North Carolina pie mont—April–mid Oct. RS to Indiana, Ohio (1 record).
MAJOR FOODPLANT	Mistletoe (*Phoradendron*).
COMMENTS	The origin of the name "Great Purple Hairstreak" is hazy. B when this tropically-oriented beauty kisses the sky with its br liant iridescent blue topside, you will soar as high as Ji Hendrix's music.

	MAR	APR	MAY	JUN	JUL	AUG	SEP	OCT
WI								
NY								
NC								
LA								

Amethyst Hairstreak *Chlorostrymon maesites* **Plate 19**

SIZE   << Banded Hairstreak.

SIMILAR SPECIES   Silver-banded Hairstreak.

IDENTIFICATION   This tiny green hairstreak has a maroon marginal patch on the HW below, not extending to the HW leading edge and **lacks a FW white postmedian line**. Silver-banded Hairstreak has a HW maroon marginal border extending to the HW leading edge and has a white postmedian line on the FW below.

HABITAT   Tropical hardwood hammocks.

RANGE   Also, the Bahamas and the Antilles.

ABUNDANCE   LR or no longer found in our region. Probably all year, but mainly late May–mid June.

MAJOR FOODPLANT   Uncertain; 1 report from Jamaica on balloon-vine (*Cardiospermum*), other reports suggest that it may use a wide variety of caterpillar foodplants.

COMMENTS   I know of no reports of this species in the past five years. Perhaps a combination of rarity with a behavioral pattern that keeps this species high in the trees has caused it to be overlooked. But, with the continuing destruction of hammock environments in the Florida Keys, it is possible that this species has been extirpated.

Silver-banded Hairstreak *Chlorostrymon simaethis* Plate 19

SIZE   < Banded Hairstreak.

SIMILAR SPECIES   Amethyst Hairstreak.

IDENTIFICATION   Bright acid green below with a prominent **white, straight, postmedian line**. Above, males are iridescent purple, females blue-gray (sometimes opening their wings while landed).

HABITAT   Areas with balloon-vine, including tropical scrub, hardwood hammock edges, and disturbed areas.

RANGE   Also southern Texas and southern California, West Indies, south through tropical Americas.

ABUNDANCE   LR-LU. All year.

MAJOR FOODPLANT   Balloon-vine (*Cardiospermum*; *C. halicacabum* in Florida); the caterpillar lives within the seedpod (the "balloon").

COMMENTS   Established in south Florida in 1974 but now declining.

Plantings of its caterpillar foodplant by south Florida butterfly gardeners should increase the population of this tiny, but brilliant, butterfly.

Soapberry Hairstreak *Phaeostrymon alcestis* Plate 17

SIZE	≥ Banded Hairstreak.
SIMILAR SPECIES	Southern Hairstreak (northern form), White M Hairstreak, *Satyrium* hairstreaks.
IDENTIFICATION	Our only hairstreak with **cell-end bars with white centers**. White M and Southern hairstreaks lack distinctly white cell-end bars. *Satyrium* hairstreaks can have cell-end bars edged with white, but these have dark centers.
HABITAT	Bottomlands in arid country with its caterpillar foodplant.
RANGE	Also west to Arizona and northern Mexico.
ABUNDANCE	LC Dallas-Fort Worth area. 1 brood. April–June. Northward, LR-LU—June–mid July. RS east to Houston and northeast to south western Missouri.
MAJOR FOODPLANT	Western soapberry (*Sapindus drummondii*).
COMMENTS	Closely associated with its hostplant. Although not yet recorded from easternmost Texas and western Louisiana, western soapberry has been found in these areas and so the Soapberry Hairstreak may occur here as well.

Satyrium Hairstreaks

The eight *Satyrium* hairstreaks in our area are similar. All are basically brown to brownish-gray to gray. Although they have rapid and very erratic flight paths, they are easier to follow than one would think since they often alight not far from where they began! Like many groups of hairstreaks, male *Satyrium* hairstreaks have scent pads on the FWs above. These pads contain specialized scales through which a pheromone (a specialized type of scent) is released. Females sniff the male's perfume during courtship rituals and, presumably, how good he smells influences her decision to mate or reject her suitor.

Coral Hairstreak *Satyrium titus* Plate 17

SIZE	= Banded Hairstreak.
SIMILAR SPECIES	Acadian Hairstreak.
IDENTIFICATION	A brown, **tailless** hairstreak. It has a prominent marginal row red-orange spots but no blue marginal eye-spot. Acadian Hairstreak

has a tail, gray ground color and a blue eye-spot.

HABITAT	More a denizen of brushy fields, overgrown orchards, and the like than our other *Satyrium* hairstreaks.
RANGE	Also, west to Oregon and British Columbia.
ABUNDANCE	Mainly U-LC but LR at southern and northern edges of range. 1 brood mainly mid June–July; late May–June at southern edge of range, July–August extreme north.
MAJOR FOODPLANT	Wild cherry and wild plum (*Prunus*).
COMMENTS	Orange milkweed (*Asclepias tuberosa*) is a magnet for this butterfly, much more so than for any other hairstreak.

	MAR	APR	MAY	JUN	JUL	AUG	SEP	OCT
WI								
NY								
NC								
LA								

Acadian Hairstreak *Satyrium acadica* **Plate 18**

SIZE	= Banded Hairstreak.
SIMILAR SPECIES	Gray Hairstreak, Edwards' Hairstreak, Coral Hairstreak.
IDENTIFICATION	A tailed, pale gray hairstreak with a **HW postmedian band of black spots**. Gray Hairstreak has a postmedian **line**. Edwards' and Coral hairstreaks have brown ground color and Coral Hairstreak also lacks a tail.
HABITAT	Open areas and thickets near streams and marshy places where willows grow.
RANGE	Also, west to Montana.
ABUNDANCE	LU over most of range, more common Wisconsin, Ontario, LR at south edge of range. 1 brood. Generally late June–mid July; Maine and Manitoba—July.
MAJOR FOODPLANT	Willows (*Salix sericea* and others).
COMMENTS	This species seems to be fairly colonial; so if you find one, you'll probably find more.

	MAR	APR	MAY	JUN	JUL	AUG	SEP	OCT
WI								
NY								
NC								
LA								

Hickory Hairstreak *Satyrium caryaevorum* **Plate 18**

SIZE	= Banded Hairstreak.
SIMILAR SPECIES	Banded Hairstreak, Edwards' Hairstreak.
IDENTIFICATION	Very similar to Banded Hairstreak. Best separated by the HW blue outer angle spot. In Hickory Hairstreak this spot usually: 1. **extends farther inward, breaking the arc of the marginal**

spots and usually reaching, or almost reaching, the arc of the white postmedian band, 2. is usually more pointed inwardly, and 3. is a paler, more shining blue. Also, Hickory Hairstreak almost always has the FW postmedian band bordered by white **on both sides**. Banded usually has this band bordered by white only on the distal side (but sometimes on both sides). Lastly, note the HW cell-end double white bar. Hickory usually has these lines aligned with the first lines of the postmedian band, just above it. Banded usually has these offset. Except with known colonies, you will want to see all of these field marks before concluding that you are observing a Hickory Hairstreak.

HABITAT Prefers open fields or glades with nectar sources adjacent to deciduous woods. Probably prefers richer soil than Banded Hairstreak.

ABUNDANCE R-U. 1 brood, mid/late June–mid/late July.

MAJOR FOODPLANT Hickories (*Carya*), especially *C. cordiformis*.

COMMENTS This poorly known hairstreak seems to be genuinely rare over much of its range, rather than being under-reported due to confusion with Banded Hairstreak.

	MAR	APR	MAY	JUN	JUL	AUG	SEP	OCT
WI								
NY								
NC								
LA								

Edwards' Hairstreak *Satyrium edwardsii* **Plate 18**

SIZE = Banded Hairstreak.

SIMILAR SPECIES Banded Hairstreak, Acadian Hairstreak.

IDENTIFICATION Very similar to Banded Hairstreak but usually browner with HW postmedian band broken into **spots surrounded by white**. Note the prominent orange outer angle spot, more prominent than in Banded Hairstreak. Edwards' Hairstreaks frequently have some orange scales running from the outer angle spot to the adjacent blue lunule. Banded Hairstreaks almost never have any orange over the blue lunule. Acadian Hairstreak has a HW postmedian band of solid black spots and is grayer.

HABITAT Woodlands with scrubby oaks and adjacent clearings. These are usually poor-soil areas: pine barrens, rocky hill-tops, prairie ridges, shale barrens, etc.

ABUNDANCE Mainly LR-LC. Throughout much of its range, this species occurs in isolated colonies. 1 brood, mainly mid June–mid July, but in May–June in Georgia and July–early Aug. in Mass., Maine, Ontario, Wisconsin, Manitoba.

| | MAJOR FOODPLANT | Small oaks, especially scrub oak (*Quercus ilicifolia*). |

MAJOR FOODPLANT   Small oaks, especially scrub oak (*Quercus ilicifolia*).

COMMENTS   Usually local but can be abundant where it occurs.

	MAR	APR	MAY	JUN	JUL	AUG	SEP	OCT
WI					—			
NY				▬▬				
NC								
LA								

Banded Hairstreak *Satyrium calanus* **Plate 18**

SIZE   10/16 in.

SIMILAR SPECIES   Hickory Hairstreak, Edwards' Hairstreak.

IDENTIFICATION   A widespread and variable hairstreak, Banded Hairstreak has well-marked postmedian bands on both FWs and HWs. The band is outwardly strongly edged with white while inwardly the white edging varies from absent to strong. Banded Hairstreak is very similar to the more uncommon Hickory Hairstreak and they can often be found together. See Hickory and Edwards' hairstreaks for discussions.

HABITAT   Prefers open fields or glades, with nectar sources, adjacent to oak woodlands.

RANGE   Also west to Utah.

ABUNDANCE   U-C. 1 brood. Florida—April–May; Southern Georgia west to East Texas—May–early June; North Carolina west to northeastern Oklahoma—late May–early July. Northward—mainly mid/late June–mid/late July. July in New Brunswick.

MAJOR FOODPLANT   Oaks (*Quercus*) and hickories (*Carya*).

COMMENTS   Although often common, the abundance of this species exhibits massive fluctuations. Some years this appears to happen synchronously over large areas.

	MAR	APR	MAY	JUN	JUL	AUG	SEP	OCT
WI				—		▪		
NY				▬▬▬				
NC			▬▬					
LA								

King's Hairstreak *Satyrium kingi* **Plate 18**

SIZE   = Banded Hairstreak.

SIMILAR SPECIES   Edwards' Hairstreak, Striped Hairstreak, Banded Hairstreak.

IDENTIFICATION   Looks like a Banded Hairstreak with a **strong orange bar over blue "thecla" spot**. Striped Hairstreak also has orange over its blue "thecla" spot, but this orange is usually (but not always) in the form of an inwardly directed chevron, not a flat bar. Also, note **2 nearly equal dash marks** as the 2 last marks of the HW postmedian band, the **white dash (almost) touching the white edge of the blue**

"thecla" spot. Unlike Striped, FW white cell-end bars are set from the postmedian band and two white dashes closest to HW leaing margin are not aligned with white cell-end bars below. Edwar often has some orange over blue "thecla" spot but has more exte sive orange at HW outer angle and has postmedian band as sp rather than bars. The flight of King's Hairstreak is more dire easier to follow, than the whirling flight of Banded Hairstreak.

HABITAT Moist woodlands where the caterpillar foodplant is present.

ABUNDANCE LR. 1 brood. Mid/late May–mid June on the coastal pla June–early July on the piedmont; mid July–mid Aug. in sour ern Appalachians. Not yet recorded from Louisiana but it pro ably occurs there.

MAJOR FOODPLANT Common sweetleaf (*Symplocos tinctoria*).

COMMENTS The range of this species essentially follows the range of its cate pillar foodplant, but within that range it is inexplicably local a rare. Males perch at about 3–4 ft., often on the hostplant, du ing the middle of the day.

	MAR	APR	MAY	JUN	JUL	AUG	SEP	OCT
WI								
NY								
NC			—					
LA								

Striped Hairstreak *Satyrium liparops* Plate 18

SIZE = Banded Hairstreak.

SIMILAR SPECIES Banded Hairstreak.

IDENTIFICATION On first impression appears to have many more white lines a be "stripier" but actual differences are rather subtle. The wh lines are set farther apart and **aligned** so as to form stripes. A note the **orange cap** on the blue outer angle eye-spot.

HABITAT Thickets, woodland openings and brushy edges. This spec tends to stay closer to woodlands than related species.

RANGE Also west to Montana.

ABUNDANCE R-U. 1 brood. Florida, south Georgia, west to east Texas—Ma Central Georgia, central Louisiana, Missouri, Oklahom Kansas—late May–June; Appalachians, New York, Ohio, Indian Illinois, Nebraska, South Dakota—mid June–July; Mair Massachusetts, Ontario, Wisconsin, Manitoba—July–early Aug.

MAJOR FOODPLANT Wild cherry (*Prunus*), blueberry (*Vaccinium*), and many others

COMMENTS Although widespread, and sometimes common, unlike relate hairstreaks, one will not see a swarm of them. Their occurren and behavior seems to be much more solitary. Males perch about 3–4 ft.

	MAR	APR	MAY	JUN	JUL	AUG	SEP	OCT
WI					—			
NY								
NC								
LA								

Southern Hairstreak *Fixsenia favonius* Plate 17

SIZE ≤ Banded Hairstreak.

SIMILAR SPECIES White M Hairstreak, Gray Hairstreak.

IDENTIFICATION This species has a "clean" appearance (as do White M and Gray hairstreaks) due to the lack of cell-end bars. On the Florida peninsula and north along the Georgia coast, most individuals have an extensive HW red-orange patch, running from the blue eye-spot to the leading edge of the HW. Northward and westward, this patch is much less extensive, more orange, and broken into individual spots. Southern individuals are distinctive. Elsewhere, note that the large red-orange spot outwardly edged with black reaches, or almost reaches, the HW margin. White M Hairstreak has this spot displaced inwardly. Distinguished from Gray Hairstreak by brownish (rather than gray) ground color.

HABITAT A wide variety of woodland-edge situations including pine-oak woodlands and the edges of rich mixed deciduous woods.

ABUNDANCE R but U-LC Florida and coastal Georgia. 1 brood. Florida, coastal Georgia, southern Mississippi, Louisiana, east Texas—April–May; North Carolina, West Virginia, Missouri, Oklahoma, Kansas—mid May–June; New York, Ohio, Indiana—mid June–early July; Mass.—late June–mid July.

MAJOR FOODPLANT Various oaks (*Quercus*).

COMMENTS Until recently, the Florida and more northern populations were considered separate species, Southern and Northern hairstreaks, respectively. But there is a blend zone where every combination of characters can be found.

	MAR	APR	MAY	JUN	JUL	AUG	SEP	OCT
WI								
NY				—				
NC								
LA								

Brown Elfin *Callophrys augustinus* Plate 20

SIZE < Banded Hairstreak.

SIMILAR SPECIES Henry's Elfin, Hoary Elfin.

IDENTIFICATION A small hairstreak of the early spring and our most widespread elfin. Flight is weak and low. Rich brown below (fresh individu-

als have a purplish sheen) with the area inward of the po
median line dark brown and the area outward a brighter re
dish-brown. Usually lacks white on the FW postmedian ba
and lacks frosting on the HW margin.

HABITAT Generally distributed in acid, poor-soil woodlands, pine barre
acid bogs, and extensive rocky outcroppings with its hostplan

RANGE Also west to California and Alaska.

ABUNDANCE LC-LA east of Appalachians; LR-LU west of Appalachians.
brood. Georgia, North Carolina—March–April; West Virgin
New York, Mass.—late April–May; Maine, Ontario, Wiscons
Manitoba —May–early/mid June.

MAJOR FOODPLANT Blueberries, especially low bush blueberry (*Vaccinium vacilla*
and related heaths.

COMMENTS A strong hilltopper in some areas, this species can often be fou
by climbing to the top of a rocky outcrop in the appropria
habitat.

	MAR	APR	MAY	JUN	JUL	AUG	SEP	OCT
WI								
NY								
NC								
LA								

Hoary Elfin *Callophrys polios* **Plate 20**

SIZE < Banded Hairstreak.

SIMILAR SPECIES Frosted Elfin, Henry's Elfin, Brown Elfin.

IDENTIFICATION A small, very dark elfin of low sand barrens. Note the "frostin
(grayish-white scales) on the HW margins and the **FW margir**
Frosted Elfin is larger, with much paler ground color and h
tail-like protuberances on the HW. Brown Elfin lacks frostin
Henry's Elfin lacks frosting on the FW, has beginning and end
HW postmedian band bounded by strong white mark, and us
ally is found in a different habitat (although they can occ
together).

HABITAT Dwarf pine barrens and other barrens with good amounts of
foodplant. Rarely forest edges.

RANGE Also, west to Alaska and south in the Rockies to New Mexic
Historically recorded from eastern Long Island; Clearfield Co., P
Kanawha Co., WV; and Highland and Augusta Cos. VA. Any are
with extensive amounts of either foodplant should be searched

ABUNDANCE LR-LU. 1 brood. Late April–mid May. Ontario, Manitoba
May–early June.

MAJOR FOODPLANT Bearberry (*Arctostaphylos uva-ursi*) and trailing arbut
(*Epigaea repens*).

COMMENTS   This butterfly is almost always found right on its caterpillar food-plant. Local and rare in most of our region, in areas that have extensive heathlands, such as central Wisconsin, this species can occur widely.

	MAR	APR	MAY	JUN	JUL	AUG	SEP	OCT
WI			▬■▬					
NY								
NC								
LA								

Frosted Elfin *Callophrys irus* **Plate 20**

SIZE   ≤ Banded Hairstreak

SIMILAR SPECIES   Brown Elfin, Hoary Elfin, Henry's Elfin.

IDENTIFICATION   A larger than average elfin with "frosted" HW margin and short tail-like protuberances. Note the **black spot on the HW near the "tailed" area**. FW white postmedian line is not smooth. Hoary Elfin is smaller, darker, and has frosting on FW margin also. Henry's Elfin has richer, reddish-brown color and has a smooth continuous white FW postmedian line below. Also note pale area between FW postmedian and marginal lines of Frosted Elfin. Henry's Elfin lacks this. Brown Elfin lacks frosting.

HABITAT   Sandy or rocky acidic areas cleared by fire or, much more often, by man; such as power-line cuts, railroad right-of-ways, and roadsides with good stands of one of its foodplants.

ABUNDANCE   LR-LU. 1 brood. Florida, coastal Georgia—March–April; North Carolina—April; East Texas/Louisiana/Arkansas—April–May; northward—May–early/mid June.

MAJOR FOODPLANT   Wild indigo (*Baptisia*) in most localities; also lupine (*Lupinus*).

COMMENTS   Extremely local, with isolated colonies (some by hundreds of miles) within the range shown. Thought by many to be declining over wide areas. Great Lakes populations seem most affected.

	MAR	APR	MAY	JUN	JUL	AUG	SEP	OCT
WI			■▬					
NY			■▬▬					
NC		—						
LA								

Henry's Elfin *Callophrys henrici* **Plate 20**

SIZE   < Banded Hairstreak.

SIMILAR SPECIES   Brown Elfin, Frosted Elfin.

IDENTIFICATION   A bright brown elfin of woodlands. Note the frosted HW margin and the bold white marks at either end of the HW postmedian line. Tail-like protuberances are usually visible. Brown Elfin lacks frosting and white marks (occasionally has faint white), and "tails." Frosted Elfin has a black spot on the HW near the "tailed" area, has duller, paler ground color and little contrast between ground color on either side of postmedian line.

HABITAT A wide variety of woodlands with brushy understories; brushy barrens, and bog edges.

RANGE Also, west Texas and southeastern New Mexico.

ABUNDANCE LR-U. 1 brood. Florida, coastal Georgia, coastal North Carolina, west to Texas—March–April; New York, Mass., Ohio, Indiana, Illinois, Missouri, Kansas—April–May; Wisconsin, Ontario—May–early June.

MAJOR FOODPLANT Redbud (*Cercis canadensis*), American holly (*Ilex opaca*), European buckthorn (*Rhamnus frangula*), blueberries (*Vaccinium*).

COMMENTS In most areas only one foodplant is used. Mainly redbud west of the Appalachians, American holly on the Atlantic coast, blueberries in Great Lakes region. Apparently the recent use of European buckthorn as a foodplant in the Boston area has led to increased abundance and more varied habitat utilization.

	MAR	APR	MAY	JUN	JUL	AUG	SEP	OCT
WI								
NY								
NC								
LA								

Bog Elfin *Callophrys lanoraieensis* **Plate 20**

SIZE < Banded Hairstreak.

SIMILAR SPECIES Eastern Pine Elfin, Western Pine Elfin.

IDENTIFICATION A small elfin (there is little, if any, size overlap between this tiny dull elfin and the other pine elfins) of northern bogs with an evanescent mauve sheen that quickly dulls. The submarginal black line on the HW below is thick and fairly smooth. Other pine elfins have this line more jagged.

HABITAT Black spruce bogs.

RANGE Known from only a few locations within the range shown, mainly extreme eastern Maine, and Quebec. Recent report from a bog near Syracuse, New York and in Worcester Co, Mass., may mean this local species is more widely distributed in the black spruce bogs of the Adirondacks and New England than previously realized.

ABUNDANCE LR. 1 brood. Mid May–early June.

MAJOR FOODPLANT Black spruce (*Picea mariana*).

COMMENTS A poorly known, rarely encountered species, this, the most "elfin-like" of our elfins, resists sightings. In its fantasy land of high spruce tops and low bog mosses, it scampers on elfin wings and sends its forces of mosquitoes and black flies to guard the perimeter. At the tops of black spruces or down at ground level it flies with a slow weak flight. Landing on low vegetation, it crawls along the ground and over grasses and mosses.

Eastern Pine Elfin *Callophrys niphon* **Plate 20**

SIZE	= Banded Hairstreak.
IDENTIFICATION	Stunningly banded with rich reddish-brown and black.
HABITAT	Most common in pine barrens, this elfin can also be found in deciduous woodlands with groves of white pine.
RANGE	Also, west in Canada to Alberta.
ABUNDANCE	LU-C, but R Ohio, southern Wisconsin, 2 records Indiana. 1 brood. Florida, south Georgia, south Mississippi—March–April; North Carolina, West Virginia, Ohio, Missouri—April–May; New York, Mass., Maine, Ontario, Wisconsin, Manitoba—May–mid June.
MAJOR FOODPLANT	Hard pines; especially pitch pine (*Pinus rigida*) and jack pine (*Pinus banksiana*) but also the soft pine, white pine (*P. strobus*).
COMMENTS	It appears to be much less common in areas with white pine. Whether this is real, due to inefficient utilization of this food-plant, or a function of the difficulty of observing butterflies at the tops of 50 foot pines, is not certain.

	MAR	APR	MAY	JUN	JUL	AUG	SEP	OCT
WI								
NY								
NC								
LA								

Western Pine Elfin *Callophrys eryphon* **Plate 20**

SIZE	= Banded Hairstreak.
SIMILAR SPECIES	Eastern Pine Elfin, Bog Elfin.
IDENTIFICATION	Note the very pointed, black arrowheads of the HW submarginal line and the lack of much gray on the HW margin. Eastern Pine Elfin has HW submarginal markings that are less pointed, more crescent-like, and has much gray on the HW marginal band. Also, Eastern Pine Elfins usually have a dark bar within the FW cell that Western Pine Elfins lack.
HABITAT	Pinewoods and black spruce bogs (in the east).
RANGE	Also west in Canada to British Columbia and south throughout the western U.S. mountains.
ABUNDANCE	LR. 1 brood. May–early June.
MAJOR FOODPLANT	Jack pine (*Pinus banksiana*).
COMMENTS	In the west, this species is widespread, using various hard pines as hostplants. In our area most reports are from jack pine. But

in Maine, this rarely encountered species is reported to be ass
ciated with black spruce while reports of this species from N
Brunswick (omitted from map) include white pine as the ho
These eastern populations need further study to determine th
specific status. There are large differences of opinion amo
knowledgeable Canadians regarding the range of this species
may actually be much more restricted than indicated on t
map. Additionally, I have included parts of Wisconsin, Vermo
and New Hampshire within the range because I believe that t
species may occur there, but there are, as yet, no records fr
these states.

Juniper Hairstreak *Callophrys gryneus* **Plate 19**

SIZE
: ≤ Banded Hairstreak.

SIMILAR SPECIES
: Hessel's Hairstreak.

IDENTIFICATION
: Over most of our area, its bright olive-green color separates t
crowd pleaser from all our other hairstreaks except its close r
ative, Hessel's Hairstreak.

HABITAT
: Dry fields (especially hilly ones) or ridge tops with good stands of r
cedar, some brushy undergrowth, and nectar sources for both the spri
and summer broods. In boom years can be found on single red ceda

RANGE
: Also, west to California (as 'Siva' Juniper Hairstreak).

ABUNDANCE
: LU, Florida. 2 broods—mid March–early May, Sept.–Oct. LR-L
southeast; LC-LA northeast; LA, Ozarks; LR-LU, Midwest. 2 broo
Georgia north to New York and west to northeastern Tex
Kansas—mainly April–May, July–August; Mass., Ontario—n
May–mid June, August; Wisconsin—May, July.

MAJOR FOODPLANT
: Red cedar (*Juniperus virginiana*).

COMMENTS
: This butterfly tends to remain very close to (usually on) its ho
Best found by thumping on the red cedars and watching t
Juniper Hairstreaks whirl up. Seemingly not as fond of flowers
other hairstreaks (but if you see a hairstreak on orange mil
weed, if it is not a Coral Hairstreak, it is probably this species)
can sometimes be found on damp sand early in the morning
late in the afternoon. Our populations are 'Olive' Junip
Hairstreak (*C.g.gryneus*) and 'Sweadner's' Juniper Hairstre
(*C.g.sweadneri*). The latter is the Florida subspecies and is more
a flower visitor. 'Siva' Juniper Hairstreak (*C.g.siva*) may just ent
our area in central Nebraska and South Dakota. It lacks the tw
basal white spots on the HW. A broad blend zone between 'Oliv
and 'Siva' Juniper Hairstreaks exists in the southwest. Status
other western populations in this group is controversial.

	MAR	APR	MAY	JUN	JUL	AUG	SEP	OCT
WI								
NY								
NC								
LA								

Hessel's Hairstreak *Callophrys hesseli* **Plate 19**

SIZE < Banded Hairstreak.

SIMILAR SPECIES Juniper Hairstreak.

IDENTIFICATION Normally, only found in Atlantic white cedar swamps (although individuals must disperse to new areas). Brighter, **more emerald green** than Juniper Hairstreak from which it can usually be separated by habitat preference alone. Juniper Hairstreaks inhabit dry, often hilly fields with good stands of their host, red cedar. Hessel's Hairstreak are found in white cedar swamps. Note the **top white spot on the FW postmedian band displaced outwardly** and the **brown patches distal to the postmedian line**, especially on the HW. Juniper Hairstreak has the top white spot of the FW postmedian band aligned with the spot below it and lacks the brown patches distal to the postmedian line.

HABITAT Atlantic white cedar swamps.

ABUNDANCE LR-LU. 2 broods south, 1 + partial in north. Florida north to New York—mid/late April–mid/late May, July–early Aug.; Mass.—mid May–mid June.

MAJOR FOODPLANT Atlantic white cedar (*Chamaecyparis thyoides*).

COMMENTS This fascinating butterfly was not discovered until 1949 when, during a boom year, some spilled out of the uninviting white cedar swamps in Lakehurst, New Jersey and were found by Sid Hessel. Best searched for early or late in the day (after 4:00 p.m.) when they will come down from the tops of the white cedars to nectar on blueberries, sand myrtles, sweet pepperbushes or chokecherries. Very local with widely separated colonies within the range show. Perhaps most common in the New Jersey pine barrens.

	MAR	APR	MAY	JUN	JUL	AUG	SEP	OCT
WI								
NY								
NC								
LA								

White M Hairstreak *Parrhasius m-album* **Plate 17**

SIZE ≥ Banded Hairstreak.

SIMILAR SPECIES Southern Hairstreak.

IDENTIFICATION With its flashing iridescent blue upper wings, White M Hairstreak is a worthy representative of a largely tropical group.

Unfortunately for us, its beautiful blue is usually only visible during its rapid and erratic flight. Below, the white spot near the base of the HW separates this species from all our other hairstreaks except Southern. Note the inwardly displaced orange and black spot on the HW. 'Northern' Southern Hairstreaks have this spot at the usual position at the HW margin. 'Southern' Southern Hairstreaks have an extensive red-orange patch near the HW margin.

HABITAT Open brushy areas adjacent to, or within, oak woodlands, especially on hilltops.

ABUNDANCE U-C, Florida, south Georgia, to east Texas; LR farther north. Temporary colonist north to Massachusetts. RS north to Iowa and Michigan. Probably 3 broods. Florida, south Georgia west to east Texas—Feb./March–Oct. Northward—late April–mid May, late June–July, late Aug.–Sept./Oct.

MAJOR FOODPLANT Oaks (*Quercus*).

COMMENTS This essentially southern species has been extending its range northward and is capable of flying farther than one might think. One report is of an itinerant individual who landed on the reflective sunglasses of a boy who was boating with his mother about 1/2 mile from shore in Chesapeake Bay!

	MAR	APR	MAY	JUN	JUL	AUG	SEP	OCT
WI								
NY								
NC								
LA								

Scrub-Hairstreaks
(*Strymon*)

There are about 60 species of scrub-hairstreaks, all restricted to the New World. Only one species of this essentially tropical group—Gray Hairstreak—is widespread in the East. Unlike our other hairstreaks, scrub-hairstreaks sometimes sun themselves with their wings open and thus allow a view of their topsides.

Gray Hairstreak *Strymon melinus* **Plate 21**

SIZE = Banded Hairstreak.

SIMILAR SPECIES Acadian Hairstreak, Southern Hairstreak.

IDENTIFICATION A widespread hairstreak with a true gray ground color below (rarely gray-brown). Note the prominent HW postmedian line, white outwardly and black inwardly (often with reddish-orange inwards of the black).

HABITAT Commonest in disturbed open habitats but can be encountered in almost any habitat. A strong hilltopper (males perch in the late afternoon and early evening).

RANGE Also, the entire North American West and south through Central America to northern South America.

ABUNDANCE U-C south, LR-U near northern edge of range. Florida, south Georgia west to east Texas—Feb./March–Oct. Probably 3 broods north to New York, Indiana, Missouri, Kansas—mainly Mid April–mid Oct. 2 broods northward, mid May–Aug/Sept.

MAJOR FOODPLANT A great variety.

COMMENTS The shade of gray, and intensity and coloration of the HW postmedian line, is quite variable. Late in the summer, when this species becomes most common, it tends to spread more widely into suburban areas. Males have dull orange abdomens (Legend to photo 4, plate 10, *Butterflies Through Binoculars: Boston-New York-Washington,* incorrectly identifies photo as a male).

	MAR	APR	MAY	JUN	JUL	AUG	SEP	OCT
WI								
NY								
NC								
LA								

Martial Scrub-Hairstreak *Strymon martialis* Plate 21

SIZE = Banded Hairstreak.

SIMILAR SPECIES Gray Hairstreak, Bartram's Hairstreak.

IDENTIFICATION Both sexes with some blue above. Below, note the **bold white postmedian line** on both HW and FW. Gray Hairstreak's white postmedian line is more divided into dashes, not so bold, not so straight, and not as angled inwards. Bartram's Hairstreak has 2 white basal spots on the HW that this species lacks.

HABITAT Coastal areas with the foodplant.

RANGE Also, Bahamas, Cuba, Cayman Islands, and Jamaica.

ABUNDANCE LU-LC, all year.

MAJOR FOODPLANT Bay cedar (*Suriana maritima*) and Florida trema (*Trema micrantha*).

COMMENTS Although local, this species can sometimes be quite common on Big Pine Key.

Bartram's Scrub-Hairstreak *Strymon acis* Plate 21

SIZE ≤ Banded Hairstreak.

SIMILAR SPECIES Gray Hairstreak, Martial Scrub-Hairstreak.

IDENTIFICATION Below, note the **bold white postmedian line** on both HW and FW and the **2 white basal spots on the HW**. Gray Hairstreak's white postmedian line is more divided into dashes, not so bold, not so straight, and not as angled inwards. Martial Scrub-Hairstreak lacks the 2 white HW basal spots.

HABITAT Subtropical pine flatlands with the hostplant.

RANGE Also, West Indies.

ABUNDANCE LU, all year.

MAJOR FOODPLANT Narrow-leaved croton (*Croton linearis*).

COMMENTS Usually seen right on croton, nectaring, courting, or egg-laying. Now restricted to Big Pine Key and Long Pine Key in Everglades NP.

Mallow Scrub-Hairstreak *Strymon columella* Plate 21

SIZE < Banded Hairstreak.

SIMILAR SPECIES Gray Hairstreak, Ceraunus Blue.

IDENTIFICATION This is a small, relatively inconspicuous hairstreak. HW below has a prominent black postmedian line and **2 basal black spots** (sometimes the more distal spot is faint). Florida population often has tail spot tricolored—black, red, orange—but the Texas population doesn't. Gray Hairstreak lacks the basal spots. Ceraunus Blue lacks tails, has extra dark spots on the basal half of the HW, and flies more slowly and less erratically.

HABITAT Disturbed, weedy fields and roadsides.

RANGE Also south to the West Indies and through Central America to Bolivia.

ABUNDANCE U-C, all year. RS north to Dallas.

MAJOR FOODPLANT Various mallows (Malvaceae). Also, bay cedar (*Suriana maritima*) (at least on Big Pine Key).

COMMENTS Can be confusingly variable.

Fulvous Hairstreak *Electrostrymon angelia* Plate 17

SIZE < Banded Hairstreak.

SIMILAR SPECIES Southern Hairstreak, White M Hairstreak.

IDENTIFICATION Note the disrupted HW postmedian line with an isolated prominent white spot along the HW leading edge. In flight the copper colored upperside can sometimes be seen. Southern and White M hairstreaks have more continuous HW postmedian lines and have white postmedian lines on the FW that this species lacks.

HABITAT Gardens, disturbed shrubby areas.

RANGE Also, West Indies.

ABUNDANCE Recently established in south Florida (1974). LU, all year.

MAJOR FOODPLANT Brazilian pepper (*Schinus terebinthifolius*).

Fulvous Hairstreaks formed a beachhead in southern Florida in
the early 1970s, feeding on the introduced Brazilian pepper.

Red-banded Hairstreak *Calycopis cecrops* Plate 16

SIZE   < Banded Hairstreak.

SIMILAR SPECIES   Dusky-blue Groundstreak.

IDENTIFICATION   A small dark hairstreak with an **obvious red postmedian band** on both the HW and FW below. Above, shows some bright blue in flight.

HABITAT   A wide variety of woodland openings and edges; brushy, overgrown, sandy fields. In late summer, this species can be found in an even broader range of habitats.

ABUNDANCE   C-A north to North Carolina, the Ozarks, and Oklahoma; R-U elsewhere. Probably 3 broods in extreme south—Feb.–Nov.; Probably 2 extended broods northward. North Carolina, West Virginia, and Missouri—April–Oct.; New York, Ohio, Indiana, and Kansas—May–mid June, late July–mid-Sept. Has strayed north to Michigan.

MAJOR FOODPLANT   A wide variety of detritus (rotting leaves), although sumac seems a favorite.

COMMENTS   This is the only species of the approximately 70 species of groundstreaks—a genus of tropical hairstreaks, most of which look very similar—that ranges widely into the United States. Recent range expansion northward has brought this species north of Long Island, with records from Rockland and Westchester counties, NY and Rhode Island.

	MAR	APR	MAY	JUN	JUL	AUG	SEP	OCT
WI								
NY								
NC								
LA								

Dusky-blue Groundstreak *Calycopis isobeon* Plate 16

SIZE   < Banded Hairstreak.

SIMILAR SPECIES   Red-banded Hairstreak.

IDENTIFICATION   Usually with much more red-orange at HW outer angle than Red-banded Hairstreak, which often has black spot (above blue lunule) without any orange cap at all. Red postmedian bands of Dusky-blue Groundstreak usually are narrower than on Red-banded Hairstreak. Also, blue lunule usually with orange cap, usually lacking in Red-banded Hairstreak. However Red-banded Hairstreak is very variable and one can find the occasional individual in Ohio, for example, that closely matches a Dusky-blue Groundstreak.

HABITAT   Tropical woodlands.

RANGE	Also south through Central America to northern South America.
ABUNDANCE	RS to east Texas, mainly late summer–fall.
MAJOR FOODPLANT	A variety of detritus (decaying fallen leaves and other organic matter).
COMMENTS	Questionably distinct from Red-banded Hairstreak—many intermediate forms are found in the area from Houston to the Rio Grande Valley.

Gray Ministreak *Ministrymon azia* **Plate 16**

SIZE	<< Banded Hairstreak.
SIMILAR SPECIES	Red-banded Hairstreak.
IDENTIFICATION	A tiny, pale-gray hairstreak with irregular red postmedian bands. Note red marginal lines on FW and leading half of HW, and **red on head**. Red-banded Hairstreak is browner with much straighter HW postmedian band and lacks red marginal line and red on head.
HABITAT	Open scrub and disturbed areas.
RANGE	Also, West Indies and southern Texas south to Argentina.
ABUNDANCE	R, April–Dec. RS north to Kansas (1 record).
MAJOR FOODPLANT	Lead tree (*Leucaena leucocephala*) in Florida, *Mimosa malacophylla* in south Texas.
COMMENTS	Found in south Florida for the first time in 1974. Although rare, it apparently still occurs in this area. It is very closely associated with its caterpillar foodplant—find it and you may see the butterfly.

Early Hairstreak *Erora laeta* **Plate 19**

SIZE	<< Banded Hairstreak.
SIMILAR SPECIES	Juniper Hairstreak.
IDENTIFICATION	Unmistakable; pale mint green with red-orange postmedian and submarginal bands. Above, females have much bright blue, males with blue more restricted. Juniper Hairstreaks are dark olive green and have white postmedian markings, not red-orange ones.
HABITAT	Beech forests. Fond of landing on unpaved roads and trails.
ABUNDANCE	R-U. Probably 3 broods southward, 2 northward. North Carolina, late April–mid May, late June–late July, late Aug.–early Sept. Maine and Ontario, mid May–mid June, early July–mid Aug.
MAJOR FOODPLANT	Beech (*Fagus grandifolia*).
COMMENTS	When this pale mint-green delight unexpectedly parachutes down from the crown of beeches, it raises smiles on our faces. The paucity of Early Hairstreak sightings may reflect this species' penchant for tree-top living.

Blues

Most blues can be recognized as blues on the wing. They are generally blue above (surprise!) and their flight is usually less rapid and erratic than hairstreaks. In the Western Hemisphere, although some species are tropical, the blues are essentially a northern temperate zone group with a number of species restricted to Arctic areas. This was the group of butterflies most studied by the famous novelist Vladimir Nabokov.

Western Pygmy-Blue *Brephidium exile* Plate 22

SIZE	< Eastern Tailed-Blue.
SIMILAR SPECIES	Eastern Pygmy-Blue.
IDENTIFICATION	Tiny. Copper-colored above. Below, note the 4 bold HW marginal eye-spots. These are surrounded by pale gray. **FW strongly two-toned**—pale gray basally, copper-colored distally. Eastern Pygmy-Blue has HW marginal black spots surrounded by orange-brown, FW is not strongly two-toned.
HABITAT	Mainly coastal scrub in our area.
RANGE	Also, the West Indies and west to California and south to northern Mexico.
ABUNDANCE	R-C Houston area, Perhaps 3 broods, May–Nov. RS northeast to southeastern Nebraska, eastern Kansas, and Missouri (mainly Aug.).
MAJOR FOODPLANT	Saltbushes (*Atriplex*), lambsquarters (*Chenipodium album*) and others.
COMMENTS	Very common in much of the West, this species barely makes it into our area. In the Houston area, most pygmy-blues look like Western Pygmy-Blues, but one can encounter individuals that seem to be Eastern Pygmy-Blues as well. Whether both species co-exist in this area or whether Western and Eastern pygmy-blues are just one species is somewhat controversial.

Eastern Pygmy-Blue *Brephidium isophthalma* Plate 22

SIZE	≤ Eastern Tailed-Blue.
SIMILAR SPECIES	Western Pygmy-Blue.
IDENTIFICATION	A tiny blue of salt marsh tidal flats, where it may be abundant but inconspicuous, flying very close to the ground. Note the **4 prominent black marginal HW eye-spots**. See Western Pygmy-Blue for separation from that species.
HABITAT	Coastal flats.
RANGE	Also, North Bimini Island (Bahamas).
ABUNDANCE	LR-LA. All year south Florida; May–Sept. on the Georgia coast.

MAJOR FOODPLANT	Glassworts (*Salicornia*).
COMMENTS	Abundance fluctuates markedly from season to season, and from year to year. The caterpillars of this species are tended by ants, which may be a factor causing its distribution to be local.

Cassius Blue *Leptotes cassius* **Plate 22**

SIZE	= Eastern Tailed-Blue.
SIMILAR SPECIES	Marine Blue.
IDENTIFICATION	Its zebra-striping distinguishes Cassius Blue from all our other blues except Marine Blue. In southern Florida, where Cassius Blue is most common, Marine Blue does not occur. Distinguished from Marine Blue by whiter appearance—Marine Blue has longer and more continuous black-brown stripings. On the FW below, note that the **4th dark band in from the outer wing margin stops after 4 veins**, leaving a white patch. Marine Blue has this band extending one stop farther down the wing and so lacks the white patch.
HABITAT	Generally distributed in open habitats, including pine wood and the edges of hardwood hammocks.
RANGE	Also, West Indies and south Texas to Argentina.
ABUNDANCE	C south Florida, all year; R immigrant to northern Florida and East Texas; RS to eastern Kansas (1 record) and Missouri.
MAJOR FOODPLANT	A wide variety, especially legumes.
COMMENTS	Although often found low to the ground, it is not uncommon to find Cassius Blues nectaring high in flowering trees. Unlike Marine Blue, this species is not known to undertake long range migration.

Marine Blue *Leptotes marina* **Plate 22**

SIZE	= Eastern Tailed-Blue.
SIMILAR SPECIES	Cassius Blue.
IDENTIFICATION	A zebra-striped blue that periodically sweeps northward out Mexico. See Cassius Blue to distinguish from that species.
HABITAT	Generally distributed in open habitats.
RANGE	Also, west to California and south to Guatemala.
ABUNDANCE	Resident southwestern U.S. and Mexico, often straying northward late summer. Irregular immigrant northeast to Dallas-Fort Worth. South Dakota, Missouri, Wisconsin, Ontario, New York (1 record)
MAJOR FOODPLANT	A wide variety, especially legumes.
COMMENTS	Often emigrating northward from its stronghold in the American Southwest and northern Mexico, a remarkable movement of the species took place in 1993. Individuals appeared throughout the Midwest, and reached southern Ontario; Buffalo, New York; and Brooklyn. It is extremely likely that the individual that landed

Brooklyn flew at least 500 miles, and probably more than 1000 miles, before alighting! It seems doubtful that this tiny butterfly flew 1000 miles under its own power. A more attractive hypothesis is that some small butterflies are swept up into strong, high air currents and then carried for long distances.

Miami Blue *Hemiargus thomasi* Plate 22

SIZE	= Eastern Tailed-Blue.
SIMILAR SPECIES	Ceraunus Blue, Cassius Blue.
IDENTIFICATION	Below, note the white postmedian band, **especially on the FW** and the **2 eyespots near the HW outer angle**. Ceraunus Blues in Florida normally have only a single eyespot near the outer angle (some individuals have a partial eye-spot) and have a more uniform ground color. Cassius Blues lack bold black spots at HW leading margin.
HABITAT	Beach scrub and hammock edges.
RANGE	Also, West Indies.
ABUNDANCE	LR, all year.
MAJOR FOODPLANT	Balloon-vine (*Cardiospermum halicacabum*).
COMMENTS	This butterfly used to be common around Miami and was reported from much of south Florida (with strays to north Florida). More recently it has been restricted to the Florida Keys, but finding it even there has become problematic.

Ceraunus Blue *Hemiargus ceraunus* Plate 22

SIZE	= Eastern Tailed-Blue.
SIMILAR SPECIES	Reakirt's Blue, Miami Blue, Mallow Scrub-Hairstreak.
IDENTIFICATION	Ceraunus, Reakirt's, and Miami blues all have two prominent black spots on the HW leading margin below. Other blues may have black spots here, but they are not so prominent relative to the other HW spots. See Reakirt's and Miami Blues. Mallow Scrub-Hairstreak has tails, has fewer spots on the basal half of the HW, and flies faster and more erratically.
HABITAT	Generally distributed in open areas, especially in those that are disturbed.
RANGE	Also, west to southern California and south to Costa Rica and the West Indies.
ABUNDANCE	U-C, Florida and Georgia coast, all year. RS north to North Carolina and west to Mississippi and RS to east Texas (Mexican subspecies).
MAJOR FOODPLANT	Flowers and young leaves of a wide variety of legumes.
COMMENTS	Although Ceraunus Blues weakly flutter very close to the ground, like many blues, they usually try your patience waiting for them to actually alight.

Reakirt's Blue *Hemiargus isola* Plate 22

SIZE	= Eastern Tailed-Blue.
SIMILAR SPECIES	Ceraunus Blue, Silvery Blue.
IDENTIFICATION	Below, the **FW has a postmedian band of bold black spots**. Ceraunus Blue lacks the bold FW postmedian band. Silvery Blue is darker below and lacks black spot near HW outer angle.
HABITAT	Many types of open situations, including prairies and weedy fields.
RANGE	Also, west to southern California and south to Costa Rica.
ABUNDANCE	Regular immigrant northeast to Dallas-Fort Worth and Houston—April–Oct.; irregular immigrant to Oklahoma, Kansas and Missouri, and South Dakota. RS to North Dakota, Wisconsin, Michigan, Ohio (3 records), and Mississippi.
MAJOR FOODPLANT	A wide variety of legumes.
COMMENTS	A common to abundant resident of the southwestern U.S.

Eastern Tailed-Blue *Everes comyntas* Plate 24

SIZE	8/16 in.
SIMILAR SPECIES	Spring Azure.
IDENTIFICATION	The "tails" are diagnostic but occasionally are worn. Both above and below note the orange spot (often two or three) by the HW tails. Can usually be distinguished from Spring Azure by its ground-hugging flight and the darker blue of its males and some females and the brown color in other females.
HABITAT	Open areas in general, especially disturbed areas.
RANGE	Also, California (an introduction?) and southeastern Arizona south to Costa Rica.
ABUNDANCE	C-A. Continuously brooded during warm weather. Florida and the Deep South, Feb.–Nov.; North Carolina, West Virginia, New York, Ohio, Indiana, Illinois, Missouri, northeast Texas, Kansas, April–Oct.; Mass., Maine, Ontario, South Dakota, May–Sept.
MAJOR FOODPLANT	Pea family.
COMMENTS	A widespread, abundant species that adds welcome bursts of brilliant blue to weedy urban and suburban lots.

	MAR	APR	MAY	JUN	JUL	AUG	SEP	OCT
WI								
NY								
NC								
LA								

Western Tailed-Blue *Everes amyntula* Plate 24

SIZE	= Eastern Tailed-Blue.
SIMILAR SPECIES	Eastern Tailed-Blue.
IDENTIFICATION	Below, usually has a more "washed out" look than Eastern

Tailed-Blue, especially the orange spots near the tail (usually only 1, sometimes 2). Males above are without the orange HW tail-spots that Eastern Tailed-Blues *usually* have. Females have at least some gray or blue above, especially basally, while most female Eastern Tailed-Blues are flat brown above. Some individuals cannot be confidently identified in the field.

HABITAT	Open situations with a mixture of low vegetation and some low shrubs.
RANGE	Western U.S. and Canada.
ABUNDANCE	LR-LU. Mainly 1 brood, mid May–June; later in Manitoba, Ontario, and New Brunswick.
⏸OR FOODPLANT	Pea family.
COMMENTS	This common western species is only marginally a part of our fauna.

Azures

ere are about 120 species of azures, with the greatest diversity occurring in utheast Asia. The American azures have been called "our blue heaven" by vid Wright, and rightly so.

Spring Azure *Celastrina ladon* Plate 23

SIZE	≥ Eastern Tailed-Blue.
⏸MILAR SPECIES	Eastern Tailed-Blue, Summer Azure, Appalachian Azure.
IDENTIFICATION	Clear azure blue above (females with black borders). Unlike Eastern Tailed-Blue, there are no tails and no orange. Flight is usually higher and stronger than Eastern Tailed-Blue. Below, ground color is pale with various dark markings. Three color forms. "Lucia" has a dark blotch in the center of the HW below and has a dark brown margin, "marginata" lacks the central mark but retains the marginal brown, "violacea" lacks both marks.
HABITAT	Because a number of species are undoubtedly subsumed under this name (see Comments), "Spring Azures" are found in a wide variety of habitats including woodlands in general, bogs, pine barrens, swamps, overgrown fields, and suburban yards.
RANGE	Also western U.S., Canada, and south in the Mexican mountains.
ABUNDANCE	C-A. 1 brood. Georgia, North Carolina, Oklahoma—early March–early May; New York, Mass., Ohio, Illinois, Nebraska—April–May; Maine, Ontario, North Dakota—May–June.
⏸OR FOODPLANT	Many.
COMMENTS	Although recent years have seen progress in our understanding

of the American azures, they still present a bewildering array
forms, subspecies, and species and their story is far from unr
eled. Apart from the species treated here, other subspecies a
forms, including 'Edwards' Spring Azure, 'Cherry Gall' Spr
Azure, and 'Pine Barrens' Spring Azure may eventually be fou
to merit full species status. David Wright reports that FW sca
of male 'Edwards' Spring Azures are arranged differently fr
those of other azures, giving a matte finish to the blue wi
Other male Spring Azures have a brilliant blue effect. 'Che
Gall' Spring Azures generally fly in poor soil areas after the fli
of Spring Azure and before the flight of Summer Azures.

	MAR	APR	MAY	JUN	JUL	AUG	SEP	OCT
WI								
NY								
NC								
LA								

Summer Azure *Celastrina ladon neglecta* **Plate 23**

SIZE
≥ Eastern Tailed-Blue.

SIMILAR SPECIES
Eastern Tailed-Blue, Spring Azure, Appalachian Azure.

IDENTIFICATION
Flying throughout the summer months, Summer Azures tend
have more white overscaling than our other azures. "Lucia" a
"marginata" forms are absent or very, very rare. Otherwise, ve
similar to Spring Azure.

HABITAT
Open woodlands and surrounding fields and suburbs.

ABUNDANCE
U-C. 2-3 broods southward, 1 brood near northern edge of ran
North Carolina—early May–mid Sept.; Ohio—late May–ea
Sept.; New York—early June–Sept.; Nebraska—mid June–Au
Maine, Ontario, Wisconsin—July–Aug.

MAJOR FOODPLANT
A wide variety of plants from many different families.

COMMENTS
Although previously considered to be a 2nd brood of the Spr
Azure, these summer-flying azures are almost certainly a disti
species—*Celastrina neglecta*. I have listed them as subspecies *negle*
to be conservative and to be consistent with the NABA
(although subspecies do not normally occur together, it is possi
for two populations of the same species to be temporally separate

Appalachian Azure *Celastrina neglectamajor* **Plate**

SIZE
>> Eastern Tailed-Blue.

SIMILAR SPECIES
Summer Azure, Spring Azure.

IDENTIFICATION
If you find very large azures laying eggs on black cohosh in t
late spring, then you've got a pretty good ID. Since individu
are, so far as we know, phenotypically indistinguishable fro

other populations of azures that also fly between flights of Spring Azures and Summer Azures, anything less is a guess.

HABITAT Rich transition zone woodlands and their borders.

ABUNDANCE LR. 1 brood. Mid May–early June (through June in the mountains).

MAJOR FOODPLANT Black cohosh (*Cimicifuga racemosa*).

COMMENTS Only recently recognized as a distinct species, this species flies between the flights of Spring and Summer azures (or, in the South, with the first Summer Azures) and is much less common. The caterpillars are reported to be yellow when very young (unlike other azures) and then turn green or red.

	MAR	APR	MAY	JUN	JUL	AUG	SEP	OCT
WI								
NY			—▬					
NC								
LA								

Dusky Azure *Celastrina nigra* **Plate 23**

SIZE ≥ Eastern Tailed-Blue.

SIMILAR SPECIES Spring Azure, female Eastern Tailed-Blue.

IDENTIFICATION Below, very similar to, perhaps not separable from, Spring Azure. But males in flight are distinctive. Rather than showing off the bright blue glint of Spring Azures, these azures are a dark gray above. But remember, female Eastern Tailed-Blues are also dark gray above. Make sure that you are looking at an azure. Females above are darker blue than Spring Azures with black veining. Unlike female Spring Azures, female Dusky Azures frequently open their wings while landed.

HABITAT Stream banks and ravines in rich woodlands.

ABUNDANCE LR-LU. 1 brood. April–early May.

MAJOR FOODPLANT Goatsbeard (*Aruncus dioicus*).

COMMENTS Males can most easily be found at mud puddles.

Silvery Blue *Glaucopsyche lygdamus* **Plate 25**

SIZE ≥ Eastern Tailed-Blue.

SIMILAR SPECIES Reakirt's Blue.

IDENTIFICATION Below, note the **big, bold black-spotted postmedian band on both FW and HW**. Reakirt's Blue has bold postmedian band only on FW.

HABITAT Open fields, dry prairies, dunes; and woodland openings and banks (Appalachian population).

RANGE Also, Western U.S. and Canada.

ABUNDANCE 1 brood. Appalachian and Ozark populations, LR-LU, mainly April–May; northeastern populations C-A, late May–late June; Wisconsin, North Dakota, LR, mid May–early June.

MAJOR FOODPLANT Wood Vetch (*Vicia caroliniana*) and Tufted Vetch (*Vicia cracca*).

COMMENTS   Like many blues, this deeply satisfying butterfly often can be found at damp sand. In the East, although the populations are not in contact, the northern subspecies is advancing southward (at least in the Northeast) while the Appalachian subspecies has retreated southward.

	MAR	APR	MAY	JUN	JUL	AUG	SEP	OCT
WI			▬					
NY								
NC								
LA								

Northern Blue *Lycaeides idas* **Plates 24 & 25**

SIZE   ≥ Eastern Tailed-Blue.

SIMILAR SPECIES   Melissa Blue.

IDENTIFICATION   Very similar to the more common and widespread Melissa Blue. Below, the HW orange submarginal spots tend to be narrower and less intense on Northern Blues than on Melissa Blues and seem to be set farther inward. Extremely similar to 'Karner' Melissa Blue whose range does not overlap. Differs from nominate Melissa Blue in having less orange below, especially on the FW, and in females having less orange above, especially on the FW. In our region, ranges may only overlap in southern Manitoba.

HABITAT   Openings in northern woodlands, including roadsides.

RANGE   Also, mountains of western U.S. and west through Canada to Alaska and boreal Asia and Europe.

ABUNDANCE   R. 1 brood. Late June–late July/early Aug.

MAJOR FOODPLANT   Various heaths.

Melissa Blue *Lycaeides melissa* **Plates 24 & 25**

SIZE   ≥ Eastern Tailed-Blue.

SIMILAR SPECIES   Northern Blue.

IDENTIFICATION   This is the only eastern blue (aside from the geographically restricted and rare Northern Blue) with a submarginal orange spot band on the HW below.

HABITAT   Pine-oak barrens for 'Karner' Melissa Blue; western populations in many open and weedy situations.

ABUNDANCE   LR-U. 2 broods. Ohio—mid May–early June, July–mid Aug; Wisconsin—late May–June, August; Iowa, South Dakota—late May–Sept.; North Dakota—mid June–July; mid Aug.–early Sep.

MAJOR FOODPLANT   Lupines (*Lupinus*) for 'Karner' Melissa Blue; many legumes for western populations.

COMMENTS   Although 'Karner' Blue has traditionally been treated as a subspecies of Melissa Blue, there is no convincing evidence to su port this placement. Karner Blues look different from Melissa Blues, they occur only in pine-oak barrens while Melissa Blues occur in a wide variety of habitats, they use only lupine as a caterpillar food-plant while Melissa Blues use a large assortment of caterpillar food-plants (rarely lupines), and there is no hybrid blend zone between the populations. 'Karner' Melissa Blues occur west to eastern Minnesota and are threatened or endangered almost everywhere.

	MAR	APR	MAY	JUN	JUL	AUG	SEP	OCT
WI								
NY								
NC								
LA								

Greenish Blue *Plebejus saepiolus* **Plate 25**

SIZE ≥ Eastern Tailed-Blue.

SIMILAR SPECIES Silvery Blue.

IDENTIFICATION Below, in addition to postmedian black spot-band, note the row of submarginal spots, usually with some orange between the spots at the outer angle. Male above has **black FW cell-end bar**. Female above is dark bluish-gray to brown with some sub-marginal orangish-brown on the HW and a black FW cell-end bar. Silvery Blue lacks submarginal spot-bands below and FW cell-end bars above.

HABITAT Moist open situations in colder regions.

ABUNDANCE R-U. 1 brood. Mid May–mid July. Most common in June.

MAJOR FOODPLANT Flowerheads of clovers (*Trifolium*).

COMMENTS A major range extension in the early part of this century brought this species into southeastern Canada and northern Maine.

Arctic Blue *Agriades glandon* Not Illustrated

SIZE = Eastern Tailed-Blue.

SIMILAR SPECIES Silvery Blue.

IDENTIFICATION Like Silvery Blue, this species has black postmedian spots on the FW below and a postmedian band of white ringed spots on the HW below. But, the HW is more yellow-brown than on Silvery Blue and white markings are more extensive. Note that in addition to a black cell-end bar, there is a **black spot within the FW cell** that Silvery Blues lack.

HABITAT Alpine and arctic meadows, rocky outcrops.

RANGE Northern Canada south in the mountains to New Mexico and California, and across northern Asia and Europe.

ABUNDANCE Rare resident of Manitoba, where it flies mainly in June.

MAJOR FOODPLANT Poorly known, a number of different reports.

Metalmarks
(family Riodinidae)

Metalmarks derive their name, naturally enough, from the metallic ma[...] that are often present on their wings. The variety of wing size, shape, and p[...] tern of this very large tropical group is truly amazing. Some resemble ha[...] streaks, some resemble skippers, some resemble crescents, and some resem[...] heliconians! Compared to many of the brilliantly colored and patterned tr[...] ical species, our three closely related representatives of this family are rat[...] plain Janes, but still handsome nonetheless.

Little Metalmark *Calephelis virginiensis* **Plate 15**

SIZE	= Eastern Tailed-Blue.
SIMILAR SPECIES	Northern Metalmark, Swamp Metalmark.
IDENTIFICATION	A small, but bright inhabitant of open pine woods. Abo[...] bright, rich, red-orange-brown with silver metallic markin[...] Often with **vertical orange-brown and black stripes on** **thorax** (some individuals have a blackened thorax), the [...] marily orange-brown abdomen, and the lack of white on [...] FW fringe just below the apex. Northern Metalmark is dar[...] above, with blackish thorax and abdomen, and with a w[...] patch on the FW fringe just below the apex. Swamp Metalm[...] also has a blackish thorax and abdomen.
HABITAT	Open pine flats.
ABUNDANCE	LR-LC. 3 broods, April–Oct.
MAJOR FOODPLANT	Yellow thistle (*Cirsium horridulum*).
COMMENTS	Range doesn't overlap with either Northern or Swamp metalma[...]

	MAR	APR	MAY	JUN	JUL	AUG	SEP	OCT
WI								
NY								
NC								
LA								

Northern Metalmark *Calephelis borealis* **Plate 15**

SIZE	< Banded Hairstreak.
SIMILAR SPECIES	Swamp Metalmark, Little Metalmark.
IDENTIFICATION	A small orange-brown butterfly. During its slow and weak fli[...] it displays a strong contrast between its dark upper surface a[...] its bright orange under surface. Almost always lands with [...] **wings held flat**. Above, note the metallic silvery postmed[...]

and marginal bands, and the **very dark and prominent median band**. Swamp Metalmark's median band is not nearly so prominent. See Little Metalmark.

HABITAT	Open glades or ridges (or artificial power line cuts) within limestone soil woodlands.
ABUNDANCE	LR. 1 brood. Mid/late June–July.
MAJOR FOODPLANT	Round-leaved ragwort (*Senecio obovatus*).
COMMENTS	Search for this highly colonial butterfly in the afternoon when it is much more active, laying eggs on ragwort and nectaring on black-eyed susans. In cloudy weather it will sometimes pitch under leaves and land, moth-like, upside down—a characteristic behavior of the metalmark family.

	MAR	APR	MAY	JUN	JUL	AUG	SEP	OCT
WI								
NY				—				
NC								
LA								

Swamp Metalmark *Calephelis muticum* **Plate 15**

SIZE	< Banded Hairstreak.
SIMILAR SPECIES	Northern Metalmark, Little Metalmark.
IDENTIFICATION	A small orange-brown butterfly with metallic markings. Usually lands with its wings held open. Above, Northern Metalmark has a prominent very dark median band that this species lacks. Little Metalmark is brighter orange with more orange on the thorax and abdomen and ranges do not overlap.
HABITAT	Although found in moister habitats than related metalmarks, this species is not usually found in swamps, rather it prefers moist to wet meadows in peatland.
ABUNDANCE	LR. Missouri and southern Indiana, 2 broods—June, Aug.–early Sept.; Farther north 1 brood—July–mid Aug.
MAJOR FOODPLANT	Swamp thistle (*Cirsium muticum*).
COMMENTS	As a Swamp Metalmark came into view for the first time, I was struck by the strange similarity to a Mulberry Wing—fairly slow flight with bright yellow-orange underwings contrasting with very dark upperwings. This species needs immediate protection and an ongoing recovery plan. Now down to just a few known colonies in Wisconsin, Michigan, and Indiana and probably some others in Missouri. Many colonies were lost by habitat destruction, but it has also disappeared from a number of former haunts for no known reason. For the world to lose this gorgeous animal would be a true scandal. Join NABA and work to protect this and other species in trouble.

Brushfoots
(family Nymphalidae)

Called brushfoots because of the greatly reduced male forelegs, this family includes many of our best known and most conspicuous butterflies. They constitute a very diverse collection of species and some consider a number of the groups included here (such as the satyrs and the monarchs) as separate families. Quite a few of our species overwinter as adults, which may explain why these are the only butterflies in our region to exhibit classical migration patterns (south in the fall, north in the spring).

American Snout *Libytheana carinenta* Plate 36

SIZE	> Pearl Crescent.
IDENTIFICATION	The extremely long snout (palps) is obvious on this mainly orange and brown butterfly. It is dimorphic below, either pale or dark and mottled. While its flight can be rapid, it often seems erratic and mothlike.
HABITAT	Thickets and open woodlands with hackberries.
RANGE	Also, west to southern California and south to Argentina and the West Indies.
ABUNDANCE	R-C. 2 broods. North to North Carolina, Oklahoma—March–Oct. West Virginia, New York, Ohio, Illinois, Iowa—June–Sept. Generally R and erratic northward. RS to North Dakota, Ontario, northern New York.
MAJOR FOODPLANT	Hackberry (*Celtis*)
COMMENTS	This butterfly is often enormously abundant in the southwestern U.S. and Mexico, sometimes literally darkening the sky with millions of wings.

	MAR	APR	MAY	JUN	JUL	AUG	SEP	OCT
WI								
NY								
NC								
LA								

Gulf Fritillary *Agraulis vanillae* Plate 26

SIZE	≤ Great Spangled Fritillary
SIMILAR SPECIES	Great Spangled Fritillary, Julia.
IDENTIFICATION	A long-winged, low-flying nymphalid. Deep reddish-orange above and heavily silvered below. Above, note the black-ringed white spots in the FW cell. There is essentially no resident range

overlap with Great Spangled Fritillary (or other greater fritillaries) but Gulf Fritillaries do spread northward as the summer progresses. Gulf Fritillary wingbeats are shallower than the greater fritillaries and color above is red-orange (greater fritillaries are orange-brown).

HABITAT Open scrub, coastal areas, gardens.

RANGE Also, west to California and south to Argentina and the West Indies.

ABUNDANCE C-A, resident Florida, Georgia west to east Texas, most common late summer/early fall. Irregular immigrant north to North Carolina, Missouri and Kansas. RS to New Jersey, Wisconsin, Michigan (1 record), North Dakota (1 record), and Manitoba (1 record).

MAJOR FOODPLANT Passion-vines (*Passiflora*).

COMMENTS Truly a spangled dazzler, this is one of our most extravagant butterflies. Luckily for us, it is common and widespread. Butterfly gardeners can help make it even more common and widespread by planting plenty of passion-vines. I'm getting excited just thinking about it!

	MAR	APR	MAY	JUN	JUL	AUG	SEP	OCT
WI								
NY								
NC								
LA								

Julia *Dryas iulia* **Plate 26**

SIZE ≤ Great Spangled Fritillary

SIMILAR SPECIES Gulf Fritillary.

IDENTIFICATION Flying on narrow, stiff wings with shallow wingbeats, this orange heliconian is resident only in subtropical and tropical areas. Males are bright orange-brown, females duller orange-brown with a black band across the FW. Gulf Fritillaries are red-orange rather than orange-brown and have bright silvered spots below.

HABITAT A generalist, found in open and disturbed situations near tropical and subtropical woodlands.

RANGE Also, West Indies and south Texas south to Brazil.

ABUNDANCE C, all year south Florida. R fall immigrant to Houston area. RS north to Missouri, and eastern Nebraska (1 record).

MAJOR FOODPLANT Passion-vines (*Passiflora*).

COMMENTS Flight is much faster and directional than that of the closely related Zebra. Widespread and very common in the tropics.

Zebra (Heliconian) *Heliconius charitonius* **Plate 26**

SIZE ≤ Great Spangled Fritillary.

IDENTIFICATION   It is difficult to misidentify the black and yellow striped Zebra (Heliconian) although I'm sure some have succeeded. Flying slowly and gracefully, usually in the dappled light of semi-shade, this species is characteristic of disturbed habitats throughout the tropics and subtropics.

HABITAT   Woodland and hammock edges.

RANGE   Also, West Indies and south Texas south to Ecuador.

ABUNDANCE   C, all year south Florida; occasional immigrant north to Dallas-Fort Worth. RS north to Missouri (Aug.–Dec.) and Nebraska (1 recent record). Strays from Florida north to South Carolina, North Carolina and west to Louisiana, mainly in late summer/fall.

MAJOR FOODPLANT   Passion-vines (*Passiflora*).

COMMENTS   A Zebra (Heliconian) found in Westchester, New York in 1995 was almost certainly a transported and released butterfly. I know of at least one New Jersey commercial dealer in live butterflies that sells this species. The transport, sale and release of exotic (species not native to the region where they are released) live butterflies should be stopped.

Variegated Fritillary *Euptoieta claudia* Plate 26

SIZE   > American Lady.

IDENTIFICATION   A **dull, orange-brown** fritillary whose behavior and overall appearance is more similar to an American Lady than to the Greater Fritillaries. Our other fritillaries are brighter orange above. Below, it is unlike any of our other butterflies, with pale, very wide, postmedian band on the HW.

HABITAT   Open fields with flowers, coastal scrub.

RANGE   Also west to southern California and south to Argentina and the West Indies.

ABUNDANCE   Resident in the Deep South and common north to North Carolina, West Virginia and Kansas. A progressively decreasing breeding immigrant northward, but can sometimes become common as far north as Massachusetts and North Dakota. Stray to Ontario and Quebec. Usually appearing in late April from North Carolina to Kansas, in June from New York, Ohio, Indiana, Wisconsin, and South Dakota.

MAJOR FOODPLANT   Violets (*Viola*) and passion-vines (*Passiflora*).

COMMENTS   Abundance in the North is very variable.

	MAR	APR	MAY	JUN	JUL	AUG	SEP	OCT
WI					—	▬ —	▬	
NY					—			
NC		—						
LA	—							

Greater Fritillaries
(genus *Speyeria*)

These are the really big guys ardently swirling above open fields and meadows. Most of the 14 species are found in the American West where they present the greatest identification and systematics challenges of North American butterflies. At this time, no one really understands the relationships among the remarkable number of exceptionally variable western populations. However, in the East, the situation is much simpler. Most of the species have a long flight period, with the females emerging after the males and then flying later in the season. Perhaps uniquely among our butterflies, the greater fritillaries routinely do not lay their eggs on the caterpillar foodplant—violets. Rather, the females lay eggs seemingly at random in a meadow, amongst the grasses. The caterpillars hatch, hibernate over the winter, and then crawl to nearby violets in the springtime.

Diana Fritillary *Speyeria diana* Plate 27

SIZE
≥ Great Spangled Fritillary

IDENTIFICATION
A very large and striking fritillary. Males and females are dissimilar. Males are orange and chocolate while females are black and blue. (Is there no justice?) Unlike other fritillaries, both sexes have the HW below relatively unmarked.

HABITAT
Glades and other open areas within rich, moist mountain forests.

RANGE
·Also, formerly occurred throughout the Ohio River Valley and in southeastern VA and northeastern NC.

ABUNDANCE
LR-LU. 1 brood. Males appear before females. Late June–Sept.

MAJOR FOODPLANT
Violets (*Viola*).

COMMENTS
As Charlie Covell of Kentucky would say, an "Oh my!" butterfly.

Great Spangled Fritillary *Speyeria cybele* Plate 28

SIZE
1 11/16 in.

SIMILAR SPECIES
Aphrodite Fritillary, Atlantis Fritillary.

IDENTIFICATION
With their large size, bright orange color above, and silvered spots below, Great Spangled Fritillaries are some of our most conspicuous summer butterflies. Above, note the dark bands and spots on warm orange ground. Below, note the **wide cream-colored band** between postmedian and marginal silvered spotbands. Females are much larger and darker than males.

HABITAT	Open fields and meadows, roadsides, etc. Prefers moist areas on rich soil.
RANGE	Also west to Alberta and California.
ABUNDANCE	C. 1 brood. North to New York, Ohio, Indiana, Illinois, Nebraska, late May/June–Sept.; Mass., Ontario, Wisconsin, South Dakota, North Dakota, late June–mid Sept.
MAJOR FOODPLANT	Violets (*Viola*).
COMMENTS	Most late season individuals are females.

	MAR	APR	MAY	JUN	JUL	AUG	SEP	OCT
WI								
NY								
NC								
LA								

Aphrodite Fritillary *Speyeria aphrodite* Plate 28

SIZE	≤ Great Spangled Fritillary
SIMILAR SPECIES	Great Spangled Fritillary, Atlantis Fritillary.
IDENTIFICATION	Above, note the **black spot at the base of the FW** (below th cell). Great Spangled Fritillary lacks this spot. Below, the dar cinnamon-brown ground color **extends past the postmedi an spot-band** so that the **cream-colored band is narrowe** than in Great Spangled. The disc of the FW below is usuall noticeably rosy. Some midwestern populations ('Alcestis') hav males whose HWs below are dark reddish-brown and lack an cream-colored band, resembling Regal Fritillaries. These male and some in the southern Appalachians, also tend to lack th black spot at the base of the FW above. (Hey, if life were simp you'd probably run out of things to learn *before* you ran out energy.)
HABITAT	Prefers more wooded, cooler areas than Great Spangl Fritillary but often occurs with it; in Midwest moist prairies a also used.
RANGE	Also west to Montana.
ABUNDANCE	R-U north to New York, Ohio, Indiana, Illinois, Iowa, Nebrask U-C northward. 1 brood. Mid/late June–Aug./early Sept.
MAJOR FOODPLANT	Violets (*Viola*).
COMMENTS	Although very similar to Great Spangled Fritillary, Aphrod Fritillary is more beautiful in a subtle way. The silver below see to flash with more contrast than in Great Spangled Fritillary.

	MAR	APR	MAY	JUN	JUL	AUG	SEP	OCT
WI								
NY								
NC								
LA								

Regal Fritillary *Speyeria idalia* **Plate 27**

SIZE	≥ Great Spangled Fritillary
SIMILAR SPECIES	Aphrodite Fritillary, Great Spangled Fritillary.
IDENTIFICATION	Distinctive. Above, HW extremely dark brown to black with white spots. Below, HW completely dark brown with white spots. Some Aphrodite Fritillary populations in the northern Midwest ('Alcestis') can have the HW below completely dark brown with white spots, but spots at the base and bottom of the wing are not so prominent and long. Also note brownish-black body (Great Spangled and Aphrodite fritillaries have orange-brown bodies).
HABITAT	In the Midwest, tall-grass prairie and wet fields and meadows. Formerly ranged over much of the East in a variety of largely unnatural open situations, such as pastures and hayfields, usually wet.
RANGE	Also, west to the western Dakotas.
ABUNDANCE	LU. Extirpated from most of former range. Currently, there is only one major colony known (in central Pennsylvania) east of the Mississippi. 1 brood. Mainly mid June–mid Sept.
MAJOR FOODPLANT	Violets (*Viola*).
COMMENTS	This magnificent animal, one of our most splendiferous butterflies, has declined drastically in recent years. Although previously found throughout much of the Midwest and Northeast, the only viable colony now known from outside this species' tall-grass prairie stronghold is at Fort Indiantown Gap, Pennsylvania. Reasons for the decline are not known, although it seems likely that changes in agricultural practices, reforestation, and development have played major roles.

	MAR	APR	MAY	JUN	JUL	AUG	SEP	OCT
WI				▬	■■■	■■	■	
NY								
NC								
LA								

Callippe Fritillary *Speyeria callippe* Not illustrated

SIZE	< Great Spangled Fritillary.
SIMILAR SPECIES	Edwards' Fritillary.
IDENTIFICATION	HW below is tinged grayish-green with dull silver spots. Edwards' Fritillary is also green-tinged below (but is usually a darker brown, tinged with green) but is larger (almost the size of Great Spangled Fritillary while Callippe Fritillary is about the size of an Atlantis Fritillary).
HABITAT	Prairie hills and ridges.

RANGE — Manitoba south to Colorado, west to British Columbia and California.

ABUNDANCE — Rare resident in southwestern Manitoba, flying mid June–mid July.

MAJOR FOODPLANT — Violets (*Viola*).

Atlantis Fritillary *Speyeria atlantis* **Plate 28**

SIZE — < Great Spangled Fritillary.

SIMILAR SPECIES — Aphrodite Fritillary, Silver-bordered Fritillary.

IDENTIFICATION — Usually smaller than our other greater fritillaries. Solid black borders along most of the FWs distinguish it from most Aphrodite Fritillaries but some Aphrodites do have quite dark borders. Atlantis Fritillaries tend to have only a faint spot at the base of the FW above while Aphrodite Fritillaries usually have a strong spot. Silver-bordered Fritillaries are smaller and don't have brown on the inner portions of the FWs above. Below, unlike Aphrodite, dark ground color rarely extends much, if at all, past the postmedian spot-band. Instead, outward of most of the postmedian spots are small dark-brown spots that I refer to as **follow-spots**. Aphrodite may sometimes also have follow-spots but because the dark ground color surrounds these spots they are not so obvious.

HABITAT — Open, mixed-growth woodlands, especially in glades or boggy areas.

RANGE — Also, west to California.

ABUNDANCE — C. 1 brood. Mid June–mid Sept.

MAJOR FOODPLANT — Violets (*Viola*).

COMMENTS — A characteristic butterfly of northern meadows.

Mormon Fritillary *Speyeria mormonia* **Not Illustrated**

SIZE — << Great Spangled Fritillary.

SIMILAR SPECIES — Atlantis Fritillary.

IDENTIFICATION — A very small, variably marked, greater fritillary. Below, ground color is usually a creamy tan that is present on at least some of the HW base. Atlantis Fritillary has the HW base a darker, more uniform brown.

HABITAT — Mainly mountain meadows.

RANGE — Rocky Mountains north and west to Alaska and California.

ABUNDANCE — R in southwestern Manitoba. RS? to eastern North Dakota and western Minnesota (a few reports).

MAJOR FOODPLANT — Violets (*Viola*).

Lesser Fritillaries
(genus *Boloria*)

These delightful, diminutive, but intricately marked, fritillaries of the North can sometimes cause frustration because of their tendency to be constantly in motion—viewing their much more distinctive undersides can be a problem. Of the almost 30 species found worldwide, six are found in our region, and only two of these are widespread. Above, they are orange with black markings, as are crescents and checkerspots. But the lesser (and greater) fritillaries have a complete FW submarginal band of black spots that these other groups lack.

Bog Fritillary *Boloria eunomia* Plate 29

SIZE	≥ Pearl Crescent.
SIMILAR SPECIES	Silver-bordered Fritillary.
IDENTIFICATION	Note the rows of white spot-bands on the HW below, including a **postmedian row of white spots**, outlined in black. Silver-bordered Fritillaries have a postmedian row of black spots. Above, similar to Silver-bordered Fritillary but with darker overscaling.
HABITAT	Acid bogs.
RANGE	Also, north to the Arctic and west through Eurasia.
ABUNDANCE	LR-LU. 1 brood. Mid June–early July.
MAJOR FOODPLANT	Shrubby willows (*Salix*) and violets (*Viola*).

Silver-bordered Fritillary *Boloria selene* Plate 29

SIZE	> Pearl Crescent.
SIMILAR SPECIES	Meadow Fritillary, Harris' Checkerspot.
IDENTIFICATION	Smaller than the greater fritillaries (*Speyeria*) but larger than the crescents (*Phyciodes*). Below, distinctive. Note the median and marginal bands of silvered white. Harris' Checkerspot also has white bands below, but has an orange margin. Above, the **narrow black borders enclose orange spots** (especially on the HW). Meadow Fritillaries lack these borders.
HABITAT	Bogs, wet meadows, wet prairies, marshes.
RANGE	Also, north to the Arctic and west through Eurasia.
ABUNDANCE	LR toward southern edge of range, LC-C elsewhere. 2-3 broods. Mainly May–mid Sept. Northeastern South Dakota, North Dakota and far north—mid June–Aug.
MAJOR FOODPLANT	Violets (*Viola*).

COMMENTS This species and the next are our two common lesser fritillaries. In general they divide up the habitat with Silver-bordered Fritillaries occurring in wetter areas than Meadow Fritillaries. However, as one goes northward, Silver-bordered Fritillaries become more widespread and can be found in fairly dry situations.

	MAR	APR	MAY	JUN	JUL	AUG	SEP	OCT
WI					—	–		
NY								
NC								
LA								

Meadow Fritillary *Boloria bellona* **Plate 29**

SIZE > Pearl Crescent.

SIMILAR SPECIES Silver-bordered Fritillary.

IDENTIFICATION Dull orange-brown above. Flight is weak with stiff wingbeats. Note the lack of black borders above and the **blunt FW apex**. Below, an indistinct smudged pattern, palest outside the post-median line.

HABITAT Grassy fields and meadows, especially moist ones.

RANGE Also, west to British Columbia.

ABUNDANCE LC-C. Mainly 3 broods. Late April–mid Sept. 2 broods Maine, Ontario, Wisconsin, North Dakota, mid May–Aug./early Sept.

MAJOR FOODPLANT Violets (*Viola*).

COMMENTS Has expanded its range and become much more common over the past 30 years. Until recently, only known as far southwest as northeastern Tennessee, but recent reports of individuals from central Tennessee and northern Mississippi! may indicate that its southward colonization is continuing.

	MAR	APR	MAY	JUN	JUL	AUG	SEP	OCT
WI								
NY								
NC								
LA								

Frigga Fritillary *Boloria frigga* **Plate 29**

SIZE > Pearl Crescent.

SIMILAR SPECIES Meadow Fritillary.

IDENTIFICATION Below, the HW is more well-marked than Meadow Fritillary with the white spot at the base of the HW leading margin especially prominent. FW apex is rounded in Frigga Fritillary, not squared off as in Meadow Fritillary. Above, usually darker basally than Meadow Fritillary with the HW margin darker and with the FW cell-end bar solid black. Meadow Fritillary has the FW cell-end bar enclosing some orange ground color.

HABITAT	Northern bogs and swamps.
RANGE	Also, north to the Arctic and west through Eurasia.
ABUNDANCE	LR. 1 brood. Late May–early July.
MAJOR FOODPLANT	Shrubby willows (*Salix*) and dwarf birch (*Betula glandulosa*).
COMMENTS	Frigga was the wife of Odin in Norse mythology.

Freija Fritillary *Boloria freija* **Plate 29**

SIZE	≥ Pearl Crescent.
SIMILAR SPECIES	Arctic Fritillary, Silver-bordered Fritillary, Frigga Fritillary.
IDENTIFICATION	HW below, note the **duck head** pattern formed by a combination of the dark cell with a black "eye," and the adjacent silver-white "bill." The "bill" points to a small white crescent or patch. Arctic Fritillary is similar but lacks the white crescent and on the HW has a marginal row of flat white spots (Freija Fritillary has marginal row of white spots that point inwardly). Both Freija and Arctic fritillaries have white horizontal lines near the FW margins below. Above, the black median FW band is very connected and very angular.
HABITAT	Northern bogs and clearings in northern coniferous forests.
RANGE	Also, north to the Arctic and west through Eurasia.
ABUNDANCE	LR. 1 brood. Late May/early June–June/early July.
MAJOR FOODPLANT	Bearberry (*Arctostaphylos uva-ursi*), blueberry (*Vaccinium*) and other Ericaceae.
COMMENTS	The Norse goddess Freija is known to favor love songs and so it may become a tradition among butterflier lovers to seek this northern fritillary to invoke her blessing.

Arctic Fritillary *Boloria chariclea* **Plate 29**

SIZE	> Pearl Crescent.
SIMILAR SPECIES	Freija Fritillary, Silver-bordered Fritillary.
IDENTIFICATION	Below, many populations of this species are tinged purplish (but not the one in the White Mountains of New Hampshire). Note the white horizontal lines along the FW margin. The **HW marginal row of flat, white spots** distinguishes this from our other species. Above, only this species and Freija Fritillary has black inwardly pointing triangles **with flat bottoms** along the HW submargin.
HABITAT	In our region, dwarf willow bogs. More general farther north.
RANGE	Also, north to the Arctic and west through Eurasia.
ABUNDANCE	LU. 1 brood. New Hampshire—late July–Aug.; Ontario, Manitoba—mid July–mid Aug.
MAJOR FOODPLANT	Willows (*Salix*), violets (*Viola*), and others.

COMMENTS Recent evidence suggests that populations in North America previously referred to as *Boloria titania* are best placed as subspecies of *Boloria chariclea*, true *titania* being limited to Europe. Probably the easiest place to find this butterfly in our region is along the road to the top of Mt. Washington, at about 4700 ft.

Gorgone Checkerspot *Chlosyne gorgone* **Plate 30**

SIZE ≥ Pearl Crescent.

SIMILAR SPECIES Silvery Checkerspot, Harris' Checkerspot.

IDENTIFICATION Below, unmistakable, with a bold HW pattern of hypnotic power. Above, very similar to Silvery and Harris' checkerspots but usually has more pronounced pale chevrons in the HW black border (when pale spots are present in Silvery or Harris' borders they tend to be relatively flat). Also, averages smaller.

HABITAT Although the heart of its range is the prairie province, this species can occur in a great variety of open situations.

RANGE Also, west to Alberta and Utah.

ABUNDANCE LU-C western part of our region; LR in the Southeast. Mainly 2/3 broods. April/May–Sept.; 1 brood Manitoba—June.

MAJOR FOODPLANT Sunflowers (*Helianthus*) and other Compositae.

COMMENTS A widely wandering, colonizing species, there are isolated reports of its occurrence from (for example), Mississippi, Kentucky, West Virginia, Pennsylvania, and the Tug Hill Plateau of New York. Very recently, a number of colonies have been discovered in southern Ontario. May not still be present in Alabama and most of Georgia, outside of the extreme northeast

	MAR	APR	MAY	JUN	JUL	AUG	SEP	OCT
WI								
NY								
NC								
LA								

Silvery Checkerspot *Chlosyne nycteis* **Plate 30**

SIZE > Pearl Crescent.

SIMILAR SPECIES Pearl Crescent, Harris' Checkerspot, Gorgone Checkerspot.

IDENTIFICATION A small, orange and black nymphalid of woodland glades. Larger than Pearl Crescent with **wider FW black borders above**. Below, note the very broad **white median band** on the HW, and the **interrupted marginal white spot band**. Over most of the East, Harris' Checkerspot has much brighter, silvered white spot bands below, but in the northern Midwest, Harris' can look a lot like this species except that it has a continuous marginal white spot-band. Above, similar to Harris' and Gorgone checkerspots but

Silvery has HW black submarginal spots that are surrounded by orange and no (or faint) marginal pale chevrons. Harris' has the HW black submarginal spots either directly attached to the black marginal band or with black line attached to the spots distally.

HABITAT Open deciduous woodlands and edges; stream edges in open country.

RANGE Also, west to Colorado and Arizona.

ABUNDANCE Mainly LU-LC. Houston area and Florida panhandle (near Marianna)—Mar.–Sept.; Georgia, North Carolina, Philadelphia, Ohio, Missouri, Oklahoma, Kansas, 2 broods—mid May–early June, mid July–early Sept.; New York, Ontario, Michigan, Wisconsin, North Dakota, 1 brood—mainly mid June–early July.

MAJOR FOODPLANT Sunflowers (*Helianthus*) and other Compositae.

COMMENTS Usually flies within one foot of the ground or shrubs. Often difficult to see the underside well.

	MAR	APR	MAY	JUN	JUL	AUG	SEP	OCT
WI								
NY								
NC								
LA								

Harris' Checkerspot *Chlosyne harrisii* **Plate 30**

SIZE > Pearl Crescent.

SIMILAR SPECIES Silvery Checkerspot, Gorgone Checkerspot, Pearl Crescent.

IDENTIFICATION Below, one of our more striking butterflies. Alternating white and orange-brown bands make Harris' Checkerspot a real show-off. Some individuals in the northern Midwest have the HW central band more tan than white and resemble Silvery Checkerspots. Note the HW margin with a complete row of large white spots. Above, larger and darker than Pearl Crescent. Above, very similar to Silvery and Gorgone checkerspots; see them for discussion.

HABITAT Wet shrubby meadows and marsh borders with its foodplant.

ABUNDANCE LR-LU. 1 brood. June in southern parts of range, mid June–mid July farther north.

MAJOR FOODPLANT Flat-topped white aster (*Aster umbellatus*).

COMMENTS Eggs are laid in clusters and the caterpillars are colonial, sometimes causing small colonies to eat themselves out of house and home!

	MAR	APR	MAY	JUN	JUL	AUG	SEP	OCT
WI								
NY								
NC								
LA								

Texan Crescent *Phyciodes texana* Plate 31

SIZE	≥ Pearl Crescent
IDENTIFICATION	Black with white median spot-band and some red-brown basally. Darker than our other crescents.
HABITAT	Roadside ditches, parks, and other open situations.
RANGE	Also, the American southwest and south to Guatemala.
ABUNDANCE	Generally LR-LU, but LU-LC northeastern Texas. 3 broods? Florida, northeastern Texas—Mar.–Oct.; south Georgia and coastal South Carolina—late May–early Sept. Irregular immigrant north to Kansas. RS to Nebraska, western Missouri, South Dakota (1 record), and Minnesota (1 record).
MAJOR FOODPLANT	*Dicliptera*, shrimpflower (*Beloperone*), *Ruellia* and other small Acanthaceae.
COMMENTS	A more leisurely flyer than our other crescents. Some consider the Florida subspecies, 'Seminole' Texan Crescent, to be a distinct species.

	MAR	APR	MAY	JUN	JUL	AUG	SEP	OCT
WI								
NY								
NC								
LA								

Cuban Crescent *Phyciodes frisia* Plate 31

SIZE	= Pearl Crescent.
SIMILAR SPECIES	Pearl Crescent, Phaon Crescent.
IDENTIFICATION	This crescent has the FW above with three large orange-brown spots against a black ground color. Below, note the pale zigzag submarginal bands.
HABITAT	Edges of subtropical hammocks and other open situations.
RANGE	Also, West Indies and (as 'Tulcis' Cuban Crescent) southern Texas south through South America.
ABUNDANCE	U, south Florida, all year. RS and temporary colonist north to Volusia and Alachua counties, Florida. 1 record of 'Tulcis' Cuban Crescent from Missouri.
MAJOR FOODPLANT	*Dicliptera*, shrimpflower (*Beloperone*), *Ruellia*, and other small Acanthacae.
COMMENTS	'Tulcis' Cuban Crescent is probably a distinct species, not a subspecies of Cuban Crescent. It is black and white rather than black and orange-brown.

Phaon Crescent *Phyciodes phaon* Plate 31

SIZE	≤ Pearl Crescent.
SIMILAR SPECIES	Pearl Crescent.

IDENTIFICATION Above, note the **cream-colored FW median band**, contrasting with the orange postmedian band. Below, the pale crescent in the middle of the FW outer margin is inwardly bounded by a continuous black line. In Pearl Crescent this black line is missing or incomplete.

HABITAT Moist open situations with its low, mat-forming hostplants. Often along roadsides, trails, or lake beds.

RANGE Also, west to southern California and Cuba and Mexico south to Guatemala.

ABUNDANCE C-A, Florida—all year. U-C, Immediate Gulf Coast—March–November. Decreasing in abundance north along Atlantic coast north to Dare Co., North Carolina—mainly May–mid–October. C north to northeastern Texas—May mid October. LR north to eastern Kansas and Missouri—July–Oct.

MAJOR FOODPLANT Fogfruit (*Lippia*).

COMMENTS It is easy to overlook these small crescents, even when they swarm on roadsides and lawns, because they fly very close to the ground.

	MAR	APR	MAY	JUN	JUL	AUG	SEP	OCT
WI								
NY								
NC								
LA								

Pearl Crescent *Phyciodes tharos* **Plate 32**

SIZE 11/16 in.

SIMILAR SPECIES Northern Crescent, Silvery Checkerspot, Phaon Crescent.

IDENTIFICATION Small, bright orange (when fresh) with a flight that is low to the ground and often involves gliding. Exact pattern can be quite variable. Males and females and different broods also differ to some degree. Note the orange above with extensive reticulate black markings. Below, note the brown smudge on HW border enclosing a pale crescent. See Northern Crescent.

HABITAT Widespread in open situations, fields, meadows, power-line cuts, suburbia, etc.

RANGE Also, west to Montana and south through Mexico.

ABUNDANCE C-A. Florida and south Georgia west along coast—all year. North to Philadelphia, Indiana, Illinois, Iowa, Nebraska, 3 broods—April–October. 2 broods farther north—mainly mid May–June, July–Sept.

MAJOR FOODPLANT Asters.

COMMENTS This is one of the most common and widespread butterflies in North America. It is also quite beautiful. Sometimes we get lucky!

BRUSHFOOTS

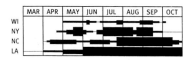

	MAR	APR	MAY	JUN	JUL	AUG	SEP	OCT
WI								
NY								
NC								
LA								

Northern Crescent *Phyciodes selenis* **Plate 32**

SIZE ≥ Pearl Crescent.

SIMILAR SPECIES Pearl Crescent, Tawny Crescent.

IDENTIFICATION Northern Crescents can be extremely difficult to distinguish from Pearl Crescents. The major identification difference has been stated to be that males of this species have orange and black antennal clubs while the antennal clubs of male Pearl Crescents are entirely black. Unfortunately, even putting aside the fact that female Pearl Crescents have orange and black antennal clubs, this character varies widely among bona fide Pearl Crescents. General differences are that Northern Crescents tend to be large (but populations in northern Minnesota look like Northern Crescents but are no larger than Pearl Crescents) and have less prominent black reticulations on the HW above (giving a more open appearance to the orange area of the HW). Females tend to have the FW above postmedian band a paler (more yellow orange than the rest of the wing while Pearl Crescent females tend to have a more uniform orange color. Some females are quite dark, resembling Tawny Crescents. Behavioral differences are often cited, such as speed of flight and willingness to fly over bushes, but I saw little difference in this regard in populations have seen. It is probably best to study a whole colony before concluding that this species might be present.

HABITAT A wide variety of open situations.

RANGE Also, west to British Columbia and south through the Rockies New Mexico.

ABUNDANCE C-A, except R at southern edges of range and in the Appalachians. 1 brood. Mid June-mid July, some population have a partial second brood in August.

MAJOR FOODPLANT Asters

COMMENTS I remain unconvinced that this is a valid species. When there are so few valid characters to differentiate these "species," how would one know the extent of a zone of hybridization? Sure, you look at individuals from northern Canada and Maryland you can call them a Northern Crescent and a Pearl Crescent respectively. But, if you look at an individual from central New Hampshire, you can probably call it anything you want! T

complex probably does not comfortably fit within the neat boxes
we like to construct. The two entities fall somewhere between
species and subspecies.

	MAR	APR	MAY	JUN	JUL	AUG	SEP	OCT
WI								
NY								
NC								
LA								

Tawny Crescent *Phyciodes batesii* **Plate 32**

SIZE   = Pearl Crescent.

SIMILAR SPECIES   Pearl Crescent, Northern Crescent.

IDENTIFICATION   Easy to confuse with its relatives. Easiest to distinguish below—the **entire HW is straw yellow**, generally with just a few darker brown markings (some individuals have brown at the margin). Pearl and Northern crescents have various dark markings on the HW below, especially around the pale crescent toward the middle of the outer margin. The **FW subapex by the outer margin is clear** in Tawny crescent but has darker markings in Pearl and Northern crescents. Also, look at the black median bar that is perpendicular to the FW costal margin. In Tawny Crescents it is characteristically (but not always) longer, with straighter sides (more rectangular) than in Northern and Pearl crescents. Above, tends to be darker than Northern and Pearl crescents (especially comparing males) but I would hesitate to make any determination from only an upperside view.

HABITAT   Reported from both dry situations, such as pastures and moister woodland openings.

RANGE   Also, west through Canada to Alberta with some isolated colonies in the U.S. western plains.

ABUNDANCE   LR. 1 brood. June–early/mid July.

MAJOR FOODPLANT   Asters.

COMMENTS   This species has declined over large areas of the Northeast for no apparent reason (although many old reports were misidentifications). Previously reported from much of New York and Pennsylvania, the only populations currently known to exist southeast of Lakes Erie and Ontario are in the mountains of extreme southwestern North Carolina and adjacent Georgia.

Baltimore Checkerspot *Euphydryas phaeton* **Plate 30**

SIZE   = American Lady.

IDENTIFICATION   One of our most dazzling butterflies. Black, white, and orange.

The underside is particularly arresting.

HABITAT Usually marshes/wet meadows with turtlehead but recently found in enormous concentrations in dry fields, feeding on English plantain. In MA, this is now the habitat in which this species is most frequently found.

ABUNDANCE Mainly LU. 1 brood. Early June–mid July. LR, Appalachians; LA eastern Ozarks and southeastern Mass.

MAJOR FOODPLANT Turtlehead (*Chelone glabra*) and English plantain (*Plantago lanceolata*).

COMMENTS Even very small areas with turtlehead will often have a population of Baltimore Checkerspots. Named for the orange and black colors of Lord Baltimore.

	MAR	APR	MAY	JUN	JUL	AUG	SEP	OCT
WI				■	■■			
NY								
NC								
LA								

Anglewings and Tortoiseshells
(genus *Polygonia*) (genus *Nymphalis*

These two groups are best considered together, since they share many trait and are very closely related. Unlike most of our butterflies, adult anglewing and tortoiseshells do not usually nectar at flowers. Instead, they can often b seen taking sap from trees, congregating at rotting fruit, or even deriving sus tenance from animal scat or carrion. These are the butterflies one is most like ly to see landed on dirt roads through woodlands. Also unlike any of our othe butterflies, species in these groups overwinter in cold areas as adults. Th adult butterflies crawl into narrow cavities in trees, or into cracks in huma dwellings. On warm days in the dead of winter, they can sometimes be foun flying in the sunshine! The overwintering adults usually mate in the earl springtime.

Species in these groups can be migratory. Certainly, Question Marks an Mourning Cloaks routinely fly southward in the fall. It is not known wheth they randomly disperse or congregate at some yet unknown location Compton Tortoiseshells can also have strong southern movements, and Europe, Small Tortoiseshells are famous for their migrations.

Although these butterflies are essentially northern (also found througho Eurasia), Question Marks, Eastern Commas, and Mourning Cloaks are fou throughout most of our region.

SIZE	> American Lady.
SIMILAR SPECIES	Eastern Comma.
IDENTIFICATION	A medium-sized orangish butterfly of the woods and nearby open area. Flight is rapid but usually not very directional, often returning to the same area. Above, the only anglewing with a small black horizontal bar in the subapical FW. Also note the violaceous margin of the HW. Below, note the silvered "question-mark." Above, the black or "summer" form has much black on the HWs while the orange, or "fall" form is mainly orangish-brown. These forms correspond largely, but not completely, with the summer and fall broods. There are also two forms below, either fairly uni-colored or heavily mottled. Question Marks can usually be told from Eastern Commas, even on the wing, by their generally larger size and more robust flight with slower wingbeats.
HABITAT	Woodlands and adjacent open areas. More wide-ranging than Eastern Comma.
RANGE	Also west to Colorado and southeastern Arizona and south through the Mexican highlands.
ABUNDANCE	U-C. 2 broods. Late May/late June–mid Oct. 2nd brood over-wintering as adults and flying again next spring, mainly April–May. Occasionally move northward to southern Manitoba and southern New Brunswick.
MAJOR FOODPLANT	Nettles (*Urtica*), elm family (Ulmaceae), hackberry (*Celtis*), and others.
COMMENTS	Late in the fall, Question Marks move south along the coast in a dramatic migration. In the spring, these individuals move back north in a migration that isn't as dramatic as the fall's but is noticeable nonetheless. It is these individuals who are largely responsible for repopulating most of the North each season. From New York north, some do overwinter, but their numbers are generally low and vary with the severity of the winters.

	MAR	APR	MAY	JUN	JUL	AUG	SEP	OCT
WI		▬		▬	▬	▬▬	▬▬	▬
NY								
NC	▬▬▬▬	▬▬	▬▬	▬				
LA			▬▬▬▬▬▬▬▬▬▬▬▬▬▬▬					

Eastern Comma *Polygonia comma* **Plate 33**

SIZE	≤ American Lady.
SIMILAR SPECIES	Question Mark, Green Comma, Gray Comma.
IDENTIFICATION	Note the size, generally smaller than a Question Mark. Above, very similar to Question Mark but **lacks the horizontal black,**

subapical spot of that species. Below, note silvered "comma." Like Question Mark there is an orange above "fall" form and a "summer" form with black on the HW. See discussions under Green and Gray commas.

HABITAT	More closely restricted to woodlands than Question Mark, but found in a wide variety of situations.
ABUNDANCE	U-C. 2 broods. Late May/late June–mid Oct. 2nd brood over–wintering as adults and flying again next spring, mainly April–May. RS south to the Florida panhandle.
MAJOR FOODPLANT	Elms and nettles (*Urtica*).
COMMENTS	The only comma restricted to the East. Unlike Question Marks, Eastern Commas, and the other commas, do not seem to migrate.

	MAR	APR	MAY	JUN	JUL	AUG	SEP	OCT
WI								
NY								
NC								
LA								

Satyr Comma *Polygonia satyrus* **Plate 34**

SIZE	≤ American Lady.
SIMILAR SPECIES	Eastern Comma.
IDENTIFICATION	Unlike Eastern Comma, there is no black form. Above, this rarely encountered species is more **golden colored** than Eastern Comma with a tan HW margin and a pale submarginal HW band that is continuous (or almost so). Eastern Comma has a pale gray HW margin and a submarginal HW band that is broken into spots. Below, Satyr Comma tend to be **unicolorous at the FW apex** while Eastern Commas are two-toned here. The HW margin between the outer angle and tail is not particularly darkened in Satyr Commas while Eastern Commas usually have a dark brown band in this region. In addition, the HW median line of Satyr Commas tends to be straighter than that of Eastern Commas.
HABITAT	Generally, but rather sparsely, distributed in northern woodland.
RANGE	Also, west to British Columbia and California, south through the Rockies.
ABUNDANCE	R. 1 brood July–Oct., overwintering adults fly again April–May.
MAJOR FOODPLANT	Nettles (*Urtica*).
COMMENTS	A Satyr Comma is a good find anywhere in our region.

Green Comma *Polygonia faunus* **Plate 34**

SIZE	≤ American Lady.
SIMILAR SPECIES	Eastern Comma, Gray Comma, Hoary Comma.
IDENTIFICATION	Wings usually more jagged than other anglewings. Above, no

the **2 black spots** on the inner margin of the FW. Eastern Comma, Gray Comma, and Hoary Comma usually have only the bottom spot or if the top spot is present it is faint. Also note black HW border with yellowish spots. Below, note the **bluish-green submarginal band** and the **comma mark with the thick hooked end**. Gray Comma can also occasionally have some bluish-green below, but is more unicolorous dark gray, and heavily striated.

HABITAT Canadian zone forests.

RANGE Also, west to Alaska and south through the Rockies.

ABUNDANCE LR, Appalachians, 1 brood. Late June–Aug., overwintering adults fly again April–May. LC, Adirondacks, northern New England. R-U, Michigan, Wisconsin, North Dakota.

MAJOR FOODPLANT Willows (*Salix*) and birches (*Betula*).

COMMENTS A rare "chocolate" form of the Green Comma is all dark below, like a Gray Comma and even has the comma mark thin and unhooked like a Gray Comma. But even this form lacks Gray Comma's dark striations. The underside of this color form is illustrated (although the reproduction is quite poor) in *Butterflies through Binoculars: Boston-New York-Washington*— misidentified as a Gray Comma. Thanks to Jeff Ingraham for pointing this out to me.

Hoary Comma *Polygonia gracilis* **Plate 34**

SIZE ≤ American Lady.

SIMILAR SPECIES Eastern Comma, Green Comma, Gray Comma.

IDENTIFICATION Below, note the very **two-toned appearance** with the outer 1/3 of the wings very hoary. Other commas are not so hoary, especially on the HW. Above, Hoary Commas can usually be distinguished from Green Commas by the absence of HW black median spot and by the absence of a paler gray margin on the HW. Also note the black mark at the end of the FW cell. In Hoary Commas this mark is curved on both sides, while in Green Commas it is much straighter. Eastern Commas and Gray Commas usually have the HW base suffused with red.

HABITAT Canadian zone forest.

RANGE Also, west to Alaska and (as 'Zephyr' Hoary Comma) south through the Rockies.

ABUNDANCE R. July–Sept., overwintering adults in April–May.

MAJOR FOODPLANT Currants (*Ribes*).

COMMENTS Some consider the western 'Zephyr' Hoary Comma to be a distinct species.

Gray Comma *Polygonia progne* **Plate 34**

SIZE	≤ American Lady.
SIMILAR SPECIES	Eastern Comma, Green Comma, Hoary Comma, Compton Tortoiseshell.
IDENTIFICATION	Above, very similar to Eastern Comma. HW black border is usually broader than on other anglewings ("summer" form Eastern Commas have extensive black). Below, **dark gray and often heavily striated. Comma is thin and tapers at both ends**. Very similar below to the much larger Compton Tortoiseshell. Wingbeats slower than other commas.
HABITAT	Mainly rich deciduous woodlands with northern elements.
RANGE	Also, west to British Columbia.
ABUNDANCE	R-U. 2 broods. Mainly June–July, Aug.–early Oct., overwintering adults in April–May. Strays south to Westchester Co., New York and northwestern New Jersey.
MAJOR FOODPLANT	Currants (*Ribes*).
COMMENTS	This species may be more common in parts of its southern range than thought, because it is most common in woodlands in September and October when butterfliers become rare.

	MAR	APR	MAY	JUN	JUL	AUG	SEP	OCT
WI				▬ ▬	▬▬▬	—	—	—
NY								
NC								
LA								

Compton Tortoiseshell *Nymphalis vau-album* **Plate 3**

SIZE	< Mourning Cloak.
SIMILAR SPECIES	Gray Comma.
IDENTIFICATION	The aristocratic and boldly patterned reddish-brown, black, and orange Compton Tortoiseshell often glides through the woodlands, seemingly surveying its realm. Above, note the white spot on the HW. Below, dark gray and heavily striated. Often attracted to tree sap. Gray Comma, similar below, is much smaller.
HABITAT	A wide variety of wooded situations.
RANGE	Also, west to British Columbia.
ABUNDANCE	R-U. 1 brood. Adults emerge late June/early July, often aestivate during summer, fly Sept.–Oct., overwinter, fly and mate early spring, mid March–May. RS south to southern New Jersey, the North Carolina coast (1 recent record), Missouri, southern Nebraska (1 record).
MAJOR FOODPLANT	Birches (*Betula*) and willows (*Salix*).
COMMENTS	Named after Compton County, Quebec, so, like Virginia bluebell (not Virginia's bluebells) this species is Compton Tortoiseshell, n

Compton's Tortoiseshell. Subject to cyclical population explosions and range expansions, it has recently been found regularly as far south as western Maryland. Next year its range may contract again.

	MAR	APR	MAY	JUN	JUL	AUG	SEP	OCT
WI		▬		▬			▬	▬ ▬
NY	▬				▬		▬	
NC								
LA		·						

Mourning Cloak *Nymphalis antiopa* **Plate 35**

SIZE   1 10/16 in.

DENTIFICATION   Unmistakable. A large, dark nymphalid. Dark brown above with yellow borders and blue submarginal spots. Below, dark striated brown with pale yellow borders. Often glides in flight.

HABITAT   One of our most widespread butterflies. Though characteristic of hardwood forests, Mourning Cloaks can be found in almost any habitat including, woodlands, fields, suburbs, and downtown Manhattan!

RANGE   Also, all of North America, west through Eurasia, south through Mexico.

ABUNDANCE   U-C. 1 brood (perhaps a partial second). Adults emerge late June/early July, usually aestivate during summer, fly Sept.–Oct., overwinter, fly and mate early spring, April–early June. R at south edge of range, where perhaps normally only a winter resident. R immigrant south to the Florida panhandle and Houston.

JOR FOODPLANT   Willows (*Salix*) and many other trees and shrubs.

COMMENTS   To some extent, migrates south in the fall, especially along the beaches. I have lived in New York, Massachusetts, New Jersey, Texas, and California, and this species and Cabbage White are the only two butterflies that have been in my yard at each location.

	MAR	APR	MAY	JUN	JUL	AUG	SEP	OCT
WI		▬		▬			▬	
NY	▬ ▬			▬			▬	
NC			▬					
LA								

Milbert's Tortoiseshell *Nymphalis milberti* **Plate 35**

SIZE   < American Lady.

MILAR SPECIES   Mourning Cloak (underside).

IDENTIFICATION   This colorful northern nymphalid has bright orange and yellow FW borders above. Below, dark, striated brown with a **pale submarginal band**. Mourning Cloak is much larger and has pale marginal band.

HABITAT   Open fields, usually moist, near woodlands.

RANGE   Also, west to Alaska and California.

ABUNDANCE   R-C. 2 broods? Late June–early Oct., overwintering adults April–June.

MAJOR FOODPLANT   Nettles (*Urtica*).

COMMENTS   Formerly occurred more commonly to the southeast. Irrup[tive] movements and sporadic breeding still occur to regions south[of] the range shown.

	MAR	APR	MAY	JUN	JUL	AUG	SEP	OCT
WI								
NY								
NC								
LA								

American Lady *Vanessa virginiensis* **Plate 36**

SIZE   1 2/16 in.

SIMILAR SPECIES   Painted Lady.

IDENTIFICATION   A medium-sized dull-orange butterfly with white spots on [the] black upper FW apex. Below, note the distinctive cobweb p[at]tern on the HW and the pink patch on the FW. To distingu[ish] from similar Painted Lady remember, "American Ladies have [big] eyes and an open mind." The big eyes refer to the 2 large e[ye]spots on the HW below. Painted Ladies have 4 smallish eye-sp[ots] on the HW below. The open mind refers to the lack of a ho[ri]zontal "closing" line connecting the black lines in the lower m[id]dle FW above. Most individuals have a white spot on the [FW] above that Painted Ladies lack.

HABITAT   Open spaces, including fields, meadows, roadsides, a[nd] coastal dunes.

RANGE   Also, west to California and south through Mexico.

ABUNDANCE   U-C. Florida, all year resident. Broods irregular. Farther no[rth] mainly Apr.–Oct.; R immigrant north to Manitoba and N[ew] Brunswick, mainly June–July.

MAJOR FOODPLANT   Pearly everlastings (*Anaphalis*) and other Compositae.

COMMENTS   Migrates south in the fall, north in the spring; sometimes [in] large numbers.

	MAR	APR	MAY	JUN	JUL	AUG	SEP	OCT
WI								
NY								
NC								
LA								

Painted Lady *Vanessa cardui* **Plate 36**

SIZE   ≥ American Lady.

SIMILAR SPECIES   American Lady.

IDENTIFICATION This widespread immigrant is generally larger than American Lady and has a pinkish suffusion (American Lady is more orange). The median black FW band is much bolder (in fact, the entire gestalt of the butterfly is more dramatic). Above, American Lady usually has a white spot on the FW orange ground (sometimes small) that Painted Lady lacks. Below, note 4 roughly equal eye-spots on the HW. American Lady has 2 large eye-spots.

HABITAT Can be encountered in any type of open habitat.

RANGE Also, the rest of North America, south to northern South America, Eurasia, Africa, and India.

ABUNDANCE R-A. Each year, Painted Ladies stream out of northern Mexico during March and April in impressive migratory swarms to repopulate our region. This repopulation, both as to numbers of butterflies and to the extent of the territory they reach, varies widely from year to year. Due to the path of the migration, butterflies often reach the Northeast (usually by May) and the northern plains (June) before they reach the southeast (North Carolina, June; Georgia and Florida, Aug.). They remain on the wing into Oct.

MAJOR FOODPLANT Thistles and many other species.

COMMENTS The most cosmopolitan butterfly in the world.

	MAR	APR	MAY	JUN	JUL	AUG	SEP	OCT
WI								
NY								
NC								
LA								

Red Admiral *Vanessa atalanta* **Plate 36**

SIZE = American Lady.

IDENTIFICATION A rapidly flying (often), medium-sized dark nymphalid. Naturally enough, Red Admirals are patriotic—sporting red, white and blue along the FW costa below. Above, the reddish-orange bands on both FWs and HWs make confusion of this species with any other very difficult.

HABITAT Open situations with flowers, including fields, beaches, suburbia, and especially moist meadows near woodlands.

RANGE Also, the rest of North America and south through Central America, Eurasia, and Africa.

ABUNDANCE C-A. Florida and south Georgia west to east Texas, all year resident. Emigrants move northward mainly in April to repopulate northward. This northward movement is very rapid, butterflies appearing in New York in mid April, only a week or two after they have appeared in North Carolina. Individuals of the brood move southward in Sept.–Oct. Occasionally, these mo\[...] ments are spectacular.

MAJOR FOODPLANT Nettles (*Urtica*).

COMMENTS Another species that can be strongly migratory. Tens of th\[...] sands streamed north through the New York area in the spr\[...] and summer of 1990.

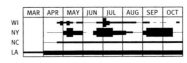

Mimic *Hypolimnas misippus* **Plate 38**

SIZE Between American Lady and Mourning Cloak.

SIMILAR SPECIES Male, Caribbean Peacock; Female, Monarch.

IDENTIFICATION Males and females look very different. Males above are black \[...] a few bold white spots and are distinctive. Below, males h\[...] approximately the same white spots on a brown backgrou\[...] Caribbean Peacocks lack Mimic's white apical spot and are bro\[...] not black. Females are orange with a black FW apex and a s\[...] apical white stripe. Monarchs lack the bold white stripes.

HABITAT Open tropical areas.

RANGE Antilles, Africa, and Asia.

ABUNDANCE RS to south Florida, North Carolina (1 record), and Mississ\[...] (1 record).

MAJOR FOODPLANT Morning glory (*Ipoema*), purslanes (Portulacaceae) and mall\[...] (Malvaceae).

COMMENTS Apparently an immigrant to the New World in historic tim\[...] either unaided or assisted by boats over trade routes.

Common Buckeye *Junonia coenia* **Plate 37**

SIZE ≤ American Lady.

SIMILAR SPECIES In south Florida see Mangrove and Tropical buckeyes.

IDENTIFICATION A brown nymphalid with **prominent eye-spots** along margins of both wings and **2 orange bars** in the FW cell.

HABITAT Open fields, beaches, and many disturbed situations. Especi\[...] fond of sandy areas and paths where they can rest on the grou\[...]

RANGE Also, west to California and south through the West Indies \[...] Mexico.

ABUNDANCE C, resident all year Florida and south Georgia west to Houst\[...] progressively rarer immigrant northward. More common al\[...] migration pathways—coastline and river valleys. Reaches No\[...]

Carolina and Oklahoma in April, north to New York, Indiana, Illinois, in May, north to Mass., Ontario, Michigan, Wisconsin, South Dakota in June, RS to Maine, Manitoba—July. Some of fall brood moves southward in Sept.–Oct.

JOR FOODPLANT   Gerardias (*Gerardia*), toadflax (*Linaria*), and plantain (*Plantago*).

COMMENTS   This is one of the most familiar butterflies of the South, as it is easily identified and is found around lawns, and gardens—close to human habitations.

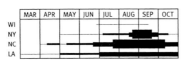

Mangrove Buckeye *Junonia evarete* **Plate 37**

SIZE   = American Lady.

MILAR SPECIES   Common Buckeye, Tropical Buckeye.

IDENTIFICATION   A large buckeye with much orange. Above, the FW subapical patch is pale to strong orange. Common Buckeyes have this patch white. Note that the **large FW eye-spot is surrounded by orange.** Common Buckeyes usually have some white on the inner edge of the FW eye-spot and have a contrasting bright orange patch adjacent to the FW eye-spot by the FW tornus. Tropical Buckeyes lack orange on the inner edge of the FW eye-spot. The 2 HW eye-spots tend to be more similar in size in Mangrove Buckeyes than in Common Buckeyes.

HABITAT   Edges of black mangrove swamps and adjacent areas.

RANGE   Also, the Antilles and the Caribbean coast of north Mexico and south Texas.

ABUNDANCE   LU south Florida and the Keys, all year.

JOR FOODPLANT   Black mangrove (*Avicennia germinans*).

COMMENTS   Until very recently, the buckeye species situation was quite confused, and there are still some uncertainties.

Tropical Buckeye *Junonia genoveva* **Plate 37**

SIZE   ≤ American Lady.

MILAR SPECIES   Common Buckeye, Mangrove Buckeye.

IDENTIFICATION   Above, **FW pale median band is wide and flushed with pink. Inner edge of the large FW eye-spot is usually brown, or pale brown** (very occasionally with some orange). **HW orange submarginal band is narrow.** Below, note the prominent pale median stripe. Common Buckeye usually has white along inner edge of FW eye-spot, very unequal HW eye-spots, and a broad orange HW submarginal band. Mangr⟨ Buckeye has orange FW median band and FW eye-spot co⟨ pletely surrounded by orange.

HABITAT	Open and/or disturbed areas in the tropics and subtropics.
RANGE	Also, south throughout the American tropics.
ABUNDANCE	Present in variable numbers in south Florida, mainly on ⟨ Largo.
MAJOR FOODPLANT	Verbena family (Verbenaceae).
COMMENTS	Not really part of our fauna, this species may periodica become established in southern Florida, only to eventually out. A very dark buckeye flies in southern Texas and south⟨ Arizona. These populations have been placed as a subspecies this species (*J.g.nigrosuffusa*), but this placement is uncertain. these forms the pale FW band is either suffused with d⟨ brown, or absent altogether. While not yet recorded in our ar⟨ strays into the Houston area are possible.

White Peacock *Anartia jatrophae* Plate 37

SIZE	= American Lady.
IDENTIFICATION	An easy call—silvery white all over with an orange border.
HABITAT	Open and/or disturbed areas in the tropics and subtropics.
RANGE	Also, throughout tropical Americas.
ABUNDANCE	C, south Florida, all year. Late summer immigrant to no⟨ Florida. Strays north to Georgia, North Carolina, and Misso⟨ very rarely to southern NJ, Mass. (1 record).
MAJOR FOODPLANT	Mainly bacopa (Scrophulariaceae) and various verbe⟨ (Verbenaceae).
COMMENTS	Florida populations are brighter, Texas populations duller.

Malachite *Siproeta stelenes* Plate 40

SIZE	= Mourning Cloak.
IDENTIFICATION	How many other big, bright green butterflies have you s⟨ flying around?
HABITAT	Tropical hardwood hammocks and overgrown avocado a⟨ citrus groves.
RANGE	Also, south throughout tropical Americas.
ABUNDANCE	LC, all year in south Florida and the Keys. Numbers increasi⟨
MAJOR FOODPLANT	Green shrimp-plant (*Blechum brownei*).
COMMENTS	Not many people can remain stoic after sighting one of these ⟨ ing emeralds. Established in southern Florida within the rec⟨ past, Malachites are becoming more common and expand⟨ their range.

Red-spotted Admiral
(*Limenitis arthemis*)

Our two well-marked subspecies were long considered separate species (and are still so regarded by some). The strikingly different Red-spotted Purple and White Admiral hybridize and intergrade along a very broad zone stretching from southern Maine south to Connecticut, and in the mountains to Maryland, and west to southern Minnesota. In this blend zone, all possible combinations of the traits of the two subspecies can be found. Because their appearances and distributions are so different, I give each of these a separate treatment, operationally calling individuals with any white banding "White Admirals."

White Admiral *Limenitis arthemis arthemis* Plate 38

SIZE	= Mourning Cloak.
IDENTIFICATION	White bands on the velvet-black ground color are striking and give rise to the alternate name, Banded Purple. The alternately gliding and flapping flight usually affords an opportunity for good views.
HABITAT	Northern forests, especially along watercourses, and adjacent open areas.
RANGE	Also, west to Alaska.
ABUNDANCE	U-C. Mainly 2 broods. Mainly June, Aug. 1 brood, mainly July, South Dakota north.
MAJOR FOODPLANT	Birch (*Betula*), poplar (*Populus*), and many others.

Red-spotted Purple *Limenitis arthemis astyanax* Plate 38

SIZE	= Mourning Cloak.
SIMILAR SPECIES	Pipevine Swallowtail.
IDENTIFICATION	This magnificent butterfly is common in the south, less so in the north. Above, black with extensive iridescent blue. It has no tails. Below there are **red-orange spots** both in a submarginal band and **at the base of the wings**. Pipevine Swallowtail has tails and lacks the spots at the wing base.
HABITAT	Rich moist woodlands are preferred but Red-spotted Purples are widely distributed and are often found in suburban areas.
RANGE	Also, west Texas west to southeast Arizona and south into northern Mexico.
ABUNDANCE	U-C. 3 broods north to New York, Ohio, Indiana, Illinois, Iowa, southern Nebraska—April/May–Sept./Oct.; 2 broods northward—June–Aug.

| MAJOR FOODPLANT | Cherry (*Prunus*) and others. |
| COMMENTS | Often attracted to mud puddles and animal feces. |

	MAR	APR	MAY	JUN	JUL	AUG	SEP	OCT
WI								
NY								
NC								
LA								

Viceroy *Limenitis archippus* Plates 38 & 45

SIZE	≤ Mourning Cloak.
SIMILAR SPECIES	Monarch, Queen.
IDENTIFICATION	Fairly large and **uniformly orange**. Much darker brown-orange in Florida. Distinguished from Monarchs and Queens by the black postmedian band on the HW. Viceroys can be readily separated from Monarchs and Queens in flight by their smaller size and less powerful wingbeats. They often glide on flat wings while Monarchs and Queens sail with their wings in a "V."
HABITAT	Open areas adjacent to watercourses or wet areas with willows.
RANGE	Also, west to Washington State and south into northern Mexico
ABUNDANCE	C (but U-R in poor soil areas). 2 broods. April/May–Oct. north to Philadelphia, West Virginia, Ohio, Illinois, Missouri, Kansas June–Sept. northward.
MAJOR FOODPLANT	Willows (*Salix*), especially small shrubby species.
COMMENTS	Well known as a mimic of the Monarch. For a long time it was thought that birds avoided eating palatable Viceroys because they confused them with distasteful Monarchs. Recent evidence suggest that, at least in Florida, Viceroys are also distasteful to birds. Presumably, a greater number of similar-looking, unpalatable individuals in an area results in a faster learning curve for birds, sparing butterflies.

	MAR	APR	MAY	JUN	JUL	AUG	SEP	OCT
WI								
NY								
NC								
LA								

Dingy Purplewing *Eunica monima* Plate 40

SIZE	< American Lady.
SIMILAR SPECIES	Florida Purplewing.
IDENTIFICATION	Above, a dull, iridescent purple. Unfortunately, it doesn't normally open its wings while landed—usually on leaves on trees. Below, a warm gray-brown tinged with mauve. Note the HW postmedian circular areas, the upper circular area containing spots—the top one gray-white. Florida Purplewing is larger, h

a falcate FW apex, has a FW black subapical spot that this species lacks, and usually lacks the gray-white HW spot.

HABITAT   Tropical hardwood hammocks.

RANGE   Also, the Greater Antilles and southern Texas south to northern South America.

ABUNDANCE   LR or no longer found in our region. July–Dec.

MAJOR FOODPLANT   Gumbo limbo (*Bursera simaruba*)(a small tree).

COMMENTS   In the 1970s through the 1980s this species was regularly found in southern Florida but searches over the past few years have failed to find any. Given to strong migratory movements in the tropics.

Florida Purplewing *Eunica tatila* Plate 40

SIZE   = American Lady.

SIMILAR SPECIES   Dingy Purplewing.

IDENTIFICATION   Iridescent purple above. Below, bark brown, with a falcate FW apex. Usually one can see a black FW subapical spot between two white spots. See Dingy Purplewing.

HABITAT   Tropical hardwood hammocks.

RANGE   Also, West Indies and southern Texas south to Argentina.

ABUNDANCE   LR. All year. RS north to Kansas (1 record).

MAJOR FOODPLANT   Reported to be crabwood (*Gymnanthes lucida*) by Minno and Emmel (1993).

COMMENTS   It is difficult to see this species' bright iridescent purple upperside, because it usually flies within the shade of tropical hardwood hammocks, lands on tree trunks, and keeps its wings closed while landed.

Ruddy Daggerwing *Marpesia petreus* Plate 39

SIZE   = Mourning Cloak.

SIMILAR SPECIES   Julia.

IDENTIFICATION   A good-sized orange nymphalid of the tropics and subtropics. In flight it could be mistaken for a bright orange Julia (but of course it isn't potable). Seen well, the straight black lines across the wings and especially the characteristically-shaped wings and tails are unmistakable. Usually lands with its head facing down, except when on the ground.

HABITAT   Hardwood hammock edges and openings.

RANGE   Also, some Caribbean islands and south Texas south through the American tropics.

ABUNDANCE   LC. All year, south Florida. R north to St. Augustine and Tampa. RS north to Nebraska (1 record)

MAJOR FOODPLANT   Figs (*Ficus*).

COMMENTS	Territorial males will often come down from on high to investigate bright orange objects. Try throwing an orange into the air or waving an orange cloth.

Florida Leafwing *Anaea floridalis* **Plate 39**

SIZE	≤ Mourning Cloak.
SIMILAR SPECIES	Goatweed Leafwing.
IDENTIFICATION	Bright red-orange above, mottled grayish below, these boldly marked leafwings rush about the pine scrub barrens then suddenly alight on a tree limb with their wings closed. Goatweed Leafwings are similar, browner below and more orange above, but the 2 species are not normally found together. Also, Florida Leafwings have slightly uneven wing margins.
HABITAT	Open pine scrub.
ABUNDANCE	LC. Extreme south Florida and the Keys. All year.
MAJOR FOODPLANT	Narrow-leaved croton (*Croton linearis*).
COMMENTS	Some consider the Florida Leafwing a subspecies of the Tropical Leafwing.

Goatweed Leafwing *Anaea andria* **Plate 39**

SIZE	≤ Mourning Cloak.
IDENTIFICATION	Larger than anglewings. Red-orange to orange-brown above (males brighter), with a short HW tail. Behavior, flight, and wing-shape is different from other orange butterflies in its range.
HABITAT	Open woodlands with its foodplant and adjacent areas.
ABUNDANCE	LC, Oklahoma, Kansas, Arkansas, Missouri, northern Louisiana, northern Mississippi; LR, southern Illinois, southern Nebraska; LP southeast, RS north to North Carolina, Ohio, Michigan, Wisconsin, Iowa, South Dakota. 2 broods, generally June/July–Aug, Aug.–Oct. overwintering as adults and flying April–May.
MAJOR FOODPLANT	Goatweed (*Croton monanthogynus*) and other crotons.
COMMENTS	Often flies as if swooping up and down on ocean waves. Overwintering individuals have more pointed FWs than summer individuals.

	MAR	APR	MAY	JUN	JUL	AUG	SEP	OCT
WI								
NY								
NC								
LA								

Hackberry Emperor *Asterocampa celtis* **Plate 40**

SIZE	= American Lady. Females usually much larger than males.
SIMILAR SPECIES	Tawny Emperor.

IDENTIFICATION A nervous, rapidly flying nymphalid that often appears quite pale in flight as the sun flashes off the creamy gray-brown undersurface. Above, warm brown. Note the **white subapical FW spots** above and the **black FW marginal eye-spot** both above and below. Tawny Emperor is a warm orange-brown above and lacks the white subapical spots and the black FW eye-spot.

HABITAT Closely tied to hackberry trees.

ABUNDANCE LU-C. Perhaps 3 broods in Deep South—April–Oct.; 2 broods northward—May–June, July–Sept.

MAJOR FOODPLANT Hackberries (*Celtis*).

COMMENTS An infrequent flower visitor, Hackberry Emperors can, not surprisingly, most often be found flying around a hackberry tree. When not on hackberry trees they often alight on people in search of the salts in our perspiration. Geographically variable, some populations have previously been considered separate species.

	MAR	APR	MAY	JUN	JUL	AUG	SEP	OCT
WI								
NY								
NC								
LA								

Tawny Emperor *Asterocampa clyton* **Plate 40**

SIZE = American Lady. Females usually much larger than males.

SIMILAR SPECIES Hackberry Emperor, Painted Lady.

IDENTIFICATION Above, warm orange-brown with HW borders that can be either mainly orange or mainly black. Note the prominent series of eye-spots on the HW on both surfaces. Hackberry Emperor has white spots above, is paler and grayer below, and has black eye-spots on the FW. Painted Lady is much paler below.

HABITAT Closely tied to hackberry trees but seems to disperse more than Hackberry Emperor.

ABUNDANCE Perhaps 3 broods in Deep South, April–Oct.; 2 broods most of range, mainly June–July, Aug.–early Sept.; LR-U, east of Appalachians, Ozarks; U-C, Missouri, Kansas, Iowa, Illinois, Indiana, Ohio.

MAJOR FOODPLANT Hackberries (*Celtis*).

COMMENTS One frequently sees both Tawny Emperors and Hackberry Emperors in the same vicinity—if you are a really proficient butterflier you find them both alighted on you at the same time! Geographically variable, some populations have previously been considered separate species.

	MAR	APR	MAY	JUN	JUL	AUG	SEP	OCT
WI								
NY								
NC								
LA								

Satyrs or Browns
(subfamily Satyrinae)

The satyrs are a group of brown, medium-sized butterflies with a characteristically bouncy flight. They tend to remain low and weave among the grasses or sedges that are their caterpillar foodplants.

Southern Pearly-eye *Enodia portlandia* Plate 42

SIZE	> Little Wood-Satyr, < Common Wood-Nymph.
SIMILAR SPECIES	Northern Pearly-eye, Appalachian Brown.
IDENTIFICATION	A large, dark, woodland satyr. Below, note the prominent HW submarginal eye-spots that are **surrounded as a group, by one continuous white line**. Appalachian Brown is much paler brown and has HW submarginal eye-spots that are individually surrounded by white circles. Note the **orange-yellow antennal clubs**. FW eye-spots usually curve slightly toward the apex. Northern Pearly-eye is quite similar but has black bases of the antennal clubs and usually its FW eye-spots are in a relatively straight line.
HABITAT	Rich southern bottomlands with cane.
ABUNDANCE	LC (LR south Missouri). Probably 3 broods. April/early May–Oct.
MAJOR FOODPLANT	Cane (*Arundinaria*).
COMMENTS	Our most common cane-feeding butterfly.

	MAR	APR	MAY	JUN	JUL	AUG	SEP	OCT
WI								
NY								
NC								
LA								

Northern Pearly-eye *Enodia anthedon* Plate 42

SIZE	> Little Wood-Satyr, < Common Wood-Nymph.
SIMILAR SPECIES	Southern Pearly-eye, Appalachian Brown.
IDENTIFICATION	See Southern Pearly-eye for general discussion. Distinguish from Southern Pearly-eye by the **black base of the antennal clubs**. Southern Pearly-eye has orange-yellow antennal clubs, usually more extensive white markings, and usually has its FW eye-spots slightly curved outward toward the apex.
HABITAT	Prefers the edges and glades of rocky deciduous woodlands in the vicinity of brooks and other water sources.

| | ABUNDANCE | U-LC north to New York, Ohio, Illinois, Missouri, Nebraska. 2 broods. Mainly May–early Sept. Farther north generally LC-A. 1 brood. New Hampshire, northern New York, Wisconsin, South Dakota—Late June–early Aug. |

ABUNDANCE U-LC north to New York, Ohio, Illinois, Missouri, Nebraska. 2 broods. Mainly May–early Sept. Farther north generally LC-A. 1 brood. New Hampshire, northern New York, Wisconsin, South Dakota—Late June–early Aug.

MAJOR FOODPLANT Grasses.

COMMENTS Look for this elegant satyr near the end of the day in the dappled light of dirt roads and trails through rocky damp woodlands. Often alights on tree trunks with its head facing downward.

	MAR	APR	MAY	JUN	JUL	AUG	SEP	OCT
WI								
NY								
NC								
LA								

Creole Pearly-eye *Enodia creola* **Plate 42**

SIZE > Little Wood-Satyr, < Common Wood-Nymph.

SIMILAR SPECIES Southern Pearly-eye; Northern Pearly-eye.

IDENTIFICATION Below, near the costal margin, Creole Pearly-eyes have the **FW postmedian line pushed outward, in the shape of a fist** (with "knuckles" showing). Southern Pearly-eyes (and usually Northerns) have this line differently shaped, coming to a point toward the center of the wing. On the HW below, note that the **submarginal eye-spots are individually surrounded by white**. Northern and Southern pearly-eyes have these eye-spots surrounded as a group by white. Also, Creoles *usually* have 5 FW eye-spots in a straight line while Southerns usually have 4 eye-spots in a curved line.

HABITAT Canebrakes in dense southern woodlands.

ABUNDANCE LR-U. 2 broods. Mid April–early June, early July–mid Sept.

MAJOR FOODPLANT Cane (*Arundinaria*).

COMMENTS Our rarest and most local pearly-eye. Its habits and habitats are very similar to those of Southern Pearly-eyes and these species are often found together.

	MAR	APR	MAY	JUN	JUL	AUG	SEP	OCT
WI								
NY								
NC								
LA								

Eyed Brown *Satyrodes eurydice* **Plate 41**

SIZE > Little Wood-Satyr.

SIMILAR SPECIES Appalachian Brown, Little Wood-Satyr.

IDENTIFICATION See discussion under Appalachian Brown.

BRUSHFOOTS

	HABITAT	Very wet meadows, marshes with sedges.

HABITAT Very wet meadows, marshes with sedges.

ABUNDANCE LR-U near southern edge of range. Elsewhere U-A. 1 brood. Late June–early August.

MAJOR FOODPLANT Sedges (*Carex*).

COMMENTS In parts of the Midwest some populations of Eyed Browns are darker and have five FW eye-spots rather than four. These populations of 'Smoky' Eyed Browns intergrade into the surrounding populations.

	MAR	APR	MAY	JUN	JUL	AUG	SEP	OCT
WI						–		
NY								
NC								
LA								

Appalachian Brown *Satyrodes appalachia* Plate 41

SIZE > Little Wood-Satyr.

SIMILAR SPECIES Eyed Brown, Northern Pearly-eye, Southern Pearly-eye, Little Wood-Satyr.

IDENTIFICATION Our two browns are easily distinguished from Little Wood-Satyrs by their larger size and large HW eye-spots below. They can be distinguished from Northern and Southern pearly-eyes by their paler more subdued coloration and below, by the presence of a white outer ring around each HW eye-spot. Separating Appalachian Brown from Eyed Brown can be tricky. Although the preferred habitats differ, wet wooded habitats tend to intergrade with wet open habitats so that often both species can be found on the same patch of land. Usually, Appalachian Browns are darker; have less jagged postmedian lines on the FW and HW below; and have the FW eye-spots below of unequal size and intensity (at least one of the middle two usually being smaller and paler). Below, note the HW postbasal line. Appalachian has this line straight, Eyed has an inward directed "tooth" at the 2nd vein. Also below, Appalachian has the lowest FW eye-spot surrounded by a white ring thus making this spot look like a bull's eye. Eyed has this (and the other FW spots as well) only partially surrounded by white—thus looking like a pea pod.

HABITAT Wet wooded situations adjacent to open areas.

ABUNDANCE R-U. 3 broods Florida, April–Oct. 2 broods north to Maryland and southern New Jersey—late May/early June–July/Aug., late Aug.–Sept. Northward, 1 brood. Mid/late June–Aug.

MAJOR FOODPLANT Sedges (*Carex*).

COMMENTS Often, populations of both browns live in close proximity. the 1960s there were large populations of both species

Lynnfield Marsh in Massachusetts and more recently, I found both flying in nearby habitats at Baileys Harbor, Door Co., Wisconsin.

	MAR	APR	MAY	JUN	JUL	AUG	SEP	OCT
WI								
NY								
NC								
LA								

Gemmed Satyr *Cyllopsis gemma* Plate 43

SIZE
: < Little Wood-Satyr.

SIMILAR SPECIES
: Carolina Satyr, Little Wood-Satyr.

IDENTIFICATION
: On the HW below, "gemmed" with a **silver-gray HW patch** containing marginal eye-spots.

HABITAT
: Moist grassy areas within woodlands and, paradoxically, dry ridgetops (in the northern parts of its range).

RANGE
: Also, south into northeastern Mexico.

ABUNDANCE
: R-LC, mainly U. Probably 3 broods. March/April–Oct.

MAJOR FOODPLANT
: Grasses.

COMMENTS
: Can often be recognized as a non-Carolina Satyr in flight by its slightly larger size and paler appearance, but you'll need to wait for it to land to confirm its identity.

	MAR	APR	MAY	JUN	JUL	AUG	SEP	OCT
WI								
NY								
NC								
LA								

Carolina Satyr *Hermeuptychia sosybius* Plate 43

SIZE
: < Little Wood-Satyr.

SIMILAR SPECIES
: Little Wood-Satyr.

IDENTIFICATION
: A small satyr, common throughout southern woodlands. Much more at home **within** woodlands than is Little Wood-Satyr. Below, very similar to Little Wood-Satyr but note the HW cell-end bar. FW lacks the lower large eye-spot of Little Wood-Satyr. Above, uniform dark brown, lacking the eye-spots of Little Wood-Satyr.

HABITAT
: A wide variety of woodland situations, especially moist forests.

RANGE
: Also, south into Mexico.

ABUNDANCE
: C-A, all year Florida and the Deep South, C, April–Sept./early Oct. northward. RS north to Kansas (1 record).

MAJOR FOODPLANT
: Grasses.

COMMENTS
: One of the most frequently seen butterflies along bottomland trails in the South.

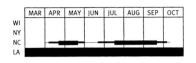

	MAR	APR	MAY	JUN	JUL	AUG	SEP	OCT
WI								
NY								
NC								
LA								

Georgia Satyr *Neonympha areolata* **Plate 43**

SIZE = Little Wood-Satyr.

IDENTIFICATION On the HW below, note the orange-brown ring surrounding the elliptical, postmedian eye-spots.

HABITAT Open pine-barrens bogs in New Jersey; grass savannas in open pine woods farther south.

ABUNDANCE LC. South Florida—all year; northern Florida, Georgia, Mississippi east Texas, 2 broods—March/April–Sept./Oct.; North Carolina– mid May–early Sept.; New Jersey, 1 brood—late June–mid July (except reportedly 2 broods on Fort Dix!—June, Aug.)

MAJOR FOODPLANT Probably sedges although grasses have also been reported.

COMMENTS Although its flight is slow, this constantly bobbing satyr can b frustrating to see well.

	MAR	APR	MAY	JUN	JUL	AUG	SEP	OCT
WI								
NY								
NC								
LA								

Mitchell's Satyr *Neonympha mitchellii* **Plate 43**

SIZE = Little Wood-Satyr.

SIMILAR SPECIES Georgia Satyr.

IDENTIFICATION Note the presence of **prominent, relatively round, pos median eye-spots on both the FW (3 or 4) and the H** Georgia Satyr lacks the FW spots (or has 1 or 2 weak ones) a has the HW spots more oval and elongated.

HABITAT Fens (alkaline bogs) in Michigan and New Jersey; dense, se shaded bogs in North Carolina.

ABUNDANCE LR. North Carolina, late May–late June, late July–late Au Michigan, late June–mid July; extirpated from New Jers Ohio, Indiana, formerly early July–mid July.

MAJOR FOODPLANT Sedges (*Carex*).

COMMENTS This is one of the real horror stories of American butterflies. beautiful and mysterious little butterfly was literally hunte extinction in New Jersey. A group of greedy, immoral indivi als returned day after day, year after year, to the few, very sr fens where it was found. They illegally collected and killed th animals for their own "amusement" and in some cases pr

Toward the end, even chain-link fences, guard dogs, and a security man could not keep the poachers out. Mitchell's Satyr is now listed as federally endangered due to similar problems throughout its range.

	MAR	APR	MAY	JUN	JUL	AUG	SEP	OCT
WI								
NY								
NC			—		—			
LA								

Little Wood-Satyr *Megisto cymela* **Plate 43**

SIZE
: 13/16 in.

SIMILAR SPECIES
: Carolina Satyr.

IDENTIFICATION
: A medium-brown butterfly that "bounces" along the tops of the grasses, shrubs, and just inside the canopy of small trees. Its characteristic flight, color, and size make it immediately recognizable on the wing. This is good because it rarely rests. When it does, note the two large eye-spots on each wing both above and below.

HABITAT
: Most at home in the grassland/woodland interface, this satyr may be found in the middle of quite large opens fields or (more rarely) deep in the woods.

ABUNDANCE
: C-A. 1 brood. Mainly April/May–July. A partial 2nd brood in the South—Aug.–Sept.

OR FOODPLANT
: Grasses.

COMMENTS
: In most areas there is a large synchronized emergence in May, followed, about three weeks later, by a much smaller emergence. It is unknown whether these later emergers (which fly too soon after the emergence of the first wave to be a second brood) are a second sibling species, or are simply some type of delayed hatch.

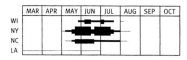

Viola's Wood-Satyr *Megisto viola* **Plate 43**

SIZE
: ≥ Little Wood-Satyr

SIMILAR SPECIES
: Little Wood-Satyr.

IDENTIFICATION
: Slightly bigger and brighter than Little Wood-Satyr, with more prominent silver iridescence. Eye-rings tend to be a richer golden color than on Little Wood-Satyrs. The FW postmedian line is usually slightly more curved inwardly than on Little Wood-Satyr, but some Little Wood-Satyrs also have this trait. Best to go by locality.

HABITAT	Woodlands.
ABUNDANCE	LC-A. 1 brood. Mid March–early May.
MAJOR FOODPLANT	Grasses.
COMMENTS	There appears to be a broad blend zone in northern Florida along the southeastern coast between Viola and Little wo satyrs. It seems likely that when all the evidence is in, Vic Wood-Satyr will be considered a subspecies of Little Wood-Sa

Common Ringlet *Coenonympha tullia* **Plate 44**

SIZE	< Little Wood-Satyr.
SIMILAR SPECIES	Little Wood-Satyr.
IDENTIFICATION	A small, **very pale**, satyr with an orange-red flush that bou through the grasses, continually stopping to nectar at flov (unlike other satyrs). The gray-brown HW below has a w postmedian line and no eye-spots. Little Wood-Satyr is lar much darker, and has prominent eye-spots on the HW belo
HABITAT	Low grassy fields, seemingly with a preference for moist fiel
RANGE	Also, west to Alaska and California.
ABUNDANCE	C-A. 1 brood east to Michigan—late May/June–July. 2 bro Ontario east—mainly late May/June and Aug.
MAJOR FOODPLANT	Grasses.
COMMENTS	Especially in northern fields, this species can be so abunc that the grass seems to be shimmering with butterflies. Form not found in the northeastern U.S., the appearance (in the e 1960s) of a two-brood phenotype in eastern Canada has allo this species to drive southward. It reached New Jersey in 1 and I expect that it will eventually reach Georgia.

	MAR	APR	MAY	JUN	JUL	AUG	SEP	OCT
WI								
NY				—		—		
NC								
LA								

Common Wood-Nymph *Cercyonis pegala* **Plate 41**

SIZE	1 4/16 inch.
SIMILAR SPECIES	(For populations without yellow-orange patches) North Pearly-eye, browns.
IDENTIFICATION	A large, very dark satyr of open brushy fields. Over most of East, the yellow-orange postmedian FW patches are distinct From the Maine interior north and west to northern Illinois the Dakotas, populations of Common Wood-Nymphs lack bright patches and more closely resemble other large sat Intermediate populations bridge the color gap. Below, note

large, isolated FW subapical eye-spot. Other large satyrs are not so dark, and do not have a large, isolated FW subapical eye-spot.

HABITAT   Brushy fields, prairies, woodland edges, etc. and salt marshes (in Mass.).

RANGE   Also, west to California.

ABUNDANCE   U-A, mainly C. 1 brood. Late May–Sept. in the Deep South, mid/late June–Aug/early Sept. farther north.

MAJOR FOODPLANT   Grasses.

COMMENTS   In favored localities, concentrations of this butterfly can be very impressive. Unlike many of our other satyrs, this species is frequently seen nectaring at flowers.

	MAR	APR	MAY	JUN	JUL	AUG	SEP	OCT
WI								
NY								
NC								
LA								

Alpines and Arctics
(genus *Erebia*) (genus *Oeneis*)

Alpines and Arctics are specialities of the far north. Perhaps because the growing season is so short in these regions, many of these species require two years to complete their life cycle. So, in some regions a particular species only (or mainly) appears once every two years.

Disa Alpine *Erebia disa* Not Illustrated

SIZE   = Little Wood-Satyr.

SIMILAR SPECIES   Common Alpine, Red-disked Alpine.

IDENTIFICATION   Dark. Below, FW with 4 black eye-spots ringed with yellow-brown. **HW with small pale gray spot at the end of the cell**. Above, FW with 4 black eye-spots ringed with yellow or chestnut.

HABITAT   Black spruce sphagnum bogs.

RANGE   Circumpolar, south in North America to southern Manitoba and extreme northern Minnesota.

ABUNDANCE   LR. 1 brood. June–mid July. Most common mid June in odd-numbered years.

MAJOR FOODPLANT   Unknown.

COMMENTS   Very poorly known from our region.

Red-disked Alpine *Erebia discoidalis* **Plate 44**

SIZE	= Little Wood-Satyr.
SIMILAR SPECIES	Disa Alpine.
IDENTIFICATION	Below, HW dark with outer 1/3 heavily frosted. Both below and above, **FW disc reddish-brown**.
HABITAT	A wide variety of open situations, including pine forest glades, dry ridge tops, and sedge marshes.
RANGE	Also, holarctic.
ABUNDANCE	LR-LU. 1 brood. Mid May–early June.
MAJOR FOODPLANT	Bluegrass (*Poa*).
COMMENTS	Probably the best location in our region to see this northern beauty is the Sandilands Provincial Forest in Manitoba.

Common Alpine *Erebia epipsodea* Not Illustrated

SIZE	> Little Wood-Satyr.
SIMILAR SPECIES	Disa Alpine.
IDENTIFICATION	The FW subapex below has 2 prominent black spots surrounded by yellow, with no spot (or a small one) below them. Disa Alpine has 4 spots on the FW below, of almost equal size. HW above has yellow-ringed black spots. Disa Alpine lacks these and has a small gray spot at the end of the cell on the HW below that Common Alpine lacks.
HABITAT	Meadows and moist virgin prairie.
RANGE	Manitoba west to Alaska and south in the Rockies to New Mexico.
ABUNDANCE	R-U, southern Manitoba. Mainly flying in June.
MAJOR FOODPLANT	Grasses.
COMMENTS	This is the most widespread alpine in the West, but barely enters our region in western Manitoba.

Macoun's Arctic *Oeneis macounii* **Plate 44**

SIZE	= Common Wood-Nymph.
SIMILAR SPECIES	Chryxus Arctic.
IDENTIFICATION	Our **largest arctic** sports its **bright tawny-orange uppersurface** as it flies back and forth along a northern forest road. Below, usually with **some frosting at FW and HW apexes**. FW with disc and area around eye-spot, orange. Chryxus Arctic is similar but much smaller, not so bright above, and lacks HW frosting below.
HABITAT	Jack pine forest.
RANGE	Also, west to British Columbia.
ABUNDANCE	LR. 1 brood. June–early July. Biennial, flying in even-numbered years in our area.

OR FOODPLANT	Grasses and sedges (*Carex*).
COMMENTS	Males are quite pugnacious and territorial.

Chryxus Arctic *Oeneis chryxus* Plate 44

SIZE	< Common Wood-Nymph.
MILAR SPECIES	Uhler's Arctic, Macoun's Arctic.
DENTIFICATION	A variable species. Below, mottled brown and off-white with the HW basal and median dark bands of about equal intensity. See Macoun's Arctic. Uhler's Arctic is smaller with multiple eye-spots on the HW below.
HABITAT	Rocky grassy hilltops, meadows.
RANGE	Also, west to Alaska and south in the mountains to the California Sierra Nevadas and New Mexico.
ABUNDANCE	LR. 1 brood. Northwestern Wisconsin, Ontario, mid May–mid June.
JOR FOODPLANT	Grasses.
COMMENTS	These inhabitants of colder climes can often be found sunning themselves on rocks or bare patches of ground.

Uhler's Arctic *Oeneis uhleri* Plate 44

SIZE	≥ Little Wood-Satyr.
MILAR SPECIES	Chryxus Arctic.
IDENTIFICATION	This small prairie arctic usually has **multiple prominent black eye-spots on the HW**, both above and below. Tawny above with obvious veining. Chryxus Arctic is tawny above but is much larger and lacks the multiple eye-spots on the HW.
HABITAT	Dry prairie, grassy ridges in woodlands.
RANGE	Also, west to Alberta and south to northern New Mexico.
ABUNDANCE	LR-LU. 1 brood. Late May/June–early July.
JOR FOODPLANT	Grasses.

Alberta Arctic *Oeneis alberta* Not Illustrated

SIZE	≥ Little Wood-Satyr.
MILAR SPECIES	Chyrxus Arctic, Uhler's Arctic.
IDENTIFICATION	Another small, prairie arctic. Unlike Uhler's Arctic, its lacks multiple black eye-spots on the HW and is not so bright above. The FW below has a noticeable postmedian band with a "bird beak" protrusion. Uhler's lacks a definite FW postmedian band. Chryxus Arctic is larger and darker.
HABITAT	Short-grass prairie hills and ridges.
RANGE	Southern Alberta and possibly north-central North Dakota. Also, west to Saskatchewan and isolated populations in the Rockies.

ABUNDANCE   LU in southern Manitoba, flying in May–June.

MAJOR FOODPLANT   Grasses.

Jutta Arctic *Oeneis jutta* **Plate 44**

SIZE   = Common Wood-Nymph.

SIMILAR SPECIES   Macoun's Arctic, Chryxus Arctic.

IDENTIFICATION   A large arctic with a **small tawny or yellow ring around** FW **black subapical eye-spot** above and below. Dull bro above. Macoun's and Chryxus arctics have FW eyespot s rounded by a large area of tawny orange.

HABITAT   Black spruce and tamarack sphagnum bogs.

RANGE   Also, holarctic.

ABUNDANCE   LR. 1 brood. Late May/early June–June/early July.

MAJOR FOODPLANT   Cottongrass (*Eriophorum spissum*).

COMMENTS   As do many northern butterflies, Jutta Arctics take two year complete their life cycle. Adults fly mainly in odd-numbe years in southeastern Manitoba, Wisconsin and Michigan; ev numbered years in southwestern Manitoba; each year eas the Great Lakes.

Melissa Arctic *Oeneis melissa* **Plate 44**

SIZE   ≥ Little Wood-Satyr.

SIMILAR SPECIES   Polixenes Arctic.

IDENTIFICATION   FW translucent. HW below dark mottled brown. FW below e spot absent (or very faint). Polixenes Arctic is not as dark bel In our area, ranges don't overlap.

HABITAT   Rocky slopes near mountain summits.

ABUNDANCE   LC. 1 brood. Late June–July.

MAJOR FOODPLANT   Bigelow's sedge (*Carex rigida*).

COMMENTS   In our area, found only near the highest peaks in the Wl Mountains of New Hampshire. Easy to find by taking the r to just below the summit of Mt. Washington in early July. In clouds and wind these glacial relics look much like the lich covered rocks on which they rest. Sunshine causes brief, skit ing, low flight.

Polixenes Arctic *Oeneis polixenes* **Plate 44**

SIZE   ≥ Little Wood-Satyr.

SIMILAR SPECIES   Melissa Arctic.

IDENTIFICATION   If you see an arctic in our region, the best way to know whet it is this species is to get out your GPS transponder and det mine where you are. If you are near the summit of Mt. Katah

in Maine, then the arctic is a Polixenes Arctic. If you are anywhere else, it is not. Otherwise, very similar to Melissa Arctic
which averages darker below. In our area, ranges don't overlap.

HABITAT   Rocky slopes above treeline on Mt. Katahdin.

RANGE   In our area, found only on Mt. Katahdin in Maine. Also, across
the entire North American arctic and south in the Rockies to
New Mexico.

ABUNDANCE   LC. 1 brood. Late June–July.

MAJOR FOODPLANT   Grasses.

Monarchs or Milkweed Butterflies (subfamily Danainae)

Milkweed butterflies are found throughout the tropical world. Many species
are distasteful to predators because of the accumulation of toxic chemicals
derived from the caterpillar foodplants. They signal this distastefulness to
potential predators by sporting bold coloration. For a thorough treatment of
this group, see Ackery and Vane-Wright (1984).

Monarch *Danaus plexippus* Plate 45

SIZE   2 in.

SIMILAR SPECIES   Viceroy, Queen, Great Spangled Fritillary.

IDENTIFICATION   Probably the best known butterfly of North America. A large
orange butterfly with a powerful flight. often sails with its wings
held in a "V." The male has a black scent patch on a HW vein
above. Viceroy is smaller and has a weaker flight on shallower
wingbeats, often gliding on flat wings. Viceroys have a black
postmedian line on the HW. See Queen.

HABITAT   Open fields, roadsides, suburban areas. While migrating it can be
anywhere, but strongly concentrates on the immediate coast
and along river valleys.

RANGE   Also, all of North America, south to South America. Now established on New Zealand, Australia, Canary Islands, India, etc.

ABUNDANCE   C. Mainly April/May–Oct./Nov.

MAJOR FOODPLANT   Milkweeds (*Asclepias*).

COMMENTS   Huge numbers of Monarchs move south throughout the East in
September and October. The spectacle at congregation points is
awe-inspiring. Millions of Monarchs from North America even-

tually overwinter in communal sites high in the fir-clad Mexican mountains. These enormous roosts are rapidly becoming a major tourist attraction, but face pressures from logging and other development activities that are jeopardizing this vast migratory phenomenon. In very early spring, the overwintering adults mate and begin to move north and lay eggs. Their offspring then continue moving north, reaching much of the East in April or May. See Comments under Viceroy for a discussion of mimicry.

	MAR	APR	MAY	JUN	JUL	AUG	SEP	OCT
WI								
NY								
NC								
LA								

Queen *Danaus gilippus* **Plate 45**

SIZE	≤ Monarch.
SIMILAR SPECIES	Monarch, Viceroy.
IDENTIFICATION	Queens are a **rich mahogany brown**, darker than Monarchs. This closely related species lacks the Monarch's black subapical band and has **white spots in the FW postmedian area** that are visible either from above or below. Viceroys are smaller, lack the white spots, and have a black HW postmedian line.
HABITAT	General in open areas, brushy fields, roadsides, etc.
RANGE	Also, west to southern California and south throughout tropical Americas.
ABUNDANCE	U. South Florida, all year resident. R north to north Florida, Georgia coast, April–Sept., R irregular immigrant north to North Carolina coast and Kansas. RS north to Mass. (1 record), Ohio (1 record), Illinois (1 record), Michigan, North Dakota.
MAJOR FOODPLANT	Milkweed (*Asclepias*) and milkweed family vines (*Sarcostemma* and *Cynanchum*).
COMMENTS	Although Monarch migrations are famous, it is little known that Queens also undertake mass movements. Many falls, in southern Texas and northern Mexico, tremendous numbers Queens migrate southward. Whether these butterflies congregate at specific sites, a la Monarchs, is unknown.

Soldier *Danaus eresimus* **Plate 45**

SIZE	≤ Monarch.
SIMILAR SPECIES	Queen, Monarch.
IDENTIFICATION	Soldiers are mahogany brown, like Queens, but Texas individuals **lack the white spots in the FW postmedian area.** Florida, many individuals have 2 faint pale (usually yellowish

spots in the FW postmedian area but are not as dark nor so richly colored. Note the **blackened FW veins**. Queens veins are not blackened. Below, the HW postmedian area is paler.

HABITAT Open areas and woodland edges.

RANGE Also, south through tropical Americas.

ABUNDANCE U. South Florida, mainly Feb.–Oct.

MAJOR FOODPLANT Milkweeds (*Asclepias*) and milkweed family vines (*Sarcostemma* and *Cynanchum*).

COMMENTS Apparently only established in south Florida since 1970, Soldiers may still be increasing their range.

The Skippers
(family Hesperiidae)

>kippers, which derive their name from their characteristic rapid darting ﬂight, can be the agony and the ecstasy of butterﬂying. The agony results ⁀rom trying to identify individual species in the many difﬁcult (some would say ⁀npossible) to identify groups. Ecstasy is the result of success. With roughly ₀000 species worldwide, there is ample opportunity for pleasure. Skippers are ₁enerally distinguishable from the true butterﬂies by their relatively large ₁odies (compared to their wings), their relatively small, very angular wings, ⁀nd by the presence of a thin extension (the apiculus) of the antennal club. ▌here are three subfamilies of skippers in our area. The spread-winged skippers ⁀e generally large (for skippers). When these skippers alight they generally ⁀old their wings open ﬂat—hence the name spread-winged skippers. ⁀lthough they sometimes hold their wings closed or partially open, the FWs ⁀d the HWs are always moved in unison. In contrast, the grass-skippers ▌ther alight with their wings completely closed (often) or with the HWs more ⁀ less completely open but with the FWs only partially opened, forming a ⁀"or "U." The third subfamily, the intermediate skippers, have caterpillars ⁀at feed on grasses, like the grass-skippers, look like grass-skippers, but hold ⁀d move their wings more like spread-winged skippers.

Spread-winged Skippers
(subfamily Pyrginae)

▌most all of our species are essentially dark brown with some spotting. This ⁀ludes two of our most difﬁcult groups, the cloudywings and the duskywings.

Mangrove Skipper *Phocides pigmalion* Plate 48

SIZE = Silver-spotted Skipper.

SIMILAR SPECIES Hammock Skipper.

IDENTIFICATION Very large and dark. Fresh individuals have an **overall cobalt blue iridescence**. Note the lighter **iridescent turquoise blue stripes on the HW and body**. Hammock Skipper can have much iridescent blue above, but is smaller, has bold white spots on the FW, and lacks the lighter iridescent blue on the HW and body.

HABITAT Mangrove swamps and nearby areas, including hardwood hammocks and flower gardens.

RANGE Also, south through tropical Americas.

ABUNDANCE LC. South Florida, all year

MAJOR FOODPLANT Red mangrove (*Rhizophora mangle*).

COMMENTS Powerfully winging through hammock trails in south Florida, these guys are so big and so dark that they make one think of bats. Maybe that's why the old scientific name for this species was *batabano*.

Zestos Skipper *Epargyreus zestos* Plate 46

SIZE ≤ Silver-spotted Skipper

SIMILAR SPECIES Silver-spotted Skipper.

IDENTIFICATION Looks like a Silver-spotted Skipper without the silver spot (although there is a broad pale median stripe on the HW below) but Silver-spotted Skippers are not normally found on the Florida Keys (soon, neither will be Zestos Skippers—see Comments). Its flight is surprisingly slow compared to a Silver-spotted Skipper and it often lands upside-down under leaves. Fresh individuals have a violaceous sheen below.

HABITAT Tropical hardwood hammocks.

RANGE Also, the Bahamas and eastern Antilles.

ABUNDANCE LR. All year in the Florida Keys.

MAJOR FOODPLANT *Galactia striata* (a legume).

COMMENTS This species has greatly declined in recent years. This is not surprising since there are almost no hardwood hammocks left in the keys and the few native areas remaining are usually treated with anti-mosquito sprays that kill butterflies. Formerly found on the mainland in south Florida, recently common on the Upper Keys, this species now barely hangs on, on the Lower Keys.

Silver-spotted Skipper *Epargyreus clarus* Plate 46

SIZE 1 2/16 in.

SIMILAR SPECIES Hoary Edge.

IDENTIFICATION A large, powerful skipper that flashes its **silvered spot in the middle of the HW below** even as it flies. Above the brown-gold FW spots are in an open configuration. The somewhat smaller Hoary Edge has these spots enclosing some dark brown ground color. The Hoary Edge also has a large white patch below, but it is located on the HW margin.

HABITAT Wide-ranging in open habitats. Woodland borders and opening, fields, gardens, meadows, etc.

RANGE Also, west to California.

ABUNDANCE C-A. Florida, Georgia, Mississippi—March–Oct.; Probably 3 broods north to Virginia, Indiana, Nebraska—early April–mid Oct; 2 broods north to Connecticut, Michigan, South Dakotas—mid April/early May–Sept.; 1 brood northward, June–July/Aug.

MAJOR FOODPLANT Black locust (*Robina pseudacacia*) and many other legumes.

COMMENTS One of the most widespread, conspicuous, and easily identified skippers, common in gardens—a favorite!

	MAR	APR	MAY	JUN	JUL	AUG	SEP	OCT
WI								
NY								
NC								
LA								

Hammock Skipper *Polygonus leo* **Plate 48**

SIZE ≤ Silver-spotted Skipper

SIMILAR SPECIES Mangrove Skipper.

IDENTIFICATION Above, blackish-brown (with blue iridescent sheen) with 3 large white spots on the FW and 3 small subapical spots. Below, blue-tinged gray-brown with a prominent black spot near the base of the HW. Mangrove Skipper lacks the FW white spots, below it is blacker with iridescent blue streaks.

HABITAT Tropical hardwood hammocks.

RANGE Also, south through tropical Americas.

ABUNDANCE C. All year.

MAJOR FOODPLANT Jamaican dogwood (*Piscidia piscipula*).

COMMENTS Often pitches under a leaf and lands upside down with its wings closed.

White-striped Longtail *Chioides catillus* **Plate 47**

SIZE < Silver-spotted Skipper.

SIMILAR SPECIES Long-tailed Skipper.

IDENTIFICATION Look for that **white stripe** going straight across the middle of the HW below. Note the very long tails (so long that—unlike other longtails' tails—they dangle as the butterfly flies) and the black upside-down triangle at the FW subapex. Long-tailed Skippers lack the HW white stripe and are iridescent blue-green above.

HABITAT	Tropical and subtropical scrub and open woodlands.
RANGE	Also, south through tropical Americas.
ABUNDANCE	R-U immigrant to Brazoria Co., TX.
MAJOR FOODPLANT	Legume family vines.
COMMENTS	Has bred at Brazos Bend State Park.

Long-tailed Skipper *Urbanus proteus* **Plate 47**

SIZE	≤ Silver-spotted Skipper.
SIMILAR SPECIES	Dorantes Longtail.
IDENTIFICATION	Note the **long, broad "tails."** Over most of our area, no other skipper has these tails. Above, note the striking blue-green iridescence. In Florida and southeastern Texas, Dorantes Longtail also have tails. See discussion under that species.
HABITAT	Open fields and woodland edges, especially brushy and disturbed situations.
RANGE	Also west to southern Arizona and California and south through tropical Americas.
ABUNDANCE	C-A all year resident in South Florida. C immigrant north to southeastern North Carolina, southern Mississippi, and east-central Texas—late Aug.–mid Oct.; RS north to Massachusetts, New York, Ohio (1 record), Missouri, eastern Kansas (2 records).
MAJOR FOODPLANT	Legume family vines (including beans).
COMMENTS	Often a minor pest of bean farms in the South. After an absence of about 40 years, the species has recently been appearing in good numbers in the northeastern United States in late summer.

	MAR	APR	MAY	JUN	JUL	AUG	SEP	OCT
WI								
NY								
NC								
LA								

Dorantes Longtail *Urbanus dorantes* **Plate 47**

SIZE	≤ Silver-spotted Skipper.
SIMILAR SPECIES	Long-tailed Skipper.
IDENTIFICATION	Immediately identifiable as a longtail by its long tails. Above brown with yellowish spots and no blue-green color. Long-tailed Skipper has iridescent blue-green above. Below, look at the dark brown FW submarginal band. Note how it is almost completely interrupted by a finger of the paler interior ground color pushing through from the inside. Long-tailed Skipper has this band solid through its entire length.

HABITAT	Woodland edges, brushy fields, and gardens.
RANGE	Also, west to southern California and south through tropical Americas.
ABUNDANCE	C-A all year resident in South Florida. C immigrant north to Gainesville area, U north to Houston area. RS north to Dallas Co. and Missouri.
MAJOR FOODPLANT	Legume family vines.
COMMENTS	Unlike Long-tailed Skipper, this species rarely lands with its wings open. Established in Florida only since the late 1960s and possibly still spreading northward.

Golden-banded Skipper *Autochton cellus* Plate 46

SIZE	≥ Northern Cloudywing.
SIMILAR SPECIES	Hoary Edge.
IDENTIFICATION	A large, dark skipper with very broad, luminous yellow FW bands. FW band of Hoary Edge is a series of orange-brown spots. Below, the Golden-banded Skipper has no white patch.
HABITAT	Wooded ravines with a stream or other water.
RANGE	Also west to southeastern Arizona and south into northern Mexico.
ABUNDANCE	LR. 1 main brood mid May–mid June; smaller 2nd brood July-Aug.
MAJOR FOODPLANT	Hog peanut (*Amphicarpa bracteata*).
COMMENTS	Always one of the rarest and most elusive butterflies in the East, this species has now retreated from some of its former range in the Northeast.

Cloudywings
(*Achalarus* and *Thorybes*)

The cloudywings are large-sized skippers with an even, dark brown ground color above with pale or golden spots. The duskywings, which are generally smaller, have an upperside ground color that is very mottled. We have 4 species, another 7 occur in the West.

Hoary Edge *Achalarus lyciades* Plate 46

SIZE	< Silver-spotted Skipper.
SIMILAR SPECIES	Silver-spotted Skipper.
IDENTIFICATION	A large dark skipper with a conspicuous white patch on the mar-

gin of the HW below. Silver-spotted Skipper has more angled wings and its silvered spot is in the middle of the HW below. Above, note the brown-gold spot-band enclosing dark brown ground color.

HABITAT Widespread in open areas near woodlands.

ABUNDANCE U. 2 broods north to Washington, D.C., West Virginia, Ohio, Illinois, Missouri, Nebraska—Mainly May–June, July–Sept. 1 brood northward. June–July. RS north to Ontario.

MAJOR FOODPLANT Tick-trefoils (*Desmodium*).

COMMENTS Prefers sandier or rockier areas than Silver-spotted Skipper.

	MAR	APR	MAY	JUN	JUL	AUG	SEP	OCT
WI								
NY								
NC								
LA								

Southern Cloudywing *Thorybes bathyllus* **Plate 49**

SIZE = Northern Cloudywing.

SIMILAR SPECIES Northern Cloudywing, Confused Cloudywing.

IDENTIFICATION A large brown, spread-wing skipper with prominent white markings above and complex dark markings and frosting below. Often lands with its wings folded over its back. Separable from the duskywings by its uniform ground color above (duskywings are heavily mottled) and the bright white line behind the eye. Southern Cloudywings have more extensive and aligned spots than do Northern Cloudywings. Note especially the 2nd spot from the FW margin. This spot is prominent and hourglass shaped in Southern Cloudywings but is usually a small dot or absent in Northern Cloudywings. Look at the antennal club. Southern Cloudywings have a **white patch just where the antennal clubs bend**, Northern Cloudywings lack this white patch. Some Confused Cloudywings can have as extensive spotting as do Southern Cloudywings, but they also lack the white antennal club patch. Below, note the **white or pale gray "face"** of the Southern. Northern has a dark brown or dark gray "face".

HABITAT A wide variety of open situations, especially dry fields with low brushy areas (for perching).

ABUNDANCE Mainly U-C. 2 broods southward. North Florida, North Carolina, Missouri, Oklahoma—March/April–May, Aug.–Oct.; southern Pennsylvania, West Virginia, Ohio, Illinois, Nebraska—May–June, late July–Aug.; 1 brood northward. Mainly mid/late June–mid/late July. RS to northern New York and Maine.

MAJOR FOODPLANT Legumes.

Males often behave territorially, returning again and again to   *151*
the same perch.

	MAR	APR	MAY	JUN	JUL	AUG	SEP	OCT
WI								
NY								
NC								
LA								

Northern Cloudywing *Thorybes pylades* **Plate 49**

SIZE | 12/16 in.

SIMILAR SPECIES | Southern Cloudywing, Confused Cloudywing.

IDENTIFICATION | A large skipper, evenly brown above with restricted white spots. See
Southern and Confused cloudywings for discussion of differences.

HABITAT | Widespread in open situations, such as power-line cuts,
Andropogon fields, moist meadows, etc.

RANGE | Also, west to California.

ABUNDANCE | U-C. 2 broods southward. North Florida—March–May,
Aug–Oct.; North Carolina, northeastern Oklahoma—mid
April–mid June, late July–Aug.; Washington, D.C., Missouri,
Kansas—mid May–mid July, late July–Sept. (partial). 1 brood
northward. New Jersey, West Virginia, Ohio, Indiana, central
Illinois, Nebraska, South Dakota—mid/late May–mid July.

MAJOR FOODPLANT | Legumes.

COMMENTS | On average, probably somewhat more common and widespread
than Southern Cloudywing.

	MAR	APR	MAY	JUN	JUL	AUG	SEP	OCT
WI								
NY								
NC								
LA								

Confused Cloudywing *Thorybes confusis* **Plate 49**

SIZE | = Northern Cloudywing.

SIMILAR SPECIES | Northern Cloudywing, Southern Cloudywing.

IDENTIFICATION | Called Confused Cloudywing for good reason, the identification of
this essentially southern butterfly is extremely tricky, and many
individuals cannot be identified in the field. Spot pattern above
varies from usually very restricted (like Northern Cloudywing) to
extensive (like Southern Cloudywing). "Face" (palps) tends to be
grayish white, as in Southern. The genitalia are diagnostic but, for
most people this is difficult (actually impossible) to determine in
the field (examination of genitalia, usually with a microscope, for
species determinations is standard fare for lepidopterists).
Although, as indicated above, **many individuals cannot be**

identified, individuals strongly exhibiting the following com
tion of markings can probably be assigned to this species. 1. A
with very reduced white markings. In the grouping of the l
three white spots, the central mark (if present at all) is a very
pale white line aligned with the spot adjacent to the leading
gin (Southern Cloudywing has this spot much thicker and *
prominent). 2. Face (palps) white (Northern Cloudywing has
gray or brown palps). 3. Antennal clubs with no white at
bend (Southern Cloudywing has a white patch here).

HABITAT Dry open situations, such as dry prairie, hillside fields, and sand bar

ABUNDANCE R-U. 2 broods. March–May, July/Aug.–Sept.

MAJOR FOODPLANT Probably legumes.

COMMENTS While Southern and/or Northern Cloudywings often occur
Confused Cloudywings, this species seems to be more ha
restricted, favoring even drier situations than those species.

	MAR	APR	MAY	JUN	JUL	AUG	SEP	OCT
WI								
NY								
NC								
LA								

Outis Skipper *Cogia outis* Plate 48

SIZE = Northern Cloudywing.

SIMILAR SPECIES Cloudywings.

IDENTIFICATION Note the **semi-circle of white spots on the FW** and
white patch just below the antennal club. Cloudywing
spot patterns do not appear as a semi-circle and cloudyw
lack white patches **below** the antennal clubs.

HABITAT Acacia prairie, parks.

RANGE Also, south into northern Mexico.

ABUNDANCE U just to the west, in the Fort Worth and Austin area
broods—April–May, July–Aug. RS to northeastern Texas, e
ern Oklahoma, northern Arkansas, and southwestern Misso

MAJOR FOODPLANT Acacias.

COMMENTS One of our least known butterflies, it seems to have disappe
from the Dallas area in the past 10 years.

Mazans Scallopwing *Staphylus mazans* Plate 54

SIZE = Common Sootywing.

SIMILAR SPECIES Hayhurst's Scallopwing, Common Sootywing.

IDENTIFICATION Many individuals are not distinguishable in the field f
Hayhurst's Scallopwing, except by location. Best guess is to l
at the fringes at the bottom of the HW. This species has unchec

fringes (sometimes alternating black and gray) while many Hayhurst's Scallopwings, in Texas, have definite white checks to the fringes (Hayhurst's Scallopwings in Florida seem to be unchecked). But worn fringes quickly look unchecked. So, if you're in the Houston area and see a scallopwing with white on its HW fringe, you can be pretty sure its a Hayhurst's Scallopwing; if the fringe is dark and unchecked, you're on your own.

HABITAT	Small open areas within and adjacent to woodlands.
RANGE	Southern Texas south into Mexico.
ABUNDANCE	R-U immigrant northeast to Houston and Dallas-Fort Worth—June–Sept.
MAJOR FOODPLANT	Lambsquarters (*Chenopodium album*) and *Amaranthus*.

Hayhurst's Scallopwing *Staphylus hayhurstii* **Plate 54**

SIZE	= Common Sootywing.
SIMILAR SPECIES	Common Sootywing.
IDENTIFICATION	A small, very dark spread-winged skipper with even **darker bands forming concentric semicircles on the HW above**. Above, **variably strewn with tiny pale silver or gold flecks**. Also, note the **scalloped HW margin**. Common Sootywing lacks the gray or gold flecks and scalloped HW, has bright white spots above and on the head, and is more uniformly black.
HABITAT	Formerly restricted to moist open woodlands but now also adapted to disturbed areas and gardens due to use of an introduced foodplant.
ABUNDANCE	R-U. 2 broods (probably 3 in south Florida). Mainly April–June, July–Sept. RS north to Wisconsin.
MAJOR FOODPLANT	Lambsquarters (*Chenopodium album*).
COMMENTS	The most northern member of the large and easily recognizable (due to the scalloped HW and metallic flecking) scallopwing genus. Surprisingly scarce given its use of a common weedy caterpillar foodplant. An isolated colony is on Pelee Island in southern Ontario.

	MAR	APR	MAY	JUN	JUL	AUG	SEP	OCT
WI								
NY								
NC								
LA								

Sickle-winged Skipper *Achlyodes thraso* **Plate 48**

SIZE	= Northern Cloudywing.
IDENTIFICATION	**FW apex curved outward—like a sickle**. Above, with various mottled bluish-purplish sheens.

HABITAT	Tropical woodlands and adjacent gardens.
RANGE	South Texas and the West Indies south through tropical Americas
ABUNDANCE	R immigrant to Houston area. RS north to Dallas area, Kansas (2 records), and Arkansas—mainly Sept.–Oct.
MAJOR FOODPLANT	Lime prickly-ash (*Zanthoxylum fagara*).
COMMENTS	Just completed work by Andrew Warren indicates that the correct scientific name for this species may well be *Eantis tamenund* with the genus *Achlyodes* split and *thraso* referring to a Central American species. But, to be conservative, I have used the NABA checklist name.

Duskywings

... and rising up like a dark cloud—the duskywings spread across the land, sowing confusion and dissension among butterfliers, the instrument of the Erinnyes revenge.

—*The Rites of an Ancient Aurelian*, Anonymous. Unpublished.

The duskywings constitute one of our most difficult identification problems. Many duskywings are so similar that it is common to find misidentified museum specimens. Thus the astute observer will often say "That's a duskywing" or "That's a Wild Indigo group duskywing." Not considering the geographically limited False and Florida duskywings, there are essentially three groups species in our area. First there are the large, well-marked duskywings with large pale spots on the FWs, Juvenal's and Horace's duskywings. Second there are the medium-sized species with less extensive pale spots on the FWs, Wild Indigo, Columbine, Persius, Mottled, and Zarucco duskywings. The first three of these species are particularly closely related and difficult to separate. Last there are the species that lack white on the FWs (although even these species occasionally have small white spots at the FW subapexes)—Dreamy and Sleepy duskywings.

Florida Duskywing *Ephyriades brunneus* Plate 50

SIZE	= Northern Cloudywing.
SIMILAR SPECIES	Horace's and Zarucco duskywings.
IDENTIFICATION	Males and females look different, but on both above, note semi-circle of white spots on the apical portion of the FW. Males are dark brown with a broad paler brown margin on HW. Females are a paler brown with a violaceous sheen over

FW. Other duskywings lack the semi-circle of white spots.

HABITAT	Open pinelands.
ABUNDANCE	C. All year
MAJOR FOODPLANT	Locustberry (*Byrsonima lucida*)(Malpighiaceae).

Dreamy Duskywing *Erynnis icelus* Plate 51

SIZE	< Wild Indigo Duskywing.
SIMILAR SPECIES	Sleepy Duskywing.
IDENTIFICATION	Dreamy and Sleepy duskywings lack white spots above and have broad, chain-like postmedian bands. Dreamy Duskywing is 1. smaller, 2. has a bright silver-gray spot on the FW costa above as its most conspicuous feature (Sleepy females are brown in this area, males have some gray but not so extensive nor so bright and silvered); 3. has the last segment of the palps longer than does Sleepy Duskywing, 4. has the inner one-third of the FW above blacker than the rest of the ground color, 5. flies later in the year (although there is overlap), 6. tends to fly lower to the ground (about 1 ft. above the ground as compared with 2-3 ft. for Sleepy) with a less powerful flight.
HABITAT	Open woodlands and areas adjacent to woodlands.
RANGE	Also, west to California.
ABUNDANCE	U-C. 1 brood. North to Washington D.C., Ohio, Missouri —mid April–mid June; northward mid May–June/early July.
MAJOR FOODPLANT	Willows (*Salix*) and poplars (*Populus*).
COMMENTS	Dreamy and Sleepy Duskywing got their names not because of their flight characteristics, but because they lack eye-spots, thus their eyes are closed and they are "sleepy."

	MAR	APR	MAY	JUN	JUL	AUG	SEP	OCT
WI								
NY								
NC								
LA								

Sleepy Duskywing *Erynnis brizo* Plate 51

SIZE	= Wild Indigo Duskywing.
SIMILAR SPECIES	Dreamy Duskywing.
IDENTIFICATION	A medium-sized duskywing, without white spots above and with a broad, chain-like postmedian band on the FW above. See Dreamy Duskywing for comparison.
HABITAT	Mainly dry habitats with oaks, especially pine-oak woodlands and barrens, but in West Virginia it is common in rich, moist woodland. Go figure.
RANGE	Also, west to California.

ABUNDANCE U-C most of range. C-A Florida and Ozarks. 1 brood. North to South Carolina, Georgia, Alabama, Louisiana, Arkansas and east Texas—mainly March–April; North to New York, Ohio, Indiana, Illinois, Iowa, Missouri, southern Nebraska—mid/late April–May; northward May–June.

MAJOR FOODPLANT Scrub oak (*Quercus ilicifolia*), black oak (*Q. velutina*).

	MAR	APR	MAY	JUN	JUL	AUG	SEP	OCT
WI								
NY								
NC								
LA								

Juvenal's Duskywing *Erynnis juvenalis* Plate 50

SIZE = Northern Cloudywing.

SIMILAR SPECIES Horace's Duskywing.

IDENTIFICATION A large, strong-flying duskywing that is very common and widespread. Larger size and extensive white spots above (especially the one in the FW cell) separate this species from all our other duskywings but Horace's (see it for distinction).

HABITAT Open oak woodlands and adjacent areas.

ABUNDANCE C-A. 1 brood. Florida—mid Feb.–early April; South Carolina Georgia, Alabama, Mississippi, Louisiana, Arkansas, east Texas—mid March–April; north to Massachusetts, New York, Ohio Illinois, Michigan, Iowa, Nebraska—April-June; Maine, Ontario Wisconsin, North Dakota—mid/late May–mid July.

MAJOR FOODPLANT Oaks (*Quercus*).

COMMENTS Males are territorial and quite aggressive. They will "police beat," often chasing large moving objects such as Mourning Cloaks or people, then returning to the same perch.

	MAR	APR	MAY	JUN	JUL	AUG	SEP	OCT
WI								
NY								
NC								
LA								

Horace's Duskywing *Erynnis horatius* Plate 50

SIZE = Northern Cloudywing.

SIMILAR SPECIES Juvenal's Duskywing, Wild Indigo Duskywing, Zarucco Duskywing.

IDENTIFICATION A large duskywing, very similar to Juvenal's. Below, Horace's lacks the two pale subapical spots on the HW that Juvenal **almost** always has. Horace's is more sexually dimorphic than Juvenal's. Horace's males are less mottled, more uniform, dark brown than Juvenal's males (which usually have much gray overscaling that Horace's lacks), while Horace's females are more boldly mottled than Juvenal's females. Most easily distinguished from Juvenal's in the summer when Juvenal's doesn't fly. Large, boldly marked summer female Wild Indigo Duskywings can be mistaken for Horace's. Try to note the margin of the HW below. Horace's has large dark spots, Wild Indigo has small pale spots. Male Horace's are easily confused with Zarucco Duskywing—see below.

HABITAT   Oak woodlands, especially those on poor soils and adjacent open areas.

ABUNDANCE   U-C. 3 broods Florida, Georgia, Alabama, Mississippi, Louisiana, Arkansas, east Texas—Feb.–Oct.; elsewhere, 2 broods northward—mainly March/April-early May, late June/early July-Sept. RS to eastern South Dakota.

MAJOR FOODPLANT   Oaks (*Quercus*).

COMMENTS   A number of duskywings are named for Roman poets.

	MAR	APR	MAY	JUN	JUL	AUG	SEP	OCT
WI								
NY								
NC								
LA								

Mottled Duskywing *Erynnis martialis* **Plate 51**

SIZE   = Wild Indigo Duskywing.

SIMILAR SPECIES   Wild Indigo Duskywing.

IDENTIFICATION   A brighter, more mottled skipper than our other duskywings, especially on the HW above. Usually has gray-white apical markings on the FW above that Wild Indigo Duskywing lacks. **Note the narrow and relatively sharply delineated HW postmedian dark band**. Fresh individuals have a strong purplish sheen.

HABITAT   Open wooded areas with sites for hilltopping such as hilly pine-oak woodlands or barrens.

ABUNDANCE   Mainly LR, but U in Ozark region. 2 broods. Georgia, Alabama, Mississippi—March–April, June–early July; South Carolina, Kentucky, Tennessee, Missouri—April–May, late June–July; northward mainly May–early June; July–early Aug.

MAJOR FOODPLANT   New Jersey tea (*Ceanothus americanus*).

COMMENTS   This species has disappeared from most of the Northeast, now found at only a few barrens.

	MAR	APR	MAY	JUN	JUL	AUG	SEP	OCT
WI								
NY								
NC								
LA								

Zarucco Duskywing *Erynnis zarucco* Plates 51 & 52

SIZE = Northern Cloudywing.

SIMILAR SPECIES Wild Indigo Duskywing, Horace's Duskywing.

IDENTIFICATION Slightly larger than Wild Indigo, with more angled wings. Note the **pale brown patch** at the end of the FW cell and the **absence of gray overscaling** anywhere. Males are dark and are most similar to male Horace's Duskywings. Note the gray neck on Zarucco males and the absence (or small amount) of white behind the eyes. Horace's males have white behind the eyes and lack the uniform gray neck. Above, Zaruccos usually have the **FW cell (almost) evenly black** and a **cell-spot is usually absent or faint**. Females very closely resemble some female Wild Indigo Duskywings and many individuals may not be separable. Above, Wild Indigo females usually have a faint, pale, straight and thin, HW cell-end bar which Zaruccos either lack or have less defined. Below, Zaruccos are more evenly dark than are Wild Indigos.

HABITAT Hot, sandy, situations—sandy pineland, power-line cuts, etc.

RANGE Also, Cuba and Hispaniola.

ABUNDANCE C (but Keys subspecies is R-U). 3+ broods. Feb./March–Sep (but Keys race flies all year). Regular immigrant to southern and tidewater North Carolina—June–Sept. Perhaps more regular than indicated north to central Virginia.

MAJOR FOODPLANT Various legumes, including black locust (*Robinia pseudacacia*) and *Sesbania macrocarpa* (on the Keys).

COMMENTS Often misidentified, many older records from the northeast are referable to Wild Indigo Duskywing. This species is rare even northern North Carolina. The population on the lower Flori Keys has paler, sometimes white, HW fringes.

	MAR	APR	MAY	JUN	JUL	AUG	SEP	OCT
WI								
NY								
NC								
LA								

Funereal Duskywing *Erynnis funeralis* Plate 52

SIZE = Northern Cloudywing.

IDENTIFICATION Our blackest duskywing comes with a bold white fringe attached to the HW.

HABITAT A wide variety of open situations, from woodland edges, brushy fields, to thorn scrub.

RANGE Also, west to southern California and south through Mexico southern South America.

ABUNDANCE R-U. Probably 3 broods. March–Oct. RS northeast to Nebraska, Missouri, Indiana (1 record), Arkansas, and Mississippi.

MAJOR FOODPLANT Common rattlebush (*Sesbania drummondii*) and many other legumes.

COMMENTS Some consider Zarucco and Funereal duskywing to be one species.

	MAR	APR	MAY	JUN	JUL	AUG	SEP	OCT
WI								
NY								
NC								
LA								

Columbine Duskywing *Erynnis lucilius* Plate 52

SIZE ≤ Wild Indigo Duskywing.

SIMILAR SPECIES Wild Indigo Duskywing.

IDENTIFICATION Most individuals cannot be distinguished, on the basis of appearance, from Wild Indigo Duskywing. Averages blacker and smaller. A small dark duskywing of the Wild Indigo group, flying around columbine plants, is probably this species. But even then, who knows?

HABITAT Rock outcrops or barrens with good stands of columbine.

ABUNDANCE LR (but C in Ontario). 2 broods. April/May, July/Aug.

MAJOR FOODPLANT Wild columbine (*Aquilegia canadensis*).

COMMENTS Seems to be genuinely rare, but due to its similarity to the much more common Wild Indigo Duskywing, it may be overlooked in some areas.

Wild Indigo Duskywing *Erynnis baptisiae* Plates 51 & 52

SIZE 11/16 inch.

SIMILAR SPECIES Horace's Duskywing, Zarucco Duskywing, Columbine Duskywing, Mottled Duskywing.

IDENTIFICATION A medium-sized, very variable duskywing, usually with three or four small white spots just past the FW "wrist" above. The basal one-half of the FWs is usually very dark and appears "oily." Females are more mottled with more contrast than males. Large, well-marked females can be mistaken for Horace's Duskywing females. Note the small pale spots on the HW margin below. See Zarucco Duskywing for a discussion of separation from that species.

HABITAT Widespread in open areas, especially along roadsides and railroad embankments with plantings of crown vetch.

ABUNDANCE U-LA. Now 3 broods (previously 2). April/May–Sept/Oct.

MAJOR FOODPLANT Crown vetch (*Coronilla varia*) and wild indigo (*Baptisia tinctoria*).

COMMENTS Until fairly recently this butterfly was quite uncommon. Having

adapted to the introduced crown vetch (widely planted alc
embankments for erosion control) within the past twenty yea
Wild Indigo Duskywing has undergone a tremendous popu
tion explosion and an increase in flight period as well.

	MAR	APR	MAY	JUN	JUL	AUG	SEP	OCT
WI								
NY								
NC								
LA								

Persius Duskywing *Erynnis persius* Plate 52

SIZE = Wild Indigo Duskywing.

SIMILAR SPECIES Wild Indigo Duskywing.

IDENTIFICATION Reportedly identifiable by the presence of short grayish-wh
hairs on the FW of the male. However, even many museum spe
imens are misidentified. This doesn't give one much confiden
for field identification. Then again, maybe the live butterflies a
easier to identify once we've figured out the right field mark:

HABITAT Barrens, power lines through dry woods, mountain balds, etc

RANGE Also, west to Alaska and California.

ABUNDANCE LR. Perhaps most common in Wisconsin. 1 brood. May–early Ju

MAJOR FOODPLANT Lupines (*Lupinus*).

COMMENTS While always a scarce butterfly, this very difficult to identi
duskywing seems to have greatly declined in the northea
Currently, there are only a few extant populations, in Conco
New Hampshire and in northeastern Connecticut (possibly a
in Miles Standish State Forest in Massachusetts).

	MAR	APR	MAY	JUN	JUL	AUG	SEP	OCT
WI								
NY								
NC								
LA								

'Appalachian' Grizzled Skipper *Pyrgus centaureae wyano*
Plate 53

SIZE = Common Sootywing.

SIMILAR SPECIES Common Checkered-Skipper.

IDENTIFICATION A checkered-skipper with reduced white markings. Above, t
species **lacks a white spot just below and inward of F
cell-end bar** that Common Checkered-Skipper has. Look at t
3 lowest white spots of the FW postmedian band. Note that t
**top 2 of these spots are not aligned—the top spot
inward of the spot below it**. The HW above lacks a stro
median white band. Above, Common Checkered-Skipper has

FW postmedian band with the lowest 3 white spots in a line and 161
its HW has a strong median white band.

HABITAT Open hilltops and grassy hillsides in barren areas.

RANGE Other subspecies of Grizzled Skippers are found in the Rocky
Mountains, and throughout much of Canada and northern Eurasia.

ABUNDANCE LR. 1 brood. Appalachians—mid-April–mid May; Michigan—May.

MAJOR FOODPLANT Dwarf cinquefoil (*Potentilla canadensis*).

COMMENTS "Cuter" than our other checkered-skippers, this charcoal-col-
ored fantasy, now close to extinction, is worth searching for.
Although the reasons for its decline are not known, intensive
spraying for gypsy moths is suspected. Many workers believe
that the 'Appalachian' Grizzled Skipper merits full species status.

SKIPPERS

Common Checkered-Skipper *Pyrgus communis* **Plate 53**

SIZE ≥ Common Sootywing.

SIMILAR SPECIES Tropical Checkered-Skipper, 'Appalachian' Grizzled Skipper.

IDENTIFICATION The extensive white spots on the black background coupled
with the blue-tinged hair create the effect of a blue-gray blur as
this little skipper whirs by you. Their black and white checks
make checkered-skippers distinctive. See Tropical Checkered-
Skipper and 'Appalachian' Grizzled Skipper to distinguish from
those species.

HABITAT A wide variety of open situations, usually disturbed.

RANGE Also, west to Washington State and through Mexico to Argentina.

ABUNDANCE C-A Florida, Deep South, and from Texas north to Kansas, becoming increasingly rarer northward. Areas with 3 broods—mainly
April–Oct. Areas with 2 broods—mainly July–Oct. R immigrant
north to Massachusetts, southern Ontario, and Manitoba.

MAJOR FOODPLANT Mallow family (*Malvaceae*).

COMMENTS Often does not survive the winter north of Virginia. Everywhere,
the late-summer-fall brood is by far the commonest.

	MAR	APR	MAY	JUN	JUL	AUG	SEP	OCT
WI								
NY								
NC								
LA								

Tropical Checkered-Skipper *Pyrgus oileus* **Plate 53**

SIZE ≥ Common Sootywing.

SIMILAR SPECIES Common Checkered-Skipper.

IDENTIFICATION Easily recognized as a checkered-skipper by its black & white
checks. To distinguish from Common Checkered-Skipper above,
look at the FW apex. Tropical has the **apical white spot** of the

marginal spot-band present; Common almost always lacks this spot. Look at the FW white cell-end bar. Just beyond it, between the cell-end bar and the median spot-band of white spots, Tropical has another prominent white spot. Common has only a very small white spot here, or lacks this spot entirely. Look at the HW marginal row of white spots. In Tropicals, these spots are smaller than the submarginal white spots, but are not minute. In Commons, they are generally minute. Below, Tropicals are tanner and more smudged than the more clean-cut white and brown Commons, and Tropicals have a **brown spot in the middle of the HW costa** that Commons lack.

HABITAT	Mainly disturbed, open situations.
RANGE	Also, south through the West Indies and Mexico through tropical Americas.
ABUNDANCE	C. All year in south Florida. April–Oct. to north Florida and Houston area. RS north to North Carolina (1 record), and Missouri.
MAJOR FOODPLANT	Mallow family (Malvaceae).
COMMENTS	As if distinguishing Tropical and Common checkered-skipper was not difficult enough, males patrolling for females make infrequent stops.

	MAR	APR	MAY	JUN	JUL	AUG	SEP	OCT
WI								
NY								
NC								
LA								

Common Sootywing *Pholisora catullus* **Plate 54**

SIZE	9/16 in.
SIMILAR SPECIES	Hayhurst's Scallopwing.
IDENTIFICATION	A very small, black spread-winged skipper with a variable number (but usually many) of small, bright **white dots on the head** and wings. Other black skippers lack the white dots on the head.
HABITAT	Disturbed open areas, urban lots, railroad yards, etc.
RANGE	Also, west to Washington State.
ABUNDANCE	U-C. 2/3 broods. April/May–Sept. RS north to northern Vermont, Maine and southern Quebec.
MAJOR FOODPLANT	Lambsquarters (*Chenopodium album*).
COMMENTS	Shapiro (1965) describes this as "perhaps the only butterfly benefit appreciably from urbanization."

	MAR	APR	MAY	JUN	JUL	AUG	SEP	OCT
WI								
NY								
NC								
LA								

Intermediate Skippers
(subfamily Heteropterinae)

These small skippers share some traits with grass-skippers and others with spread-winged skippers. They also lack the tapering terminal extension of the antenna (apiculus) that other skippers have. There are a number of tropical genera, but we have only one representative.

Arctic Skipper *Carterocephalus palaemon* **Plate 54**

SIZE	= Tawny-edged Skipper.
IDENTIFICATION	A small, but choice, gift from the north. Marked rather like a miniature fritillary. Above checked orange and very dark brown. Below, rows of gray-white spots on an orange-brown ground.
HABITAT	Moist, grassy open areas within or adjacent to oak-pine transition forest.
RANGE	Also, west in the Rockies and California Sierra, and circumpolar.
ABUNDANCE	LR-LC. 1 brood. Mainly June.
MAJOR FOODPLANT	Grasses.
COMMENTS	During their mating dance, males follow behind females and the pair opens and shuts their wings synchronously.

	MAR	APR	MAY	JUN	JUL	AUG	SEP	OCT
WI				▬				
NY								
NC								
LA								

Grass-Skippers
(subfamily Hesperiinae)

ur grass-skippers are generally smaller than the spread-wing skippers and eir flight is harder to follow. In many species the males have specialized ent patches or stigmas on the FWs. With a color spectrum that ranges mainfrom brown to pale orange, many of these are the LBJs (little brown jobs) of e butterfly world. Many beginning butterfliers (and even some experienced tterfliers) avoid this group entirely. While I can't fault this strategy in pain and frustration avoidance, careful study of this large and very interesting group is rewarded by some of the greatest pleasures of butterflying. In addition, because they are understudied, this is the area in which the observations of an amateur can most easily be of importance.

Swarthy Skipper *Nastra lherminier* **Plate 55**

SIZE ≥ Least Skipper.

SIMILAR SPECIES Tawny-edged Skipper.

IDENTIFICATION A very small **dark yellowish-brown** skipper with **slightly paler veining below**. Small worn Tawny-edged Skippers can look very dark below but they usually have pale subapical spots on the FW and lack the pale veining. Above, Swarthy Skippers are plain dark brown while Tawny-edged Skippers have extensive markings. In south Florida and southeastern Texas see Neamathla and Julia's skippers.

.HABITAT Areas with low vegetation and bluestem grasses, such as grassy fields, power-line cuts, roadsides, and savannas.

ABUNDANCE LU-LC. 2 broods, probably 3 in Florida. Mainly May/Jun –Aug/Sept. 1st brood March or April in Deep South. RS north to Rhode Island, Michigan, Wisconsin, Minnesota, and Kansas.

MAJOR FOODPLANT Little bluestem grass (*Andropogon scoparius*).

COMMENTS One of the plainest butterflies in the East—those slightly pale veins are the only outward manifestation of its wild heart.

	MAR	APR	MAY	JUN	JUL	AUG	SEP	OCT
WI								
NY								
NC								
LA								

Julia's Skipper *Nastra julia* **Plate 55**

SIZE ≥ Least Skipper.

SIMILAR SPECIES Neamathla Skipper, Swarthy Skipper, Eufala Skipper

IDENTIFICATION *Nastra* presents some nasty identification problems. This species, fairly common in the Rio Grande Valley, is normally a warm brown below, with some red/yellow in the ground color, than either Swarthy or Neamathla skippers and lacks the paler veining of Swarthy. Above, Julia's Skippers tend to have more prominent pale spots than do Neamathla Skippers. Eufala Skipper is usually grayer below and is larger with somewhat more elongated wings. Above, Eufala Skippers have a prom nent double spot in the FW cell that Julia's Skippers lack.

HABITAT	Woodland trails and edges, as a stray, could be found in a wide variety of habitats.
ABUNDANCE	U. April–Oct.
MAJOR FOODPLANT	Bermuda grass (*Cynodon dactylon*) and other grasses.
COMMENTS	Named for H.A. Freeman's eldest daughter.

Neamathla Skipper *Nastra neamathla* **Plate 55**

SIZE	≥ Least Skipper.
SIMILAR SPECIES	Swarthy Skipper, Julia's Skipper, Eufala Skipper
IDENTIFICATION	Very similar to the much more common and widespread Swarthy Skipper. Below, Neamathla Skippers are a duller brown **without the paler yellow veining**. Above, this species generally has 2 pale spots in the median FW and especially **2 subapical FW spots** that Swarthy Skippers almost always lack.
HABITAT	Low, grassy fields, including disturbed areas.
ABUNDANCE	U-C. March–Oct. RS to southern Louisiana and Mississippi.
MAJOR FOODPLANT	Probably bluestem grasses (*Andropogon*).

Three-spotted Skipper *Cymaenes tripunctus* **Plate 55**

SIZE	= Tawny-edged Skipper.
SIMILAR SPECIES	Eufala Skipper, Obscure Skipper.
IDENTIFICATION	This species does have 3 spots near the FW apex, but so do many others! Note the **long antennas**, about 1/2 the length of the FW. Above, often with a **bright tawny base of the FW costa**. Note the **3 white subapical spots that are separate and curve outward**. Below, yellowish-brown with faint and variable postmedian pale spot-band that is usually more distinct than on Eufala Skipper. Eufala Skipper is generally grayer and paler below, without a bright tawny base of the FW costa above, with FW subapical white spots that are in a straight line and almost touching, and with shorter antennas (about 1/3 the length of the FW). Obscure Skipper has yellower spots above, panaquin body stripe below.
HABITAT	Grassy disturbed woodlands and adjacent areas.
ABUNDANCE	U-C. All year.
MAJOR FOODPLANT	Grasses.
COMMENTS	If you are confused by this skipper, you are in good company. Close to 1/2 of the south Florida specimens of this species and Eufala Skipper in a major museum were misidentified, mainly with Three-spotted Skippers being labeled as Eufala Skippers. But the box of Three-spotted Skippers also contained Eufala Skippers and a misidentified Obscure Skipper.

SKIPPERS

Clouded Skipper *Lerema accius* **Plate 64**

SIZE	≥ Zabulon/Hobomok Skipper.
SIMILAR SPECIES	Zabulon Skipper (female), Dusted Skipper, Dun Skipper (above), Twin-spot Skipper (above).
IDENTIFICATION	A very dark southern skipper. When fresh there is much frosting below. The HW frosting (or, when worn, paler areas) at the margin and at the lower middle of the wing, sets off a dark vertical band that extends from the center of the HW trailing margin. Above, both sexes have **3 white subapical FW spots that usually curve outwardly**. Females also have a **smaller, ovate cell spot**. Female Zabulon Skipper has a white apex of the HW below and much more extensive spotting above. Dusted Skipper has white "eye-brows." Above, Dun Skippers are similar but don't have 3 white FW subapical spots or the ovate cell spot. Twin-spot Skippers do have 3 white FW subapical spots, but they are in a line, and they lack the ovate cell spot.
HABITAT	Can be found in almost any open habitat, including open woodland, but prefers moist grassy areas in or near woods.
ABUNDANCE	C-A. Southern Florida and Houston, TX areas—all year. Decreasing immigrant northward, mainly April–Oct. Common along the coast north to North Carolina, late summer – early fall. Irregular immigrant or RS north to New York, Massachusetts, Indiana, Missouri, and southeastern Kansas.
MAJOR FOODPLANT	Grasses.
COMMENTS	One of our earliest rising skippers, Clouded Skippers will be seen perching and courting early in the morning before their relatives have woken.

	MAR	APR	MAY	JUN	JUL	AUG	SEP	OCT
WI								
NY								
NC								
LA								

Least Skipper *Ancyloxypha numitor* **Plate 56**

SIZE	8/16 in.
SIMILAR SPECIES	European Skipper, Southern Skipperling.
IDENTIFICATION	A very small, bright orange skipper **weakly weaving through the grass** is sure to be this species. Contrasting black wing above (in almost all populations) can be detected in flight. Below, Least Skippers are bright orange, with **rounded wings**. Southern Skipperlings fly with much more rapid wing-beats, are even smaller, have little black above, have angular wings, and below have a white stripe. European Skippers are larger, dull

orange below and orange above.

HABITAT Wet meadows and marshes, grassy roadside ditches, etc.

ABUNDANCE C-A (but LR-U southward & to the northwest). 3 broods north to New Jersey, southern Ohio, Kansas. Mainly May/early June–early Oct. Maine, Manitoba—late June–Aug. New Brunswick—July.

OR FOODPLANT Grasses.

COMMENTS Although tiny, in the right habitat absolute numbers can be impressive.

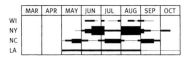

	MAR	APR	MAY	JUN	JUL	AUG	SEP	OCT
WI								
NY								
NC								
LA								

Poweshiek Skipperling *Oarisma poweshiek* **Plate 56**

SIZE ≥ Least Skipper.

MILAR SPECIES Garita Skipperling.

DENTIFICATION The striking and beautiful **white veins and overscaling on the black HW below** background, makes this species easy to pick out, even during its strange whirring flight—an awful lot of FW movement doesn't produce much forward velocity. Fresh individuals have the **outer edge of HW fringe black**. Above, largely black with a bright orange FW cell. Poweshiek Skipperling usually lands below the level of the top of the grasses (unlike most other skippers), orienting its body parallel to the blade of grass on which it is resting, i.e., vertical. Garita Skipperling lacks the black ground color of the HW below and is usually not so black above.

HABITAT High quality, tall-grass prairie.

ABUNDANCE LR. 1 brood. Mainly late June–mid July.

OR FOODPLANT Spikerush (*Eleocharis elliptica*).

COMMENTS Very restricted both by habitat and geography, this is one of a number of prairie species that are in serious trouble.

Garita Skipperling *Oarisma garita* **Plate 56**

SIZE ≥ Least Skipper

MILAR SPECIES Poweshiek Skipperling.

DENTIFICATION A very small orange skipper with **white veins and fringe on the HW below**. Above, variably blackened orange with **white FW costal margins**. Poweshiek Skipperlings (usually) have black HWs below (with much white overscaling) and orange FW costal margins.

HABITAT Short-grass prairie.

RANGE Also, west through the Rockies and south to northern Mexico.

ABUNDANCE LR. 1 brood. Mid June–mid July.

MAJOR FOODPLANT	Grasses.
COMMENTS	Recently, small populations have been found twice, a numb[...] years apart, on Manitoulin Island in southern Ontario, so it [...] be resident there, almost 1000 miles east of the rest of its kn[...] range!

Orange Skipperling *Copaeodes aurantiacus* **Plate [...]**

SIZE	= Least Skipper.
SIMILAR SPECIES	Southern Skipperling.
IDENTIFICATION	A very small, bright orange skipper with very angular wings[...] **orange below**, while Southern Skipperling has a white ra[...] the HW below. Above, very similar to Southern Skipper[...] Orange Skipperling usually has a black band along leading [...] of HW above; in Southern Skipperling the black is ma[...] restricted to the basal half of the HW leading edge. Best to ch[...] out the underwing.
HABITAT	Grassy situations within arid regions.
RANGE	Southern Texas west to southern California and south to Pana[...]
ABUNDANCE	R immigrant to Houston and Dallas, RS late summer/fall n[...] to Arkansas and southern Kansas.
MAJOR FOODPLANT	Bermuda grass (*Cynodon dactylon*) and other grasses.
COMMENTS	More at home in arid regions than is Southern Skipperling[...] our area the range of these two species overlaps only in so[...] and central Texas.

Southern Skipperling *Copaeodes minimus* **Plate 5[...]**

SIZE	≤ Least Skipper.
SIMILAR SPECIES	Least Skipper.
IDENTIFICATION	A tiny, bright orange skipper with very angular wings. Br[...] orange with a **narrow white ray on the HW below**. L[...] Skipper is larger, with more rounded wings, much black ab[...] and without the white ray below. In Texas, see Ora[...] Skipperling.
HABITAT	A wide variety of open grassy habitats, but usually not in v[...] wet situations.
RANGE	Also, Mexico to Costa Rica.
ABUNDANCE	U-C. Probably 3 broods in peninsula Florida and north to ab[...] Houston—March–Nov. 2 broods northward—April/May–J[...] Aug–Oct. RS north to Oklahoma, central Arkansas, and Ohi[...]
MAJOR FOODPLANT	Bermuda grass (*Cynodon dactylon*) and other grasses.
COMMENTS	Our smallest skipper makes up for its lack of size with its sn[...] good looks.

	MAR	APR	MAY	JUN	JUL	AUG	SEP	OCT
WI								
NY								
NC								
LA								

European Skipper *Thymelicus lineola* Plate 56

SIZE	≤ Tawny-edged Skipper.
SIMILAR SPECIES	Least Skipper, Delaware Skipper.
IDENTIFICATION	A small, weak-flying skipper that is completely orange (usually with a fair amount of white dusting below). Note the short reddish antennas with blunt ends. Delaware Skipper is larger (usually), a much more powerful, faster flyer, with longer antennas with hooked, pointed ends. Least Skipper is smaller brighter orange. Both Delaware and Least Skippers have more black markings above.
HABITAT	Dry grassy fields, especially those with tall grasses.
RANGE	Also, North Africa, Europe, and northern Asia.
ABUNDANCE	C-A. 1 brood. late May/June–early July.
MAJOR FOODPLANT	Timothy (*Phleum pratense*).
COMMENTS	A native of Europe, this skipper was introduced into Ontario in 1910 and is still expanding its range in our region. Although not native, it has certainly found itself at home here and is now one of the commonest skippers in North America. Some NABA 4th of July Butterfly Counts tally over 10,000 individuals within their count circle.

	MAR	APR	MAY	JUN	JUL	AUG	SEP	OCT
WI				–				
NY								
NC								
LA								

Fiery Skipper *Hylephila phyleus* Plate 57

SIZE	≤ Zabulon/Hobomok Skipper.
SIMILAR SPECIES	Whirlabout.
IDENTIFICATION	This common species has the "measles"—many small black spots on the HW below—giving it a fever and making it "fiery." Males are bright orange, with spots varying from faint dull brown to sharp black. Whirlabouts have fewer, larger brown to black blotches. Note the **very wavy black borders on the FW and HW above**. Whirlabout has HW border smooth. Female Fiery Skippers are similar to males but the ground color is dull yellow-brown with a greenish tinge. Above, they are brown with yellow spots. Note the **"arrow" on the HW above**.

HABITAT Lawns and other low open grassy areas such as dry fields and roadsides.

ABUNDANCE C. Florida, Georgia, west to east Texas—Feb.–Nov. Decreasingly common immigrant northward. R-U north to New York, Ohio, Indiana, Illinois, northern Missouri, Kansas. RS north to Massachusetts, southern Ontario, Michigan, Wisconsin, South Dakota (1 record).

MAJOR FOODPLANT Bermuda grass (*Cynodon dactylon*).

COMMENTS Along with Whirlabout and Sachem, one of the three "wizards"—active, orange skippers that are widespread and common throughout the South, and often occur together.

	MAR	APR	MAY	JUN	JUL	AUG	SEP	OCT
WI								
NY								
NC								
LA								

Hesperia Skippers

In many areas, hesperia skippers replace one another throughout the butterfly year. Just as brownish Cobweb Skippers are fading into fields of bluestem grasses in early spring, bright orange Indian Skippers appear to take their place! Ottoe Skippers rule the prairies mid June–July, Common Branded Skippers buzz low in northern meadows in late July–Aug., while Leonard Skippers go on bombing runs in late Aug.–Sept. Unlike most of our other butterflies, when disturbed, hesperia skippers will most likely fly rapidly out of sight. On the other hand, sometimes they can be quite confiding, as when a mated pair of Dakota Skippers climbed onto my outstretched finger (see photo 15, plate 59).

Uncas Skipper *Hesperia uncas* Not Illustrated

SIZE = Zabulon/Hobomok Skipper.

SIMILAR SPECIES Common Branded Skipper, Cobweb Skipper.

IDENTIFICATION HW below, note the **white veining** and areas of dark brown. Below and above, often has a **white vein connecting the two patches of FW subapical spots**. Common Branded Skipper lacks the white veining. Cobweb Skipper flies in the spring.

HABITAT Dry short-grass prairies.

RANGE Southern Saskatchewan and Alberta south through much of western United States.

| ABUNDANCE | R or not now occurring in southern Manitoba and eastern South Dakota. RS to eastern Nebraska, Minnesota, and Iowa. 2 broods—mainly June–Aug. |
| MAJOR FOODPLANT | Grama grasses (*Bouteloua*) and needle grasses (*Stipa*). |

Common Branded Skipper *Hesperia comma* **Plate 58**

SIZE	≤ Zabulon/Hobomok Skipper.
SIMILAR SPECIES	Leonard's Skipper.
IDENTIFICATION	Variable throughout its range. Below, note the bold white postmedian spot-band and the **central, large, hooked white spot**. Male above, area distal to FW stigma is not so dark—contrasts with stigma. Leonard's Skipper is generally larger, redder below, has a simple central spot, and males above have the area distal to the FW stigma about as black as the stigma. Northern prairie populations (*H.c.assiniboia*) are a pale dirty-gray-green-yellow below.
HABITAT	Meadows, roadsides, open fields.
RANGE	Also, montane western North America and northern Europe and Asia.
ABUNDANCE	U-C. 1 brood. Late July–Aug.
MAJOR FOODPLANT	Grasses.
COMMENTS	Some believe that the subspecies *assiniboia*, a prairie skipper just entering our area in southern Manitoba and North Dakota, warrants species status.

Ottoe Skipper *Hesperia ottoe* **Plate 59**

SIZE	≥ Zabulon/Hobomok Skipper.
SIMILAR SPECIES	'Pawnee' Leonard's Skipper, Dakota Skipper.
IDENTIFICATION	The skipper-king of the tall-grass prairies—the biggest and strongest prairie grass-skipper. Below, dull yellow-orange with a faint, or absent, postmedian spot-band. 'Pawnee' Leonard's Skipper is very, very similar but flies later in the year and has yellow (Ottoe Skipper—gray) in the center of male's stigmas, but this is very difficult to see in the field. Dakota Skipper males are extremely similar except that they are much smaller.
HABITAT	High quality, tall-grass prairie, especially along ridge-tops.
RANGE	Also, west to Montana and Colorado.
ABUNDANCE	LR. 1 brood. Mid June-July/early Aug.
MAJOR FOODPLANT	Grasses.
COMMENTS	Extremely local within the range shown, not now occurring in large areas of Nebraska and South Dakota. Prairie destruction has greatly affected this species.

SKIPPERS

	MAR	APR	MAY	JUN	JUL	AUG	SEP	OCT
WI					▪ ▪▪▮			
NY								
NC								
LA								

Leonard's Skipper *Hesperia leonardus* **Plates 58 & 59**

SIZE ≥ Zabulon/Hobomok Skipper.

SIMILAR SPECIES Common Branded Skipper (for *H.l.leonardus*); Ottoe Skipper, Dotted Skipper (for *H.l.pawnee*).

IDENTIFICATION Throughout most of the East, Leonard's Skipper is easily identified. A large reddish-brown skipper bombing around a large open field in very late summer is almost certainly this species. Note the very conspicuous white (or yellowish) postmedian spot-band on the HW below. Common Branded Skipper is smaller and not so reddish. The western subspecies (considered by some to be a full species), 'Pawnee' Leonard's Skipper looks quite different below, tending toward a pale yellow-brown with a very faint (or absent) postmedian spot-band. Ottoe Skipper is very similar but flies in July–early Aug. Dotted Skipper's range doesn't overlap.

HABITAT Open fields with thick low vegetation and nectar sources. Seems to prefer a combination of dry *Andropogon*-covered hillside juxtaposed with an area with a profusion of fall-blooming purple flowers, often in a moist open meadow. 'Pawnee' prefers prairie hilltops.

RANGE 'Pawnee' ranges from extreme western Minnesota and Iowa west to Montana and Colorado.

ABUNDANCE LR-U. 1 brood. Mainly mid/late Aug.–Sept., but flying Sept.–mid Oct. in southern parts of range.

MAJOR FOODPLANT Grasses.

COMMENTS Our only fall-flying, single-brooded butterfly. Leonard's Skipper populations from Manitoba south to Iowa are a blend of nominate Leonard's and 'Pawnee.'

	MAR	APR	MAY	JUN	JUL	AUG	SEP	OCT
WI						▬▮▬		
NY						▬		
NC								
LA								

Cobweb Skipper *Hesperia metea* **Plate 58**

SIZE = Tawny-edged Skipper.

SIMILAR SPECIES Female Sachem.

IDENTIFICATION A small, often inconspicuous, dark **springtime skipper**. Usually flies low among or at the top of bluestem grasses. Note the pale, **chevron-shaped postmedian band on the HW below and above** and the **white FW costal margin**. Female Sachem also has a chevron-shaped band below but is larger and much paler yellowish-brown and lacks the white FW costal margin.

HABITAT : Dry open fields with bluestem grasses, often on hillsides but also power-line cuts, open hilltops, etc.

ABUNDANCE : LR-LC. 1 brood. April–May/early June.

MAJOR FOODPLANT : Bluestem grasses (*Andropogon*).

COMMENTS : Although this early spring skipper is easily overlooked and some might call this a "Little Brown Job," I think that close inspection will open your eyes to its beauty.

	MAR	APR	MAY	JUN	JUL	AUG	SEP	OCT
WI			▬▬					
NY		▬▬▬						
NC		▬						
LA								

Green Skipper *Hesperia viridis* Plate 58

SIZE : = Zabulon/Hobomok Skipper.

SIMILAR SPECIES : Common Branded Skipper.

IDENTIFICATION : You need to look quickly at a very fresh individual to see the greenish sheen for which this species is named. The bold white postmedian spot-band, in the shape of a chevron, and white basal and median spots on the HW below are characteristic of many hesperia skippers. Note that the **bottom white spot of the postmedian spot-band bends outward**. Also, both the basal white spot and the top spot of the postmedian band are prominent. Common Branded Skipper does not co-occur with Green Skipper in our region and doesn't have the bottom white spot bent outward.

HABITAT : Dry grasslands such as occur in prairie gulches, ridgetops, and canyon hillsides.

RANGE : Also, Wyoming and western Nebraska south into northern Mexico.

ABUNDANCE : C. 2 broods. April–June; Aug.–Oct. RS to southwestern Missouri.

MAJOR FOODPLANT : Grasses.

COMMENTS : The population in Pontotoc Co., Oklahoma is the only one known in our area, although another population occurs just outside our area on the west side of Fort Worth, TX.

Dotted Skipper *Hesperia attalus* Plates 59 & 61

SIZE : ≥ Zabulon/Hobomok Skipper.

SIMILAR SPECIES : Crossline Skipper, 'Pawnee' Leonard's Skipper, female Sachem.

IDENTIFICATION Large. Below, quite variable, from rich yellowish-brown with well-separated **bold white spots forming a postmedian chevron** on the HW to dull pale brownish-yellow with weak pale spots. Boldly marked individuals are unmistakable but individuals with weak spots could be confused with Crossline Skippers or 'Pawnee' Leonard's Skippers. Note the presence of **two subapical FW spots** (characteristic of hesperia skippers) that Crossline Skipper lacks. 'Pawnee' Leonard's Skipper is more yellow-orange below, but Dotted Skipper prairie populations are yellower than are Atlantic populations. Female Sachems below have a more pronounced postmedian spot-band with outwardly concave spots.

HABITAT Atlantic coast (*H.a.slossonae*)—sandy barrens, including pine barrens and associated railroad tracks, airport runways, and power line cuts. Kansas-Texas (*H.a.attalus*)—short-grass prairie.

ABUNDANCE LR–LU. Mainly 2 broods—May–mid June, mid Aug.–Sept.; 1 brood New Jersey—early July–early August. RS to southwestern Missouri.

MAJOR FOODPLANT Grasses.

COMMENTS Old reports from Nantucket, MA and Staten Island, NY, Virginia and Georgia were probably of strays rather than of residents, but it is possible that this easily overlooked skipper still inhabits the sandhills region from southern North Carolina through central South Carolina into Georgia.

	MAR	APR	MAY	JUN	JUL	AUG	SEP	OCT
WI								
NY								
NC								
LA								

Meske's Skipper *Hesperia meskei* **Plate 59**

SIZE > Tawny-edged Skipper.

SIMILAR SPECIES Dotted Skipper, Delaware Skipper, Arogos Skipper.

IDENTIFICATION Yellow-orange to rusty-orange below, often with some sooty overscaling. HW usually with a postmedian spot-band, although this varies from quite prominent and distinct spots to a faint indistinct band. Female above has an unbroken postmedian spot-band. Dotted Skippers are larger and, along the Atlantic coast are much browner (prairie Dotteds can be quite yellow). Below, Delaware and Arogos Skippers lack any HW postmedian band or FW spots. They look very different above.

HABITAT Open dry or sandy pinelands and adjacent areas.

RANGE A recent report from southern Louisiana may mean that there populations connecting the east Texas and Florida populations

	ABUNDANCE	LR-LU. 2 broods. May–June, Sept.–Oct.
	OR FOODPLANT	Little bluestem and other grasses.
	COMMENTS	One of our more elusive and rarely seen skippers. A population that inhabited Big Pine Key in the Florida Keys may now be extirpated.

	MAR	APR	MAY	JUN	JUL	AUG	SEP	OCT
WI								
NY								
NC					—			—
LA								

Dakota Skipper *Hesperia dacotae* **Plate 59**

SIZE
= Tawny-edged Skipper.

SIMILAR SPECIES
Ottoe Skipper, Dotted Skipper, Sachem (female).

IDENTIFICATION
Males below are dull yellow-brown with a faint postmedian band. Females below vary from mouse brown with strong spots (most common form) to gray-yellow (similar to male) but usually have a basal white spot at the leading margin of the HW below. Dotted Skippers lack this basal spot and are larger. Females' flight is very heavy bodied with lots of wing-beats for a substandard result. Female Sachems above look surprisingly similar but have a black patch at the center of the FW that Dakota Skippers lack.

HABITAT
Moist or dry, ungrazed, calcareous (alkaline) prairies. Moist habitat almost always has wood lily, harebell, and alkali grass blooming during Dakotas flight. Dry habitats have pale purple coneflowers, and Indian blanket.

ABUNDANCE
LR. 1 brood. Mid/late June–mid July.

MAJOR FOODPLANT
Grasses.

COMMENTS
The few remaining colonies of this prairie species need all the help they can get. Small, isolated colonies are certain to die out, the only question is when. Since native prairie is one of our most endangered habitats, prairie restoration is the only hope for this and similarly situated species.

Indian Skipper *Hesperia sassacus* **Plate 58**

SIZE
≤ Zabulon/Hobomok Skipper.

SIMILAR SPECIES
Long Dash.

IDENTIFICATION
A spring skipper with an indistinct pattern below. HW below is yellow-orange to rusty-orange with a pale yellow postmedian chevron that is usually indistinct but sometimes obvious. Note that the chevron spots are **somewhat concave distally**. Above, note clear orange HW with black border. Long Dash pat-

tern below is more distinct and spots are not concave dist
Above, male is bright orange with a thin black stigma. L
Dash has black "cobwebbing" in the center of HW and n
black on the FW.

HABITAT	Brushy fields and open meadows near woodlands, both and moist.
ABUNDANCE	R-U (locally C). 1 brood. Mainly May–June but June–mid in Maine, Ontario, Wisconsin, Manitoba.
MAJOR FOODPLANT	Grasses.
COMMENTS	You may have noticed that many of the scientific name American skippers are based on Native-American names.

	MAR	APR	MAY	JUN	JUL	AUG	SEP	OCT
WI								
NY								
NC								
LA								

Peck's Skipper *Polites peckius* **Plates 60 & 61**

SIZE	= Tawny-edged Skipper.
SIMILAR SPECIES	Long Dash, Tawny-edged Skipper (above).
IDENTIFICATION	HW below has 2 "patches" of yellow separated by the w brown ground color but bridged by yellow. The amount of brown between the two patches is quite variable. Remem that **Peck's is a pointer**—the HW surfaces of both sexes h postmedian spot-bands with the central spot extending outw toward the wing margin. Male above, note the prominent b stigma separating orange FW margin from the dark distal t thirds of the wing. Tawny-edged Skipper is similar above note dark HW. Long Dash has less contrast below with mor a postmedian band and less of a "patch."
HABITAT	Any open grassy areas with nectar sources, including meado power-line cuts, suburban habitats, and roadsides.
RANGE	Also, west to Washington State.
ABUNDANCE	Mainly C-A, U at edges of range. 2 broods north to New Y (Catskills), Massachusetts, Ontario, Wisconsin, South Dakot mid/late May–Sept./Oct. 1 brood northward—June–Aug.
MAJOR FOODPLANT	Grasses.
COMMENTS	One of the most common skippers through much of its ran this active butterfly is very fond of clovers.

	MAR	APR	MAY	JUN	JUL	AUG	SEP	OCT
WI								
NY								
NC								
LA								

Baracoa Skipper *Polites baracoa* Plate 60

SIZE   ≤ Tawny-edged Skipper.

SIMILAR SPECIES   Tawny-edged Skipper.

IDENTIFICATION   A small, dark Florida polites. HW below usually with a chunky pale postmedian band. On the male above, note the short, narrow stigma and the dark ray that extends inward from the FW margin past the end of the stigma. Tawny-edged Skipper is slightly larger, usually not so dark below, usually lacks spots on the HW below and, in males, the stigma is thicker and longer and the dark FW ray doesn't extend past the end of the stigma.

HABITAT   Open situations with low grasses, especially lawns.

RANGE   Also Cuba and Hispaniola.

ABUNDANCE   South Florida, C—all year. North Florida, U—April–Oct.

MAJOR FOODPLANT   Low grasses.

COMMENTS   Baracoa Skippers have a great mating dance. Male and female face each other with antennas touching, or almost so. The male starts on the female's right, rapidly dances to her left, then back to her right, then back to her left. The female then waggles her body, tilting her wings first to the left then to the right.

Tawny-edged Skipper *Polites themistocles* Plates 60 & 61

SIZE   9/16 in.

SIMILAR SPECIES   Crossline Skipper.

IDENTIFICATION   A small, dull to darkish skipper below. Below, usually unicolorous drab olive except for tawny orange FW margin and 3 white spots on the FW subapex (sometimes HW has a faint postmedian band). Male above has intense **thick black stigma** bordering bright orange FW margin. Rest of FW and HW dull brown. Below, usually has sharp contrast between HW color and the brighter FW costal margin. See Crossline Skipper.

HABITAT   Open grassy areas with nectar sources, including suburban habitats and roadsides.

RANGE   Also, west to Washington State and south in the mountains to New Mexico and Arizona.

ABUNDANCE   C-A. Mainly 2 broods. Mainly May–June, Aug.–Sept. 1 brood Michigan, Wisconsin, South Dakota, northward—June–July. Perhaps 3 broods northern Florida and along the immediate Gulf Coast, where it is U, April–Oct.

MAJOR FOODPLANT   Grasses.

COMMENTS   Very common, very widespread, and quite variable.

	MAR	APR	MAY	JUN	JUL	AUG	SEP	OCT
WI								
NY								
NC								
LA								

Crossline Skipper *Polites origenes* **Plates 60 & 61**

SIZE ≥ Tawny-edged Skipper.

SIMILAR SPECIES Tawny-edged Skipper, female Sachem, Dotted Skipper.

IDENTIFICATION A small to medium-sized dull skipper. Below, distinguished fr
Tawny-edged Skipper by 1. larger size (usually), 2. ligh
ground color, yellowish-brown, often with a "brassy" l
(compared to dull olive for Tawny-edged), 3. presence (usua
of at least some (often marked) postmedian spot-band (Taw
edged Skipper usually lacks a HW postmedian spot-band);
4. less contrast between the HW color and the color of the
costal margin. Above, the male is distinguished from Taw
edged Skipper by the **less intense stigma that narrows s
nificantly toward the base of the FW** and by the presence
an **additional pale yellow spot distally adjacent to t
stigma**. Female above is very similar to Tawny-edged Skip
but on the HW usually has a broad dark border and a hin
orange. Tawny-edged females lack these features.

HABITAT Dry grassy fields, prairies, power-line cuts, especially in p
soil area.

RANGE Also, west to Colorado.

ABUNDANCE U-C. 2 broods north to Philadelphia, Ohio, Indiana, Illin
Missouri, Kansas—mainly May–June/early July, Aug.–Sept
brood New York, Ontario, Michigan, Wisconsin, Nebra
northward–mid/late June–July/early Aug.

MAJOR FOODPLANT Purple top (*Tridens flavus*) and other grasses.

COMMENTS More restricted in habitat than Tawny-edged Skipper, Cross
Skipper still often flies in the same locality.

	MAR	APR	MAY	JUN	JUL	AUG	SEP	OCT
WI								
NY								
NC								
LA								

Long Dash *Polites mystic* **Plates 60 & 61**

SIZE ≤ Zabulon/Hobomok Skipper.

SIMILAR SPECIES Indian Skipper, Peck's Skipper.

IDENTIFICATION Clear orange-brown and yellow pattern below with wide y
low-spotted postmedian band and yellow cell spot. Usually s

arable from Indian Skipper by much sharper pattern. HW postmedian band is smoother than is the Indian Skipper chevron. Occasionally has yellow spots almost as extensive as Peck's Skipper. On the FW, note the 3 elongated subapical spots with the lowest of the 3 closest to the wing margin (straight in Indian and Peck's skippers) and the elongated FW postmedian spot.

HABITAT Toward the south, wet meadows and marshes, often with blue flag (wild iris). More tolerant of drier conditions in the north where it is more common.

ABUNDANCE U-C. 1 brood—June (mid June–mid July northward), with a partial second brood late Aug.–early Sept.

MAJOR FOODPLANT Grasses.

COMMENTS Often nectars at blue flag (*Iris versicolor*).

	MAR	APR	MAY	JUN	JUL	AUG	SEP	OCT
WI				▬ ▬	▬	—		
NY			▬▬▬	▬▬▬	—			
NC								
LA								

Whirlabout *Polites vibex* **Plate 57**

SIZE ≥ Tawny-edged Skipper.

SIMILAR SPECIES Fiery Skipper.

IDENTIFICATION Male below, orange-yellow with **large smudged brown or black spots**. These spots are larger and not as numerous as in Fiery Skipper. Male above, note smooth black border on the HW (Fiery Skipper has jagged black border). Female below, dull olive-gray with smudged brown spots.

HABITAT Disturbed grassy fields, roadsides, woodland edges.

RANGE Also south through Mexico to Argentina.

ABUNDANCE C. All year resident south Florida, Feb.–Dec. in north Florida. 2 broods northward, mid May–mid July, Aug.–Sept. RS north to Staten Island, NY, West Virginia, and Iowa.

MAJOR FOODPLANT Grasses.

COMMENTS Its flight pattern lives up to its name.

	MAR	APR	MAY	JUN	JUL	AUG	SEP	OCT
WI								
NY								
NC			—	▬▬▬	—	▬▬▬	▬	
LA	—	▬▬▬	▬▬▬	▬▬▬▬	▬▬▬	▬▬▬	▬▬▬	▬▬

Southern Broken-Dash *Wallengrenia otho* **Plate 62**

SIZE ≥ Tawny-edged Skipper.

SIMILAR SPECIES Northern Broken-Dash, Black Dash.

IDENTIFICATION Similar to Northern Broken Dash but **ground color is a rich**

reddish brown. Note the **broad gray FW fringe** contrasting with the buffy HW fringe. Above, both males and females have a **rectangular flag-like yellow spot near the FW center.** Northern Broken-Dash has a yellowish-brown ground color below and brownish fringes on both wings. Black Dash male above has extensive orange on both sides of the FW black stigma

HABITAT Moist woodland edges and trails and adjacent open areas.

ABUNDANCE C along southern coastal strip north to eastern Texas and northern North Carolina. LR-U northward. Southern Florida & southern Texas—all year. 2 broods northward mainly April/May–June Aug.–Sept./early Oct.

MAJOR FOODPLANT Grasses.

COMMENTS Not that long ago this species and the Northern Broken-Dash were considered to be the same species.

	MAR	APR	MAY	JUN	JUL	AUG	SEP	OCT
WI								
NY								
NC								
LA								

Northern Broken-Dash *Wallengrenia egeremet* **Plate 61 & 62**

SIZE ≥ Tawny-edged Skipper.

SIMILAR SPECIES Little Glassywing, Dun Skipper, Black Dash, Southern Broken-Dash

IDENTIFICATION Below, ground color yellowish-brown often with a **violaceous sheen.** HW has a fairly wide, but often indistinct, cream-colored spot-band that is usually **vaguely in the shape of a "3."** Male above, usually has tawny FW margin and two-part **black stigma.** Above, both males and females have a **rectangular flag-like yellow spot near the FW center.** Below, Little Glassywing and Dun Skipper have darker brown ground colors and narrower HW postmedian bands with smaller spots. Black Dash and Southern Broken-Dash have reddish brown ground color. Distinguish worn Black Dash with brown ground color "chunky" postmedian mark as opposed to a spot-band.

HABITAT Open fields and meadows, most common in moist but not wet situations.

ABUNDANCE U-C (locally abundant). 2 broods north to Philadelphia, southern Ohio, Indiana, Illinois, Missouri, Kansas—mainly mid June–mid Sept. (Florida, Georgia, west to east Texas—April–May, Aug–Oct. 1 brood northward—late June/early July–July/early Aug.

MAJOR FOODPLANT Panic grasses (*Panicum*).

COMMENTS Along with Little Glassywing and Dun Skipper, one of the "th witches." Jane Scott claims that they're called "the witches" because it's impossible to tell which one is which!

	MAR	APR	MAY	JUN	JUL	AUG	SEP	OCT
WI								
NY								
NC								
LA								

Little Glassywing *Pompeius verna* **Plates 61 & 62**

SIZE = Tawny-edged Skipper.

SIMILAR SPECIES Dun Skipper, Northern Broken-Dash.

IDENTIFICATION Below, dark brown ground color with postmedian line of discrete pale spots. Above, dark brown with a large square (female) or rectangular (male) pale spot. Female also has a white spot *in* the cell (but this can be small). Note **white areas just before the antennal clubs.** Other similar skippers lack these white areas. Dun Skipper below has HW spot-band usually less extensive, usually lacks FW subapical white spots along costa (usually prominent in Little Glassywing). Northern Broken-Dash has a somewhat paler yellowish-brown-mauve ground color and wider postmedian band usually forming a "3."

HABITAT Moist brushy fields near woodlands, rarer in poor soil areas.

ABUNDANCE U-C. 2 broods north to Washington, DC, Missouri—May–mid June, mid/late July–Sept. 1 brood northward—mid/late June–July.

MAJOR FOODPLANT Purple top grass (*Tridens flavus*).

COMMENTS All of the witches are generally common. Some years all three swarm at the milkweeds at Ward Pound Ridge Reservation in Westchester County, New York, creating an unparalled opportunity to misidentify thousands of butterflies in a single day.

	MAR	APR	MAY	JUN	JUL	AUG	SEP	OCT
WI								
NY								
NC								
LA								

Sachem *Atalopedes campestris* **Plate 57**

SIZE = Zabulon/Hobomok Skipper.

SIMILAR SPECIES Cobweb Skipper.

IDENTIFICATION Male below, note the **squarish brown patch at center of HW bottom margin surrounded by yellow.** Broad borders are similar to Hobomok Skipper but Sachem male lacks the large brown patch at the base of the HW. Male above, the **large, black rectangular stigma** is unmistakable. Female below, very large, pale yellow postmedian chevron on the HW. Cobweb

Skipper is much smaller and flies only in the spring. Female above, note the **2 very large, white hyaline spots on the FW** and the **black patch at the center of the FW**.

HABITAT
Open disturbed fields, roadsides, suburban and urban lots, barrens

RANGE
Also, south through Mexico to Brazil.

ABUNDANCE
C-A along southern coastal strip from South Carolina west to east Texas. South Florida—all year resident; southern Georgia west to east Texas—Feb.–Nov.; C-A immigrant, Washington, DC southern West Virginia west to Kansas—mainly May–Oct Decreasing immigrant northward, mainly July–Sept. RS north to Massachusetts, southern Ontario, and Michigan.

MAJOR FOODPLANT
Bermuda Grass (*Cynodon dactylon*) and crabgrass (*Digitaria*).

COMMENTS
Widespread and often abundant. Along with Fiery Skipper an Whirlabout, one of the "three wizards."

	MAR	APR	MAY	JUN	JUL	AUG	SEP	OCT
WI								
NY								
NC								
LA								

Arogos Skipper *Atrytone arogos* Plate 63

SIZE
= Tawny-edged Skipper.

SIMILAR SPECIES
Delaware Skipper, Byssus Skipper.

IDENTIFICATION
Above, note **broad blackish borders**. Male with orange portion of FW above unmarked, female with black streak in cent of orange portion. Below, orange yellow, usually with **whi HW fringe** and **whitish HW veins**. Delaware Skipper brighter orange below, with orange or tan (not white) HW frin and without whitish veining. Byssus Skippers below usua have a paler patch in middle of HW and above have more exte sive black areas.

HABITAT
Tall-grass prairie in the Midwest; Grassy barrens, including pi flats and serpentine barrens on Atlantic Coast.

ABUNDANCE
Subspecies *A.arogos arogos*: LR. 2 broods north to No Carolina—April/May–June, Aug.–Oct. 1 brood New Jersey July (partial 2nd brood Aug–Sept.). Subspecies *A. arogos io* LU-LC. 2 broods north to Nebraska—May–early July, Aug.–Se 1 brood northward—June–July.

MAJOR FOODPLANT
Midwest, big bluestem grass (*Andropogon gerardia*); New Jers perhaps pine barrens reed grass (*Calamovilfa brevipilis*)(Cromar Dowdell, & Schweitzer, personal communication); Florida, l sided Indian grass (*Sorghastrum secundum*).

COMMENTS
Very wary; and when it decides to go, it's gone in a fla

Perhaps Ted Williams could follow its flight, but not us mere mortals. Unfortunately, with only one known extant population in North Carolina and the mismanagement of the Ocala National Forest site (burned by the U.S. Forest Service), Atlantic Coast Arogos, may soon, like Ted Williams, become only a memory. A 1996 Florida survey found Arogos Skippers at only three sites in Duval and Polk counties. I don't show it as extirpated in south Florida because it is still possible that there are remnants of the population that inhabited Jonathon Dickson State Park in Martin Co. The status of the Louisiana population is unknown. The rediscovery of this species in both central and northern New Jersey in 1995 is a bright spot.

Delaware Skipper *Anatrytone logan* Plate 63

SIZE	≤ Zabulon/Hobomok Skipper, but very variable.
SIMILAR SPECIES	European Skipper.
IDENTIFICATION	An active skipper, **clear bright unmarked yellow-orange below**. Above, orange with black borders and **black FW cell-end bar** and at least some **black veining**. Fringes orange to tan. European Skipper has short reddish antennas and is duller orange usually with some whitish overscaling and with whitish fringes.
HABITAT	Open brushy fields, moist meadows, prairies, sedge marshes, and coastal marshes.
RANGE	Also, west to Montana.
ABUNDANCE	U-C. 2 broods north to Virginia, central Illinois, Nebraska—May–mid July, late July/Aug.–Sept. 1 brood northward—late June–Aug.
MAJOR FOODPLANT	Grasses.
COMMENTS	This widespread and common skipper is often present at the same place and time as the very similar true rarities Arogos Skipper and Rare Skipper.

	MAR	APR	MAY	JUN	JUL	AUG	SEP	OCT
WI					—		—	
NY								
NC								
LA								

Byssus Skipper *Problema byssus* Plates 63 & 67

SIZE	≥ Zabulon/Hobomok Skipper.
SIMILAR SPECIES	Delaware Skipper.
IDENTIFICATION	Below bright orange to ochre, usually with a **pale area in middle of HW** but some Midwestern males are fairly evenly dull

yellow-brown. Fringes white to tan. Above, almost always with a **continuous band on FW**. Very rarely, lack of two subapical spots interrupts the band. Below, most individuals show dark shading in the FW margin.

HABITAT   Strikingly different for East and Midwest populations. A butterfly of the edges of wooded wetlands, savannas, and marshes along the Atlantic coast, while inhabiting tall-grass prairie farther west.

ABUNDANCE   LR-LC. 2 broods east—May–June, mid Aug–Oct. 1 brood Midwest—mid June–July.

MAJOR FOODPLANT   Grasses.

COMMENTS   Males will perch early in the morning and again late in the afternoon.

Rare Skipper *Problema bulenta* Plate 63

SIZE   > Zabulon/Hobomok Skipper.

SIMILAR SPECIES   Delaware Skipper, Byssus Skipper.

IDENTIFICATION   Very similar to the tremendously more common and widespread Delaware Skipper. Below, unmarked bright yellow-orange but not so bright nor so orange as Delaware Skipper. Of course, worn Delaware Skippers quickly fade in brightness! On average, Rare Skippers are larger than Delaware Skippers. This is especially true of females where there is little, if any, size overlap. On males, note the FW black cell-end bar that can often be seen clearly from below. This spot is generally not seen in Delaware Skipper both because it tends to be weaker and less distinct below and because when Delaware Skippers sit with their wings folded this spot is almost always hidden by the HW. Above, the male is a glowing golden-orange with wide black FW borders. The female above has extensive black markings. In both sexes, note the **white lines separating the abdominal segments**. Delaware Skipper is deep orange above with narrower black FW borders and has a dull-orange abdomen whose segments are not separated by white lines.

HABITAT   Brackish river tidal marshes near the coast.

ABUNDANCE   LR. 2 broods in the South—June–Aug. 1 brood New Jersey—July.

MAJOR FOODPLANT   Intertidal cordgrass (*Spartina cynosuroides*) reported from New Jersey, wild rice (*Zizania* and *Zizaniopsis*) farther south.

COMMENTS   At some locations this skipper can be common but only because the colonies are so intensely localized and the individual butterflies concentrate on flowers.

Mulberry Wing *Poanes massasoit* **Plate 65**

SIZE = Tawny-edged Skipper.

IDENTIFICATION The distinctive bright yellow patch on the reddish brown HW below is striking. Very rarely individuals are entirely suffused with the reddish-brown color below. Above, males are black with a purplish sheen when fresh (like a mulberry) and females are black with a few small white spots. The black upper surface is often visible during its low and weak flight.

HABITAT Wet meadows, open freshwater marshes, fens, or bogs.

ABUNDANCE LR-LC. 1 brood. late June/early July–early Aug.

MAJOR FOODPLANT Sedges (*Carex*).

COMMENTS Generally associated with the Black Dash.

	MAR	APR	MAY	JUN	JUL	AUG	SEP	OCT
WI								
NY								
NC								
LA								

Hobomok Skipper *Poanes hobomok* **Plate 64**

SIZE 10/16 in.

SIMILAR SPECIES Zabulon Skipper.

IDENTIFICATION Males and most females below—postmedian portion of the HW yellow with an **extensive brown patch at HW base** and **broad brown borders**. Zabulon Skipper has narrower borders and yellow within a smaller basal brown patch. Some females below (form pocahontas) are suffused with dark brown but usually retain some of the usual pattern. Distinguish from female Zabulon by lack of silvery white on the HW apex. Female pocahontas above, dark with pale spots. Note **pale cell spot**, lacking in female Zabulon. Males above can usually be distinguished from Zabulon Skipper males by the HW orange. Zabulons have the orange curved back outward toward the HW apex while Hobomoks lack this feature—remember **Hobos don't return**.

HABITAT Deciduous woodland edges and openings.

RANGE Also, south-central Colorado.

ABUNDANCE C-A. 1 brood. Mainly late May–early July.

MAJOR FOODPLANT Grasses.

COMMENTS Although this species is territorial and the males fly rapidly along the edges of trees lining woodland trails and edges, they do not appear to return to the same perch as frequently as Zabulon Skipper do. Hobomoks also don't seem as closely tied to woodland edges, often wandering farther afield than Zabulons.

	MAR	APR	MAY	JUN	JUL	AUG	SEP	OCT
WI								
NY								
NC								
LA								

Zabulon Skipper *Poanes zabulon* Plate 64

SIZE
10/16 in.

SIMILAR SPECIES
Hobomok Skipper, Clouded Skipper.

IDENTIFICATION
Male below, mainly yellow with HW post-basal **brown patch enclosing yellow at wing base**. Female below, dark rust brown with vague darker blotches. Note **silvery white HW apex**. Dark female Hobomok Skippers, and Clouded Skippers lack this mark. Dark female above, dark brown with extensive white spots on the FW but not in the cell. Female Hobomok Skipper form Pocahontas has spot in the cell.

HABITAT
Woodland openings, edges, and adjacent fields; suburban habitat Generally in moist situations.

RANGE
Also, the mountains of northeastern Mexico south to Panama

ABUNDANCE
U-C. 2 broods. Mainly May–June, late July–early Sept. RS north southern Ontario (2 records), Michigan, South Dakota (1 record

MAJOR FOODPLANT
Grasses.

COMMENTS
Unlike most of our grass-skippers, which fly close to the groun Zabulon Skippers often fly about 3 or four 4 high. The male sally forth from perches on leaves overhanging woodland tra and edges.

	MAR	APR	MAY	JUN	JUL	AUG	SEP	OCT
WI								
NY								
NC								
LA								

Aaron's Skipper *Poanes aaroni* Plate 65

SIZE
= Zabulon/Hobomok Skipper.

SIMILAR SPECIES
Broad-winged Skipper, Dion Skipper.

IDENTIFICATION
A large dingy orange-brown skipper of the salt marsh and ad cent fields. Below, note the **pale HW ray that goes the wid of the wing**, often flanked by 2 pale dots. Broad-winged Skipp is similar but has 1 or 2, well-defined white spots on the F below and is larger. Dion Skipper is usually brighter red-oran and its paler HW ray rarely goes the entire width of the wing

HABITAT
Salt and brackish and fresh-water marshes, roadside ditches.

ABUNDANCE
LR-LC. 2 broods. April/May–June, Aug.–Sept.

MAJOR FOODPLANT
Unknown.

COMMENTS — Often found nectaring outside of marshes. Range map indicates known populations but actual range may extend all along Gulf Coast.

Yehl Skipper *Poanes yehl* **Plate 65**

SIZE — = Zabulon/Hobomok Skipper.

SIMILAR SPECIES — Broad-winged Skipper.

IDENTIFICATION — Below, HW bright rusty-orange (male) or orange-brown (female) with **3 or 4 pale postmedian spots** bisected by a faint pale ray. Female above is very similar to Broad-winged Skipper but lacks the narrow yellow ray that species has at the HW outer angle. Male above looks similar to *Euphyes* but, unlike them, black border along leading edge of the HW greatly narrows near the apex.

HABITAT — Heavily wooded swamps and adjacent open areas.

ABUNDANCE — LR-U. 2 broods. Mid May–June, Aug.–mid Oct. RS north to Missouri.

MAJOR FOODPLANT — Probably cane (*Arundinaria*).

COMMENTS — The pale HW spots below become larger with wear, as do those of Broad-winged Skippers. Fresh male Yehls are rather stunning, with their bright rusty-orange color, but older individuals wear a dull yellow-orange garb.

	MAR	APR	MAY	JUN	JUL	AUG	SEP	OCT
WI								
NY								
NC								
LA								

Broad-winged Skipper *Poanes viator* **Plate 65**

SIZE — Very variable, usually > Zabulon/Hobomok Skipper.

SIMILAR SPECIES — Aaron's Skipper, Mulberry Wing.

IDENTIFICATION — A large, dull-colored, weak-flying marsh skipper. Below, dull orangish-brown with a somewhat pale ray. Usually with two pale spots below the ray and one above it. Usually **lands with its head up** and its body oriented perpendicularly to the ground. Aaron's Skipper is generally smaller and lacks the well-defined FW subapical spot(s) below that this species has. Mulberry Wing is much smaller with much sharper contrasting pattern.

HABITAT — Tidal and fresh-water marshes, especially those with tall grasses.

ABUNDANCE — **Atlantic Coast:** LC-A. 2 broods north to Virginia. The 1st, April–May (Georgia west to east Texas) or mid May–mid July (North Carolina-Virginia westward), the 2nd, Aug.–Sept./early Oct. 1 brood northward—mainly early/mid July–Aug. **North Central:** LR-U. 1 brood. Mid/late June–July/early Aug. **Gulf Coast:** LR-U. 2 broods? April–Oct.

MAJOR FOODPLANT — Common reed (*Phragmites communis*) and wild rice (*Zizania aquatica*).

COMMENTS — Historically, one population inhabited mainly tidal marshes along the Atlantic and Gulf coasts while another inhabited fresh-water marshes in the Great Lakes region. But the coastal population is now following phragmites into inland fresh-water marshes and expanding its range northwestward.

	MAR	APR	MAY	JUN	JUL	AUG	SEP	OCT
WI					—			
NY								
NC								
LA								

Palmetto Skipper *Euphyes arpa* **Plate 67**

SIZE >> Zabulon/Hobomok Skipper.

SIMILAR SPECIES Byssus Skipper.

IDENTIFICATION A large skipper, orange below with a **golden head** and mantle. Male above with a very long, narrow black stigma.

HABITAT Open pine flats with saw palmetto.

ABUNDANCE R-U. 2 broods. May–Oct. Florida Keys race (probably extinct) flew March–May, Oct.–Jan.

MAJOR FOODPLANT Saw palmetto (*Serenoa repens*).

COMMENTS Obviously foodplant availability is not the factor limiting populations of this species since saw palmetto are abundant and widespread while Palmetto Skippers are quite scarce. They are also quite wary

Palatka Skipper *Euphyes pilatka* **Plate 67**

SIZE >> Zabulon/Hobomok Skipper.

SIMILAR SPECIES Broad-winged Skipper.

IDENTIFICATION A **very large** coastal grass-skipper. **Below, rusty-brown**, fairly unicolorous but sometimes with a faint pale postmedian patch. Broad-winged Skipper is not so rusty-colored, has a FW subapical spot that Palatka Skipper lacks, and usually has a pale ray with flanking spots on the HW below.

HABITAT Brackish marshes and adjacent areas.

ABUNDANCE LU-LC. 2 broods. Mid May–mid July, mid Aug.–Sept. Possibly broods on Florida Keys.

MAJOR FOODPLANT Sawgrass (*Cladium jamaicense*).

Dion Skipper *Euphyes dion* **Plate 66**

SIZE ≥ Zabulon/Hobomok Skipper.

SIMILAR SPECIES Delaware Skipper, Broad-winged Skipper, Aaron's Skipper.

IDENTIFICATION A large wetland skipper. Bright orange to duller reddish-orange below with **1 or 2 pale rays on the HW**, the top ray usually extending the entire width of the wing. Delaware Skipper lacks pale rays and is smaller. Aaron's Skipper is duller with a ray usually extends the entire width of the wing and is flanked by pale spots. Broad-winged Skipper has a pale HW ray but is duller, its wings are more rounded, and the pale ray is flanked by pale spots.

HABITAT Calcareous fens and other alkaline to neutral wetlands from northern NJ north; bogs, roadside ditches, and other acidic wetlands from southern NJ south.

ABUNDANCE LR-U. 2 broods—Florida, southern Georgia, southern Mississippi—May, Sept.; 2 broods north to Washington, DC in the East, Illinois, Missouri in the Midwest—June–July, Aug.–Sept. 1 brood northward—mainly July. South central New Jersey—mid July–early Aug.

MAJOR FOODPLANT Sedges (*Carex*).

COMMENTS The northern populations are not only found in different habitats than the southern populations, but they also behave differently. They are very nervous and active, powerful flyers. In contrast, the southern populations seem more sluggish. Perhaps these are sibling species.

	MAR	APR	MAY	JUN	JUL	AUG	SEP	OCT
WI								
NY								
NC								
LA								

Bay Skipper *Euphyes bayensis* Not Illustrated

SIZE ≥ Zabulon/Hobomok Skipper.

SIMILAR SPECIES Dion Skipper.

IDENTIFICATION This recently described butterfly is virtually identical to Dion Skipper. Males are reported to have a slightly narrower FW stigma with slightly more extensive orange.

HABITAT Brackish marsh.

RANGE Recently described (1989) from Bay St. Louis, Hancock Co., Mississippi. Also reported from Sabine Pass, Jefferson Co., Texas.

ABUNDANCE LR. 2 broods. May, Sept.

MAJOR FOODPLANT Unknown.

COMMENTS Although this may be a valid species, the evidence so far available does not, in my opinion, force that conclusion. There are quite a few other wetland skippers that inhabit both fresh-water and brackish situations. If you travel to Bay St. Louis (or live there) and see a "Dion" Skipper in the brackish marsh, then you've seen a member of this population, whatever it is.

Dukes' Skipper *Euphyes dukesi* Plate 66

SIZE ≥ Zabulon/Hobomok Skipper.

SIMILAR SPECIES Dion Skipper.

IDENTIFICATION Below, a rich orange-brown to sooty-brown with **1 or 2 HW yellow rays** and a **black FW disc**. Above, both sexes are **quite black**, males usually with some tawny-orange along the FW costa and on the HW, females with or without 2 small white spots in the postmedian FW. Dion Skipper is not as dark below, lacks the black FW disc, and is not blackish above.

HABITAT Shady, freshwater swamps and roadside ditches.

ABUNDANCE LR-LU. 2 broods on East Coast. Florida—May–early June, Sept.–early Oct.; farther north—mid June–mid July, late July–early Sept. 2 broods lower Mississippi Valley—mid May–June, mid Aug.–early Oct. 1 brood Ohio, southern Ontario, southeastern Michigan, northern Indiana—mainly July.

MAJOR FOODPLANT Sedges (*Carex* and *Rhynchospora*).

COMMENTS Rather slow flying.

	MAR	APR	MAY	JUN	JUL	AUG	SEP	OCT
WI								
NY								
NC								
LA								

Black Dash *Euphyes conspicua* **Plate 66**

SIZE = Zabulon/Hobomok Skipper.

SIMILAR SPECIES Northern Broken-Dash, Southern Broken-Dash.

IDENTIFICATION A rusty-yellow-brown skipper with a characteristic chunky postmedian HW patch. Northern Broken-Dash is smaller and is more reddish below. Southern Broken-Dash range doesn't overlap.

HABITAT Wet meadows and fresh-water marshes.

ABUNDANCE LR-LC. 1 brood. Late June/July–early Aug.

MAJOR FOODPLANT Sedges (*Carex*).

COMMENTS Usually flies with Mulberry Wing. The presence of swamp milkweed is a good indicator for these species.

	MAR	APR	MAY	JUN	JUL	AUG	SEP	OCT
WI								
NY								
NC								
LA								

Berry's Skipper *Euphyes berryi* **Plate 67**

SIZE ≥ Zabulon/Hobomok Skipper.

SIMILAR SPECIES Byssus Skipper, Palmetto Skipper.

IDENTIFICATION Below, dull brownish-orange with **whitened HW veins**. Male above with much orange, thin FW stigma and a black ray coming in about 1/3 the FW length from the distal border. Females darker with a FW cell spot and some tawny on the HW. Palmetto

Skippers are brighter yellow-orange below, without such pronounced white veins (in some light, Palmetto Skipper HW veins do appear paler), and have golden-yellow heads that Berry's Skippers lack. Byssus Skipper below can have pronounced whitening of the HW veins but usually has a pale HW postmedian patch that Berry's Skipper lack. Female Palmetto Skippers above lack the FW cell-spot and the tawny HW.

HABITAT Swamps and swamp edges.

ABUNDANCE LR. 2 broods. March–May, Aug.–Oct. Generally most common late Sept.–early Oct. Whether there is a resident population along the North Carolina coast is unknown. The North Carolina portion of the range map is based upon only 2 records, an old one from Dare Co. and a recent report from Carteret Co.

MAJOR FOODPLANT Unknown.

COMMENTS A rarely encountered, very poorly known skipper. Most commonly found in Florida, near Daytona Beach, Volusia Co., in Big Cypress Preserve, Collier Co., and in parts of the panhandle.

Two-spotted Skipper *Euphyes bimacula* **Plate 66**

SIZE ≥ Zabulon/Hobomok Skipper.

IDENTIFICATION Orange to brownish-orange below with **paler veining** and striking **white ray along HW trailing margin**. Above, male has restricted dull orange on both sides of the stigma.

HABITAT Wet acid-soil areas such as bogs, acid marshes, and meadows with sedges.

RANGE Also, west to northeastern Colorado.

ABUNDANCE LR. 2 broods north to southeastern Virginia—May–mid June, mid July–mid Aug.; 1 brood northward—mid/late June–early/mid July.

MAJOR FOODPLANT Sedges (*Carex*).

COMMENTS Perhaps the rarest and most local of any northern butterfly with an extensive range. The very widely scattered colonies generally have a very low population density—usually only a few individuals are seen. Extensive wetland draining has made this species even rarer than it was historically.

	MAR	APR	MAY	JUN	JUL	AUG	SEP	OCT
WI								
NY								
NC								
LA								

Dun Skipper *Euphyes vestris* **Plates 61 & 62**

SIZE = Tawny-edged Skipper.

SIMILAR SPECIES Little Glassywing, Northern Broken-Dash, Clouded Skipper (above).

SKIPPERS

IDENTIFICATION Dark brown all over. Above, male is **all dark brown** with black stigma. In many populations, the **head is bright golden-orange**. Female is all dark brown above with **2 small pale spots**. Little Glassywing has a better defined HW spot-band, white at base of antennal clubs, and is very different above. Northern Broken-Dash has paler yellow-brown ground color and HW post-median band in the shape of a 3. Northern Broken-Dash female above has distinctive elongated pale spot past the FW cell. On the FW above, Dun Skippers lack the 3 white, outwardly curving, subapical spots that Clouded Skippers have (female Duns often have 2 white FW subapical spots that do not curve outward).

HABITAT Moist open situations near deciduous woodlands.

ABUNDANCE C-A. 2 broods north to north central New Jersey, Ohio, Indiana, Illinois, Missouri, Nebraska—1st brood Florida, southern Georgia,—mid/late March–May; North Carolina, West Virginia, southeastern Penn., southern Ohio west to Kansas—mid May–June/early July; Indiana, Illinois, Nebraska—June–July; 2nd brood Aug.–Sept. brood northward—late June/July–early/mid Aug.

MAJOR FOODPLANT Sedges (*Carex*).

COMMENTS Probably because it tolerates much drier conditions than its relatives, this is the most common and widespread *Euphyes*.

	MAR	APR	MAY	JUN	JUL	AUG	SEP	OCT
WI								
NY								
NC								
LA								

Monk Skipper *Asbolis capucinus* Plate 71

SIZE ≤ Silver-spotted Skipper.

IDENTIFICATION A very, very large grass-skipper. Tawny dark reddish-brown below and rich chestnut above, makes one think of a giant *Euphyes*.

HABITAT Gardens and woodland edges near palms.

ABUNDANCE U. All year resident.

MAJOR FOODPLANT Palms (Arecaceae).

COMMENTS A Cuban species that became established in the Miami area 1947. As Minno and Emmel point out, the widespread use palms for urban and suburban landscaping in southern Flori has helped this species' spread.

Dusted Skipper *Atrytonopsis hianna* Plate 71

SIZE ≥ Zabulon/Hobomok Skipper.

SIMILAR SPECIES Female Zabulon Skipper, cloudywings, Common Roadside Skipper, Clouded Skipper.

IDENTIFICATION A large dark grass-skipper with much frosting of the marginal wing areas below. When (usually) present, the **white spot at the base of the HW below** is diagnostic. Its **"masked" appearance**, due to its dark eye being bordered by the white palps below and a white eye stripe above, separates this species from our other dark skippers with frosting. Populations in the southeast (*A.h.loammi*) have white postmedian spots on the HW below.

HABITAT Dry fields, prairies, barrens, and power-line cuts in association with its foodplant.

RANGE Also, west to New Mexico, Colorado, and Wyoming.

ABUNDANCE LR-U. 2 broods Florida—mainly March–April, and Oct. 1 brood northward. North to Virginia, Ohio, Missouri, Kansas —late April–early June; northward—mid/late May–mid June.

MAJOR FOODPLANT Bluestem grasses (*Andropogon*).

COMMENTS Widespread but often local, the few individuals present in a bluestem field are usually easy to see because this skipper is active over a wide area.

	MAR	APR	MAY	JUN	JUL	AUG	SEP	OCT
WI			▬	▬				
NY								
NC		▬	▬					
LA		▬						

Roadside-Skippers
(genus *Amblyscirtes*)

The great pleasure derived from learning the roadside-skippers is fortunately as close as most of us will get to understanding sado-masochism. Under similar species, I have listed the species that most closely resemble each other, but the other roadside-skippers are not far off! For many species, the preferred habitat is the grass-woods interface, a habitat that roadways do an excellent job of creating—hence the name roadside-skipper. Roadside-skippers typically hold their wings open with the FWs held almost perpendicularly to the flat HWs (other skippers hold the FWs at a much more oblique angle). Also, most species have strongly checkered fringes and have their abdomens prominently ringed with black (or gray) and white.

Linda's Roadside-Skipper *Amblyscirtes linda* **Plate 69**

SIZE ≥ Least Skipper.

SIMILAR SPECIES Common Roadside-Skipper, Bell's Roadside-Skipper.

IDENTIFICATION	Below, very similar to Common Roadside-Skipper. Note that the **entire HW is "frosted"** (silvery-gray scales) and that there are **copper-colored scales on the FW disc**. Above, note the smattering of copper-colored scales on the FW. Common Roadside-Skipper has the leading margin of the HW below unfrosted and lacks the extensive copper-colored scales both above and below. Bell's Roadside-Skipper is darker, not so frosted, and lacks the copper-colored scales.
HABITAT	Rich, moist, woodlands.
ABUNDANCE	LR. 2 broods. Mid April–early June, July–early Sept.
MAJOR FOODPLANT	Broadleaf uniola (*Uniola latifolia*) and probably other grasses.
COMMENTS	Named for one of H.A. Freeman's daughters. Very closely related to (some believe conspecific with) the more western Bronze Roadside-Skipper (although habitats used are quite different).

Pepper and Salt Skipper *Amblyscirtes hegon* Plate 69

SIZE	= Least Skipper.
IDENTIFICATION	Below, olive-tinged gray-brown ground with prominent cream-colored HW postmedian band. Above, with more extensive white spotting than Common, Bell's, or Linda's roadside-skippers.
HABITAT	Edges, and openings within, of northern or mountain woodlands, especially along grass-lined watercourses.
ABUNDANCE	LR-U. 1 brood + partial second north to Virginia and Missouri–mid April–May, rare partial July–Aug. 1 brood northward–mainly May–June.
MAJOR FOODPLANT	Grasses.
COMMENTS	Most common in New England.

	MAR	APR	MAY	JUN	JUL	AUG	SEP	OCT
WI								
NY								
NC								
LA								

Lace-winged Roadside-Skipper *Amblyscirtes aesculapius* Plate 68

SIZE	= Tawny-edged Skipper.
IDENTIFICATION	An arresting underside pattern of **cobwebby white veins and median and postmedian lines** makes this roadside-skipper an easy call.
HABITAT	Moist woodlands (mainly deciduous) with cane.
ABUNDANCE	U. 2 broods. Mid April–mid June, mid/late July–mid/late Sept.
MAJOR FOODPLANT	Cane (*Arundinaria*).
COMMENTS	The commonest of the cane-feeding roadside-skippers.

	MAR	APR	MAY	JUN	JUL	AUG	SEP	OCT
WI								
NY								
NC			▬		▬			
LA								

Carolina Roadside-Skipper *Amblyscirtes carolina* **Plate 68**

SIZE ≥ Least Skipper.

SIMILAR SPECIES ♀ Fiery Skipper.

IDENTIFICATION This small **dirty-yellow roadside-skipper with darker chestnut spots and veins** is closely associated with cane brakes. Usually has a row of black spots on the abdomen. Above, black with white spots on both FW and HW. Female Fiery Skipper below has longer, more pointed wings, darker spots are brown or black, not chestnut, and lacks black spots on the abdomen.

HABITAT Moist woodlands (mainly deciduous) with cane.

ABUNDANCE LR-U. Probably 3 broods. April–May, June–July and Aug.–Sept.

MAJOR FOODPLANT Cane (*Arundinaria*).

COMMENTS Generally rarer than Lace-winged Roadside-Skipper but more common than Reversed Roadside-Skipper.

	MAR	APR	MAY	JUN	JUL	AUG	SEP	OCT
WI								
NY								
NC		—		—	—			
LA								

Reversed Roadside-Skipper *Amblyscirtes reversa* **Plate 68**

SIZE ≥ Least Skipper.

SIMILAR SPECIES Carolina Roadside-Skipper.

IDENTIFICATION Essentially the reverse of a Carolina Roadside-Skipper. Basic ground color below is **chestnut with yellow veins** and other pale markings. Often has a wavy yellow ray splitting pale spots. Above, similar to Carolina Roadside-Skipper but FW has 2 white cell-spots usually separate while Carolina has these spots fused.

HABITAT Moist woodlands (mainly pine) with cane, Harry LeGrand reports that it is probably more associated with longleaf or pond pine wetlands that the other cane-feeding roadside-skippers.

ABUNDANCE LR-LU. Probably 3 broods. April–May, June–July, Aug.–Sept.

MAJOR FOODPLANT Cane (*Arundinaria*).

COMMENTS Reports from southern Illinois and central Arkansas may be of strays or transient populations. Previously considered to be a color phase of Carolina Roadside-Skipper, this is one of the very few species found in our region that I have not yet seen.

	MAR	APR	MAY	JUN	JUL	AUG	SEP	OCT
WI								
NY								
NC			—			—		
LA								

Nysa Roadside-Skipper *Amblyscirtes nysa* Plate 68

SIZE = Least Skipper.

IDENTIFICATION The **mottled pattern below** nysally distinguishes this species from our other roadside-skippers (to paraphrase Klots).

HABITAT Dry rocky gulches and suburban and urban lawns and gardens

ABUNDANCE R-U. Probably 2 broods. May–mid Oct, mainly July–Aug. RS to southeastern Nebraska (1 record).

MAJOR FOODPLANT Grasses.

Common Roadside-Skipper *Amblyscirtes vialis* Plate 6

SIZE = Least Skipper.

SIMILAR SPECIES Dusted Skipper, female Zabulon Skipper, other roadside-skipper

IDENTIFICATION A **very small black** skipper. Below, frosted on the outer por tions of the wings. FW subapical spots are usually wider at cost margin, tending to form a white wedge. Note **strongly check ered fringes**. Dusted and Zabulon Skippers are much larger ar lack checkered fringes. See other roadside-skippers.

HABITAT Roadsides and other edge areas where woodlands meet gras lands. Barrens.

ABUNDANCE R-LC. 2 broods (the second brood apparently partial ar scarce)—mainly April–May, June/July–Aug./Sept. Massachuse west to South Dakota and northward, mainly June and Augus

MAJOR FOODPLANT Grasses.

COMMENTS Although widespread, this species is seldom really very con mon. In fact, over much of its range it is a real rarity. Since appears to be a habitat generalist, this rarity is a puzzle. Ve rarely individuals lack the frosting below, creating confusion.

	MAR	APR	MAY	JUN	JUL	AUG	SEP	OCT
WI			▬▬		—	▬ ■	—	
NY								
NC		—			—			
LA								

Celia's Roadside-Skipper *Amblyscirtes celia* Plate 6

SIZE ≥ Least Skipper.

SIMILAR SPECIES Bell's Roadside-Skipper, Common Roadside-Skipper, Lin Roadside-Skipper.

IDENTIFICATION Overall appearance below is dark grayish-brown. Pale spots

HW are more developed than on Common or Linda's roadside-skippers. Above, brown with a few pale spots, often including a small spot near the end of the FW cell. Very similar to Bell's Roadside-Skipper, with which it was long confused. In general, Bell's is blacker both below, and especially above but worn Bell's become browner. On the HW below, Celia's postmedian spots tend to be separate and well-defined, while Bell's postmedian spots are usually indistinct and form a zigzag line. Above, look at the inner of the (usually) 2 median pale spots. In Celia's this spot is irregularly shaped while in Bell's, it usually is shaped like a "V" or "U" with the bottom portion of the "V" or "U" facing inward. Also, Bell's lacks the FW spot that Celia's often has.

HABITAT Woodland trails, creek bottoms, moist open woodland, suburban lawns and gardens.

ABUNDANCE U. Probably 2 long broods, possibly 3. April/May–early June, late June–early Sept.

MAJOR FOODPLANT Grasses.

COMMENTS Can be found in H.A. Freeman's yard in Garland, Texas and named for another of H.A. Freeman's daughters.

Bell's Roadside-Skipper *Amblyscirtes belli* **Plate 69**

SIZE ≥ Least Skipper.

SIMILAR SPECIES Celia's Roadside-Skipper, Pepper and Salt Skipper, Common Roadside-Skipper.

IDENTIFICATION Below, **quite black**, often with a purplish sheen but the **HW apex area is not frosted**. HW pale spots are often indistinct, forming a zigzag partial postmedian line. Unlike Common Roadside-Skipper, the FW subapical white spots are not usually much wider at the costal margin. See Celia's Roadside-Skipper for separation from that species.

HABITAT Trails through moist, rich woodlands, woodland creeksides.

ABUNDANCE LR-LU. 2 broods. April/May–early June, July–early Sept. (mainly Aug.). RS along Ohio River to Ohio.

MAJOR FOODPLANT Grasses, including broad-leaved uniola (*Uniola latifolia*) and Johnson grass (*Sorghum halepense*). (I have seen females repeatedly laying eggs on the underside of blades of the latter grass in McKinney, Texas.)

COMMENTS Females lay eggs on the underside of young leaves. An easy place to see this species is the Heard Museum in McKinney, Texas.

Dusky Roadside-Skipper *Amblyscirtes alternata* **Plate 68**

SIZE = Least Skipper.

SIMILAR SPECIES Common, Linda's, Celia's, Bell's roadside-skippers.

IDENTIFICATION Small and blackish with very few markings. Below, **bottom 2/3 of HW frosted with bluish scales**. Above, brown with a purplish sheen and with the only pale spots being a few faint FW subapical spots. **Note the blunt antennal clubs, without a tapered extension (apiculus)**. Similar roadside-skippers have antennal clubs that taper at their ends.

HABITAT Open pine flats with low grasses.

ABUNDANCE R. 2 broods. Mainly late March–May, Aug–Sept.

MAJOR FOODPLANT Unknown, but presumably grasses.

COMMENTS The fact that there are almost no records of this delightful little butterfly from most of Louisiana probably says more about the distribution of butterfliers than it does about the distribution of this species.

	MAR	APR	MAY	JUN	JUL	AUG	SEP	OCT
WI								
NY								
NC								
LA								

Eufala Skipper *Lerodea eufala* **Plate 55**

SIZE = Tawny-edged Skipper.

SIMILAR SPECIES Three-spotted Skipper, Swarthy Skipper, Little Glassywing, Tawny-edged Skipper.

IDENTIFICATION A small, grayish-brown nondescript skipper with a **pale body**. Can often be identified at a distance because it frequently gives quick "wing-claps" after landing. Below, often with **faint trace of a pale HW postmedian band vaguely shaped like a "3"**. There are a series of 3 white spots on the FW subapex (visible from above and below) that Swarthy Skipper lacks. Above, FW cell often with 1 or 2 small pale spots. Distinguish from Little Glassywing by the less extensive white spots above, the much paler gray-brown ground color below, and the narrower wings. Swarthy Skipper is darker with pale veining. Three-spotted Skipper is browner, usually with a more developed HW postmedian spot-band below, with longer antennas, and usually with brighter orange-tawny on the costal margin of the FW above.

HABITAT A wide variety of open situations.

RANGE Also, Cuba, Jamaica and south through Mexico to Argentina.

ABUNDANCE U-C Florida and the Gulf Coast—Feb.–Oct. Regular late summer immigrant north to Virginia, Missouri, Kansas. Increasingly rare northward. RS north to New Jersey (3 recent records), Ohio (1 record), Michigan, Wisconsin, North Dakota.

MAJOR FOODPLANT Grasses.

	MAR	APR	MAY	JUN	JUL	AUG	SEP	OCT
WI								
NY								
NC								
LA								

Twin-spot Skipper *Oligoria maculata* **Plate 70**

SIZE = Zabulon/Hobomok Skipper.

SIMILAR SPECIES Brazilian Skipper, Clouded Skipper (above), Dun Skipper (above).

IDENTIFICATION Note the **3 bold white spots on the rich-brown HW below, 2 together (the twins), 1 apart.** Some individuals have these spots reduced. Brazilian Skipper is much larger and has bold white or translucent HW spots that angle outward. Above, Dun and Clouded skippers are similar, see them for discussion.

HABITAT Pinelands and wetlands.

ABUNDANCE U-C. All year south Florida. 2 broods northward. North Florida, immediate Gulf Coast—April–Oct.; northward—mid/late May–late June, early Aug.–mid Sept. RS north to northern Mississippi and Georgia, Maryland and New Jersey (1 report).

MAJOR FOODPLANT Unknown.

COMMENTS Thistles are a favorite nectar source.

	MAR	APR	MAY	JUN	JUL	AUG	SEP	OCT
WI								
NY								
NC								
LA								

Brazilian Skipper *Calpodes ethlius* **Plate 71**

SIZE >> Zabulon/Hobomok Skipper.

SIMILAR SPECIES Twin-spot Skipper.

IDENTIFICATION This very large grass-skipper (about the size of Hoary Edge) is a rich reddish-tinged brown below with **3 or 4 large white or translucent spots in an angled line on the HW below.**

HABITAT Wetlands and suburban and urban gardens with cannas.

RANGE Also, West Indies and southern Texas south to Argentina.

ABUNDANCE U. All year resident south Florida. R-U north Florida and Houston area—May–Oct. R immigrant north to North Carolina, Dallas area—Aug.–Oct. Irregular immigrant to southern Louisiana. RS north to New Jersey, Massachusetts (1 record), southern Ontario (1 recent record), Ohio (1 record), Missouri, and Nebraska (1 record).

MAJOR FOODPLANT Cannas (*Canna*).

COMMENTS Brazilian Skippers are one of our few crepuscular butterflies, although they certainly also can be seen in the middle of the day. But, these powerful flyers are difficult to follow as the buzz in and out of canna stands. It is often easier to locate th caterpillars, rolled up in a canna leaf. In the late 1800s and earl 1900s, cannas became a rage in the eastern United State Consequently, Brazilian Skipper populations exploded, an there are many old records from that time period from far nort of their current range. But, gardeners soon tired of canna because something was eating them and making them look ver ragged! But a moth, not Brazilian Skipper, was to blame. Aft the canna fad collapsed, Brazilian Skippers fell back to the more historical range. Today, cannas are becoming more pop lar again, and Brazilian Skippers are on the move. Become butterfly gardener and encourage this trend.

	MAR	APR	MAY	JUN	JUL	AUG	SEP	OCT
WI								
NY								
NC								
LA								

Salt Marsh Skipper *Panoquina panoquin* **Plate 70**

SIZE = Zabulon/Hobomok Skipper.

IDENTIFICATION A very long-winged, yellow-brown skipper with **paler yellow veini** and **a cream-colored streak distal to the HW cell below**. Note **dark line running along the side of the abdomen**. This, along w the very long wings is characteristic of panoquins.

HABITAT Salt marshes and adjacent fields.

ABUNDANCE U-A. Florida and Texas, probably 3 broods—March–Oct broods northward. Gulf Coast—April/May–July, July–Se Northward—mainly June, Aug–Sept.

MAJOR FOODPLANT Saltgrass (*Distichlis spicata*).

COMMENTS Recently found for the first time on the southern Connecticut cc

	MAR	APR	MAY	JUN	JUL	AUG	SEP	OCT
WI								
NY								
NC								
LA								

Obscure Skipper *Panoquina panoquinoides* **Plate**

SIZE = Tawny-edged Skipper.

SIMILAR SPECIES Twin-spot Skipper, Salt Marsh Skipper, Three-spotted Skipp

IDENTIFICATION This tiny inhabitant of salt marshes is smaller than Salt M Skipper and duller brown. Like other panoquins, it has a line running along the side of its abdomen and has paler v ing. On the HW below there are usually **2 small white s** in the lower postmedian area. The intensity of these spots varies from bold, to obvious (as in the individual on plate 70), to faint, to absent. Unlike Salt Marsh Skipper, there is no cream-colored streak on the HW below. Twin-spot Skipper is larger, has a richer, reddish-brown ground color, lacks paler veining, and has 3 FW subapical white spots (Obscure Skipper has 2). Three-spotted Skipper has longer antennas, usually has more white spots in the postmedian band and has 3 FW subapical spots.

HABITAT	Salt marshes and adjacent areas.
RANGE	Also, south through the West Indies and Mexico to South America.
ABUNDANCE	U-C. All year resident.
MAJOR FOODPLANT	Saltgrass (*Distichlis spicata*).

Ocola Skipper *Panoquina ocola* Plate 70

SIZE	≥ Zabulon/Hobomok Skipper.
SIMILAR SPECIES	Little Glassywing.
IDENTIFICATION	Note the long and narrow wings, Plain, dull yellowish-brown below with **distal one-quarter of wings darker brown**. Sometimes with purple sheen when fresh. Note the **striped abdomen**. Above, the white or yellowish median pale spot is bullet-shaped. Little Glassywing doesn't have the distal one-quarter of its wings below sharply darker and lacks the striped abdomen.
HABITAT	Almost any open moist areas, including salt marsh, open pine woodlands, and gardens.
RANGE	Also, south through the West Indies and Mexico to South America.
ABUNDANCE	C-A north to Georgia and the immediate Gulf Coast. All year south Florida, northward most common Aug.–Oct. Decreasing but regular immigrant northward to Washington, DC, southern West Virginia and southeastern Arkansas. RS north to Massachusetts (2 recent records), Ontario (1 recent record), northern Indiana, Missouri.
MAJOR FOODPLANT	Aquatic and semiaquatic grasses.
COMMENTS	A very variable immigrant northward, in some years there are major population explosions and migrations of this skipper. In recent years this species has become more common northward than it has been for a long time.

	MAR	APR	MAY	JUN	JUL	AUG	SEP	OCT
WI								
NY								
NC								
LA								

Giant-Skippers
(subfamily Megathyminae)

The aptly named giant-skippers are big, fat, and powerful. If you are so luck as to have one whirr by you, you will hear the quite audible sound made b their wingbeats. There are numerous species of these impressive butterflies in the Southwest, but only two species in the East.

Yucca Giant-Skipper *Megathymus yuccae* Plate 71

SIZE	≥ Silver-spotted Skipper.
IDENTIFICATION	A huge, big-bodied skipper. Very dark brown-black below wi some marginal frosting, a white spot near the leading edge of t HW, and tan-yellow HW fringe.
HABITAT	Open situations with yuccas, especially pine flats and coastal dune
RANGE	Also west to southern California and northern Mexico.
ABUNDANCE	R-U. 1 brood. Mid March–April.
MAJOR FOODPLANT	Yucca.
COMMENTS	Many active butterfliers have never seen a wild adult. It is us ally much easier to find caterpillars by looking for the you caterpillars' silk nests among the yucca leaf tips or the ol caterpillar's silk-covered tubes to the yucca roots.

	MAR	APR	MAY	JUN	JUL	AUG	SEP	OCT
WI								
NY								
NC								
LA								

Cofaqui Giant-Skipper *Megathymus cofaqui* Plate

SIZE	= Silver-spotted Skipper.
SIMILAR SPECIES	Yucca Giant-Skipper.
IDENTIFICATION	Similar to Yucca Giant-Skipper but HW below is paler g white spot near the leading margin is much less prominent, there are a variable number of other small white spots in postmedian area.
HABITAT	Open situations with yuccas, especially pine flats and coastal du
ABUNDANCE	R. 2 broods Florida—March–April, Sept.–Oct.; 1 brood Georg July–Aug.
MAJOR FOODPLANT	Yucca.
COMMENTS	Even less known and seen than Yucca Giant-Skipper.

Species Occurring in the East Only as Strays

Cuban Kite-Swallowtail *Eurytides celadon* Not Illustrated

SIZE	< Black Swallowtail.
SIMILAR SPECIES	Zebra Swallowtail.
IDENTIFICATION	Above, basal area of FW has more extensive white than does Zebra Swallowtail. Note the **uneven FW marginal band**. In Zebra Swallowtail this band is smooth. **Lacks red HW median stripe** below that Zebra Swallowtail has.
HABITAT	As a stray, could occur in any habitat.
RANGE	Cuba.
ABUNDANCE	Two reports, neither certain. If it occurs in our area at all, it is as an extremely rare stray to southern Florida. Most likely in May, during its major flight in Cuba.
MAJOR FOODPLANT	Not known.

Baird's Swallowtail *Papilio bairdi* Not Illustrated

SIZE	= Black Swallowtail.
SIMILAR SPECIES	Black Swallowtail.
IDENTIFICATION	The orange-red HW eyespot has a black spot within it that is flattened and extends to the inner edge of the HW. Black Swallowtails (and Anise Swallowtails) have this black spot centered within the orange-red spot.
HABITAT	Grasslands.
RANGE	Also western U.S.
ABUNDANCE	RS east to Valley and Buffalo Counties, Nebraska.
MAJOR FOODPLANT	Wild tarragon (*Artemisia dracunculus*).
COMMENTS	Baird's Swallowtail has usually been considered a separate species from Old World Swallowtail (*Papilio machaon*), but recent work by Felix Sperling comparing proteins and mitochondrial DNA strongly suggests that these populations should be grouped together.

Anise Swallowtail *Papilio zelicaon* Not Illustrated

SIZE	= Black Swallowtail.
SIMILAR SPECIES	Black Swallowtail, Baird's Swallowtail.
IDENTIFICATION	Yellow-form Anise Swallowtails have much more extensive yellow than do Black Swallowtails. They can usually be distinguished from

Yellow-form Baird's Swallowtail by the centered black spot in the HW orange-red eye-spot. Black-form Anise Swallowtails (nitra) are more problematical. These tend to have a single row of yellow abdominal spots, while Black Swallowtails usually have a double row.

HABITAT	A wide variety of open situations.
RANGE	Western North America.
ABUNDANCE	RS to eastern North Dakota.
MAJOR FOODPLANT	Introduced sweet fennel (*Foeniculum vulgare*), others in the carrot family (umbelliferae), and recently, citrus.
COMMENTS	The switch to sweet fennel has made this butterfly much more common on the West Coast.

Thoas Swallowtail *Papilio thoas* Not Illustrated

SIZE	≤ Eastern Tiger Swallowtail.
SIMILAR SPECIES	Giant Swallowtail.
IDENTIFICATION	Extremely similar to Giant Swallowtail. In Thoas Swallowtails the outer margins of the spots in FW median spot-band tend to be straight while in Giant Swallowtails the margins usually bulge outward.
HABITAT	Open situations in the tropics and subtropics.
RANGE	Mexico through South America.
ABUNDANCE	Reported as RS to eastern Texas and southern Oklahoma.
MAJOR FOODPLANT	Piperaceae.

Ornythion Swallowtail *Papilio ornythion* Not Illustrated

SIZE	≤ Eastern Tiger Swallowtail.
SIMILAR SPECIES	Giant Swallowtail.
IDENTIFICATION	Above, yellow bands are duller than on Giant Swallowtails and unlike Giant Swallowtail, **bands do not form an X near the FW subapex**. Ornythion Swallowtails lack yellow in the tail while Giant Swallowtails almost always have yellow in the tail. Below, the **median band of rusty-colored spots is complete**. Giant Swallowtails have only two central reddish spots.
RANGE	Northern Mexico south to Guatemala.
ABUNDANCE	Strays north into the Rio Grande Valley of Texas. RS north eastern Kansas.
MAJOR FOODPLANT	Citrus.

Androgeus Swallowtail *Papilio androgeus* Not Illustrated

SIZE	≥ Eastern Tiger Swallowtail.
SIMILAR SPECIES	Giant Swallowtail (male), Pipevine Swallowtail (female).
IDENTIFICATION	Males: note the extremely wide yellow bands on the FW and especially on the HW above covering the entire base of HW. Below, FW lacks cream-colored marginal spots that G

Swallowtail has. Female is dark with iridescent blue area on HW above and **5 short pointed tails**.

HABITAT	Overgrown citrus plantations.
RANGE	Tropical Americas. Formerly found in Broward and Dade Counties, Florida.
ABUNDANCE	There is no current population in our region. Formerly April–Oct.
MAJOR FOODPLANT	Citrus.
COMMENTS	A colony of this tropical species became established in southern Florida in 1976 and then disappeared by 1983. May occur as a stray or become established again.

Two-tailed Swallowtail *Papilio multicaudata* Not Illustrated

SIZE	= Eastern Tiger Swallowtail.
SIMILAR SPECIES	Eastern Tiger Swallowtail.
IDENTIFICATION	Note the **2 tails**, rather than the one of Eastern Tiger Swallowtail. Above, HW cell-end bar is weak and thin, or absent and black stripes are narrow. Eastern Tiger Swallowtail has thick, bold HW cell-end bar and wider black stripes.
HABITAT	Moist canyons, suburban gardens.
RANGE	Western United States south to Guatemala.
ABUNDANCE	RS east to eastern Nebraska, central South and North Dakota.
MAJOR FOODPLANT	Many Rosaceae and Oleaceae.

White Angled-Sulphur *Anteos clorinde* Plate 12

SIZE	≥ Cloudless Sulphur.
SIMILAR SPECIES	Cloudless Sulphur, Yellow Angled-Sulphur, Lyside Sulphur.
IDENTIFICATION	Stray only. Seen well, the reticulated greenish-white underside with prominent veining, and curved wing shape, distinguish angled-sulphurs from phoebis. Above, white with a bright yellow patch on the FW. Lyside Sulphurs which look similar below, also can be white above with bright yellow patches on the FWs, but White Angled-Sulphurs are **much** larger and have **angled wings**. Yellow Angled-Sulphur is similar below (but has a more prominent brown bar along the wing bases) but is bright yellow above.
HABITAT	Tropical scrub and disturbed areas, but could occur anywhere as a stray.
RANGE	West Indies and Mexico south through tropical Americas.
ABUNDANCE	1 report from Kansas (Sedgewick Co.).
MAJOR FOODPLANT	Cassias.
COMMENTS	A very large white sulphur with a very powerful flight. I recently drove in tandem with one for about a mile as it flew parallel to the road at 18 miles per hour.

SPECIES OCCURRING IN THE EAST ONLY AS STRAYS

Yellow Angled-Sulphur *Anteos maerula* Plate 12

SIZE ≥ Cloudless Sulphur.

SIMILAR SPECIES Cloudless Sulphur.

IDENTIFICATION Seen well, the reticulated greenish-white underside with prominent veining, and curved wing shape, distinguish angled-sulphurs from phoebis. Above bright (male) or dull (female) yellow.

HABITAT Generally distributed in open tropical areas, as a stray it could occur anywhere.

RANGE West Indies and Mexico south to Peru.

ABUNDANCE Rare stray to the Florida Keys and Mississippi (1 record).

MAJOR FOODPLANT Cassias.

COMMENTS A very large yellow sulphur with a very powerful flight.

Orbed Sulphur *Phoebis orbis* Not Illustrated

SIZE = Cloudless Sulphur.

SIMILAR SPECIES Cloudless Sulphur, Statira Sulphur, White Angled-Sulphur.

IDENTIFICATION Stray only. Above, male is pale yellowish-white with a bright orange patch at the FW base. Female deep orange.

RANGE Cuba and Hispaniola.

ABUNDANCE RS, 1 record (Cuban subspecies), April 25, 1973, Big Pine Key, Florida.

MAJOR FOODPLANT *Poinciana*.

Boisduval's Yellow *Eurema boisduvaliana* Plate 10

SIZE ≤ Cabbage White.

SIMILAR SPECIES Sleepy Orange, Little Yellow, Mexican Yellow.

IDENTIFICATION Note "tails," bright orange-yellow above, yellow below. Sleepy Orange is deep orange above and lacks "tails." Little Yellow is smaller and below lacks tails and HW diagonal line. Mexican Yellow is pale yellow to white above, has a more angular "face" on the FW above.

HABITAT Tropical forest and scrub.

RANGE West Indies and Mexico south to Costa Rica.

ABUNDANCE RS, 1 record Sept. 20, 1973, Stock Island, Florida.

MAJOR FOODPLANT Unknown.

COMMENTS May be increasing its range in the West Indies; if so, more strays to south Florida are possible.

Shy Yellow *Eurema messalina* Plate 10

SIZE ≤ Little Yellow.

SIMILAR SPECIES Little Yellow, Mimosa Yellow.

IDENTIFICATION White above with a narrow FW black border (visible through wing). Below there is a **black subapical spot on the FW** the FW disc is white. Some Little Yellows are white above, but they lack the strong black subapical FW spot below and their FW discs are not cleanly white.

HABITAT Edges of tropical hardwood hammocks and thickets.

RANGE West Indies.

ABUNDANCE Dubiously recorded from Florida in October, 1877, but given the proximity of the Bahamas, where it is common, who knows?

MAJOR FOODPLANT *Cassia.*

COMMENTS Even more than Mimosa Yellow, the aptly named Shy Yellow remains inaccessible, weaving deftly through the brushy edges of woodlands on indefatigable wing muscles. Perhaps praying for it to alight will work for you.

Disguised Scrub-Hairstreak *Strymon limenia* **Plate 21**

SIZE < Banded Hairstreak.

SIMILAR SPECIES Mallow Scrub-Hairstreak.

IDENTIFICATION This stray is very similar to the common Mallow Scrub-Hairstreak but is more brown than gray (but worn Mallow Scrub-Hairstreaks can appear brownish). Note the characteristic HW cell-end bar that looks like a pale continuation of the postmedian band, being much thinner and fainter than the distal 2 spots and, especially, the **extra black spot along the HW trailing margin**. In addition, note the HW black cell-spot, as black and prominent as the 2 black spots on the HW leading margin. Mallow Scrub-Hairstreak usually has this spot somewhat paler, less prominent, and with some reddish scales. Also, look at the 2 black spots on the HW leading margin. Disguised Scrub-Hairstreak has the more distal spot larger while Mallow Scrub-Hairstreak has the 2 spots about the same size. If you are exceptionally lucky and the butterfly opens its wings, note the diagnostic **red outer angle lobes above**.

HABITAT Disturbed, weedy fields and roadsides.

RANGE Cuba, Hispaniola, Puerto Rico, Jamaica, and St. Thomas.

ABUNDANCE RS and temporary colonist in Florida Keys. Reported April, May, December. I know of no records since 1976.

MAJOR FOODPLANT Unknown.

Cyna Blue *Zizula cyna* Not Illustrated

SIZE < Eastern Tailed-Blue.

SIMILAR SPECIES Ceraunus Blue, Reakirt's Blue, Western Pygmy-Blue.

IDENTIFICATION A tiny blue of the southwest. HW with an obscure postmedian band of small black spots. Lacks eye-spot at outer angle of HW. Ceraunus and Reakirt's blues have eye-spots at the HW outer angle. Western Pygmy-Blue has copper-color on FW and marginal black spots on HW.

HABITAT	Arid scrub.
RANGE	Southern and western Texas south to Argentina.
ABUNDANCE	RS to Dallas-Fort Worth, eastern Kansas (1 record).
MAJOR FOODPLANT	Unknown.

Edwards' Fritillary *Speyeria edwardsii* Not Illustrated

SIZE	≤ Great Spangled Fritillary.
SIMILAR SPECIES	Atlantis Fritillary, Aphrodite Fritillary.
IDENTIFICATION	Roughly the size of Aphrodite Fritillary, Edwards' Fritillary is a lighter, more yellowish orange-brown above than Atlantis or Aphrodite fritillary. Below, the **ground color usually has a greenish tinge** that **almost completely suffuses the post-median area**. The silvered spots are very large and prominent.
HABITAT	Short hill prairie, forest openings, meadows.
RANGE	Western North Dakota west through Alberta and Montana south to northern New Mexico.
ABUNDANCE	RS to Manitoba and eastern South and North Dakota. Also, west to Alberta and New Mexico.
MAJOR FOODPLANT	Violets (*Viola*).

Bordered Patch *Chlosyne lacinia* Not Illustrated

SIZE	≤ American Lady.
IDENTIFICATION	Below, usually with black ground color and strong cream-colored HW median and marginal bands. Above, usually with a bold orange/yellow median band on the HW against a black ground color with various other pale markings. Note the **bold white spot on the top of the head**.
HABITAT	As an immigrant or stray, it might be encountered in almost any type of habitat.
RANGE	Also, west to California and south through South America.
ABUNDANCE	Occasional late summer/early fall immigrant north to Houston and Dallas, TX. RS north to Nebraska and western Missouri.
MAJOR FOODPLANT	Sunflowers (*Helianthus*) and other Compositae.
COMMENTS	One of the most variable butterflies in the world. Individuals may be almost entirely orange, almost entirely black, and a million combinations and patterns in-between.

Elf *Microtia elva* Not Illustrated

SIZE	≤ Pearl Crescent
IDENTIFICATION	Small. Black with a broad median band of orange on the HW and an unusual orange band across the subapex of the FW.
HABITAT	As a stray, could be found in any type of open habitat.
RANGE	Also, Mexico south to Costa Rica.
ABUNDANCE	RS to Missouri (1 record).

Vesta Crescent *Phyciodes vesta* **Plate 31**

SIZE | = Pearl Crescent.
SIMILAR SPECIES | Pearl Crescent.
IDENTIFICATION | The postmedian chain of black encircled orange spots on the FW below is diagnostic, but difficult to see in the field. Some individuals have black lines crossing the FW cell below and these can be separated from Pearl Crescents which have much paler brown lines. Above, Vesta Crescents are highly reticulated with black.
HABITAT | Dry open situations.
RANGE | Southern and west Texas west to southern Arizona and south to Guatemala.
ABUNDANCE | RS northeast to eastern Kansas and Nebraska (1 record).
MAJOR FOODPLANT | Hairy tubetongue (*Siphonoglossa pilosella*).

California Tortoiseshell *Nymphalis californica* **Plate 35**

SIZE | ≥ American Lady.
SIMILAR SPECIES | Compton Tortoiseshell, Small Tortoiseshell.
IDENTIFICATION | Smaller and more orange above than Compton Tortoiseshell, with less dark brown basally. **HW above has a black border**. Compton Tortoiseshell has a golden-tan HW border. Small Tortoiseshell also has a black border on the HW above but is smaller yet and brighter orange, with much black-brown on the HW basally.
HABITAT | As a stray to our area, could occur anywhere.
RANGE | Western United States and southwestern Canada, straying eastward occasionally.
ABUNDANCE | RS to Missouri, North Dakota, Manitoba, and Wisconsin (1 record, perhaps artificially transported).
MAJOR FOODPLANT | Ceanothus.
COMMENTS | Even more than Compton Tortoiseshell, this species has periodic irruptions and migratory movements that are very impressive. Most old records from the East stem from artificially established colonies that long ago died out.

Small Tortoiseshell *Nymphalis urticae* **Plate 35**

SIZE | < American Lady.
SIMILAR SPECIES | Milbert's Tortoiseshell, California Tortoiseshell.
IDENTIFICATION | Bright orange above with **black and yellow stripes perpendicular to the FW margin**. Note black spots and orange ground above and strong black-brown on the HW basally. Milbert's Tortoiseshell has orange spots on black ground. California Tortoiseshell has FW stripes less regular and lacks strong black-brown on the HW basally.

HABITAT   Open areas.

RANGE   Most of Eurasia.

ABUNDANCE   Recorded 4 times in the past seven years in the New York City area, Aug.–Oct.

MAJOR FOODPLANT   Stinging Nettle (*Urtica dioica*).

COMMENTS   I previously considered the occurence of these butterflies to be most easily explained by the presence of a nascent population of this species in the lower Hudson River Valley, since the unconnected occurrence of hitch-hiking strays from Europe seems most unlikely. However, given the freshet of reports of other exotic species in the northeast, I now consider the most likely explanation to be the deliberate (and illegal) release of butterflies imported from Europe.

Caribbean (or Cuban) Peacock *Anartia chrysopelea* Not illustrated

SIZE   ≤ American Lady.

SIMILAR SPECIES   Male Mimic.

IDENTIFICATION   A small, black-brown nymphalid with a median white stripe on the FW, a central white blotch on the HW, and a small tail. Above, note the orange-red submarginal dashes. Male Mimic are larger and have subapical white spots and no tail.

RANGE   Cuba.

ABUNDANCE   RS. A few records from 1972–73 from Key West and Big Pine Key.

MAJOR FOODPLANT   Fogfruit (*Lippia*).

California Sister *Adelpha bredowii* Not Illustrated

SIZE   = Mourning Cloak.

IDENTIFICATION   This stray from the west is large, with bold median white stripe down both wings and an orange FW apical spot.

HABITAT   Riparian areas with oaks.

RANGE   Pacific coast and southwestern U.S. south through Mexico.

ABUNDANCE   RS to Dallas-Fort Worth area and Houston.

MAJOR FOODPLANT   Evergreen oaks (*Quercus*).

Common Mestra *Mestra amymone* Plate 39

SIZE   < American Lady.

IDENTIFICATION   A very small white nymphalid with an apricot-colored HW border and a very slow fluttering flight.

HABITAT   Edges of tropical and subtropical woodlands.

RANGE   Southern Texas south to Costa Rica.

ABUNDANCE   RS east to Houston and north to eastern Kansas, western Missouri, eastern South Dakota (1 record).

MAJOR FOODPLANT   Noseburn (*Tragia*).

COMMENTS	Although their flight is tremulous, Common Mestras manage very well to keep the hopeful butterflier at a distance.

Pale Cracker *Hamadryas amphichloe* Not illustrated

SIZE	≤ Mourning Cloak.
SIMILAR SPECIES	Other crackers, which could theoretically occur as strays.
IDENTIFICATION	Above, mottled bluish-gray with much white mottling on the apical half of the FW. Below, similar, but ground color is gray-white.
HABITAT	Edges of tropical woodlands.
RANGE	Greater Antilles and Mexico south to Peru.
ABUNDANCE	RS to extreme southern Florida.
MAJOR FOODPLANT	*Dalechampia*

Many-banded Daggerwing *Marpesia chiron* Plate 39

SIZE	= American Lady.
IDENTIFICATION	Banded dark-brown on light-brown, with characteristic daggerwing tails.
RANGE	West Indies and southern Texas south through the American tropics.
ABUNDANCE	RS. 1 report, Nov. 7, 1985, Big Pine Key.
MAJOR FOODPLANT	Figs (*Ficus*) and other Moraceae.

Antillean Daggerwing *Marpesia eleuchea* Not Illustrated

SIZE	= American Lady.
SIMILAR SPECIES	Ruddy Daggerwing.
IDENTIFICATION	Looks like a small Ruddy Daggerwing. Above, very similar but the **FW median line is angled** at the bottom of the cell. Ruddy Daggerwing has this line straight across the wing. Below, note the white spot where the HW postmedian line reaches the trailing margin and the **lack of white on the underside of the body**. Ruddy Daggerwing lacks the white spot and has a bright white body, contrasting strongly with the wings.
HABITAT	Native habitat is woodland edges and clearings.
RANGE	Bahamas, Cuba, Hispaniola and Jamaica.
ABUNDANCE	RS. 1 report, to the Florida Keys, Oct. 14, 1973.
MAJOR FOODPLANT	Probably figs (*Ficus*).

Tropical Leafwing *Anaea aidea* Not Illustrated

SIZE	< Mourning Cloak.
SIMILAR SPECIES	Goatweed Leafwing.
IDENTIFICATION	A slightly smaller (on average), redder-above version of the Goatweed Leafwing. Look for **slightly uneven wing margins**, pointing out at the veins, especially on the HW above the "tail." Also, secondary "tail" usually more developed in this species

than in Goatweed Leafwing.

HABITAT	Tropical woodlands.
ABUNDANCE	RS north to Missouri.
MAJOR FOODPLANT	Crotons (*Croton*).

Red Satyr *Megisto rubricata* **Plate 43**

SIZE	= Little Wood-Satyr.
SIMILAR SPECIES	Little Wood-Satyr.
IDENTIFICATION	This western satyr has the FW disc, both above and below, **flushed with a color closer to orange** than red. On the FW below, it lacks the bottom large eye-spot that Little Wood-Satyr has, but this is often difficult to see in the field. The reddish-orange flush is easy.
HABITAT	Dry, open woodlands.
RANGE	West-central Oklahoma and central Texas west to Arizona and south to Guatemala.
ABUNDANCE	RS. Populations exist just to the west of our area, in the vicinities of Austin and on the west side of Fort Worth.
MAJOR FOODPLANT	Grasses.

Mercurial Skipper *Proteides mercurius* **Plate 46**

SIZE	≥ Silver-spotted Skipper.
IDENTIFICATION	A very large skipper with **golden head and thorax**. HW below and abdomen with much pale mottling.
HABITAT	Tropical and subtropical woodlands and gardens near watercourses
RANGE	Mexico and the West Indies south through tropical Americas.
ABUNDANCE	RS. Found from Cuba and northern Mexico south, there have been a few reports of this species from Florida and Louisiana.
MAJOR FOODPLANT	Various tree and shrub legumes.

Hermit Skipper *Grais stigmatica* Not Illustrated

SIZE	> Northern Cloudywing.
SIMILAR SPECIES	Cloudywings.
IDENTIFICATION	Above, all medium brown, with darker brown median and postmedian spot-bands on both the FW and HW. FW apex with 2 small white spots. Underside of "face" (palps) is bright yellow-orange.
HABITAT	Tropical woodlands and edges.
RANGE	Northern Mexico through South America.
ABUNDANCE	RS north to Kansas (1 record).
MAJOR FOODPLANT	Unknown.
COMMENTS	Unlike cloudywings, usually rests with its wings completely fla

White-patched Skipper *Chiomara asychis* Not Illustrat

SIZE	< Wild Indigo Duskywing.

IDENTIFICATION   Mottled dark gray, black, and white. Above, both males and females have a wide white median patch on the HW. Female FW looks much like a pale version of a duskywing (close relatives) while male FW has a more prominent white median patch here also.

HABITAT   Open tropical woodlands, edges, and gardens.

ABUNDANCE   RS north to Houston area.

MAJOR FOODPLANT   Barbados Cherry (*Malpighia glabra*).

False Duskywing *Gesta gesta* Plate 51

SIZE   < Wild Indigo Duskywing.

SIMILAR SPECIES   Wild Indigo Duskywing.

IDENTIFICATION   Above, brown patch distal to FW cell curves outward in characteristic fashion partially enclosing darker black patch.

HABITAT   Open tropical scrub and disturbed situations.

RANGE   West Indies and southern Texas south through tropical Americas.

ABUNDANCE   RS north to east Texas (frequently found at Aransas NWR, about 100 miles south of our area).

MAJOR FOODPLANT   *Indigofera* and other legumes.

COMMENTS   Often wraps its wings downward when perched.

Dotted Roadside-Skipper *Amblyscirtes eos* Not Illustrated

SIZE   ≥ Least Skipper.

SIMILAR SPECIES   Other roadside-skippers.

IDENTIFICATION   More uniformly dark gray-brown below than other roadside-skippers, on the HW below this species usually has **prominent white spots that are outlined with black**.

HABITAT   Grasslands, canyons.

RANGE   Colorado south to West Texas and west to southern Arizona and northern Mexico.

ABUNDANCE   RS northeast to Dallas-Fort Worth area.

MAJOR FOODPLANT   Grasses.

Violet-banded Skipper *Nyctelius nyctelius* Plate 71

SIZE   = Tawny-edged Skipper.

IDENTIFICATION   Below, the HW has alternating pale and dark bands, the pale bands with a violaceous sheen when fresh. A black spot is near the middle of the HW leading margin. Abdomen with black and white rings. Above, FW with a double cell-spot.

HABITAT   Disturbed grassy areas.

RANGE   Southern Texas and the West Indies south through tropical Americas.

ABUNDANCE   1 record from Key Largo.

MAJOR FOODPLANT   Coarse grasses.

Plates Introduction

Photos

Photographs on the following 71 color plates show butterflies in the correct size comparison to others on the same plate. The absolute size is indicated at the top of the plate.

Unless otherwise indicated, either on the facing page or in the photo credits appendix, photographs are by the author and were taken in the wild, of unrestrained, unmanipulated butterflies.

Black and white lines have been placed on some photographs to draw your eye to field marks whose positions are difficult to explain in words.

Date and locality information are given when known. Dates are shown as month/day/year.

Maps

If an area is colored on a particular map, this means that I believe there are **resident populations** of the species in the area, or, if the species is an immigrant, that **an active field observer is likely to see the species in this area at least once every two to three years.**

Near the western edge of the maps is a diagonal line, running from just south of Houston, Texas north to the North Dakota/Canadian border. This line is the western limit of the area covered by this guide.

See the introductory text for more information about the maps.

RANGE MAP COLORS AND PLATES ABBREVIATIONS

RANGE MAP COLORS

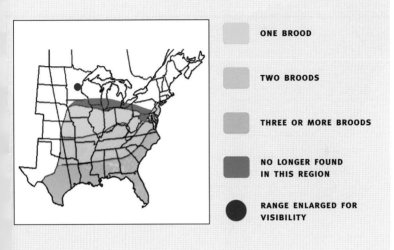

ONE BROOD

TWO BROODS

THREE OR MORE BROODS

NO LONGER FOUND
IN THIS REGION

RANGE ENLARGED FOR
VISIBILITY

PLATES ABBREVIATIONS

A	abundant	**S**	stray
C	common	**SF**	state forest
FW	forewing	**SP**	state park
HW	hindwing	**U**	uncommon
L	local	**WMA**	wildlife management area
NF	national forest	**WPR**	Ward Pound Ridge Reservation, Westchester County, NY
NP	national park		
NWR	national wildlife refuge	♂	male
R	rare	♀	female

PLATE 1 SWALLOWTAILS

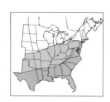

1 Pipevine Swallowtail *Battus philenor.* **p. 43**
Below. 8/16/96 Heard Museum, McKinney, TX
Single orange spot-band on iridescent blue **HW**.

2 Above. 7/30/94 Roan Mtn., Carter Co., TN
Iridescent blue **HW**.
Very dark **FW**.
No **FW** markings.

3 Polydamas Swallowtail *Battus polydamas.* **p. 44**
Below. 3/30/97 Ft. Lauderdale, Broward Co., FL
No tails.
Dull red **HW** marginal spots and red spots on the body.

4 Above. Ft. Lauderdale, Broward Co., FL
No tails.
Wide dirty-yellow postmedian band.
Constantly in motion.

5 Zebra Swallowtail *Eurytides marcellus.* **p. 44**
Spring form below. 3/17/94 Ocala NF, Marion Co., FL
Black and white and red stripes.
Long tails.

6 Spring form above. 3/17/94 Ocala NF, Marion Co., FL
Black and white stripes.
Long tails.

7 Summer form below. 6/6/87 Ocala NF, Marion Co., FL
Black and white and red stripes.
Very long tails.

8 Summer form above. 8/24/91 Ocala NF, Marion Co., FL
Black and white stripes.
Very long tails.

Pipevine Swallowtail

2 Pipevine Swallowtail

Polydamas Swallowtail

4 Polydamas Swallowtail

Zebra Swallowtail

6 Zebra Swallowtail

Zebra Swallowtail

8 Zebra Swallowtail

PLATE 2 "BLACK" SWALLOWTAILS

1 Black Swallowtail *Papilio polyxenes.* **p. 45**
Below. 8/9/90 Oakwood Cemetery, Mt. Kisco, NY.
HW median and submarginal orange spot-bands.
HW yellow/orange cell spot.

2 ♂ above. 7/28/89 Chappaqua, Westchester Co., NY.
Bright yellow spot-bands, **FW** and **HW**.

4 ♀ above. 5/19/94, Gainesville, Alachua Co., FL.
Blue on **HW**.
Yellow **FW** subapical spot.
Often flies with low non-directional flight.
Open areas and gardens.

Ozark Swallowtail *Papilio joanae.* **p. 46**
Not illustrated.
Ozark region only.
Woodland glades.
Virtually indistinguishable from Black Swallowtail.

3 Spicebush Swallowtail *Papilio troilus.* **p. 49**
Below. 8/9/90 Chappaqua, Westchester Co., NY.
HW median and submarginal orange spot-bands.
Lacks **HW** yellow/orange cell spot.

6 ♂ above. 7/30/94 Lynch Farm, Union Co., TN.
Greenish-blue cast on the **HW**.
Usually flies with rapid, directional flight.
Woodlands and adjacent fields.

8 ♀ above. 4/16/95 Devil's Den SP, Washington Co., AR.
Blue on **HW**.
Lacks yellow **FW** subapical spot.
Marginal spots greenish and large.

5 Short-tailed Swallowtail *Papilio brevicauda.* **p. 46**
Below. 6/29/73 St. John's, Newfoundland.
Very short tails.
Black pupil in orange spot at **HW** outer angle is not centere

7 Above. 6/29/73 St. John's, Newfoundland.
Some orange in yellow median **HW** band.
Very short tails.

ack Swallowtail

2 Black Swallowtail ♂

picebush Swallowtail

4 Black Swallowtail ♀

hort-tailed Swallowtail

6 Spicebush Swallowtail ♂

hort-tailed Swallowtail

8 Spicebush Swallowtail ♀

PLATE 3 BROWN-BLACK & YELLOW SWALLOWTAILS

1 Giant Swallowtail *Papilio cresphontes.* **p. 46**
Below. 6/19/96 Memorial Park, Houston, TX
Cream-colored wings and body.
HW with blue median spot-band.

2 Above. 8/25/91 Newnan's Lake, Alachua Co., FL
Brown-black.
Yellow spot-bands form x's near **FW** apexes.
Yellow spot within tail.

3 Schaus' Swallowtail *Papilio aristodemus.* **p. 47**
Below. 5/24/94 Elliott Key, Dade Co., FL
(Marked individual for population study.)
Large rusty patch in the **HW** median band.
Males with bright yellow antennal clubs.
Lacks yellow spot in tail.

4 ♂ above. 5/25/94 North Key Largo, Monroe Co., FL
Yellow bands duller than Giant or Palamedes.
Yellow bands do not form an x near **FW** apex.
Males with bright yellow antennal clubs.
Lacks yellow spot in tail.

5 Bahamian Swallowtail *Papilio andraemon.* **p. 48**
Below. 6/5/85 Elliott Key, Dade Co., FL
(Individual to be marked for population study.)
Rusty "brick" juts into the **HW** postmedian band.
Males with bright yellow antennal clubs.

6 Above. 5/9/85 Elliott Key, Dade Co., FL
Yellow bar in the **FW** cell.

7 Palamedes Swallowtail *Papilio palamedes.* **p. 50**
Below. 8/30/95 Great Dismal Swamp, NWR, Suffolk VA
Brown-black wing bases.
Yellow stripe along the base of the wings.
Inhabitant of southern swamps.

8 Above. 8/25/91 Newnan's Lake, Alachua Co., FL
Wide yellow **HW** postmedian band.
Inhabitant of southern swamps.

Giant Swallowtail

2 Giant Swallowtail

Schaus' Swallowtail

4 Schaus' Swallowtail ♂

5 Bahamian Swallowtail

6 Bahamian Swallowtail

7 Palamedes Swallowtail

8 Palamedes Swallowtail

PLATE 4 TIGER SWALLOWTAILS

1 **Canadian Tiger Swallowtail** *Papilio canadensis.* **p. 49**
♂ above. 6/12/93 Errol, NH
Smaller than Eastern Tiger Swallowtail
Occurs farther north.
One brood only, flying in spring–early summer.

3 Below. 6/28/96 McNair, Lake Co., MN
Broad black stripe along the trailing margin of the **HW** taking
 up more than 1/2 the width of the distance to the first vein.
Continuous yellow **FW** marginal band.
Occurs farther north in spring.

2 **Eastern Tiger Swallowtail** *Papilio glaucus.* **p. 48**
♂ above. 7/29/94 Blowing Rock, Watauga Co., NC
Yellow with black stripes.
HW border mainly black.

4 ♀ above. 7/27/89 WPR, Westchester Co., NY
Yellow with black stripes.
HW border with much blue.

5 Below. 8/21/94 Spruce Run Recreation Area, Hunterdon Co., NJ
Yellow with black stripes.

6 ♀ above. 9/23/94 Chassahowitzka, Citrus Co., FL
Florida populations are flushed with orange above.
Large.

7 Black ♀ below. 8/16/96 Heard Museum, McKinney, TX
No postmedian orange spot-band.
Usually retains "shadow" of tiger pattern.

8 Black ♀ above. 8/16/96 Heard Museum, McKinney, TX
Large.
Flies higher than other swallowtails.
Marginal spots yellowish and small.
(See ♀ Spicebush Swallowtail, plate 2.)

1 Canadian Tiger Swallowtail ♂

2 Eastern Tiger Swallowtail ♂

Canadian Tiger Swallowtail

4 Eastern Tiger Swallowtail ♀

Eastern Tiger Swallowtail

6 Eastern Tiger Swallowtail ♀

astern Tiger Swallowtail ♀

8 Eastern Tiger Swallowtail ♀

PLATE 5 WHITES, MAINLY SOUTHERN

1 Checkered White *Pontia protodice.* **p. 51**
♀ below. 8/16/96 Heard Museum, McKinney, TX
Black patch on mid **FW** costa.

2 ♀ above. 8/16/96 Heard Museum, McKinney, TX
Many black spots on white background.

4 ♂ above. 5/17/94 Gainesville, Alachua Co., FL
Black spots on white background, not as extensive as
on female.

Western White *Pontia occidentalis.* **p. 52**
Not illustrated.
Extremely similar to Checkered White.
See text.

3 Great Southern White *Ascia monuste.* **p. 54**
♀ below. 5/21/94 W. Summerland Key, Monroe Co., FL
Varies from white to smoky-gray-brown as shown.
Antennal clubs are phosphorescent blue.
Most common in coastal open situations.

5 ♂ below. 5/22/94 W. Summerland Key, Monroe Co., FL
Antennal clubs are phosphorescent blue.
No orange at base of **HW** leading margin.
Most common in coastal open situations.

7 Above. 5/21/94 W. Summerland Key, Monroe Co., FL
Black **FW** border tends to follow veins inward.
Antennal clubs are phosphorescent blue.
Most common in coastal open situations.

6 Florida White *Appias drusilla.* **p. 51**
Below. 3/21/90 South Miami, Dade Co., FL.
Antennal clubs are pale but not phosphorescent blue.
Orange at base of **HW** leading margin.
Usually more opalescent than Great Southern White.
Mainly in hardwood hammocks.

8 Above. 3/25/90 Matheson Hammock, Dade Co., FL
Black **FW** border, if present, doesn't follow veins inward.
Antennal clubs are pale but not phosphorescent blue.
Mainly in hardwood hammocks.

1 Checkered White ♀

2 Checkered White ♀

Great Southern White ♀

4 Checkered White ♂

Great Southern White ♂

6 Florida White

Great Southern White

8 Florida White

PLATE 6 WHITES, MAINLY NORTHERN

1 Cabbage White *Pieris rapae.* **p. 54**
Below. 7/30/94 Roan Mtn., Carter Co., TN
Black spot on **FW**.

2 ♀ above. 10/4/92 Glazier Arboretum, Chappaqua, NY
Two black spots on **FW**.

4 ♂ above. 6/14/91 WPR, Westchester Co., NY
Black spot on **FW**.

3 Clouded/Orange Sulphur *Colias philodice/eurytheme.* **p. 56**
♀ white form below. 6/20/91 WPR, Westchester Co., NY
Silvered spot in center of **HW**.
Black borders of **FW** above can be seen in flight and
   through the wing.

5 West Virginia White *Pieris virginiensis.* **p. 53**
Below. 4/28/90 Steep Rock Reservation, Litchfield Co., CT
White with veins edged in soft gray.
Rich woodlands with toothwort in spring.

6 Above. 4/18/96 Fork Creek WMA, Boone Co., WV
Unmarked white.

7 Mustard White *Pieris napi.* **p. 53**
Below. 6/12/93 Wentworths Location, NH
In spring with veins edged with dark greenish-black.
In summer, often immaculate white.

8 Above. 5/27/96 Mont-Tremblant Park, Quebec
Unmarked white.

Cabbage White

2 Cabbage White ♀

Orange/Clouded Sulphur ♀

4 Cabbage White ♂

West Virginia White

6 West Virginia White

Mustard White

8 Mustard White

PLATE 7 MARBLED WHITES

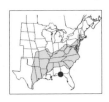

1 **Falcate Orangetip** *Anthocharis midea.* **p. 56**
♂ below. 5/12/92 Hook Mtn., Rockland Co., NY
Heavily "marbled."
Orange at **FW** apex.

2 ♂ above. 4/19/90 Hook Mtn., Rockland Co., NY
Orange wingtips.

3 ♀ below. 5/12/92 Hook Mtn., Rockland Co., NY
Heavily "marbled."

4 ♀ above. 4/28/93 Assunpink WMA, Monmouth Co., NJ
Hooked **FW** apex.
FW has checkered margins.
Low weak flight.

5 **Olympia Marble** *Euchloe olympia.* **p. 55**
Below. 4/24/94 posed photo, Larenim Park, Mineral Co., WV
Sparse green marbling.
White antennas.

6 Above. 4/23/94 Larenim Park, Mineral Co., WV
FW apexes rounded.
FW cell-end bar is longer than in Falcate Orangetip.
White antennas.

7 **Large Marble** *Euchloe ausonides.* **p. 55**
Below. 6/27/91 Coal Creek Canyon, Jefferson Co., CO
HW median greenish band with two prongs near leading
edge of **HW**.

8 Above. Same individual as 7.
Similar to Olympia Marble but antennas checked with blac

Falcate Orangetip ♂

2 Falcate Orangetip ♂

Falcate Orangetip ♀

4 Falcate Orangetip ♀

Olympia Marble

6 Olympia Marble

Large Marble

8 Large Marble

PLATE 8 SULPHURS

1 Clouded Sulphur *Colias philodice.* **p. 56**
Below. 10/14/91 Bronx Botanical Garden, Bronx, NY
Shows no orange at all.

2 Above (in flight). 7/14/93 Glazier Arboretum, Chappaqua, NY
Clear lemon yellow.

3 Orange Sulphur *Colias eurytheme.* **p. 57**
Below. 7/29/94 Blowing Rock, Watauga Co., NC
Shows at least some orange on the **FW**.

4 Above (road killed). 9/19/93 Anza-Borrego SP, CA
Ranges from extensive bright orange to just a blush of
orange on the **FW** disc.

5 Pink-edged Sulphur *Colias interior.* **p. 57**
Below. 6/28/96 McNair, Lake Co., MN
Yellow above.
Single **HW** central spot (double in Clouded Sulphur).
No **HW** postmedian spots.
Bright pink fringe.

6 Southern Dogface *Colias cesonia.* **p. 58**
Below. 10/1/95 Ocala NF, Marion Co., FL
Large.
Bold black outline of a dog's head can be seen through **FW**
Pointed **FW**.
Fall form with **HW** suffused with pink.

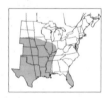

7 Dainty Sulphur *Nathalis iole.* **p. 64**
Dry season (winter) form, below. 2/3/96 Homestead, Dade Co., FL
Tiny.
Variable below.
Greenish **HW**.
Black spots in **FW** submargin.
Flies low to ground.

8 Wet season (summer) form below. 10/2/95 Daytona Beach, Volus
Co., FL

Clouded Sulphur

2 Clouded Sulphur

Orange Sulphur

4 Orange Sulphur

ink-edged Sulphur

6 Southern Dogface

ainty Sulphur

8 Dainty Sulphur

PLATE 9 YELLOWS

1 Little Yellow *Eurema lisa.* **p. 62**
♂ below. 7/26/93 Chappaqua, Westchester Co., NY
Bright yellow above. Black antennas.
Immigrant northward.
Wide black **FW** border at apex visible through wing.
Rapid, straight, and low flight in open situations.
HW with two basal black spots.

2 ♀ below. 6/8/95 Pontotoc Ridge, Pontotoc Co., OK
HW with two basal black spots.
Pink spot at **HW** apex.

3 Mimosa Yellow *Eurema nise.* **p. 63**
♂ below. 10/8/95 Bauer Park, Homestead, Dade Co., FL
Lacks **HW** basal black spots of Little Yellow.
FW black border at apex narrower than in Little Yellow.
Flies within edge of woodland.

4 ♀ below. 2/3/96 Bauer Park, Homestead, Dade Co., FL
Similar to Little Yellow.
Lacks **HW** basal black spots of Little Yellow.
FW black border at apex narrower than in Little Yellow.
Flies within edge of woodland.

5 Dina Yellow *Eurema dina.* **p. 63**
♂ below. 5/20/94 Bauer Park, Homestead, Dade Co., FL
Bright orange above.
Very narrow **FW** black border.
Pink-brown line at **FW** apex.

6 ♀ below. 5/20/94 Bauer Park, Homestead, Dade Co., FL
Yellow above.
Pink-brown line at **FW** apex.

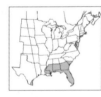

7 Barred Yellow *Eurema daira.* **p. 61**
Wet season (summer) form below. 3/23/90 Key Largo, Monroe Co
Small.
FW costal margin not yellow.
White or yellow above.
♂ above with black bar along **FW** lower margin

8 Dry season (winter) form below. 3/19/94 Gainesville, Alachua Co
Suffused with rusty-brown.
FW costal margin not yellow.

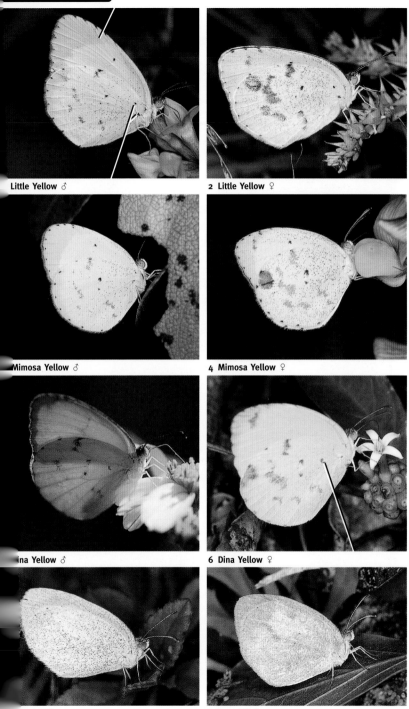

Little Yellow ♂

2 Little Yellow ♀

Mimosa Yellow ♂

4 Mimosa Yellow ♀

ina Yellow ♂

6 Dina Yellow ♀

rred Yellow

8 Barred Yellow

PLATE 10 YELLOWS

1 Sleepy Orange *Eurema nicippe.* **p. 64**
Dry season (winter) form below. 10/27/96 Peñitas, Hidalgo Co., TX
Bright orange above.
Diagonal brown markings on **HW**
FW cell-end bar.

2 Wet season (summer) form below. 9/22/94 Pasco, Pasco Co., FL
Bright orange above.
Diagonal brown markings on **HW**
FW cell-end bar.

3 Tailed Orange *Eurema proterpia.* **p. 62**
Dry season (winter) form below. 10/21/95 Santa Ana NWR, Hidalgo
  Co., TX
Rare stray from south Texas. Bright orange above.
Pointed tail.
Reticulated with brown markings below.
No **FW** cell-end bar.

4 Wet season (summer) form below. 10/21/95 Santa Ana NWR,
  Hidalgo Co., TX
Rare stray from south Texas. Unmarked orange.
HW sharply angled.

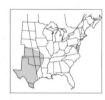

5 Mexican Yellow *Eurema mexicana.* **p. 62**
Below. 8/9/96 Box Canyon, Pima Co., AZ
Tailed, pale yellow **HW**.
Whitish above with dog's face pattern.

6 Boisduval's Yellow *Eurema boisduvaliana.* **p. 206**
Below. 2/9/95 Mismaloya, Jalisco, Mexico
1 record from Florida Keys.
Similar to Mexican Yellow.
Bright orange-yellow above. See text.

7 Shy Yellow *Eurema messalina.* **p. 206**
12/6/94 New Providence, Bahamas
Possible stray to Florida Keys.
Black subapical mark on **FW**.
White **FW** disc. See text.

8 Little Yellow *Eurema lisa.* **p. 62**
White form ♀ below. 6/18/96 Brazos Bend SP, Brazoria Co., TX
White, above and below.
Wide black border at **FW** apex above.

Sleepy Orange

2 Sleepy Orange

Tailed Orange

4 Tailed Orange

Mexican Yellow

6 Boisduval's Yellow

y Yellow

8 Little Yellow ♀

PLATE 11 PHOEBIS

1 Cloudless Sulphur *Phoebis sennae*. **p. 58**
♂ below. 10/1/96 Hutchinson Island, Savannah, GA
Larger than *Colias* sulphurs and yellows.
Bright yellow above (see plate 12).
Green-yellow below with cell-end spots on **FW** and **HW**.
Immigrant northward in late summer/fall.

2 ♀ below. 9/29/96 Black River, Savannah, GA
Larger than *Colias* sulphurs and yellows.
Cell-end spots on **FW** and **HW**.
Line from **FW** apex broken.
Above, yellow (East) or whitish (West).
Immigrant northward in late summer/fall.

3 Orange-barred Sulphur *Phoebis philea*. **p. 59**
♂ below. 3/22/94 Kendall, Dade Co., FL
Rich yellow to orange.
Can be almost unmarked orange-yellow or as well-marked
  as shown.
Line from **FW** apex broken.
Above, with large orange patches (see plate 12).

4 ♀ below. 3/31/97 Kendall, Dade Co., FL
Similar to Cloudless Sulphur but more extensive pink.
Above, with large pink-orange patches on **HW**.

5 Large Orange Sulphur *Phoebis agarithe*. **p. 60**
♂ below. 3/22/94 Kendall, Dade Co., FL
Orange.
Line from **FW** apex straight.
Bright orange above (see plate 12).

6 ♀ below. 5/24/94 Elliott Key, Dade Co., FL
Line from **FW** apex straight.
Above, orange or whitish.

loudless Sulphur ♂

2 Cloudless Sulphur ♀

range-barred Sulphur ♂

4 Orange-barred Sulphur ♀

arge Orange Sulphur ♂

6 Large Orange Sulphur ♀

PLATE 12 LARGE SULPHURS

1 Cloudless Sulphur *Phoebis sennae*. **p. 58**
♂ above (road-killed). 10/27/96 La Joya, Starr Co., TX
Larger than *Colias* sulphurs and yellows.
Bright yellow.
Immigrant northward in late summer/fall.
See plate 11.

2 Large Orange Sulphur *Phoebis agarithe*. **p. 60**
♂ above (road-killed). 10/23/95 Roma, Starr Co., TX
Bright orange. See plate 11.

3 Orange-barred Sulphur *Phoebis philea*. **p. 59**
♂ above (in flight, not to scale). 3/26/90 South Miami, Dade Co.,
Yellow with bright orange patches.
Florida. See plate 11.

4 White Angled-Sulphur *Anteos clorinde*. **p. 205**
Above. 2/6/95 Mismaloya, Jalisco, Mexico
Very rare stray only (not to scale).
White with yellow **FW** costal patch.

6 Below. 2/6/95 Mismaloya, Jalisco, Mexico.
Very large. Veined leaf effect. White above.

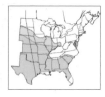

5 Southern Dogface *Colias cesonia*. **p. 58**
Above (caught in a spider web). 10/26/95 La Gloria, Starr Co., TX
Bold dog's face pattern on **FW**.
Bright yellow. See plate **8**

7 Yellow Angled-Sulphur *Anteos maerula*. **p. 206**
Below. 10/26/93 Mission, Hidalgo Co., TX
Very rare stray only. Very large. Veined leaf effect.
Bright yellow above.

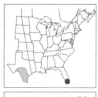

8 Lyside Sulphur *Kricogonia lyside*. **p. 61**
Below. 10/28/96 Peñitas, Hidalgo Co., TX
Usually with green tinge and whitened vein as shown bu
  can be very pale without whitened vein.
Above, varies from yellow to white.

9 Statira Sulphur *Phoebis statira*. **p. 60**
Below. 10/19/93 Santa Ana NWR, Hidalgo Co., TX
Some yellow at base of **FW** costa and along **FW** disc.
Usually with a pink patch at **FW** apex.
Outer 1/3 of the wings seem "puckered."

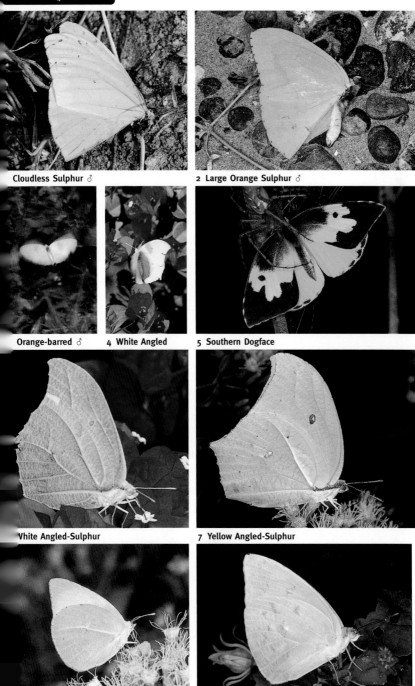

Cloudless Sulphur ♂

2 Large Orange Sulphur ♂

Orange-barred ♂   4 White Angled

5 Southern Dogface

Vhite Angled-Sulphur

7 Yellow Angled-Sulphur

side Sulphur

9 Statira Sulphur

PLATE 13 COPPERS

1 Gray Copper *Lycaena dione.* **p. 67**
Below. 6/9/95 Wagoner, Wagoner Co., OK
Large.
HW with orange marginal band.
FW disc gray.

2 ♀ above. Same individual as in 1.
Large.
Gray with orange marginal band.
FW with many black spots.

4 ♂ above. 6/11/95 Prairie SP, Barton Co., MO
Large and gray.

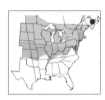

3 Bronze Copper *Lycaena hyllus.* **p. 67**
Below. 7/3/96 Dakota Dunes, Union Co., SD
Large.
Wet areas.
HW with broad orange marginal band.
FW disc orange.

6 ♂ above. 7/2/96 Pipestone NM, Pipestone Co., MN
Purplish iridescence.
HW with broad orange marginal band.
Fewer **FW** black spots than Gray Copper ♀.
Wet areas.

8 ♀ above. 6/5/90 Middle Creek WMA, Lancaster Co., PA
Large.
Wet areas.
Orange **FW**, gray **HW**.
Black spots near base of **FW** inner margin.

5 American Copper *Lycaena phlaeas.* **p. 66**
Below. 7/30/94 Roan Mtn., Carter Co., TN
Small.
Dry fields.
HW with narrow reddish-orange marginal band.

7 Above. 5/20/90 Chappaqua, Westchester Co., NY
Small.
Dry fields.
Bright orange **FW**
Gray **HW** with marginal orange band.

Gray Copper

2 Gray Copper ♀

Bronze Copper

4 Gray Copper ♂

American Copper

6 Bronze Copper ♂

American Copper

8 Bronze Copper ♀

PLATE 14 COPPERS

1 Bog Copper *Lycaena epixanthe.* **p. 68**
Below. 6/15/94 Lakehurst Bog, Ocean Co., NJ
Very small.
Pale **HW**.

2 ♀ above. 6/28/95 Lakehurst Bog, Ocean Co., NJ
Cranberry bogs.
Duller with smaller spots than other small coppers.

7 ♂ above. 7/26/90 Lakehurst Bog, Ocean Co., NJ
Cranberry bogs.
Fewer and smaller black spots than other small coppers.

3 Purplish Copper *Lycaena helloides.* **p. 69**
Below. 7/25/95 Stockton, San Joaquin Co., CA
Orange **FW** disc.
Mauve-brown **HW** with orange marginal line.

4 ♀ above. 9/10/78 Cedar Creek Preserve, Anoka Co, MN
Usually with extensive bright orange.

9 ♂ above. 9/10/78 Cedar Creek Preserve, Anoka Co, MN
Iridescent purple with strong orange **HW** marginal band.

5 Dorcas Copper *Lycaena dorcas.* **p. 68**
Below. 7/26/96 Bailey's Harbor, Door Co, WI
In wet or moist areas with shrubby cinquefoil.

6 ♀ above. Same individual as in 5.
Orange dull and restricted.

8 ♀ above. 8/8/94 Springfield, Penobscot Co., ME
Lycaena dorcas claytoni found in Maine only.
Tinged with rusty-brown, above and below.

10 ♂ above. 7/27/96 Bailey's Harbor, Door Co., WI
Iridescent purple with weak orange **HW** marginal band.

1 Bog Copper

2 Bog Copper ♀

Purplish Copper

4 Purplish Copper ♀

Dorcas Copper

6 Dorcas Copper ♀

Bog Copper ♂

8 Dorcas Copper ♀

9 Purplish Copper ♂

10 Dorcas Copper ♂

PLATE 15 HARVESTER & METALMARKS

1 **Harvester** *Feniseca tarquinius.* **p. 65**
Below. 6/12/93 Wentworths Location, NH
HW with delicate white tracings.
Found in woodlands with alders.

2 Above. 5/24/95 Morristown, Morris Co., NJ
Orange.
Inky-black spots in **FW** cell and near apex.

3 **Little Metalmark** *Calephelis virginiensis.* **p. 98**
Below. 8/26/91 Ocala NF, Marion Co., FL
Found in open pine flats.
FW fringe evenly gray.

4 Above. Same individual as in 3.
Rich orange-brown.
Metallic markings.
Thorax usually orange-brown with vertical gray stripes.

5 **Northern Metalmark** *Calephelis borealis.* **p. 98**
Below. 7/2/91 Bethel, Fairfield Co., CT

6 Above. 7/1/91 Bethel, Fairfield Co., CT
Extremely local within range shown.
Chestnut with black markings.
Metallic markings.
Thorax blackish.
Found on limestone soils.

7 **Swamp Metalmark** *Calephelis muticum.* **p. 99**
Below. 7/25/96 Kettle Moraine State Forest, Fond du Lac Co., WI
FW fringe with faint checkering.

8 Above. 7/25/96 Kettle Moraine State Forest, Fond du Lac Co., WI
Extremely local within range shown.
Rich orange-brown.
Metallic markings.
Thorax usually blackish.
Found in moist to wet areas with swamp thistle.

Harvester

2 Harvester

Little Metalmark

4 Little Metalmark

Northern Metalmark

6 Northern Metalmark

Swamp Metalmark

8 Swamp Metalmark

PLATE 16 MISCELLANEOUS HAIRSTREAKS

1 Great Purple Hairstreak *Atlides halesus*. **p. 70**

♂ above (caught by crab spider—legs at top left). 9/24/94 Gainesville, Alachua Co., FL

Brilliant iridescent blue (not purple) normally visible only in flight.

♀ above has more restricted, non-iridescent blue.

3 Below. 6/8/95 Pontotoc Ridge, Pontotoc Co., OK
Large.
Bright red spots at wing bases.
White spots on body.
Iridescent turquoise on **FW** disc.

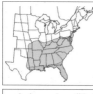

2 Gray Ministreak *Ministrymon azia*. **p. 88**

Below. 3/20/90 South Miami, Dade Co., FL
Tiny.
Pale gray ground color.
Irregular red postmedian band.
Red marginal line.
Red on crown of head.

4 Red-banded Hairstreak *Calycopis cecrops*. **p. 87**

Below. 8/8/96 Dallas Arboretum, Dallas Co., TX
Small and dark.
Prominent red postmedian band on both wings.
Some blue above in flight.

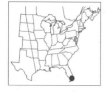

5 Dusky-blue Groundstreak *Calycopis isobeon*. **p. 87**

Below. 10/21/95 Santa Ana NWR, Hidalgo Co., TX
South Texas only.
Similar to Red-banded Hairstreak.
More red-orange at **HW** outer angle than Red-banded.
Red postmedian bands usually narrower.
Blue lunule at **HW** outer angle with red-orange cap.
Intermediates occur.

6 Atala *Eumaeus atala*. **p. 70**

Below. 3/25/90 South Miami, Dade Co., FL
Brilliant orange abdomen.
HW with phosphorescent blue spot-bands.
Caterpillars bright red and yellow on cycads.

eat Purple Hairstreak ♂

ay Ministreak

d-banded Hairstreak

ky-blue Groundstreak

3 Great Purple Hairstreak

6 Atala

PLATE 17 MISCELLANEOUS HAIRSTREAKS

1 Soapberry Hairstreak *Phaeostrymon alcestis.* **p. 72**
Below. 6/9/95 Wagoner, Wagoner Co., OK
Cell-end bars with white centers.
Near soapberry trees.

2 White M Hairstreak *Parrhasius m-album.* **p. 83**
Below. 9/26/94 Gainesville, Alachua Co., FL
White spot at center of leading edge of **HW**.
HW red spot set inward from margin.
Lacks cell-end bar.
Brilliant iridescent blue above.

3 Southern Hairstreak *Fixsenia favonius.* **p. 77**
Below. **'Northern' Southern Hairstreak** *F. f. ontario*
6/22/89 WPR, Westchester Co., NY
Lacks cell-end bar.
Usually no **HW** white spot at center of leading edge of **H**
  but sometimes present.
Brown ground color (Gray Hairstreak normally gray).
Inwardly directed white chevron over largest red spot.
(Gray Hairstreak has flat black line over orange spot.)

5 'Southern' Southern Hairstreak *F.f. favonius.* 3/24/94 Hendry C
Florida peninsula and coastal Georgia.
Extensive red-orange on **HW** submargin.
White spot at center of leading edge of **HW**.
Long tails.

4 Coral Hairstreak *Satyrium titus.* **p. 72**
Below. 6/15/94 Lakehurst, Ocean Co., NJ
Coral red marginal spots on **HW**.
No tail.
No blue marginal eye-spot.

6 Fulvous Hairstreak *Electrostrymon angelia.* **p. 86**
Below. 3/21/90 Homestead, Dade Co., FL
HW postmedian line disrupted, with an isolated white s
  at leading edge of **HW**.
FW postmedian line with no white.
Copper-colored above, sometimes visible in flight.

Soapberry Hairstreak

2 White M Hairstreak

'Northern' Southern Hairstreak

4 Coral Hairstreak

'Southern' Southern Hairstreak

6 Fulvous Hairstreak

PLATE 18 SATYRIUM HAIRSTREAKS

1 Banded Hairstreak *Satyrium calanus.* **p. 75**
Below. 7/3/96 Minneopa SP, Blue Earth Co., MN
Common and variable.
Postmedian band with white dashes outwardly, occasionally
with white on both sides of band.

2 Edwards' Hairstreak *Satyrium edwardsii.* **p. 74**
Below. 6/2/96 Weymouth Woods, Southern Pines, Moore Co., NC
HW postmedian band broken into spots, each spot com-
pletely ringed with white.
Prominent orange at **HW** outer angle.
Often with some orange over the **HW** blue lunule.

3 Hickory Hairstreak *Satyrium caryaevorum.* **p. 73**
Below. 6/30/94 Bedford, Westchester Co., NY
HW blue spot extends inward.
HW cell-end bars aligned with bars above them.
Postmedian band with white on both sides.
Rare to uncommon.

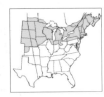

4 Acadian Hairstreak *Satyrium acadica.* **p. 73**
Below. 7/25/96 Riveredge Nature Center, Saukville, Ozaukee Co., WI
Postmedian band of solid black circles.
Orange cap on **HW** blue spot.
Whitish gray or gray ground color.
Associated with shrubby willows.

5 King's Hairstreak *Satyrium kingi.* **p. 75**
Below. 6/6/96 Weymouth Woods, Southern Pines, Moore Co., NC
Strong orange "bar" over **HW** blue spot.
Cell-end bars not aligned with bars above them.
Postmedian band composed of rectangles, not surrounded
at their ends with white (as is Edwards').
Bottom two segments of postmedian band nearly equal
(unequal in Edwards').
Local and rare.

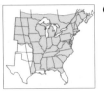

6 Striped Hairstreak *Satyrium liparops.* **p. 76**
Below. 7/4/96 Minnesota Valley NWR, Scott Co., MN
Striped appearance.
Orange cap on **HW** blue spot.
Cell-end bars aligned with bars above them.

Banded Hairstreak

2 Edwards' Hairstreak

Hickory Hairstreak

4 Acadian Hairstreak

King's Hairstreak

6 Striped Hairstreak

PLATE 19 GREEN HAIRSTREAKS

1 Juniper Hairstreak *Callophrys gryneus.* **p. 82**
Below. 7/7/91 Chappaqua, Westchester Co., NY
Smooth, olive-green ground color.
Found amidst stands of red cedars.

2 Hessel's Hairstreak *Callophrys hesseli.* **p. 83**
Below. 5/1/90 Chatsworth, Ocean Co., NJ
Emerald green ground color.
Top white spot on **FW** postmedian band displaced outwardly.
Found in white cedar swamps.
Very local, with widely separated colonies within the range
   shown.

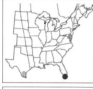

3 Silver-banded Hairstreak *Chlorostrymon simaethis.* **p. 71**
Below. 5/21/94 Tavernier, Key Largo, Monroe Co., FL
Bright acid green ground color.
HW postmedian line white and straight.

4 Amethyst Hairstreak *Chlorostrymon maesites.* **p. 71**
Below. Collected 6/25/35 Brickell Hammock, Miami, FL [This specimen was
the model for Fig. 10, Plate 15 in Klots (1951).]
No white postmedian line on **FW**.
HW with maroon marginal patch.
Extremely rare.

5 Early Hairstreak *Erora laeta.* **p. 88**
Below. 6/14/93 Mt. Greylock, Berkshire Co., MA
Mint green ground color.
Red-orange postmedian and submarginal spots.
Local and rare to uncommon.

6 ♀ above. 6/14/93 Mt. Greylock, Berkshire Co., MA

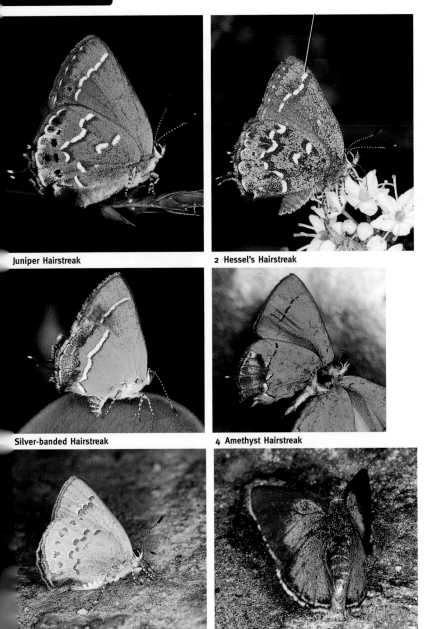

Juniper Hairstreak

2 Hessel's Hairstreak

Silver-banded Hairstreak

4 Amethyst Hairstreak

Early Hairstreak

6 Early Hairstreak ♀

PLATE 20 ELFINS

1 Henry's Elfin *Callophrys henrici.* **p. 79**
Below. 4/24/94 Larenim Park, Mineral Co., WV
Frosted **HW** margin.
Bold white marks at ends of **HW** postmedian band.
Short, tail-like protuberance on **HW**.

2 Brown Elfin *Callophrys augustinus.* **p. 77**
Below. 4/24/90 Waccabuc, Westchester Co., NY
Commonest elfin.
Rich brown, brighter reddish-brown on outer **HW**.
No frosting.
Almost always without white at postmedian line ends.

3 Frosted Elfin *Callophrys irus.* **p. 79**
Below. 4/25/94 Bratton's Run, Rockbridge Co., VA
Larger than most similar elfins.
Frosted **HW**.
Short, tail-like protuberance on **HW**.
Black spot near tailed area.
Found in barrens with lupine or wild indigo.

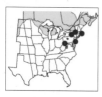

4 Hoary Elfin *Callophrys polios.* **p. 78**
Below. 4/26/97 Warren Grove, Ocean Co., NJ
Very dark.
Small.
Frosting on both **HW** and **FW** margins.
Found in low sand barrens with bearberry.

5 Eastern Pine Elfin *Callophrys niphon.* **p. 81**
Below. 5/1/90 Chatsworth, Burlington Co., NJ
Stunningly banded.

6 5/23/96 Voluntown, New London Co., CT.
Orange-brown patches on females above, visible in flight.

7 Western Pine Elfin *Callophrys eryphon.* **p. 81**
Below. 7/24/95 Carson Pass, Alpine Co., CA
HW submarginal black line with pointed black arrowheads
Not much gray on the **HW** margin.

8 Bog Elfin *Callophrys lanoraieensis.* **p. 80**
Below. 5/26/96 Lanoraie, Quebec
Much smaller than Eastern or Western pine elfins.
HW submarginal black line thick and smooth.
Extremely local in black spruce bogs within range shown

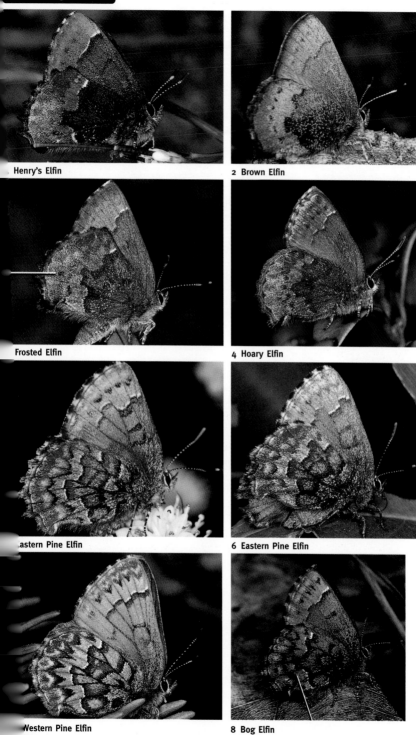

Henry's Elfin

2 Brown Elfin

Frosted Elfin

4 Hoary Elfin

Eastern Pine Elfin

6 Eastern Pine Elfin

Western Pine Elfin

8 Bog Elfin

PLATE 21 SCRUB-HAIRSTREAKS

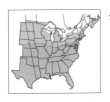

1 Gray Hairstreak *Strymon melinus.* **p. 84**
Below. 7/29/94 Blowing Rock, Watauga Co., NC
Common and widespread.
HW large orange marginal spot usually flat inwardly with
  black line on inward side.
Postmedian line with white outside, black adjacent, and
  often with some red on inward side.

2 ♀ above. 7/14/90 Gulf Shores, Baldwin Co., AL
Red-orange on crown of head.

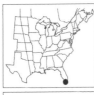

3 Martial Scrub-Hairstreak *Strymon martialis.* **p. 85**
Below. 3/24/94 Big Pine Key, Monroe Co., FL
Bold white postmedian line on both **HW** and **FW**.
HW without white basal spots.
Extreme southern Florida only.

4 Bartram's Scrub-Hairstreak *Strymon acis.* **p. 85**
Below. 5/21/94 Big Pine Key, Monroe Co., FL
Two white basal spots on **HW**.
Pine flatlands with narrow-leaved croton.
Local and threatened.
Everglades NP and Florida Keys only.

5 Mallow Scrub-Hairstreak *Strymon columella.* **p. 86**
Below. 3/25/94 Key West, Monroe Co., FL
Postmedian band of black and white crescents.
Strong black spot near base of **HW**.
Spot by tail often triple-colored—black, red, orange.
Texas population duller and spot, not triple-colored.

6 Disguised Scrub-Hairstreak *Strymon limenia.* **p. 207**
Below. 2/26/96 Vega Alta, Puerto Rico
Very rare stray to Florida Keys.
Browner than Mallow Scrub-Hairstreak.
Extra black spot along **HW** trailing margin.
Red outer angle lobes above. See text.

1 Gray Hairstreak

2 Gray Hairstreak ♀

Martial Scrub-Hairstreak

4 Bartram's Scrub-Hairstreak

allow Scrub-Hairstreak

6 Disguised Scrub-Hairstreak

PLATE 22 PYGMY-BLUES & BLACK-EYED BLUES

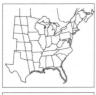

1 Eastern Pygmy-Blue *Brephidium isophthalma*. **p. 89**
Below. 9/29/96 Black River, Savannah, GA
Salt marsh tidal flats.
Four bold marginal eye-spots on **HW**.
FW unicolorous gray-brown.

2 Western Pygmy-Blue *Brephidium exile*. **p. 89**
Below. 9/11/93 Pearblossom, Los Angeles Co., CA
Four bold marginal eye-spots on **HW**.
FW strongly two-tone.

3 Above. 8/11/89 Wilcox Playa, Cochise Co., AZ
Copper-colored.

4 Miami Blue *Hemiargus thomasi*. **p. 91**
Below. 5/19/72 Islamorada, Monroe Co., FL
Broad white postmedian band on both **HW** and **FW**.
Two black eye-spots near **HW** outer angle,
Rare and local.

5 Marine Blue *Leptotes marina*. **p. 90**
Below. 8/9/96 Box Canyon, Pima Co., AZ
Zebra-striped.
Darker than Cassius Blue.

9 ♂ above. 9/13/93 Avalon, Catalina Island, CA
Purplish with strong blue basally.

6 Cassius Blue *Leptotes cassius*. **p. 90**
Below. 3/23/94 Royal Palm, Everglades NP, FL
Primarily white with darker stripes.
FW 4th dark band in from outer margin shorter than on
  Marine Blue, causing a white patch that Marine Blue lacks

7 Ceraunus Blue *Hemiargus ceraunus*. **p. 91**
Below. 9/28/95 Ocala NF, Marion Co., FL
HW with 1 or 2 strong marginal eye-spots.
HW with 2 strong black spots on the basal 1/2 of the lead
  margin.

8 ♂ above. 9/24/94 Gainesville, Alachu Co., FL
Black border around entire **HW**.

10 Reakirt's Blue *Hemiargus isola*. **p. 92**
Below. 8/9/96 Patagonia, Santa Cruz Co., AZ
FW with bold black spots.

11 ♂ above. 9/17/93 Morongo Valley, San Bernadino Co., CA

12 ♀ above. 10/21/93 Roma, Starr Co., TX

1 ...stern Pygmy-Blue

2 Western Pygmy-Blue

3 Western Pygmy-Blue

4 ...iami Blue

5 Marine Blue

6 Cassius Blue

7 ...eraunus Blue

8 Ceraunus Blue ♂

9 Marine Blue ♂

10 ...Reakirt's Blue

11 Reakirt's Blue ♂

12 Reakirt's Blue ♀

PLATE 23 AZURES

1 Spring Azure *Celastrina ladon.* **p. 93**
Form lucia below. Helmetta, Middlesex Co., NJ
Brown border. Brown patch in middle of **HW**.

2 ♂ above. 4/9/90 WPR, Westchester Co., NY
Brilliant blue. No black borders.

3 ♀ above. 4/29/93 WPR, Westchester Co., NY
Dull blue, wide black borders.

4 Form marginata below. 4/30/92 Chappaqua, NY
HW with brown border but no middle brown patch.

5 Form violacea below. 4/28/93 Monmouth Co., NJ
No brown border or patch.

6 'Cherry Gall' Spring Azure *Celastrina ladon* unnamed spp. **p.**
♀ above. 6/14/93 Mt. Greylock, Berkshire Co., MA
Flies between broods of Spring and Summer azures.

7 Appalachian Azure *Celastrina neglectamajor.* **p. 94**
5/28/97 Sourland Mtn. Park, Somerset Co., NJ
Same pattern as 'Summer' and 'Cherry Gall' Spring Azur
Generally larger.
Found with caterpillar foodplant—black cohosh.

12 ♀ above. 5/28/97 Sourland Mtn. Park, Somerset Co., NJ

8 'Edwards' Spring Azure *Celastrina ladon violacea.* **p. 93**
♂ above. 4/17/96 Fork Creek WMA, Boone Co., WV
Flatter, less brilliant blue than Spring Azure.

9 Summer Azure *Celastrina ladon neglecta.* **p. 94**
Below. 6/3/96 Lake Ashwood, Lee Co., SC
Essentially identical to Spring Azure form violacea.
Females very whitish above. See text.

10 Dusky Azure *Celastrina nigra.* **p. 95**
Below. 4/18/96 Fork Creek WMA, Boone Co., WV
Essentially identical to Spring Azure form violacea.

11 ♂ above (in flight—not to scale). 4/17/96 Fork Creek WMA, Boon
Co.,WV.
Dark gray, not blue.

Spring Azure, form lucia

2. Spring Azure ♂

3 Spring Azure ♀

Spring Azure, form marginata

5 Form violacea

6 'Cherry Gall' Azure ♀

Appalachian Azure

8 'Edwards' Azure ♂

9 'Summer' Azure

Dusky Azure

11 Dusky Azure ♂

12 Appalachian Azure ♀

PLATE 24 BLUES

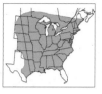

1 Eastern Tailed-Blue *Everes comyntas.* **p. 92**
Below. 5/13/96 Reston, Fairfax Co., VA
Tailed.
Orange spots by tail.

2 ♂ above. 5/13/96 Reston, Fairfax Co., VA
Tailed.
Orange spots by tail.
Darker blue than azures.

4 ♀ above. 7/29/94 Blowing Rock, Watauga Co., NC
Dark gray.
Tailed.
Orange spots by tail.
No red on head (Gray Hairstreak has red on head).

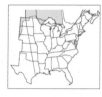

3 Western Tailed-Blue *Everes amyntula.* **p. 92**
Below. 7/20/95 Warren Creek, Mono Co., CA
Tailed.
Orange spots by tail faint.
Usually whiter than Eastern Tailed-Blue
♂ above lacks orange tail-spots. See text.

5 'Karner' Melissa Blue *Lycaeides melissa samuelis.* **p. 96**
Below. 7/19/89 Albany Pine Bush, Albany Co., NY
HW with submarginal orange band.
Black marginal dots at ends of veins.

6 ♂ above. 7/19/89 Albany Pine Bush, Albany Co., NY
Untailed. Blue.

8 ♀ above. 7/19/89 Albany Pine Bush, Albany Co., NY
Orange submarginal spots on **HW**.
See plate 25 for western ♀ Melissa Blue above.

7 Northern Blue *Lycaeides idas.* **p. 96**
Below. 7/23/95 Stanislaus NF, Tuolomne Co., CA
Extemely similar to Melissa Blue.
See female above, plate 25.

Eastern Tailed-Blue

2 Eastern Tailed-Blue ♂

Western Tailed-Blue

4 Eastern Tailed-Blue ♀

'Karner' Melissa Blue

6 'Karner' Melissa Blue ♂

rthern Blue

8 'Karner' Melissa Blue ♀

PLATE 25 BLUES

1 Silvery Blue *Glaucopsyche lygdamus.* **p. 95**
'Appalachian' Silvery Blue below. 4/17/96 Fork Creek WMA, Boone Co., WV
Postmedian band of bold black spots on both **FW** and **HW**.

2 ♀ above. 4/21/95 Los Angeles Co., CA

3 'Northern' Silvery Blue
Below. 6/12/93 Wilsons Mills, Oxford Co., ME
Postmedian band of bold black spots on **FW.**
HW postmedian band of black spots prominently ringed with white.

4 ♂ above. 4/17/96 Fork Creek WMA, Boone Co., WV

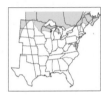

5 Greenish Blue *Plebejus saepiolus.* **p. 97**
Below. 7/18/95 Crane Flat, Yosemite NP, CA
Northern.
Usually with some orange between double spots at the **HW** outer angle.

6 ♂ above. 7/18/95 Crane Flat, Yosemite NP, CA
Black cell-end bars.

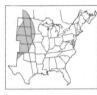

7 Melissa Blue *Lycaeides m. melissa.* **p. 96**
♀ above. 6/30/96 Glacial Lakes SP, Pope Co., MN
Orange bands on both **HW** and **FW**.

8 Northern Blue *Lycaeides idas.* **p. 96**
♀ above. 7/17/94 McNair, Lake Co., MN
Orange reduced compared to Melissa Blue (but 'Karner' Melissa Blue also has reduced orange on the **FW**).

Silvery Blue

2 Silvery Blue ♀

Silvery Blue

4 Silvery Blue ♂

Greenish Blue

6 Greenish Blue ♂

Melissa Blue ♀

8 Northern Blue ♀

PLATE 26 HELICONIANS

1 Gulf Fritillary *Agraulis vanillae*. **p. 100**
Below. 8/17/96 Heard Museum, McKinney, TX
HW heavily silvered.
FW long and narrow.

2 ♂ above. 6/19/95 Bayou Savage, New Orleans, LA
Red-orange.
Bright black-ringed white spots in **FW** cell.
♀ is similar but browner above.

3 Julia *Dryas iulia*. **p. 101**
Below. 5/23/94 Miami, Dade Co., FL
Long wings.
Brown with white and red at **HW** base.

4 ♂ above. 10/8/95 Bauer Park, Dade Co., FL
Bright brownish-orange.
Long narrow wings.

5 ♀ above. 5/20/94 Bauer Park, Dade Co., FL
Dull orange-brown.
Long narrow wings.
Black band across **FW**.

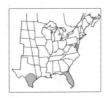

6 Zebra (Heliconian) *Heliconius charitonius*. **p. 101**
Below. 10/4/95 Royal Palm, Everglades NP, FL
Black with yellow stripes.
Long narrow wings.

7 Above. 3/21/91 Homestead, FL
Black with yellow stripes.
Long narrow wings.

8 Variegated Fritillary *Euptoieta claudia*. **p. 102**
Below. 6/29/91 Pelham Bay Park, Bronx, NY
Mottled **HW** with pale median and marginal patches.

9 Above. 5/24/87 Bogue Chitta NWR, Tammany Parish, LA
Dull orange-brown.
Chunky shape.
Black spots around submargin of **FW** and **HW**.

Gulf Fritillary

2 Gulf Fritillary ♂

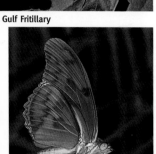

3 Julia

4 Julia ♂

5 Julia ♀

6 Zebra (Heliconian)

7 Zebra (Heliconian)

8 Variegated Fritillary

9 Variegated Fritillary

PLATE 27 DIANA & REGAL FRITILLARIES

1 Diana Fritillary *Speyeria diana.* **p. 103**
♀ below. 7/8/95 Fork Creek WMA, Boone Co., WV
Large.
Black and blue.
Moist mountain woodlands.

2 ♀ above. Western NC, date and locality unavailable.
Large.
Black and blue.
Moist mountain woodlands.

3 ♂ below. 7/31/94 Cherokee NF, Washington Co., TN
Large.
Orange-brown.
FW disc dark brown/black.
Moist mountain woodlands.

4 ♂ above. 7/31/94 Cherokee NF, Washington Co., TN
Large.
Chocolate and orange.
Moist mountain woodlands.

5 Regal Fritillary *Speyeria idalia.* **p. 105**
Below. 6/11/95 Prairie SP, Barton Co., MO
HW completely dark brown with bright white spots.
Body dark brown and black.
Open, low grassland.

6 ♀ above. 8/17/93 Fort Indiantown Gap, Lebanon Co., PA
HW black with bluish sheen and white spots.
Abdomen black.
Open, low grassland.

7 ♂ above. Same individual as 5.
HW completely black with white and orange spots.
Abdomen black.
Open, low grassland.

Diana Fritillary ♀

2 Diana Fritillary ♀

Diana Fritillary ♂

4 Diana Fritillary ♂

Regal Fritillary

6 Regal Fritillary ♀

7 Regal Fritillary ♂

PLATE 28 GREATER FRITILLARIES

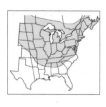

1 Great Spangled Fritillary *Speyeria cybele.* **p. 103**
Below. 6/12/95 Roaring River SP, Barry Co., MO
Widespread.
Yellowish-brown.
Silvered spots on **HW**.
Wide, cream-colored postmedian band on **HW**.

2 Above. 6/12/95 Roaring River SP, Barry Co., MO
Widespread.
Bright orange-brown.
No black spot at base of **FW**.
Females are larger and darker brown.

3 Aphrodite Fritillary *Speyeria aphrodite.* **p. 104**
Below. 7/26/96 Bailey's Harbor, Door Co., WI
HW dark brown ground color extends past the post-medi
silvered spots causing cream colored band to be narrow
FW disc usually somewhat rosy.

4 Above. 7/29/94 Blowing Rock, Watauga Co., NC
Black spot at base of **FW**.

5 Atlantis Fritillary *Speyeria atlantis.* **p. 106**
Below. 7/25/91 Moose River Plains, Inlet, Hamilton Co., NY
Relatively small.
HW ground color usually mousy gray-brown.
HW postmedian silvered spots with small dark "follow spot

6 Above. 7/26/96 Bailey's Harbor, Door Co., WI
Relatively small.
Black spot at base of **FW** usually faint or absent.
Solid black borders along most of **FW.** (Aphrodite sometin
has similar borders.)

eat Spangled Fritillary

2 Great Spangled Fritillary

hrodite Fritillary

4 Aphrodite Fritillary

lantis Fritillary

6 Atlantis Fritillary

PLATE 29 LESSER FRITILLARIES

1 Meadow Fritillary *Boloria bellona*. **p. 108**
Below. 6/25/90 WPR, Westchester Co., NY
Indistinct pattern, paler on outer 1/3 of **HW**.
FW apexes somewhat squared off.
Flies with shallow wing-beats.

2 Above. 7/30/94 Roan Mtn., Carter Co., TN
Orange.
Lacks black borders.
Moist meadows and fields.

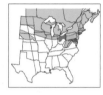

3 Silver-bordered Fritillary *Boloria selene*. **p. 107**
Below. 6/12/93 Errol, NH
Median and marginal silvered spots.

4 Above. 5/26/96 Lanorai, Quebec
Narrow black **HW** border encloses orange spots.
Wet situations.

5 Bog Fritillary *Boloria eunomia*. **p. 107**
Below. 6/13/93 Wilsons Mills, Oxford Co., ME
Bogs.
Postmedian band of small white spots (black in Silver-
bordered Fritillary).

6 Above. Same individual as 5.

7 Arctic Fritillary *Boloria chariclea*. **p. 109**
Below. 8/3/93 Mt. Washington, NH
FW margin with white horizontal lines.
HW with marginal row of flat white spots.

8 Above. 8/3/93 Mt. Washington, NH
HW with submarginal row of black inwardly pointing tri-
gles with flat bottoms

9 Freija Fritillary *Boloria freija*. **p. 109**
Below. June 1980. Floodwood Bog, Aitkin Co., MN
FW margin with white horizontal lines.
HW with "duck head" pattern (dark cell with black "eye"
and adjacent silver-white "bill"). See text.
HW marginal row of white spots not flat.

10 Frigga Fritillary *Boloria frigga*. **p. 108**
Below. May 1980. Kalavella Bog, Carlton Co., MN
Very similar to Meadow Fritillary.
White spot at base of **HW** prominent.
FW apexes rounded. (Meadow is squared off.)

Meadow Fritillary

2 Meadow Fritillary

Silver-bordered Fritillary

4 Silver-bordered Fritillary

Bog Fritillary

6 Bog Fritillary

Arctic Fritillary

8 Arctic Fritillary

eija Fritillary

10 Frigga Fritillary

PLATE 30 CHECKERSPOTS

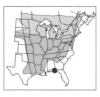

1 Silvery Checkerspot *Chlosyne nycteis*. **p. 110**
Below. 6/12/95 Roaring River SP, Barry Co., MO
HW with broad white median band.
HW submarginal white spot-band is interrupted.

2 Above. 6/12/95 Roaring River SP, Barry Co., MO
Larger than Pearl Crescent.
FW with wide black borders.
HW black submarginal spots surrounded by orange.
No (or faint) pale chevrons in the **HW** black border.

3 Harris' Checkerspot *Chlosyne harrisii*. **p. 111**
Below. 6/30/96 Glacial Lakes SP, Pope Co., MN
White and orange spot bands.
HW submarginal white spot-band is complete.

4 Above. 6/4/95 WPR, Westchester Co., NY
Very similar to Gorgone and Silvery Checkerspots.
HW black submarginal spots either rest directly on the black
    border or have black line attached distally.

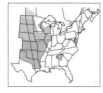

5 Gorgone Checkerspot *Chlosyne gorgone*. **p. 110**
Below. 4/17/95 Ouachita NF, Logan Co., AR
HW with bold mosaic pattern.

6 Above. Same individual as 5.
Usually with pale chevrons in the **HW** black border.

7 Baltimore Checkerspot *Euphydryas phaeton*. **p. 115**
Below. 6/24/93 Yorktown, Westchester Co., NY
Orange, black, and white spot-bands.

8 Above. 6/11/91 Oxford, Orange Co., NY
In flight, looks mainly black.

lvery Checkerspot

2 Silvery Checkerspot

arris' Checkerspot

4 Harris' Checkerspot

orgone Checkerspot

6 Gorgone Checkerspot

ltimore Checkerspot

8 Baltimore Checkerspot

PLATE 31 CRESCENTS, MAINLY SOUTHERN

1 **Phaon Crescent** *Phyciodes phaon.* **p. 112**
Below. 8/11/95 Sabine Pass, Jefferson Co., TX
HW tan with darker markings.
FW disc bright orange.
HW marginal crescent inwardly bounded by black line.

2 Above. 8/17/96 McKinney, Collin Co., TX
Cream-colored **FW** median band.

3 **Cuban Crescent** *Phyciodes frisia.* **p. 112**
Below. 5/21/94 W. Summerland Key, Monroe Co., FL

4 Above. Same individual as 3.
HW submarginal line more angled.
FW with three large orange-brown spots.

5 **Vesta Crescent** *Phyciodes vesta.* **p. 209**
Below. 11/12/89 Falcon SP, Starr Co., TX
Rare stray to eastern Kansas and Nebraska.
FW postmedian chain of black-circled orange spots.

6 Above. 10/25/95 Laguna Atascosa NWR, Cameron Co., TX
Rare stray to eastern Kansas and Nebraska.
Strongly reticulated with black.

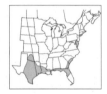

7 **Texan Crescent** *Phyciodes texana.* **p. 112**
Below. 9/29/95 Newnan's Lake, Alachua Co., FL
HW mottled dark with white median band.

8 Above. 6/19/96 Memorial Park, Houston, TX
Black with red-orange basally.
HW with white median band.

aon Crescent

2 Phaon Crescent

uban Crescent

4 Cuban Crescent

esta Crescent

6 Vesta Crescent

xan Crescent

8 Texan Crescent

PLATE 32 CRESCENTS, MAINLY NORTHERN

1 Pearl Crescent *Phyciodes tharos*. **p. 113**
♀ below. 7/7/93 Chappaqua, Westchester Co., NY
HW reticulated.
HW with pale marginal crescent.
FW with dark marginal patch below apex.
Abundant and widespread.

2 ♀ above. 7/6/96 Troy Meadows, Morris Co., NJ
Orange with black reticulations.

3 ♂ below. 8/15/96 Garland, Dallas Co., TX
HW with pale marginal crescent.
FW with dark marginal patch below apex.

4 ♂ above. 8/30/95 Great Dismal Swamp NWR, Suffolk, VA

5 Northern Crescent *Phyciodes selenis*. **p. 114**
Below. 6/12/93 Errol, NH
Probably not separable from Pearl Crescent. See text.

6 ♂ above. Same individual as 5.
Averages larger than Pearl Crescent.
HW with more "open" orange—black chevrons, inwardly
   bordering submarginal black spots, faint or absent.
See text.

9 ♀ above. 6/28/96 McNair, Lake Co., MN
Averages darker than ♀ Pearl Crescent.
See text.

7 Tawny Crescent *Phyciodes batesii*. **p. 115**
Below. 6/5/96 Jones Gap, Highlands, Macon Co., NC
HW straw yellow with only faint markings.
FW without marginal dark patch below apex.
FW black median bar usually long and rectangular.
(Pearl and Northern Crescents usually have this bar taper
   downward and curved outward.)

8 ♂ above. 6/28/96 McNair, Lake Co., MN
FW usually heavily suffused with black.

10 ♀ above. Same individual as 7.
FW usually heavily suffused with black.

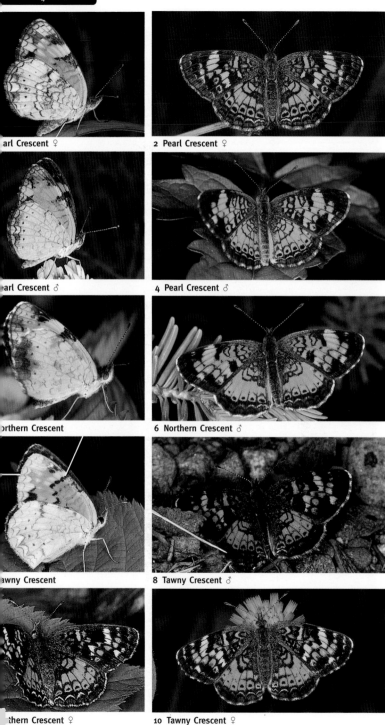

arl Crescent ♀

2 Pearl Crescent ♀

arl Crescent ♂

4 Pearl Crescent ♂

orthern Crescent

6 Northern Crescent ♂

awny Crescent

8 Tawny Crescent ♂

thern Crescent ♀

10 Tawny Crescent ♀

PLATE 33 WIDESPREAD ANGLEWINGS

1 **Question Mark** *Polygonia interrogationis.* **p. 117**
"Orange" form below. Jamaica Bay, Queens NY
HW with silvered "question-mark."

2 "Orange" form above. 10/29/94 Morristown, Morris Co., NJ
FW black horizontal subapical mark.
Violaceous **HW** margin.

5 "Black" form below. 7/9/94 Chappaqua, Westchester Co., NY
HW with silvered "question-mark."

6 "Black" form above. 7/9/95 Mt. Kisco, Westchester Co., NY
FW black horizontal subapical mark.
Violaceous **HW** margin.

3 **Eastern Comma** *Polygonia comma.* **p. 117**
"Orange" form below.
HW with silvered "comma."

4 "Orange" form above.
Smaller than Question Mark.
Lacks **FW** black horizontal subapical mark.

7 "Black" form below. 8/22/92 Great Dismal Swamp NWR, Suffolk, VA
HW with silvered "comma."

8 "Black" form above. 7/12/95 Lunenburg, Essex Co., VT
Smaller than Question Mark.
Lacks **FW** black horizontal subapical mark.

estion Mark

2 Question Mark

stern Comma

4 Eastern Comma

estion Mark

6 Question Mark

stern Comma

8 Eastern Comma

PLATE 34 NORTHERN ANGLEWINGS

1 Green Comma *Polygonia faunus.* **p. 118**

Below. 7/23/91 Moose River Plains, Hamilton Co., NY

Very jagged wings.

Blue-green submarginal band.

Comma mark with inner end thick and hooked.

2 Above. 7/26/91 Moose River Plains, Hamilton Co., NY

FW with two black spots just below two cell spots.

Yellow spots inward of black **HW** border.

3 Gray Comma *Polygonia progne.* **p. 120**

Below. 6/12/95 Roaring River SP, Barry Co., MO

Gray-brown, usually with fine striations.

Comma mark is thin and tapers at both ends.

Compton Tortoiseshell (Plate 35) is larger.

4 Above. 7/12/95 Lunenburg, Essex Co., VT

HW with broad black borders with small yellow spots.

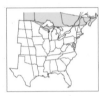

5 Satyr Comma *Polygonia satyrus.* **p. 118**

Below. 6/23/97 Burleigh Murray SP, San Mateo Co., CA

Very similar to Eastern Comma (Plate 33).

Usually unicolorous at the **FW** apex. (Eastern Comma two-toned).

HW median line straighter than Eastern Comma.

6 Above. 6/16/97 Burleigh Murray SP, San Mateo Co., CA

Golden colored.

HW margin tan (Eastern Comma gray or violet).

See text.

7 Hoary Comma *Polygonia gracilis.* **p. 119**

Below. 8/13/93 Scotts Bog, Pittsburg, NH

Two-toned appearance.

Outer 1/3 of wings very "hoary."

HW margin not pale gray.

8 Above. 8/21/93 Scotts Bog, Pittsburg, NH

FW with only one black spot below two cell spots. (Green Comma with two.)

FW cell-end bar curved on both sides. (Green Comma straighter.)

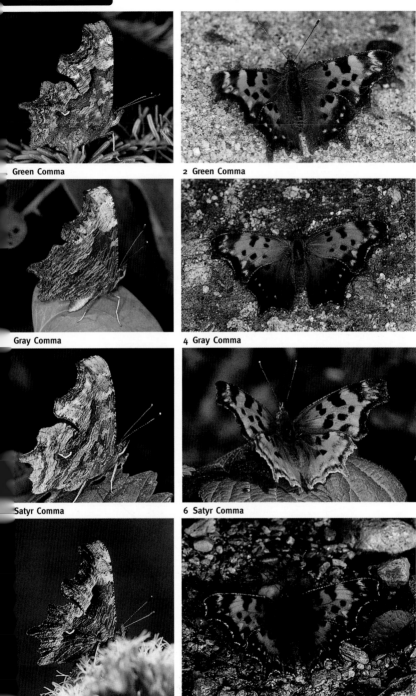

Green Comma

2 Green Comma

Gray Comma

4 Gray Comma

Satyr Comma

6 Satyr Comma

Hoary Comma

8 Hoary Comma

PLATE 35 TORTOISESHELLS

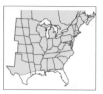

1 Mourning Cloak *Nymphalis antiopa.* **p. 121**
Below. 7/2/96 Stone SP, Woodbury Co., IA
Very dark striated brown.
Cream-yellow borders.

2 Above. 6/11/95 Prairie SP, Barton Co., MO
Deep brown.
Cream-yellow borders.

3 Compton Tortoiseshell *Nymphalis vau-album.* **p. 120**
Below. 7/7/96 Troy Meadows, Morris Co., NJ
Heavily striated dark gray.
Larger than Gray Comma.

4 Above. Same individual as 3.
Orange, black, and brown.
White spot on **HW**.

5 Milbert's Tortoiseshell *Nymphalis milberti.* **p. 121**
Below. 6/29/96 Savannah SF, Aitkin Co., MN
Very dark ground color.
Wide pale submarginal bands.

6 Above. 6/14/93 Mt. Greylock, Berkshire Co., MA
Bright orange and yellow submarginal bands.
Dark ground color.

7 Small Tortoiseshell *Nymphalis urticae.* **p. 209**
Above. 8/31/88 Jamaica Bay Wildlife Refuge, NY
Bright orange.
Black and yellow stripes along **FW** margin.
Black basal half of **HW**.
European, recent reports from New York City area.
See text.

8 California Tortoiseshell *Nymphalis californica.* **p. 209**
Above. Oct. 1989 Tahoe NF, Nevada Co., CA
Orange-brown.
Black and orange and yellow stripes along **FW** margin.
HW mostly orange.
Very rare stray only.

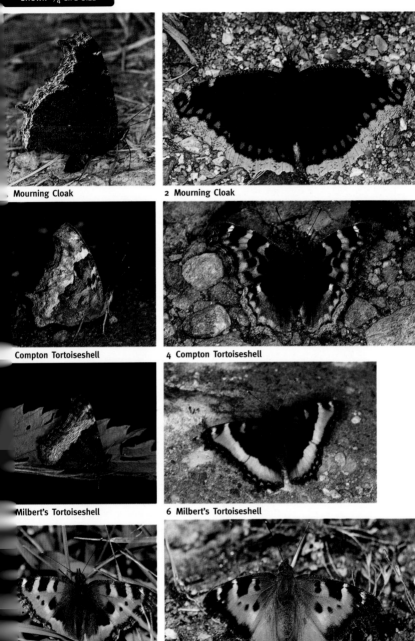

Mourning Cloak

2 Mourning Cloak

Compton Tortoiseshell

4 Compton Tortoiseshell

Milbert's Tortoiseshell

6 Milbert's Tortoiseshell

Small Tortoiseshell

8 California Tortoiseshell

PLATE 36 LADIES & AMERICAN SNOUT

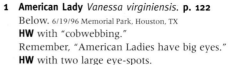

1 American Lady *Vanessa virginiensis*. **p. 122**
Below. 6/19/96 Memorial Park, Houston, TX
HW with "cobwebbing."
Remember, "American Ladies have big eyes."
HW with two large eye-spots.

2 Above. 6/30/94 WPR, Westchester Co., NY
FW black median markings usually not connected.
FW often with small white spot in orange ground.
(This spot is often more prominent than on this individual.)

3 Painted Lady *Vanessa cardui*. **p. 122**
Below. 9/13/91 Snug Harbor, Staten Island, NY
HW with "cobwebbing."
HW with four smallish eye-spots.

4 Above. 6/12/95 Roaring River SP, Barry Co., MO
FW with bold black median band forming semicircle.
FW often flushed with pink.
No white spot in orange ground.

5 Red Admiral *Vanessa atalanta*. **p. 123**
Below. 6/25/89 WPR, Westchester Co., NY
HW dark and mottled.
Red, white, and blue along the **FW** costal margin.

6 Above. 7/3/96 Homer, Dakota Co., NE
FW with bright red-orange median band.
HW with bright red-orange marginal band.
Appears small and dark during its rapid flight.

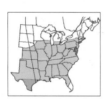

7 American Snout *Libytheana carinenta*. **p. 100**
Below. 8/22/88 Vernon, Sussex Co., NJ
Extremely long palps.
Ground color variable.

8 Above. 10/21/93 La Joya, Starr Co., TX
Extremely long palps.
Orange basally, wide blackish brown borders.
White subapical spots.

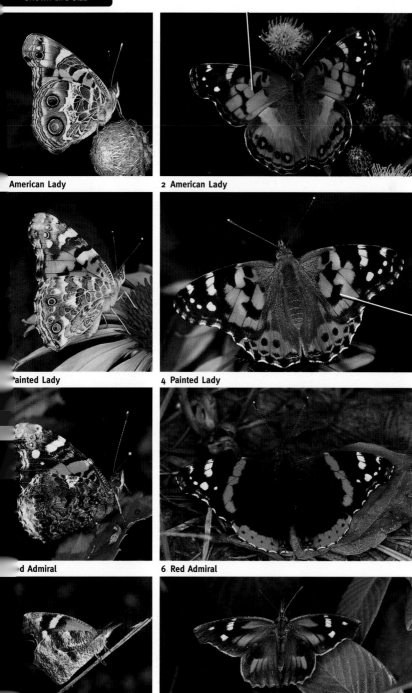

American Lady

2 American Lady

ainted Lady

4 Painted Lady

d Admiral

6 Red Admiral

merican Snout

8 American Snout

PLATE 37 BUCKEYES & PEACOCKS

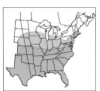

1 Common Buckeye *Junonia coenia*. **p. 124**
Below. 6/14/95 Wagoner, Wagoner Co., OK
HW pale with darker lines.
FW often with white on inside of large eye-spot
 (not visible in photo).

2 Above. 6/17/96 Big Thicket, Polk Co., TX
Prominent eye-spots on both wings.
Two orange bars in the **FW** cell.
FW usually with white on inside of large eye-spot.
FW band just past cell usually off-white.
Contrasting orange patch by **FW** eye-spot at tornus.
Two **HW** eye-spots unequal in size.
HW orange submarginal band is wide.

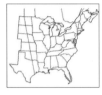

3 Mangrove Buckeye *Junonia evarete*. **p. 125**
Below. 3/23/94 Mrazek Pond, Everglades NP, FL
Most of **HW** fairly unicolorous dull brown.

4 Above. 3/25/94 Little Hamaca Park, Key West, FL
Large **FW** eye-spot completely surrounded by orange.
FW band just past cell is orange.
Two **HW** eye-spots fairly similar in size.
HW orange submarginal band is wide.

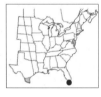

5 Tropical Buckeye *Junonia genoveva*. **p. 125**
Below. 12/4/94 New Providence, Bahamas
HW with prominent pale median stripe.

6 Above. 12/4/94 Same individual as 5.
Brown or pale brown to the inside of large **FW** eye-spot.
FW band just past cell is wide and flushed with pink.
HW orange submarginal band is narrow.

7 White Peacock *Anartia jatrophae*. **p. 126**
Below. 5/23/94 Miami, Dade Co., FL
Pearly white with darker markings.
Pale orange margins.

8 Above. 10/2/95 Tree Tops Park, Broward Co., FL
Pearly gray-white with darker markings.
Orange margins.

mmon Buckeye

2 Common Buckeye

ngrove Buckeye

4 Mangrove Buckeye

pical Buckeye

6 Tropical Buckeye

ite Peacock

8 White Peacock

PLATE 38 ADMIRALS & MIMICS

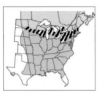

1 Red-spotted Purple *Limenitis arthemis astyanax.* **p. 127**
Below. 8/2/94 Fort Bragg, Cumberland Co., NC
Red-orange spots at wing bases and in a submarginal ba

2 Above. 4/17/95 Ouachita NF, Logan Co., AR
Iridescent blue **HW**.
No tails.
Range shown in green; black striped area indicates zone
hybrids with White Admiral.

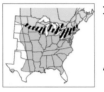

3 White Admiral *Limenitis arthemis arthemis.* **p. 127**
Below. 6/9/90 Jamesville, Onadagada Co., NY
Broad white bands.
Red-orange spots.

4 Above. 7/11/95 Moose Brook SP, Gorham, NH
Broad white bands.
Range shown in yellow; black striped area indicates zor
hybrids with Red-spotted Purple.

5 Viceroy *Limenitis archippus.* **p. 128**
Below. 6/18/96 Brazos Bend SP, Brazoria Co., TX
HW with black postmedian band.

6 Above. 8/2/89 WPR, Westchester Co., NY
Deep orange (browner and darker in Florida).
Smaller than Monarch.
HW with black postmedian band.

7 Mimic *Hypolimnas misippus.* **p. 124**
♂ above. 9/9/76 Subic Bay, Grande Island, Philippines
Rare stray to south Florida.
Extremely large white spots on black ground.

8 ♀ above. 9/23/76 Subic Bay, Grande Island, Philippines
Rare stray to south Florida.
FW with bold white subapical stripe.

Red-spotted Purple

2 Red-spotted Purple

White Admiral

4 White Admiral

Viceroy

6 Viceroy

Mimic ♂

8 Mimic ♀

PLATE 39 LEAFWINGS, DAGGERWINGS & MESTRA

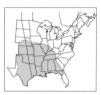

1 Goatweed Leafwing *Anaea andria.* **p. 130**
Below. 6/14/95 Delaware Co., OK
FW apex usually hooked.
Dead leaf pattern.

2 Above. 6/12/95 Roaring River SP, Barry Co., MO
Orange-brown (males brighter).
HW with short tail.

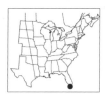

3 Florida Leafwing *Anaea floridalis.* **p. 130**
Below. 3/22/90 Everglades NP, Dade Co., FL
Mottled gray.
FW with hooked apex.
HW with short tail.
Usually lands on tree limbs or trunks.

4 Above (caught by green lynx spider). 10/4/95 Long Pine Key,
Everglades NP, Dade Co., FL
Bright red-orange.
Usually lands with wings closed.

5 Ruddy Daggerwing *Marpesia petreus.* **p. 129**
Below. 3/21/90 South Miami, Dade Co., FL
Mauve-gray-brown wings.
White body and wing bases.
FW sharply angled by apex.
HW with long tail.

6 Above. 3/25/90 Matheson Hammock, Dade Co., FL
Bright orange with black stripes across **FW** and **HW**.
FW sharply angled by apex.
HW with long tail.

7 Common Mestra *Mestra amymone.* **p. 210**
Above. 10/24/94 Peñitas, Hidalgo Co., TX
Off-white.
Slow, fluttering flight.
Apricot-colored **HW** border.

8 Many-banded Daggerwing *Marpesia chiron.* **p. 211**
Above. 2/12/95 Mismaloya, Jalisco, Mexico
Brown with black stripes across **FW** and **HW**.
HW with long tail.
Short dagger tail at **HW** outer angle.
Possible stray from West Indies and Mexico.
1 report from Florida Keys.

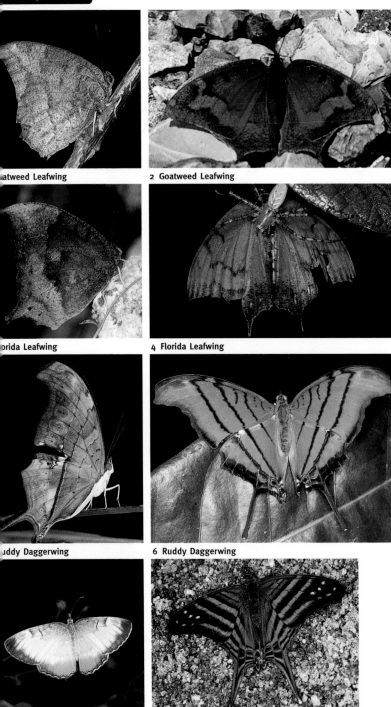

atweed Leafwing

2 Goatweed Leafwing

orida Leafwing

4 Florida Leafwing

ıddy Daggerwing

6 Ruddy Daggerwing

ommon Mestra

8 Many-banded Daggerwing

PLATE 40 EMPERORS, PURPLEWINGS, PURPLEWINGS & MALACHITE

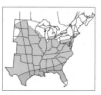

1 Hackberry Emperor *Asterocampa celtis.* **p. 130**
Below. 6/18/96 Brazos Bend SP, Brazoria Co., TX
Creamy gray-brown.
Prominent eye-spots on **HW** and **FW**.

2 Above. 7/2/96 Plymouth Co., IA
Dark brown.
FW with white spots.
FW with a black eye-spot (2 in south Texas).

3 Tawny Emperor *Asterocampa clyton.* **p. 131**
Below. 8/6/94 Darby Creek Park, Franklin Co., OH
Mauve gray-brown.
No eye-spots on **FW.**

4 Above. 7/4/96 Minnesota Valley NWR, Scott Co., MN
Warm orange-brown.
FW without white spots.
FW without black eye-spot.

5 Florida Purplewing *Eunica tatila.* **p. 129**
Below. 11/11/89 Bentsen SP, Hidalgo Co., TX
Dark brown with a squared off **FW** apex.
FW with two subapical white spots with a black spot
   between them.
Flies in the interior of hardwood hammocks.

6 Malachite *Siproeta stelenes.* **p. 126**
Above. 10/6/95 Sugarloaf Key, Monroe Co., FL
Large.
Green.

8 Below. 10/21/93 Roma, Starr Co., TX
Large.
Green.

7 Dingy Purplewing *Eunica monima.* **p. 128**
Below. 2/12/95 Mismaloya, Jalisco, Mexico
Warm mauve gray-brown.
FW apex rounded.
HW with circular line enclosing two spots, bottom spot
   black, top spot gray-white.
Local and rare.

ckberry Emperor

2 Hackberry Emperor

wny Emperor

4 Tawny Emperor

orida Purplewing

6 Malachite

ngy Purplewing

8 Malachite

PLATE 41 WOOD-NYMPHS & BROWNS

1 Common Wood-Nymph *Cercyonis pegala*. **p. 138**
Below. 8/3/93 Lunenburg, Essex Co., VT
Very dark brown.
Large, isolated **FW** subapical eye-spot.

2 Below. 6/30/94. WPR Westchester Co., NY
FW with large yellow-orange postmedian patch.

3 Appalachian Brown *Satyrodes appalachia*. **p. 134**
Below. 6/23/96 WPR, Westchester Co., NY
Pale brown.
Each **HW** eye-spot surrounded by pale circle.
Postmedian line relatively smooth.
HW basal line straight.
FW bottom eye-spot surrounded individually by pale line
yielding a "bull's-eye" effect.
FW eye-spots usually of unequal intensity.

4 Above. 6/23/96 WPR, Westchester Co., NY
Prefers wet wooded areas.

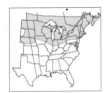

5 Eyed Brown *Satyrodes eurydice*. **p. 133**
Below. 6/30/96 Glacial Lakes SP, Pope Co., MN
Pale brown.
Each **HW** eye-spot surrounded by pale circle.
Postmedian line relatively jagged.
HW basal line with inward directed "tooth" at 2nd vein
from leading edge.
FW eye-spots surrounded as a group by pale line, yielding
"pea pod" effect.
FW eye-spots of nearly equal intensity.

6 Above. 7/26/96 Bailey's Harbor, Door Co., WI
Prefers wet open areas.

7 'Smoky' Eyed Brown *S. eurydice fumosa*. **p. 133**
Below. 7/28/96 Newark Prairie, Beloit, Rock Co., WI
Dark brown.
Usually with five eye-spots on **FW**.

8 Above. 7/28/96 Newark Prairie, Beloit, Rock Co., WI
Wet areas on prairies.
Southern Minnesota southeast to northwestern Indiana.

Common Wood-Nymph

2 Common Wood-Nymph

Appalachian Brown

4 Appalachian Brown

yed Brown

6 Eyed Brown

moky' Eyed Brown

8 'Smoky' Eyed Brown

PLATE 42 PEARLY-EYES

1 Northern Pearly-eye *Enodia anthedon.* **p. 132**
Below. 6/8/95 Pontotoc Ridge, Pontotoc Co., OK
Dark brown.
HW submarginal eye-spots are surrounded as a group by
one continuous white line.
Antennal clubs with black at their bases.
FW eye-spots in a relatively straight line.
Prefers rocky deciduous woodlands.

2 Above. 7/11/95 Gorham, NH
HW black eye-spots very large.

3 Southern Pearly-eye *Enodia portlandia.* **p. 132**
Below. 8/1/94 Fort Bragg, Moore Co., NC
Dark brown.
HW submarginal eye-spots are surrounded as a group by
one continuous white line.
Antennal clubs are orange-yellow, without black.
FW eye-spots curve slightly out toward apex.
FW postmedian line comes to a point near center of wing.
Prefers rich bottomland woods with cane.

4 Below. 9/13/80 Fulton Co., KY
South central population is more "golden."

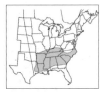

5 Creole Pearly-eye *Enodia creola.* **p. 133**
Below. 8/22/92 Great Dismal Swamp NWR, Suffolk, VA
FW postmedian line pushed outward, in the shape of a fist
with "knuckles" showing.
FW with 5 eye-spots in a relatively straight line.
HW submarginal eye-spots are individually surrounded by
white circles.

6 Above. 8/30/95 Great Dismal Swamp NWR, Suffolk, VA
Dark sex patches along veins.
Found by canebrakes in dense woodlands.

Northern Pearly-eye

2 Northern Pearly-eye

Southern Pearly-eye

4 Southern Pearly-eye

Creole Pearly-eye

6 Creole Pearly-eye

PLATE 43 SATYRS

1 Carolina Satyr *Hermeuptychia sosybius.* **p. 135**
Below. 9/29/96 Skidaway Island, Savannah, GA
No lower **FW** eye-spot. **HW** with cell-end bar.
Prefers woodlands and woodland edges.

2 Above.9/30/96 Skidaway Island, Savannah, GA
No eye-spots.

3 Little Wood-Satyr *Megisto cymela.* **p. 137**
Below. 7/2/96 Plymouth Co., IA
Two eye-spots on **FW**. **HW** without cell-end bar.
Abundant and widespread.

4 Above. 7/3/96 Homer, Dakota Co., NE
Two large eye-spots on both **FW** and **HW**.

5 Viola's Wood-Satyr *Megisto viola.* **p. 137**
Below. 3/16/94 Newnan's Lake, Alachua Co., FL
Prominent silver markings between eye-spots.
See text.

6 Above. 3/16/94 Newnan's Lake, Alachua Co., FL
Eye-spots somewhat larger than Little Wood-Satyr.

7 Gemmed Satyr *Cyllopsis gemma.* **p. 135**
Below. 4/23/94 Fork Creek WMA, Boone Co., WV
"Gemmed" with a silvery-gray **HW** marginal patch.
No **FW** eye-spots.

8 Red Satyr *Megisto rubricata.* **p. 212**
Below. 8/6/89 Ash Canyon, Cochise Co., AZ
FW disc flushed with red-orange, below and above.
RS to the west edge of our region in Texas.

9 Georgia Satyr *Neonympha areolata.* **p. 136**
Below. 6/26/94 Lakehurst Bog, Ocean Co., NJ
Orange-brown ring surrounds **HW** eye-spots.
HW eye-spots quite elongated.
FW spots faint or absent.

10 Mitchell's Satyr *Neonympha mitchellii.* **p. 136**
Below. 8/1/94 Fort Bragg, Cumberland Co., NC
HW eye-spots close to round.
FW with 3 or 4 eye-spots.
Extremely rare and local. Fens (MI) and bogs (NC).

1 Carolina Satyr

2 Carolina Satyr

Little Wood-Satyr

4 Little Wood-Satyr

Viola's Wood-Satyr

6 Viola's Wood-Satyr

Gemmed Satyr

8 Red Satyr

Georgia Satyr

10 Mitchell's Satyr

PLATE 44 RINGLET, ALPINE & ARCTICS

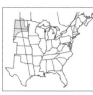

1 Uhler's Arctic *Oeneis uhleri*. **p. 141**
Below. 5/16/92 Pakowki Lake, Alberta
HW with prominent multiple eye-spots.
Small, prefers prairies.

2 Common Ringlet *Coenonympha tullia*. **p. 138**
Below. 8/26/92 WPR, Westchester Co., NY
Small. Common.
Red-orange flush on disc often visible in flight.
Often paler than individual shown.

3 Chryxus Arctic *Oeneis chryxus*. **p. 141**
Below. 7/22/95 Sonora Pass, Alpine Co., CA
Variable, mottled brown and off-white.
Extensive tawny-orange around **FW** subapical eye-spot.
No frosting at **FW** or **HW** apexes.
Not so bright above as Macoun's Arctic.

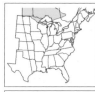

4 Red-disked Alpine *Erebia discoidalis*. **p. 140**
Below. May 1980 Kalavella Bog, Carlton Co., MN
HW dark with outer 1/3 heavily frosted.
FW disc reddish-brown below and above.

5 Macoun's Arctic *Oeneis macounii*. **p. 140**
Below. June1980 Langley Preserve, Pine Co., MN
Largest arctic in region.
Extensive tawny-orange around **FW** subapical eye-spot.
Usually with some frosting at **FW** and **HW** apexes.
Bright tawny-orange above.

6 Polixenes Arctic *Oeneis polixenes*. **p. 142**
Above. 7/4/85 Mt. Katahdin, ME
Only found above treeline on Mt. Katahdin, Maine.
Brown above with translucent **FW**.

7 Jutta Arctic *Oeneis jutta*. **p. 142**
Below. 6/12/93 Wilsons Mills, Oxford Co., ME
Large. Dull brown above. Found in black spruce bogs.
FW subapical eye-spot surrounded by tawny ring.

8 Melissa Arctic *Oeneis melissa*. **p. 142**
Below. 7/11/95 Mt. Washington, Gorham, NH
Peaks of White Mountains of New Hampshire only.
FW without subapical eye-spot (or very faint).
Brown above with translucent **FW**.

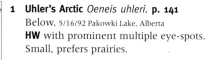

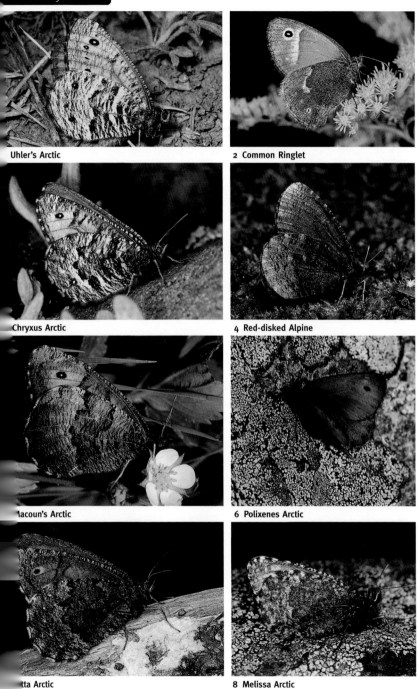

Uhler's Arctic

2 Common Ringlet

Chryxus Arctic

4 Red-disked Alpine

Macoun's Arctic

6 Polixenes Arctic

tta Arctic

8 Melissa Arctic

PLATE 45 MONARCHS

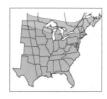

1 Monarch *Danaus plexippus.* **p. 143**
Below. 7/27/89 WPR, Westchester Co., NY
Large. Dull orange.
Black border with double marginal row of white spots.
White spots on body.

2 ♂ above. 7/30/94 Roan Mtn., Carter Co., TN
Bright orange.
HW without black postmedian band.
HW with black sex patch that ♀ lacks.
Glides with wings held in a "V."
Flies with deep powerful wingbeats.

4 ♀ above. 10/13/96 Morristown, Morris Co., NJ
Same as ♂ but lacks **HW** black sex patch.

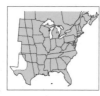

3 Viceroy *Limenitis archippus.* **p. 128**
Above. 8/21/95 Bombay Hook NWR, Kent Co., DE
Not related to monarchs, shown for comparison.
Smaller than Monarch.
HW with black postmedian band.
Glides on flat wings.
Flies with shallow wingbeats.

5 Queen *Danaus gilippus.* **p. 144**
Below. 8/15/96 McKinney, Collin Co., TX
Darker and browner than Monarch.
FW postmedian area with white spots.
FW without black subapical band.

6 ♂ above. 8/16/96 McKinney, Collin Co., TX
Rich mahogany brown.
FW postmedian area with white spots.
FW without black subapical band.
FW veins not blackened.

7 Soldier *Danaus erisimus.* **p. 144**
Below. 10/24/95 Hargill, Hidalgo Co., TX
HW with a postmedian pale patch.
FW postmedian area without white spots (area covered by **HW** in photo).
FW cell reddish.
FW veins blackened.

8 ♀ above. 10/26/95 Rio Grande City, Starr Co., TX
FW postmedian area without white spots. (Many FL individuals have two faint yellowish spots.)
FW veins blackened.

Monarch

2 Monarch ♂

Viceroy

4 Monarch ♀

Queen

6 Queen ♂

Soldier

8 Soldier ♀

PLATE 46 LARGE SKIPPERS

1 Golden-banded Skipper *Autochton cellus*. **p. 149**
Below. 8/15/89 Box Canyon, Pima Co., AZ
Luminous yellow band on **FW**.
No white patch on **HW**.

2 Above. 4/24/96 Tapoco, Graham Co., NC
Luminous yellow band on **FW**.
Local and rare.

3 Hoary Edge *Achalarus lyciades*. **p. 149**
Below. 8/1/94 Fort Bragg, Cumberland Co., NC
A large dark skipper.
Large white patch on **HW** margin.

4 Above. 8/2/94 Fort Bragg, Cumberland Co., NC
Brown-gold **FW** spot-band encloses some brown.

5 Silver-spotted Skipper *Epargyreus clarus*. **p. 146**
Below. 8/29/95 Bombay Hook NWR, Kent Co., DE
One of our largest skippers.
Large silvered spot in the middle of the **HW**.
Very common and widespread.

6 Above. 8/4/90 Lititz, Lancaster Co., PA
FW is angular.
Brown-gold **FW** spot-band doesn't enclose any brown.

7 Zestos Skipper *Epargyreus zestos*. **p. 146**
Below. 5/22/94 Stock Island, Monroe Co., FL
Looks like a Silver-spotted without the silver spot.
Local, rare and declining on the Florida Keys.

8 Mercurial Skipper *Proteides mercurius*. **p. 212**
Below. 2/7/95 Mismaloya, Jalisco, Mexico
Very large.
Golden head and thorax.
HW dark mottled with much white.
Very rare stray to southern Florida.

1 Golden-banded Skipper

2 Golden-banded Skipper

Hoary Edge

4 Hoary Edge

ilver-spotted Skipper

6 Silver-spotted Skipper

stos Skipper

8 Mercurial Skipper

PLATE 47 LONGTAILS

1 Long-tailed Skipper *Urbanus proteus*. **p. 148**
Below. 9/28/96 Savannah River, Savannah, GA
Long tail on **HW**.
FW postmedian dark band continuous.

2 Above. 9/29/96 Savannah River, Savannah, GA
Long and broad tails.
Blue-green iridescence on body and wing bases.

3 Dorantes Longtail *Urbanus dorantes*. **p. 148**
Below. 3/20/90 South Miami, Dade Co., FL
Long tail on **HW**.
FW postmedian dark band interrupted by ground color
pushing out toward wing margin.

4 Above. 9/24/94 Gainesville, Alachua Co., FL
Long tails.
No blue-green iridescence.

5 White-striped Longtail *Chioides catillus*. **p. 147**
Below. 11/10/89 Santa Ana NWR, Hidalgo Co.,TX
Very long tail on **HW**.
White stripe across middle of **HW**.
Black upside-down triangle at the **FW** subapex.
Rare immigrant to Houston area.

6 Above. 10/21/95 Santa Ana NWR, Hidalgo Co., TX
Very long broad tails.
No blue-green iridescence.
FW spots very large and white.
Rare immigrant to Houston area.

1 Long-tailed Skipper

2 Long-tailed Skipper

3 Dorantes Longtail

4 Dorantes Longtail

5 White-striped Longtail

6 White-striped Longtail

PLATE 48 LARGE SKIPPERS

1 Mangrove Skipper *Phocides pigmalion.* **p. 146**
Below. 3/23/90 Key Largo, Monroe Co., FL
Much iridescent cobalt blue.
Iridescent turquoise bands on **HW**.

2 Above. 5/22/93 Stock Island, Monroe Co., FL
Very large.
Much iridescent cobalt blue.
Iridescent turquoise on **HW**.

3 Hammock Skipper *Polygonus leo.* **p. 147**
Below. 3/25/94 Stock Island, Monroe Co., FL
Often lands upside down under a leaf.
Blue-tinged gray-brown ground color.
Black spot near base of the **HW**.

4 Above. 3/21/90 South Miami, Dade Co., FL
Blackish-brown with blue iridescent sheen.
Three large white spots on the **FW**.
Three small subapical white spots on the **FW**.

5 Outis Skipper *Cogia outis.* **p. 152**
Above. 8/10/95 Barton Creek Park, Austin, TX
Brown with a semi-circle of white spots on the **FW**.
FW long and narrow.
White patch just below the antennal club.
Areas with acacias (perched on an acacia in photo).

6 Sickle-winged Skipper *Achlyodes thraso.* **p. 153**
Above. 10/15/94 Sabal Palms, Brownsville, TX
FW curved outward at apex, like a sickle.
Purple-blue iridescence.
Pale band on **FW** postmedian costa.
Rare immigrant to Houston area.

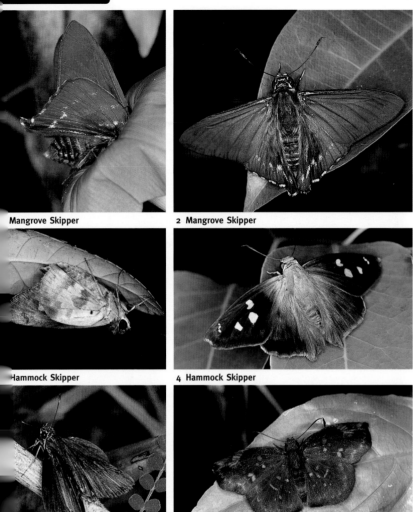

Mangrove Skipper

2 Mangrove Skipper

Hammock Skipper

4 Hammock Skipper

utis Skipper

6 Sickle-winged Skipper

PLATE 49 CLOUDYWINGS

1 Northern Cloudywing *Thorybes pylades*. **p. 151**
Below. 5/29/91 WPR, Westchester Co., NY
"Face" brown or dark gray.

2 Above. Same individual as 1.
Uniform brown ground color.
White spots usually restricted.

3 Southern Cloudywing *Thorybes bathyllus*. **p. 150**
Below. 6/28/90 Oakwood Cemetery, Mt. Kisco, NY
"Face" white or pale gray.

4 Above. 6/7/91 Oakwood Cemetery, Mt. Kisco, NY
Uniform brown ground color.
White spots usually large.
FW with second from the costa, white median spot often
shaped like an hourglass.
White patch at bend in antennal club.

5 Confused Cloudywing *Thorybes confusis*. **p. 151**
Below. 8/23/91 Gainesville, Alachua Co., FL
"Face" white or pale gray.
Outer 1/3 of **FW** often pale.
See text.

6 Above. 8/1/94 Fort Bragg, Cumberland Co., NC
White spots vary from very restricted to extensive.
Middle spot of lower group of three spots usually a pale
thin line (if present at all).
Individuals with extensive markings resemble Southern
Cloudywings but lack the white patch at the bend in
antennal club.
See text.

Northern Cloudywing

2 Northern Cloudywing

Southern Cloudywing

4 Southern Cloudywing

onfused Cloudywing

6 Confused Cloudywing

PLATE 50 LARGER DUSKYWINGS

1 Horace's Duskywing *Erynnis horatius.* **p. 156**
♂ above. 7/14/90 Gulf Shores, Baldwin Co., AL
Pale spot near end of **FW** cell (sometimes faint).
Fairly uniform brown without gray.
White line over eye.
See Zarucco Duskywing, plate 52.

2 ♀ above. 6/8/95 Pontotoc Ridge, Pontotoc Co., OK
Large for a duskywing.
White spots large on **FW**.
Pale spot near end of **FW** cell.
Very strong pattern.
Large, dark submarginal spots on paler **HW** ground.
See Wild Indigo Duskywing, plate 52.

5 Below. 7/11/91 Lakehurst, Ocean Co., NJ
No pale subapical spots on **HW**.

3 Juvenal's Duskywing *Erynnis juvenalis.* **p. 156**
♂ above. 4/23/94 Fork Creek WMA, Boone Co., WV
Large for a duskywing.
White spots large on **FW**.
Pale spot near end of **FW** cell (sometimes faint).
Usually with much gray on the **FW**.

4 ♀ above. 4/15/95 Busch, Carroll Co., AR
Large for a duskywing.
White spots large on **FW**.
Pale spot near end of **FW** cell.

6 Below. 5/22/92 Chappaqua, Westcester Co., NY
Two pale subapical spots on **HW** (almost always).

7 Florida Duskywing *Ephyriades brunneus.* **p. 154**
♂ above. 3/22/90 Long Pine Key, Everglades NP, FL
Semicircle of white spots near the **FW** apex.
Brown ground color fairly uniform.
Prefers pinelands.

8 ♀ above. 3/22/90 Long Pine Key, Everglades NP, FL
Semicircle of white spots near the **FW** apex.
Violaceous sheen when fresh.
Prefers pinelands.

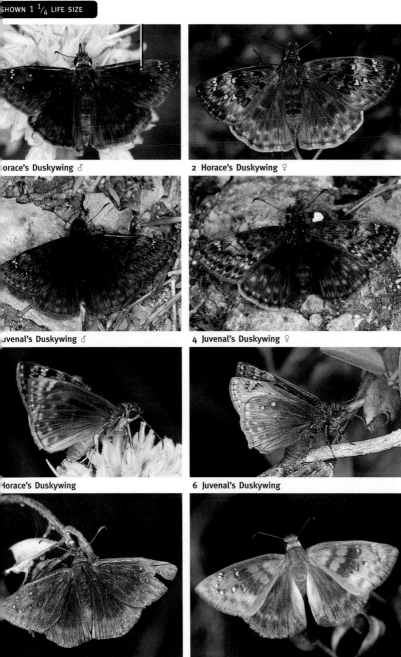

1 Horace's Duskywing ♂

2 Horace's Duskywing ♀

3 Juvenal's Duskywing ♂

4 Juvenal's Duskywing ♀

5 Horace's Duskywing

6 Juvenal's Duskywing

7 Florida Duskywing ♂

8 Florida Duskywing ♀

PLATE 51 DUSKYWINGS

1 Dreamy Duskywing *Erynnis icelus*. **p. 155**
♂ above. 5/11/96 Worthington SF, Warren Co., NJ
No white spots on **FW**.
Broad chain-like postmedian band on **FW**.
Bright gray patch along **FW** costa at "wrist."
Last segment of palps is relatively long.
Basal 1/3 of **FW** tends to be blackened.

2 ♀ above. 5/24/95 Morristown, Morris Co., NJ
See ID tips under 1.

5 Below. 5/21/92 WPR, Westchester Co., NY
Small pale spots on dark brown **HW**.

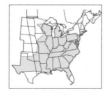

3 Sleepy Duskywing *Erynnis brizo*. **p. 155**
♂ above. 4/17/96 Fork Creek WMA, Boone Co., WV
No white spots on **FW**.
Broad chain-like postmedian band on **FW**.
Patch along **FW** costa at "wrist" not so large nor gray.
Last segment of palps is relatively short.
Basal 1/3 of **FW** tends not to be blackened.

4 ♀ above. 5/9/89 Easthampton, Suffolk Co., NY
See ID tips under 3

6 Below. 4/18/96 Fork Creek WMA, Boone Co., WV
Small pale spots on dark brown **HW**.

7 Wild Indigo Duskywing *Erynnis baptisiae*. **p. 159**
Below. 5/22/91 Chappaqua, Westchester Co., NY
Small pale spots on dark brown **HW**.
See plate 52 for map and uppersides.

8 Zarucco Duskywing *Erynnis zarucco*. **p. 158**
Below. 8/1/94 Fort Bragg, Cumberland Co., NC
Small pale spots on dark brown **HW**.
See plate 52 for map and uppersides.

9 False Duskywing *Gesta gesta*. **p. 213**
Above. 2/19/95 Mismaloya, Jalisco, Mexico
Rare stray to Houston area.
Brown patch along **FW** costa curves outward, partially
  enclosing a darker patch.

10 Mottled Duskywing *Erynnis martialis*. **p. 157**
Above. 4/15/95 Busch, Caroll Co., AR
More mottled.
Gray along **FW** submargins (usually).
Narrow and sharp **HW** postmedian dark band.
Violet sheen when fresh.

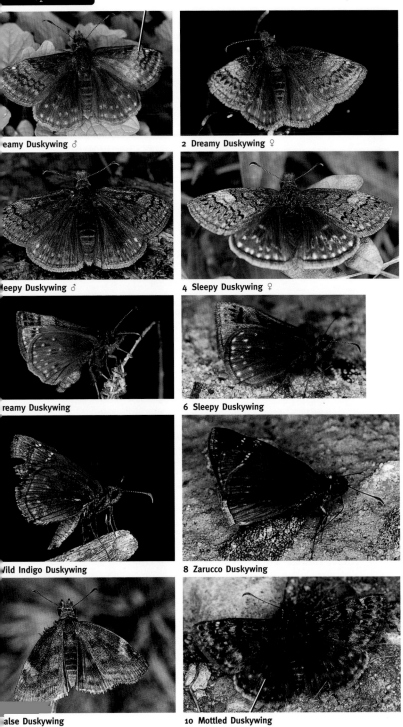

SHOWN 1½ LIFE SIZE

Dreamy Duskywing ♂

2 Dreamy Duskywing ♀

Sleepy Duskywing ♂

4 Sleepy Duskywing ♀

Dreamy Duskywing

6 Sleepy Duskywing

Wild Indigo Duskywing

8 Zarucco Duskywing

False Duskywing

10 Mottled Duskywing

PLATE 52 DUSKYWINGS

1 Wild Indigo Duskywing *Erynnis baptisiae*. **p. 159**
♂ above. 5/29/92 Oakridge, Sussex Co., NJ
Subapical white spots on **FW**.
Usually without (or faint) pale spot in **FW** cell.

2 ♀ above. 7/11/96 Troy Meadows, Morris Co., NJ
Subapical white spots on **FW**.
Usually without (or faint) pale spot in **FW** cell.
HW with small pale spots on dark brown.
HW usually with pale, straight and thin cell-end bar.
See Horace's and Zarucco Duskywings females.

3 ♀ above. 7/28/90 Chappaqua, Westchester Co., NY
Basal 1/2 of **FW** often looks very dark and "oily."

4 Zarucco Duskywing *Erynnis zarucco*. **p. 158**
♀ above. 8/23/91 Gainesville, Alachua Co., FL
Very similar to Wild Indigo Duskywing female.
HW with no cell-end bar (or an ill-defined one).

6 ♂ above. 8/1/94 Fort Bragg, Cumberland Co., NC
FW relatively narrow and angled.
Pale brown "wrist" patch at end of **FW** cell.
No gray overscaling.
FW cell usually evenly black.
FW cell-spot faint or absent.
No (or faint) white eyeline. Often with neck gray.
See male Horace's Duskywing, plate 50.

5 Columbine Duskywing *Erynnis lucilius*. **p. 159**
Above. 5/18/92 Limerick Cedars, Jefferson Co., NY
Averages smaller and blacker than Wild Indigo.
Closely associated with wild columbine.
See text.

7 Persius Duskywing *Erynnis persius*. **p. 160**
♂ above. 5/23/96 Voluntown, New London Co., CT
Short grayish-white hairs on the **FW**.
Prefers barrens.
Local and rare.
See text.

8 Funereal Duskywing *Erynnis funeralis*. **p. 158**
Above. 11/10/89 Santa Ana NWR, Hidalgo Co., TX
Bold white fringe on **HW**.
Otherwise, extremely similar to Zarucco Duskywing.

1 Wild Indigo Duskywing ♂

2 Wild Indigo Duskywing ♀

3 Wild Indigo Duskywing ♀

4 Zarucco Duskywing ♀

5 Columbine Duskywing

6 Zarucco Duskywing ♂

7 Persius Duskywing ♂

8 Funereal Duskywing

PLATE 53 CHECKERED-SKIPPERS

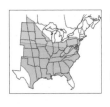

1 Common Checkered-Skipper *Pyrgus communis.* **p. 161**
Below. 9/24/94 Gainesville, Alachua Co., FL
"Clean" white and tan bands.
No brown spot in the middle of the **HW** leading margin.

2 ♂ above. 8/21/92 Great Dismal Swamp, NWR, Suffolk, VA
White and black.
Blue-gray body hairs.
FW marginal row of very small white spots missing apical sp
FW with white spot just beyond cell-end white bar abser
or very small.
HW marginal white spots usually minute.

4 ♀ above. 8/21/92 Great Dismal Swamp, NWR, VA
White and black.
See number 2 for more ID information.

3 Tropical Checkered-Skipper *Pyrgus oileus.* **p. 161**
Below. 3/20/90 South Miami, Dade Co., FL
White and tan pattern "smudged."
Brown spot in the middle of the **HW** leading margin.

6 ♂ above. 5/17/94 Newnan's Lake, Alachua Co., FL
FW marginal row of small white spots complete with apical s
FW with white spot just beyond cell-end white bar prese
and large.
HW marginal white spots usually not so small.

8 ♀ above. 5/20/94 Bauer Park, Homestead, FL
White and black.
See number 6 for more ID information.

5 'Appalachian' Grizzled Skipper *Pyrgus centaureae wyandot,* **p.**
Below. 4/24/94 Rockbridge Co., VA

7 Above. 4/24/94 Rockbridge Co., VA
Local, rare and declining.
White markings somewhat reduced.
HW with weak median white band.
Lacks white spot immediately below and inward from **F**
white cell-end bar.
Top spot of bottom three postmedian white spots is inwa
to the spot below it. (Common Checkered-Skipper has
these spots aligned).

Common Checkered-Skipper

2 Common Checkered-Skipper ♂

Tropical Checkered-Skipper

4 Common Checkered-Skipper ♀

'Appalachian' Grizzled Skipper

6 Tropical Checkered-Skipper ♂

'Appalachian' Grizzled Skipper

8 Tropical Checkered-Skipper ♀

PLATE 54 SMALL SPREADWING & INTERMEDIATE SKIPPERS

1 **Common Sootywing** *Pholisora catullus.* **p. 162**
♂ above. 5/21/93 Somers, Westchester Co., NY
Small and brown/black with many tiny white spots.
White spots on the head.

2 ♀ above. 7/29/92 Somers, Westchester Co., NY
Small and brown/black with many tiny white spots.
White spots on the head.

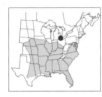

3 **Hayhurst's Scallopwing** *Staphylus hayhurstii.* **p. 153**
♂ above. 8/23/91 U. of Florida, Gainesville, FL
Dark brown/black with a few small white spots.
Gold or silver flecking.
HW with scalloped margin.
In TX, usually has fringes vaguely checkered.

4 ♀ above. 8/16/96 Heard Museum, McKinney, TX
Brown with darker concentric bands.
FW with a few small white spots.
Gold or silver flecking.
HW with scalloped margin.
Fringes usually vaguely checkered.

5 ♀ above. 8/15/96 Duck Creek Park, Garland, TX
Worn individual not showing much checkered fringe.

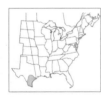

6 **Mazans Scallopwing** *Staphylus mazans.* **p. 152**
♂ above. 11/15/89 Sabal Palms, Brownsville, TX
Rare stray to eastern Texas.
Extremely similar to Hayhurst's Scallopwing.
Fringes without pale checkering.
See text.

7 **Arctic Skipper** *Carterocephalus palaemon.* **p. 163**
Below. 6/12/93 Wentworths Location, NH
Small. Like a miniature fritillary.
Orange-brown with large white spots.

8 Above. 6/28/96 McNair, Lake Co., MN
Checked orange and very dark brown.

Common Sootywing ♂

2 Common Sootywing ♀

Hayhurst's Scallopwing ♂

4 Hayhurst's Scallopwing ♀

Hayhurst's Scallopwing ♀

6 Mazans Scallopwing ♂

rctic Skipper

8 Arctic Skipper

PLATE 55 SMALL, DULL, GRASS-SKIPPERS

1 Swarthy Skipper *Nastra lherminier.* **p. 164**
Below. 8/1/91 Sandy Hook, Monmouth Co., NJ
Yellow-brown.
Veins paler.

2 Above. 8/2/94 Fort Bragg, Cumberland Co., NC
Unmarked dark brown.

3 Neamathla Skipper *Nastra neamathla.* **p. 165**
Below. 9/23/94 Chassahowitzka, Citrus Co., FL
Usually duller brown than Swarthy Skipper.
Veins not paler.

4 Above. 8/23/91 Gainesville, Alachua Co., FL
Usually with two pale spots in the median **FW**.

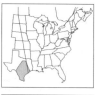

5 Julia's Skipper *Nastra julia.* **p. 164**
Below. 10/25/95 Laguna Atascosa NWR, Cameron Co., TX
Averages a warmer, redder brown than other *Nastra*.

6 Above. Same individual as 5.
Two spots in the median **FW** usually prominent.

7 Three-spotted Skipper *Cymaenes tripunctus.* **p. 165**
Below. 10/3/95 Matheson Hammock, Dade Co., FL
Long antennas—about 1/2 the **FW** length.
Yellowish-brown to brown ground.
HW usually with distinct postmedian spots.
See Eufala Skipper and Obscure Skipper, plate 70.
See text.

8 Above. 5/20/94 Bauer Park, Homestead, Dade Co., FL
Base of the **FW** costa often tawny orange.
Three white subapical spots are separate and curve out.

9 Eufala Skipper *Lerodea eufala.* **p. 198**
Below. 8/15/96 Duck Creek Park, Garland, TX
Antennas less than 1/2 the **FW** length.
Pale gray-brown ground color.
HW with indistinct postmedian spots.
Immigrant northward.
See Three-spotted Skipper, this plate.

10 Above. 8/17/96 Heard Museum, McKinney, TX
White subapical spots almost touch and are straight.

Swarthy Skipper

2 Swarthy Skipper

Neamathla Skipper

4 Neamathla Skipper

Julia's Skipper

6 Julia's Skipper

Three-spotted Skipper

8 Three-spotted Skipper

Eufala Skipper

10 Eufala Skipper

PLATE 56 SMALL ORANGE SKIPPERS

1 European Skipper *Thymelicus lineola.* **p. 169**
Below. 6/8/96 Morristown, Morris Co., NJ.
Usually with variable amount of white dusting.
Fringes pale. Antennas short.

2 Above. 7/11/95 Gorham, NH.
Short reddish antennas.

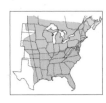

3 Least Skipper *Ancyloxypha numitor.* **p. 166**
Above. 7/30/94 Roan Mtn., Carter Co., TN.
Small.
Weak flight with black above.
Rounded wings.

4 Below. 6/22/96 WPR, Westchester Co., NY.
Very small.
Weak flight.
Rounded wings.

5 Southern Skipperling *Copaeodes minimus.* **p. 168**
Below. 9/30/96 Black River, Savannah, GA.
Tiny.
Narrow white ray on **HW**.

6 Above. 9/29/96 Black River, Savannah, GA.
Wings long and narrow.

7 Poweshiek Skipperling *Oarisma poweshiek.* **p. 167**
Below. 6/30/96 Glacial Lakes SP, Pope Co., MN.
White veins and overscaling on black **HW**.
HW outer fringe black.

12 Above. 6/30/96 Glacial Lakes SP, Pope Co., MN.
Black with bright orange **FW** cell.

8 Orange Skipperling *Copaeodes aurantiacus.* **p. 168**
Below. 9/20/93 Sentenac Canyon, San Diego Co., CA
All orange.
Wings long and narrow.

9 Above. 9/19/93 Sentenac Canyon, San Diego Co., CA.
Similar to Southern Skipperling. See text.

10 Garita Skipperling *Oarisma garita.* **p. 167**
Below. 6/27/91 Coal Creek Canyon, Jefferson Co., CO.
White veins and fringe on **HW**.

11 Above. 6/27/91 Coal Creek Canyon, Jefferson Co., CO.
Sooty.
White **FW** costal margin.

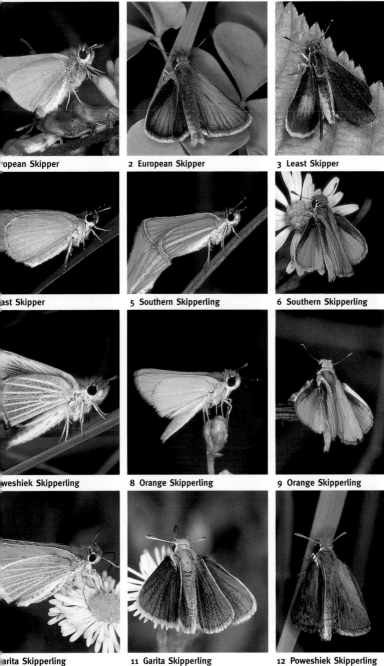

opean Skipper

2 European Skipper

3 Least Skipper

ast Skipper

5 Southern Skipperling

6 Southern Skipperling

weshiek Skipperling

8 Orange Skipperling

9 Orange Skipperling

arita Skipperling

11 Garita Skipperling

12 Poweshiek Skipperling

PLATE 57 THE WIZARDS

1 Fiery Skipper *Hylephila phyleus.* **p. 169**
♂ below. 8/15/96 Duck Creek Park, Garland, TX
Common throughout the south.
Immigrant northward.
Small dark spots on a bright orange ground.

4 ♀ below. 8/1/94 Fort Bragg, Cumberland Co., NC
Small dark spots on a dull orange ground.

7 ♂ above. 10/15/96 Duck Creek Park, Garland, TX
Jagged black borders on **FW** and **HW**.

10 ♀ above. 8/18/96 Dallas Arboretum, Dallas, TX
Jagged black border on **FW**.
"Arrow" pointing outward on **HW**.

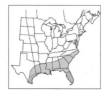

2 Whirlabout *Polites vibex.* **p. 179**
♂ below. 8/25/91 Royal Plaza, Gainesville, FL
Large smudged dark spots form the corners of a square.

5 ♀ below. 8/23/91 Gainesville, Alachua Co., FL
Dull greenish-gray-yellow.
Large smudged dark spots form the corners of a square.

8 ♂ above. 8/23/91 Gainesville, Alachua Co., FL
Jagged black border on **FW**.
Relatively smooth black border on **HW**.

11 ♀ above. 8/25/91 Gainesville, Alachua Co., FL
Brown with small pale spots on **FW**.
No spot in the **FW** cell.

3 Sachem *Atalopedes campestris.* **p. 181**
♂ below. 5/17/94 Gainesville, Alachua Co., FL
Squarish brown patch at center of **HW** trailing margin.
Immigrant northward.

6 ♀ below. 7/29/94 Blowing Rock, Watauga Co., NC
Yellow-brown.
Large, pale postmedian chevron on **HW.**

9 ♂ above. 7/30/94 Roan Mtn., Carter Co., TN
Large, black, rectangular stigma on **FW**.

12 ♀ above. 8/18/96 Dallas Arboretum, Dallas, TX
Black patch at the center of **FW**.
Two large white hyaline spots on **FW**.

ery Skipper ♂

2 Whirlabout ♂

3 Sachem ♂

ery Skipper ♀

5 Whirlabout ♀

6 Sachem ♀

ery Skipper ♂

8 Whirlabout ♂

9 Sachem ♂

Fiery Skipper ♀

11 Whirlabout ♀

12 Sachem ♀

PLATE 58 HESPERIA SKIPPERS

1 Leonard's Skipper *Hesperia leonardus.* **p. 172**
Below. 9/24/95 Wellfleet, Barnstable Co., MA
Aug.–Sept. in, or near, little bluestem fields.
Large.
Bright reddish-brown with bright white spots.

2 ♂ above. 9/3/90 Somers, Westchester Co., NY

3 ♀ above. 9/24/95 Wellfleet, Barnstable Co., MA

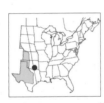

4 Common Branded Skipper *Hesperia comma.* **p. 171**
Below. 8/3/93 Lunenburg, Essex Co., VT
Bold white postmedian spot-band on **HW**.
Central, large, hooked white spot on **HW**.
North prairie populations are paler, duller and greener.

5 ♂ above. 8/3/93 Lunenburg, Essex Co., VT
Flies late July–Aug. See text.

6 ♀ above. 7/22/95 Tuolomne Co., CA

7 Green Skipper *Hesperia viridis.* **p. 173**
Below. 7/13/92 Lookout Mtn., Golden, CO
Bottom white spot of postmedian band bends outward.

8 ♂ above. 6/27/91 Lookout Mtn., Golden, CO
Thin, black "hesperia-type" stigma on **FW**.

9 ♀ above. 9/3/84 Big Arsenic Springs, Taos Co., NM

10 Cobweb Skipper *Hesperia metea.* **p. 172**
Below. 5/9/93 Oakwood Cemetery, Mt. Kisco, NY
April–May.
Flies low in bluestem fields.
Dull brown with undulating white chevron on **HW**.

11 ♂ above. 5/14/92 WPR, Westchester Co., NY
White costal margin on **FW**.

12 ♀ above. 5/14/90 WPR, Westchester Co., NY
White costal margin on **FW**.

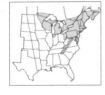

13 Indian Skipper *Hesperia sassacus.* **p. 175**
Below. 6/4/95 WPR, Westchester Co., NY
Pattern often indistinct.
Pale chevron spots concave outwardly.
Flies in late spring.

14 ♂ above. 5/29/93 WPR, Westchester Co., NY
Thin black "hesperia-type" stigma on **FW**.
HW disc bright orange.

15 ♀ above. 6/2/92 WPR, Westchester Co., NY
No black cobwebbing on **HW**.
See Long Dash, plate 60.

1 Leonard's Skipper

2 Leonard's Skipper ♂

3 Leonard's Skipper ♀

4 Common Branded Skipper

5 Common Branded Sk. ♂

6 Common Branded Skipper ♀

7 Green Skipper

8 Green Skipper ♂

9 Green Skipper ♀

10 Cobweb Skipper

11 Cobweb Skipper ♂

12 Cobweb Skipper ♀

13 Indian Skipper

14 Indian Skipper ♂

15 Indian Skipper ♀

PLATE 59 RARE HESPERIA SKIPPERS

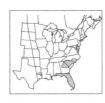

1 Meske's Skipper *Hesperia meskei.* **p. 174**
Below. 9/29/95 Gainesville, Alachua Co., FL
Yellow-orange to rusty-orange.
Scarce.
HW with pale postmedian band faint to distinct.
FW with two subapical pale spots.

2 ♂ above. 10/5/96 Sandhills Gamelands, NC

3 ♀ above. Same individual as 1.
FW costal margin white.
FW with unbroken postmedian spot-band.

4 Dotted Skipper *Hesperia attalus.* **p. 173**
Below. 6/2/96 Sandhills Gamelands, Scotland Co., NC
HW usually with distinct bright white dots.
FW with two subapical pale spots.

5 ♂ above. 7/25/90 Lakehurst, Ocean Co., NJ
Rare and local in sand barrens and short-grass prairie.
HW with postmedian spot-band.

6 ♀ above. Riverside Island, Ocala NF, Marion Co., FL
HW with postmedian spot-band.

7 Ottoe Skipper *Hesperia ottoe.* **p. 171**
Below. 7/2/96 Five Ridge Preserve, Plymouth Co., IA
Large, prairie skipper; very local and rare.
HW postmedian band faint or absent.

8 ♂ above. 7/2/96 Five Ridge Preserve, Plymouth Co., IA

9 ♀ above. 7/2/96 Five Ridge Preserve, Plymouth Co., IA

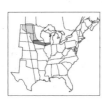

10 Dakota Skipper *Hesperia dacotae.* **p. 175**
♂ below. 6/30/96 Glacial Lakes SP, Pope Co., MN
Smaller than Ottoe Skipper.
HW postmedian band faint or absent.

11 ♂ above. 6/30/96 Glacial Lakes SP, Pope Co., MN

12 ♀ above. 7/1/96 Glacial Lakes SP, Pope Co., MN

14 ♂ below. 6/30/96 Glacial Lakes SP, Pope Co., MN
Individual with **HW** postmedian band absent.

15 ♀ below. 6/30/96 Glacial Lakes SP, Pope Co., MN
Mouse-brown.
HW with white spots, including one at wing base.

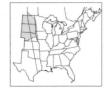

13 'Pawnee' Leonard's Skipper *Hesperia leonardus pawnee,* **p.**
Below. 8/22/78 Hole-in-the-Mountain, Lincoln Co., MN
Yellow with **HW** postmedian band faint or absent.

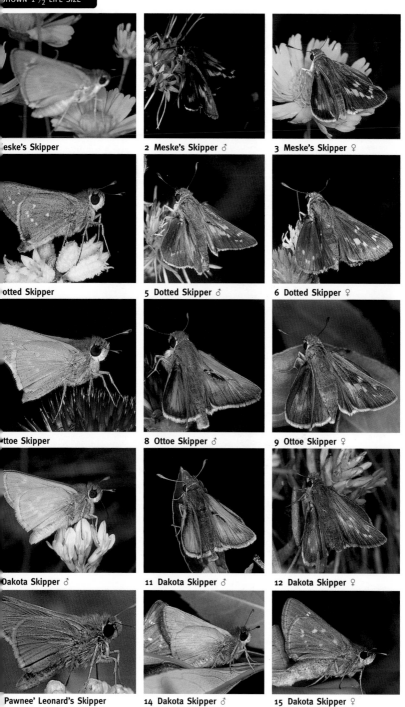

eske's Skipper

2 Meske's Skipper ♂

3 Meske's Skipper ♀

otted Skipper

5 Dotted Skipper ♂

6 Dotted Skipper ♀

ttoe Skipper

8 Ottoe Skipper ♂

9 Ottoe Skipper ♀

Dakota Skipper ♂

11 Dakota Skipper ♂

12 Dakota Skipper ♀

Pawnee' Leonard's Skipper

14 Dakota Skipper ♂

15 Dakota Skipper ♀

PLATE 60 WELL-MANNERED SKIPPERS

1 Peck's Skipper *Polites peckius.* **p. 176**
Below. 7/29/94 Blowing Rock, Watauga Co., NC
Central spot of **HW** postmedian band extends outward, b
below and above on both sexes.

2 ♂ above. 7/29/94 Blowing Rock, Watauga Co., NC

3 ♀ above. 7/25/96 Kettle Moraine SF, Fond du Lac Co., WI

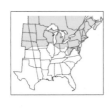

4 Long Dash *Polites mystic.* **p. 178**
Below. 7/11/95 Gorham, NH
Broad postmedian band on **HW**.
Middle spot of **HW** postmedian band not extending out.
Also see, Indian Skipper, plate 58, photo 13.

5 ♂ above. 6/26/96 Savannah SF, Aitkin Co., MN
Black divides orange on both **FW** and **HW**.

6 ♀ above. 6/4/94 WPR, Westchester Co., NY
HW postmedian band w/o spot extending outward.

7 Crossline Skipper *Polites origenes.* **p. 178**
Below. 6/28/92 Hauppauge, Suffolk Co., NY
Usually warm yellow-brown with postmedian spot-band
Low contrast between **HW** color and **FW** costal margin.

8 ♂ above. 7/9/95 Mt. Kisco, Westchester Co., NY
FW stigma not as intense as in Tawny-edged.
Stigma narrows toward the base of the **FW**.
Additional pale yellow spot distally adjacent to stigma.

9 ♀ above. 6/6/96 Sandhills Gamelands, Scotland Co., NC
HW with broad dark border and hint of orange on disc.

10 Tawny-edged Skipper *Polites themistocles.* **p. 177**
Below. 7/26/90 Arkville, Delaware Co., NY
Usually drab olive-brown with no (or faint) pale band.
Strong contrast between color of **HW** and bright **FW** costal ma

11 ♂ above 6/8/96 Morristown, Morris Co., NJ
Intense, thick, black stigma on **FW**.
Rectangular orange spot at end of stigma.

12 ♀ above. 6/4/89 Peebles, Adams Co., OH
HW with narrow dark border and very little orange.

13 Baracoa Skipper *Polites baracoa.* **p. 177**
Below. 5/23/94 Bauer Park, Dade Co., FL
Usually with chunky, pale postmedian band.

14 ♂ above. 5/25/94 Miami, Dade Co., FL
Dark ray inward from **FW** margin passes end of stigma.

15 ♀ above. 3/21/90 Homestead, Dade Co., FL

ck's Skipper

2 Peck's Skipper ♂

3 Peck's Skipper ♀

ng Dash

5 Long Dash ♂

6 Long Dash ♀

rossline Skipper

8 Crossline Skipper ♂

9 Crossline Skipper ♀

Tawny-edged Skipper

11 Tawny-edged Skipper ♂

12 Tawny-edged Skipper ♀

aracoa Skipper

14 Baracoa Skipper ♂

15 Baracoa Skipper ♀

PLATE 61 VARIATIONS

1 Long Dash *Polites mystic.* **p. 178**
Below. 6/4/95 WPR, Westchester Co., NY
Variant.
See plate 60.

2 Peck's Skipper *Polites peckius.* **p. 176**
Below. 7/28/91 Chappaqua, Westchester Co., NY
Variant with reduced central brown band.
See plate 60.

3 Below. 8/5/91 Yorktown, Westchester Co., NY
Variant with more prominent central brown band.

4 Tawny-edged Skipper *Polites themistocles.* **p. 177**
Below. 5/31/91 Chappaqua, Westchester Co., NY
Variant with pronounced **HW** postmedian band.
See plate 60.

5 Below. 6/27/96 Two Harbors, Lake Co., MN
Variant with brown **HW** ground color.

6 Crossline Skipper *Polites origenes.* **p. 178**
Below. 6/6/96 Sandhills Gamelands, Scotland Co., NC
See plate 60.

7 Below. 7/8/91 Somers, Westchester Co., NY
Variant with pronounced **HW** postmedian band.

8 Dotted Skipper *Hesperia attalus.* **p. 173**
Below. 9/27/94 Riverside Island, Ocala NF, FL
See plate 59.

9 Little Glassywing *Pompeius verna.* **p. 181**
Below. 6/22/96 WPR, Westchester Co., NY
See plate 62.

10 Below. 6/22/96 WPR, Westchester Co., NY

11 Northern Broken-Dash *Wallengrenia egeremet.* **p. 180**
Below. 7/7/96 Troy Meadows, Morris Co., NJ
Variant.
See plate 62.

12 Dun Skipper *Euphyes vestris.* **p. 191**
Below. 8/17/96 Heard Museum, McKinney, TX
Very fresh male with intense purple sheen.
See plate 62.

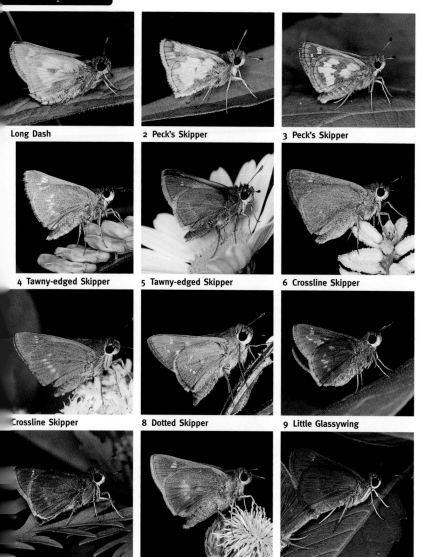

Long Dash

2 Peck's Skipper

3 Peck's Skipper

4 Tawny-edged Skipper

5 Tawny-edged Skipper

6 Crossline Skipper

Crossline Skipper

8 Dotted Skipper

9 Little Glassywing

Little Glassywing

11 Northern Broken-Dash

12 Dun Skipper

PLATE 62 THE WITCHES

1 Southern Broken-Dash *Wallengrenia otho.* **p. 179**
Below. 10/5/96 Big Pine Key, Monroe Co., FL
Reddish-brown ground color.
HW postmedian band often in shape of a 3.
Broad gray **FW** fringe.

2 ♂ above. 3/20/90 South Miami, Dade Co., FL
FW with rectangular orange spot at end of stigma.

3 ♀ above. 9/25/94 Daytona Beach, Volusia Co., FL
FW with rectangular pale spot.

4 Northern Broken-Dash *Wallengrenia egeremet.* **p. 180**
Below. 7/24/96 Fort Dix, Burlington Co., NJ
Yellow-brown ground color.
Wide postmedian **HW** band often in shape of a 3.

5 ♂ above. 7/2/91 WPR, Westchester Co., NY
Rectangular orange spot at end of stigma.

6 ♀ above. 7/7/96 Troy Meadows, Morris Co., NJ
FW with rectangular pale spot.

7 Little Glassywing *Pompeius verna.* **p. 181**
Below. 8/1/94 Fort Bragg, Cumberland Co., NC
Dark brown ground color.
White patch just below antennal club.
HW usually has postmedian line with discrete spots.

8 ♂ above. Same individual as 7.
White patch just below antennal club.
Large rectangular white spot in middle of **FW**.

9 ♀ above. 7/6/96 Troy Meadows, Morris Co., NJ
White patch just below antennal club.
Large square white spot in middle of **FW**.
White spot in **FW** cell.

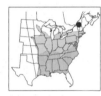

10 Dun Skipper *Euphyes vestris.* **p. 191**
Below. 7/9/90 Chappaqua, Westchester Co., NY
Faint, if any, **HW** postmedian band.
Head of males often golden.

11 ♂ above. 6/8/95 Pontotoc Ridge, Pontotoc Co., OK
Completely dark with black stigma.
Also see Clouded Skipper above, plate 64.

12 ♀ above. 7/7/91 WPR, Westchester Co., NY
FW with two small white central spots.
Also see Clouded Skipper above, plate 64 and Twin-
Skipper above, plate 70.

uthern Broken-Dash

2 Southern Broken-Dash ♂

3 Southern Broken-Dash ♀

rthern Broken-Dash

5 Northern Broken-Dash ♂

6 Northern Broken-Dash ♀

tle Glassywing

8 Little Glassywing ♂

9 Little Glassywing ♀

un Skipper

11 Dun Skipper ♂

12 Dun Skipper ♀

PLATE 63 SOME ORANGE SKIPPERS

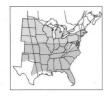

1 Delaware Skipper *Anatrytone logan.* **p. 183**
Below. 6/30/93 WPR, Westchester Co., NY
Clear, bright, unmarked yellow-orange.
HW fringe orange to tan.

2 ♂ above. 8/9/95 Fort Gibson, Cherokee Co., OK
Black **FW** cell-end bar.
Black veining on **FW**.

3 ♀ above. 7/9/95 Kitchawan, Westchester Co., NY
Black **FW** cell-end bar.
Black at base of **FW**.

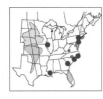

4 Arogos Skipper *Atrytone arogos.* **p. 182**
Below. 6/8/95 Pontotoc Ridge, Pontotoc Co., OK
Orange-yellow.
HW with whitish veins. **HW** fringe white.
LR, especially on Atlantic Coast.

5 ♂ above. 7/11/82 Hole-in-the-Mtn., Lincoln Co., MN
No black **FW** cell-end bar.
No black veining on **FW**.

6 ♀ above. 6/9/95 Wagoner, Wagoner Co., OK
Broad black borders on **FW** and **HW**.
Long, thin black mark in middle of basal half of **FW**.

7 Byssus Skipper *Problema byssus.* **p. 183**
Below. 6/13/95 Roaring River SP, Barry Co., MO
Variable. As shown or with pale patch in mid **HW**.
FW cell-end bar visible on males.
Wide black border on **FW** usually visible.
See plate 67 for 'Florida' Byssus Skipper.

8 ♂ above. 6/12/95 Roaring River SP, Barry Co., MO
Strong black cell-end bar on **FW**.
Black projection into orange disc on **HW**.

9 ♀ above. 6/12/95 Roaring River SP, Barry Co., MO
Strong black cell-end bar on **FW**.
Black projection into orange disc on **HW**.

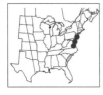

10 Rare Skipper *Problema bulenta.* **p. 184**
Below. 7/11/91 Atlantic Co., NJ
Rare and local in brackish marsh.
See text.

11 ♂ above. 7/11/91 Atlantic Co., NJ
Abdomen with white lines between segments.

12 ♀ above. 7/11/91 Atlantic Co., NJ
Abdomen with white lines between segments.

aware Skipper

2 Delaware Skipper ♂

3 Delaware Skipper ♀

gos Skipper

5 Arogos Skipper ♂

6 Arogos Skipper ♀

ssus Skipper

8 Byssus Skipper ♂

9 Byssus Skipper ♀

are Skipper

11 Rare Skipper ♂

12 Rare Skipper ♀

PLATE 64 ZABULON, HOBOMOK & CLOUDED SKIPPERS

1 Zabulon Skipper *Poanes zabulon*. **p. 186**
♂ below. 8/16/96 Heard Museum, McKinney, TX
Yellow with brown patch at **HW** base enclosing yellow.
Narrow, indistinct border.

2 ♂ above. 8/17/96 Heard Museum, McKinney, TX
Black cell-end bar on **FW**.
HW with orange recurved outward at leading margin.

3 ♀ above. 8/16/96 Heard Museum, McKinney, TX
No white spot in **FW** cell.

7 ♀ below. 8/1/91 NJ Arts Center, Monmouth Co., NJ
Silvery white margin at **HW** apex.

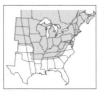

4 Hobomok Skipper *Poanes hobomok*. **p. 185**
Below. 6/8/96 Morristown, Morris Co., NJ
Large brown patch at base of **HW**.
Broad brown border on **HW**.

5 ♂ above. 5/20/90 Chappaqua, Westchester Co., NY
Black cell-end bar on **FW**.
HW with orange not recurved outward at leading margin

6 ♀ form Pocahontas above. 6/5/96 Highlands, NC
White spot in **FW** cell.

8 ♀ form Pocahontas below. 6/8/96 Morris Co., NJ
No silvery white margin at **HW** apex.

9 ♀ above. 6/4/96 Jones Gap, Highlands, Macon Co., NC

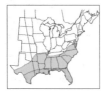

10 Clouded Skipper *Lerema accius*. **p. 166**
Below. 8/30/95 Great Dismal Swamp NWR, Suffolk, VA
FW with gray patch.
Vertical dark patch in center of wing.
Lacks 2 white submarginal spots that Hobomok has.
Immigrant northward.

11 ♂ above. 8/22/92 Great Dismal Swamp NWR, Suffolk, VA
FW subapical spots curve outward.
Also see Dun Skipper above, plate 62.

12 ♀ above. 8/30/95 Same individual as 10.
FW subapical spots curve outward.
FW with ovate cell spot.
Also see Dun Skipper above, plate 62 and Twin-spot
  Skipper above, plate 70.

ulon Skipper ♂

2 Zabulon Skipper ♂

3 Zabulon Skipper ♀

bomok Skipper

5 Hobomok Skipper ♂

6 Hobomok Skipper ♀

ulon Skipper ♀

8 Hobomok Skipper ♀

9 Hobomok Skipper ♀

ouded Skipper

11 Clouded Skipper ♂

12 Clouded Skipper ♀

PLATE 65 MARSH SKIPPERS—POANES

1 Broad-winged Skipper *Poanes viator.* **p. 187**
Below. 10/1/96 Hutchinson Island, Savannah, GA
Dull, **HW** with paler ray flanked by pale spots.
Subapical spot(s) on **FW**.
Often lands with its head up and body vertical.

2 ♂ above. 10/1/96 Hutchinson Island, Savannah, GA

3 ♀ above. 8/9/90 Kisco Swamp, Mt. Kisco, NY
Large.
Yellow ray at **HW** outer angle.

4 Yehl Skipper *Poanes yehl.* **p. 187**
Below. 8/22/92 Great Dismal Swamp NWR, Suffolk, VA
Rusty-orange fading to dull yellow.
Three or four pale postmedian spots on **HW**.

5 ♂ above. 8/22/92 Great Dismal Swamp NWR, VA
Black border along **HW** leading edge narrows near apex

6 ♀ above. 8/24/92 Great Dismal Swamp NWR, VA
Lacks yellow ray at **HW** outer angle of previous species.

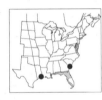

7 Aaron's Skipper *Poanes aaroni.* **p. 186**
Below. 8/26/90 Higbeetown, Atlantic Co., NJ
Dull.
HW with a narrow, pale ray that usually extends the len
of the wing.
Pale ray often flanked by two pale dots.
No subapical spot on **FW**.

8 ♂ above. 6/27/94 Port Norris, Cumberland Co., NJ
FW with small "bird head," dark patch just above cell-e
bar is "eye," small orange spot just distal is "bill."

9 ♀ above. 8/26/90 Delmont, Cumberland Co., NJ

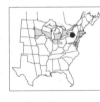

10 Mulberry Wing *Poanes massasoit.* **p. 185**
Below. 8/2/92 Glazier Arboretum, Chappaqua, NY
Yellow "airplane" on a dark reddish-brown sky.

11 ♂ above. 7/7/91 WPR, Westchester Co., NY
Black (purplish when fresh) with bright **FW** base.

12 ♀ above. 7/18/90 WPR, Westchester Co., NY
Orange-brown **FW** base contrasts with blackish wing.

ad-winged Skipper

2 Broad-winged Skipper ♂

3 Broad-winged Skipper ♀

hl Skipper

5 Yehl Skipper ♂

6 Yehl Skipper ♀

ron's Skipper

8 Aaron's Skipper ♂

9 Aaron's Skipper ♀

ulberry Wing

11 Mulberry Wing ♂

12 Mulberry Wing ♀

PLATE 66 MARSH SKIPPERS—EUPHYES

1 Dion Skipper *Euphyes dion.* **p. 188**
Below. 8/31/95 Chesapeake, VA
Bright orange to dull reddish-orange.
HW with one or two pale rays, top ray usually not exten
ing the entire length of wing.
Prefers open wetlands.

2 ♂ above. 7/11/96 Troy Meadows, Morris Co., NJ

3 ♀ above. 8/31/95 Chesapeake, VA

4 Dukes' Skipper *Euphyes dukesi.* **p. 189**
Below. 8/31/95 Chesapeake, VA
Rich orange-brown to sooty-brown.
HW with one or two pale rays.
FW disc black.
Prefers shady, fresh-water swamps.

5 ♂ above. 8/31/95 Chesapeake, VA
Very dark with black stigma.

6 ♀ above. 8/31/95 Chesapeake, VA
Dark with two small pale spots on **FW**.

7 Black Dash *Euphyes conspicua.* **p. 190**
Below. 7/4/93 Turkey Mtn., Yorktown, NY
Reddish-orange-brown.
Chunky postmedian patch on **HW**.
Prefers wet meadows and fresh-water marshes.

8 ♂ above. 7/25/96 Kettle Moraine SF, Fond du Lac Co., WI
Thick black stigma.

9 ♀ above. 7/25/96 Riveredge Preserve, Saukville, WI

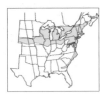

10 Two-spotted Skipper *Euphyes bimacula.* **p. 191**
Below. 6/29/89 Lakehurst Bog, Ocean Co., NJ
Orange with pale veining.
Striking white line along **HW** trailing margin.
Prefers bogs and acid marshes.

11 ♂ above. 6/29/89 Lakehurst Bog, Ocean Co., NJ
Dark brown with dull orange patch around stigma.

12 ♀ above. 6/28/95 Lakehurst Bog, Ocean Co., NJ

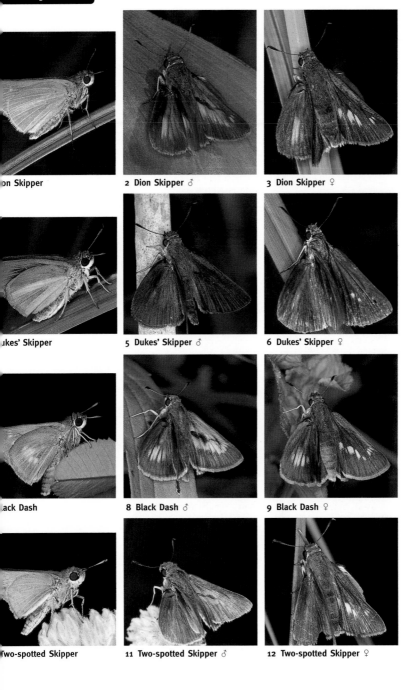

on Skipper

2 Dion Skipper ♂

3 Dion Skipper ♀

ukes' Skipper

5 Dukes' Skipper ♂

6 Dukes' Skipper ♀

ack Dash

8 Black Dash ♂

9 Black Dash ♀

wo-spotted Skipper

11 Two-spotted Skipper ♂

12 Two-spotted Skipper ♀

PLATE 67 MARSH SKIPPERS—EUPHYES & 'FLORIDA' BYSSUS SKIPPER

1 Palmetto Skipper *Euphyes arpa*. **p. 188**
Below. 9/26/94 Gainesville, Alachua Co., FL
Large and orange.
Golden head and mantle.

2 ♂ above. 8/25/91 Gainesville, Alachua Co., FL
Golden head and mantle.
Long, narrow, black stigma.

3 ♀ above. Same individual as 1.

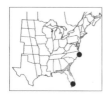

4 Berry's Skipper *Euphyes berryi*. **p. 190**
Below. 9/25/94 Daytona Beach, Volusia Co., FL
Dull brownish-orange.
Whitened **HW** veins.
FW without subapical pale spots.
Local and rare. See text.

5 ♂ above. 9/25/94 Same individual as 4.
Thin stigma on **FW**.
Black ray inward from margin about 1/3 **FW** length.

6 ♀ above. (Collected 9/16/42 Orlando, FL by Dean F. Berry—for whom th
species is named.)
FW cell spot.
Some tawny on the **HW**.

7 Palatka Skipper *Euphyes pilatka*. **p. 188**
Below. 9/28/96 Savannah River, Savannah, GA
Very large.
Rusty-brown.
Prefers brackish marshes and adjacent areas.

8 ♂ above. 3/24/90 Big Cypress Preserve, Collier Co., FL
FW usually has thin black line parallel to costal margin.

9 ♀ above. 3/26/97 Big Cypress Preserve, Collier Co., FL

10 Byssus Skipper *Problema byssus*. **p. 183**
Below. 8/25/91 Newnan's Lake, Alachua Co., FL
Bright orange-brown.
Pale area in middle of **HW**.
HW often with paler veins.
FW with subapical pale spots.

11 ♂ above. Same individual as 10.

12 ♀ above. 9/24/94 Gainesville, Alachua Co., FL

1 Palmetto Skipper

2 Palmetto Skipper ♂

3 Palmetto Skipper ♀

4 Berry's Skipper

5 Berry's Skipper ♂

6 Berry's Skipper ♀

7 Palatka Skipper

8 Palatka Skipper ♂

9 Palatka Skipper ♀

10 Byssus Skipper

11 Byssus Skipper ♂

12 Byssus Skipper ♀

PLATE 68 ROADSIDE-SKIPPERS—MAINLY SOUTHERN

1 Lace-winged Roadside-Skipper *Amblyscirtes aesculapius*. **p.**
Below. 8/30/95 Great Dismal Swamp NWR, Suffolk, VA
Cobwebby white veins.
In or near cane brakes.

2 Above. 8/30/95 Great Dismal Swamp NWR, Suffolk, VA

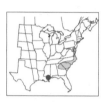

3 Carolina Roadside-Skipper *Amblyscirtes carolina*. **p. 195**
Below. 8/1/94 Fort Bragg, Cumberland Co., NC
Dirty yellow ground color.
Darker chestnut markings.
Row of spots on abdomen.
In or near cane brakes.

4 Above. 8/23/92 Northwest River Park, Chesapeake Co.,VA

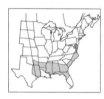

5 Reversed Roadside-Skipper *Amblyscirtes reversa*. **p. 195**
Below. 7/8/96 Francis Marion NF, SC
Chestnut ground color.
Paler yellow markings.
In or near cane brakes.

6 Above. Aug. 1994 Fort Bragg, NC

7 Dusky Roadside-Skipper *Amblyscirtes alternata*. **p. 197**
Below. 3/20/94 Riverside Island, Ocala NF, FL
Dark with some bluish scales.
Almost no white or pale markings.
Blunt antennal clubs.

8 Above. Same individual as 7.
Only a few faint **FW** subapical spots.

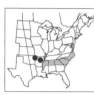

9 Nysa Roadside-Skipper *Amblyscirtes nysa*. **p. 196**
Below. 8/8/89 Guadalupe Canyon, Cochise Co., AZ
Highly mottled.

10 Above. 8/15/89 Box Canyon, Pima Co., AZ

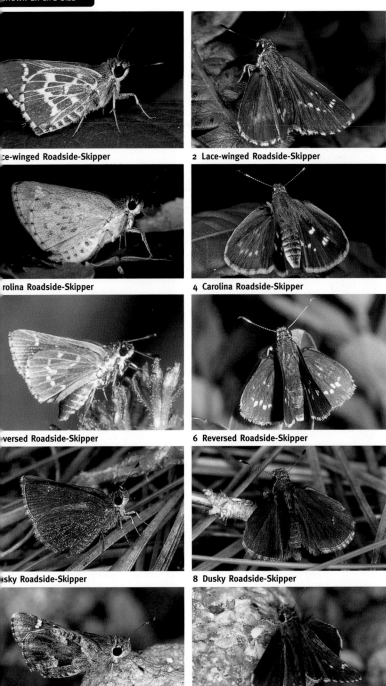

ce-winged Roadside-Skipper

2 Lace-winged Roadside-Skipper

rolina Roadside-Skipper

4 Carolina Roadside-Skipper

versed Roadside-Skipper

6 Reversed Roadside-Skipper

sky Roadside-Skipper

8 Dusky Roadside-Skipper

sa Roadside-Skipper

10 Nysa Roadside-Skipper

PLATE 69 ROADSIDE-SKIPPERS

1 Pepper and Salt Skipper *Amblyscirtes hegon.* **p. 194**
Below. 6/12/93 Wentworths Location, NH
Yellowish tinged gray-brown ground color.
Prominent cream-colored postmedian band on **HW**.

2 Above. 6/5/96 Jones Knob, Highlands, Macon Co., NC
FW with strong spot-band.

3 Common Roadside-Skipper *Amblyscirtes vialis.* **p. 196**
Below. 4/17/95 Ouachita NF, Logan Co., AR
Small and black.
Outer portions of wings are "frosted."
Fringes are strongly checkered.
FW subapical white spots usually much wider at margin.

4 Above. 8/2/94 Fort Bragg, Cumberland Co., NC

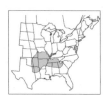

5 Linda's Roadside-Skipper *Amblyscirtes linda.* **p. 193**
Below. 4/17/95 Ouachita NF, Logan Co., AR
Similar to Common Roadside-Skipper.
Entire **HW** is "frosted," including leading margin.
Copper-colored scales on the **FW** disc.

6 Above. 4/17/95 Ouachita NF, Logan Co., AR
At least some copper-colored scales on the **FW**.

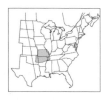

7 Bell's Roadside-Skipper *Amblyscirtes belli.* **p. 197**
Below. 8/16/96 Heard Museum, McKinney, TX
Ground color quite black.
HW pale spots often indistinct, forming zigzag line.
HW apex not frosted.
FW subapical white spots not much wider at margin.

8 Above. 8/16/96 Heard Museum, McKinney, TX
Ground color black.
Inner median spot on **FW** usually in the shape of a "V"
"U" with the base of the letter toward the body.

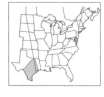

9 Celia's Roadside-Skipper *Amblyscirtes celia.* **p. 196**
Below. 8/15/96 Duck Creek Park, Garland, TX
Dark grayish-brown ground color.
HW spots usually separate and well-defined.

10 Above. 8/10/95 Barton Creek Park, Austin, TX
Inner median spot on **FW** usually irregularly shaped.

pper and Salt Skipper

2 Pepper and Salt Skipper

mmon Roadside-Skipper

4 Common Roadside-Skipper

1da's Roadside-Skipper

6 Linda's Roadside-Skipper

ell's Roadside-Skipper

8 Bell's Roadside-Skipper

elia's Roadside-Skipper

10 Celia's Roadside-Skipper

PLATE 70 PANOQUINS & TWIN-SPOT SKIPPER

1 Salt Marsh Skipper *Panoquina panoquin*. **p. 200**
Below. 9/29/96 Black River, Savannah, GA
Long narrow wings.
Dark line running along side of abdomen.
Yellow-brown ground color.
Paler yellow veining.
Cream-colored streak on **HW**.
Found in salt marshes and adjacent areas.

2 Above. Same individual as 1.
Long wings.

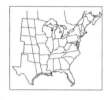

3 Obscure Skipper *Panoquina panoquinoides*. **p. 200**
Below. 3/24/94 Big Pine Key, Monroe Co., FL
Dull brown.
Dark line running along side of abdomen.
Paler veins.
Usually with two small white spots on **HW** postmedian.
No cream-colored streak on **HW**.
Found in salt marshes and adjacent areas.
Also see Three-spotted Skipper, plate 55.

4 Above. 3/26/94 Big Pine Key, Monroe Co., FL
Obscure.

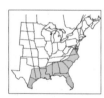

5 Ocola Skipper *Panoquina ocola*. **p. 201**
Below. 9/28/96 Savannah River, Savannah, GA
Long, narrow wings.
Dark line running along side of abdomen.
Distal 1/4 of **HW** darker.
Purplish sheen when fresh.
White postmedian spots on **HW** present or absent.
Immigrant northward.

6 Above. 8/10/95 Barton Creek Park, Austin, TX
FW median pale spot is arrowhead-shaped.

7 Twin-spot Skipper *Oligoria maculata*. **p. 199**
Below. 5/7/97 Yankeetown, Levy Co., FL
Chestnut-brown ground color.
Usually with three bold white spots on **HW**, with two
together (the twins). (Spots are occasionally faint.)

8 Above. 5/17/94 Royal Plaza, Gainesville, FL

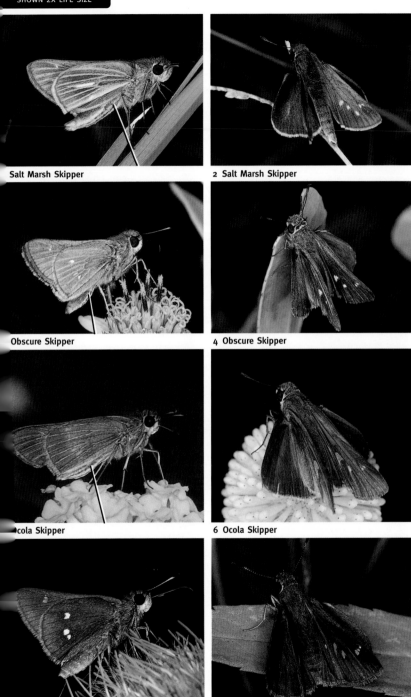

Salt Marsh Skipper

2 Salt Marsh Skipper

Obscure Skipper

4 Obscure Skipper

cola Skipper

6 Ocola Skipper

vin-spot Skipper

8 Twin-spot Skipper

PLATE 71 GIANT-SKIPPERS & OTHERS

1 Cofaqui Giant-Skipper *Megathymus cofaqui.* **p. 202**
Below. 3/18/89 Disney World, Orlando, FL
See Yucca Giant-Skipper this plate.
Gray ground color.
White spot near **HW** leading margin not so large.
Variable number of small white postmedian spots.

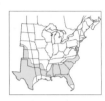

2 Yucca Giant-Skipper *Megathymus yuccae.* **p. 202**
Below. 3/19/94 Royal Plaza, Gainesville, FL
Huge.
Very dark brown with some marginal frosting.
Large white spot near the leading margin of the **HW**.
Tan-yellow **HW** fringe.

3 Monk Skipper *Asbolis capucinus.* **p. 192**
Below. 5/22/94 Key West, Monroe Co., FL
Dark red-orange-brown.

4 Above. 5/22/93 Stock Island, Monroe Co., FL
Rich chestnut color.

5 Brazilian Skipper *Calpodes ethlius.* **p. 199**
Below. 8/18/96 Dallas Arboretum, Dallas, TX
HW with 3 or 4 translucent spots in an angled line.

6 Above. 9/22/94 Trout Creek, Hillsborough Co., FL

7 Dusted Skipper *Atrytonopsis hianna.* **p. 192**
Below. 6/1/89 Chappaqua, Westchester Co., NY
"Masked" appearance.
Often with a white spot at **HW** base.
Southeastern individuals with postmedian white spots.

8 Above. 6/7/91 WPR, Westchester Co., NY
White eye-line.

9 Violet-banded Skipper *Nyctelius nyctelius.* **p. 213**
Below. 10/29/93 Mission, Hidalgo Co., TX
Alternating pale and dark bands.
Pale bands with violaceous sheen when fresh.
Black spot near the middle of **HW** leading margin.
Abdomen with black and white rings.
Possible stray north from West Indies and south Texas.
1 record from Florida Keys.

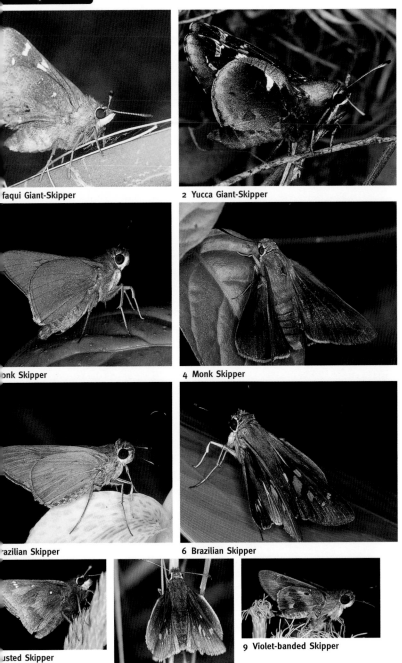

faqui Giant-Skipper

2 Yucca Giant-Skipper

onk Skipper

4 Monk Skipper

azilian Skipper

6 Brazilian Skipper

usted Skipper

8 Dusted Skipper

9 Violet-banded Skipper

Organizations Concerned with Butterflies

North American Butterfly Association (NABA) promotes public enjoyment, awareness, and conservation of butterflies and all aspects of
recreational, non-consumptive butterflying, including field identification, butterfly gardening, and photography. NABA publishes a full-color
magazine, *American Butterflies*; a newsletter *Butterfly Gardening News*; has
chapters throughout North America (There are currently 12 chapters
within our region.); and runs the annual NABA 4th of July Butterfly
Counts. These one-day counts, held mainly in June–July (centered on
the 4th of July period) are growing rapidly. Currently about 350 counts
are conducted each year, at sites across North America. They are a fun-
filled way to help monitor butterfly populations, to learn about butterfly identification, and to meet other butterfliers.

NABA
4 Delaware Rd.
Morristown, NJ 07960
Telephone: 800-503-2290 (membership inquiries only)
Web site: http://www.naba.org

Lepidopterists' Society is an international organization devoted to the
scientific study of all lepidoptera. The Society publishes the *Journal of
the Lepidopterists' Society* as well as the *News of the Lepidopterists Society*.
There are annual meetings.

Lepidopterists' Society
1608 Presidio Way
Roseville, CA 95661
Web site: http://www.furman.edu

The Xerces Society is an international organization dedicated to global protection of habitats for all invertebrates, including butterf] The Society publishes *Wings*. There are annual meetings.

Xerces Society
4828 Southeast Hawthorne Blvd.
Portland, OR 97215

The Nature Conservancy buys land to preserve natural diversity owns more than 1,300 preserves—the largest private system of nat sanctuaries in the world.

The Nature Conservancy
1815 Lynn St.
Arlington, VA 22209
Web site: http://www.tnc.org

Glossary

NTENNAL CLUB The thickened end of the antenna. Great Southern White, Plate 5, photo 5, has phosphorescent blue antennal clubs.

PEX The tip of the wing. Male Falcate Orangetip, Plate 7, photo 2, has orange FW apexes. Female Zabulon Skipper, Plate 64, photo 7, has a white HW apex.

PICAL Referring to the area at the tip of the wing.

ASAL Referring to the area near the base of the wing, adjacent to the body. Great Purple Hairstreak, Plate 16, photo 3, has red basal spots.

LL The central area of the wing, bounded on all sides by veins. Common Buckeye, Plate 37, photo 2, has two orange bars in each FW cell.

LL-END BAR A thin bar of color along the vein bounding the outer edge of the cell, contrasting with the ground color of the wing. Female Falcate Orangetip, Plate 7, photo 4, has a black FW cell-end bar.

STAL MARGIN (COSTA) The leading edge of the FW. Cobweb Skipper, Plate 58, photo 12, has a white costal margin.

SC The central area of the wing including, but larger than, the cell.

TAL Away from the body.

RSAL Toward the back. The dorsal wing surface is the upper surface.

REWINGS (FWs) The leading pair of wings.

NGES Scales that stick out from the edges of the wing membranes. Funereal Duskywing, Plate 52, photo 8, has a white HW fringe.

NS The area in the front of the head between the eyes.

UND COLOR The basic or background color of the wing.

DWINGS (HWs) The rear pair of wings.

LINE Translucent.

LEADING MARGIN The margin of the HW that is on top as the butterfly sits upright.

MARGIN Any of the wing edges, but usually referring to the outer margin.

MARGINAL LINES, BANDS, or SPOTS A series of lines or spots along the outer margin. Coral Hairstreak, Plate17, photo 4, has red HW marginal spots.

MEDIAN About one-half of the way out the wing, passing the distal end of the cell.

OUTER ANGLE The area of the HW where the outer and trailing margins meet. Miami Blue, Plate 22, photo 4, has a black eye-spot at the HW outer angle.

OUTER MARGIN The wing edge farthest from the body, it is more or less perpendicular to the ground as the butterfly sits upright.

POSTMEDIAN The wing regions farther from the body than (distal to) the median region. Silver-banded Hairstreak, Plate 19, photo has a white postmedian line on its HW.

POSTMEDIAN BAND A series of spots or lines in the postmedian region of the wing, either darker or paler than the ground color. Red-banded Hairstreak, Plate 16, photo 4, has a postmedian band that is partially red.

STIGMA A structure, usually black and visible, on the FWs of most grass-skippers, formed by specialized scales. Ottoe Skipper male, Plate 59, photo 8, has a prominent black stigma in the center the FW.

SUBAPICAL Referring to the region just before the tip of the wing.

SUBMARGINAL Referring to the region just before the area at the outside edge of the wing. 'Karner' Melissa Blue, Plate 24, photo has orange submarginal spots on the HW below.

VENTRAL Toward the belly. The ventral wing surface is the lower wing surface.

VEINS A series of visibly raised structural elements on the wings which serve as wing struts. The branching pattern of the veins important in lepidopteran systematics. Poweshiek Skipperling Plate 56, photo 7, has the HW veins covered with white scales.

Bibliography

Ackery, P.R. and Vane-Wright, R.I. 1984. *Milkweed Butterflies*. London: British Museum.

Ajilvsgi, G. 1990. *Butterfly Gardening for the South*. Dallas: Taylor Publishing Co.

Allen, T. 1997. *The Butterflies of West Virginia*. University of Pittsburg Press.

Androw, D.A., Baker, R.J., and Lane, C.P. eds. 1994. *Karner Blue Butterfly: A Symbol of a Vanishing Landscape*. University of Minnesota Miscellaneous Publication 84–1994.

Burns, J.M. 1964. *Evolution in Skipper Butterflies of the Genus* Erynnis. Berkeley: University of California Press:

Cech, R. 1993. *A Distributional Checklist of the Butterflies and Skippers of the New York City Area (50-mile Radius) and Long Island*. New York: New York City Butterfly Club.

Clark, A.H. and Clark, L.F. 1951. "The Butterflies of Virginia." Smithsonian Miscellaneous Collections, vol. 116 no. 7. Washington D.C.: Smithsonian Institution.

Conaway, C. 1997. "Definitive Destination: Pontotoc Ridge Preserve, Oklahoma." *American Butterflies*, Summer: 4–13.

Dankert, N., Nagel, H. and Nightengale, T. 1993. *Butterfly Distribution Maps—Nebraska*. Department of Biology. University of Nebraska.

Duffy, D.N. and Garland, J.A. 1978. "The skipper butterflies of the province of Quebec." Lyman Entomological Museum and Research Laboratory Memoir No. 5 (Special Publication No. 13). Quebec: McGill University Press.

Ebner, J.A. 1970. *Butterflies of Wisconsin*. Milwaukee: Milwaukee Public Museum.

Edwards, W.H. 1868–1897. *The Butterflies of North America*. 3 vols. American Entomological Society Boston: Houghton-Mifflin.

220   Ely, C.A., Schwilling, M.D., and Rolfs, M.E. 1986. *An Annotated List of the Butterflies of Kansas.* Fort Hays Studes; Third Series (Science) Number 7.

Fales, J.H. 1974. "Check-list of the Skippers and Butterflies of Maryland." *Chesapeake Science* 15:222–229.

Fales, J.H. 1984. "Status of Maryland's Less-Common Butterflies." In *Threatened and Endangered Plants and Animals of Maryland* Norden, A.W. et.al., eds. pp.273–280. Maryland Dept. of Natural Resources.

Ferguson, D.C. 1955. "The Lepidoptera of Nova Scotia. Part 1 Macrolepidoptera." Nova Scotia Museum of Science Bulletin No 1. 379 pp.

Genoways, H.H. and Brenner, F.J., eds. 1985. *Species of Special Concern in Pennsylvania.* Carnegie Museum of Natural History Special Publication No. 11.

Glassberg, J. 1993. *Butterflies through Binoculars: A Field Guide Butterflies in the Boston-New York-Washington Region.* New York Oxford University Press.

Glassberg, J. 1993. "Definitive Destination: Ward Pound Ridge Reservation, Westchester, NY." *American Butterflies,* Nov 13–18.

Gochfeld, M. and Burger, J. 1997. *Butterflies of New Jersey.* Rutgers University Press.

Grehan, J.R., et.al. 1995. *Moths and Butterflies of Vermont, a faunal check list.* Agr. Experiment Station, University of Vermont, Department of Forests, Parks and Recreation, State of Vermont Miscellaneous Publications 116.

Harris, L. 1972. *Butterflies of Georgia.* Norman: University of Oklahoma Press.

Heitzman, J.R. and Heitzman, J.E. 1987. *Butterflies and Moths Missouri.* Missouri Dept. of Conservation.

Holmes, A.M. et.al. 1991. *The Ontario Butterfly Atlas.* Toronto Entomologists' Association.

Howe, W.H. 1975. *The Butterflies of North America.* Doubleday.

Iftner, D.C., Shuey, J.A. and Calhoun, J.V. 1992. *The Butterflies Skippers of Ohio.* Columbus: The Ohio State University.

Irwin, R.R. and Downey, John C. 1973. *Annotated Checklist of the Butterflies of Illinois.* Illinois Natural History Survey Biological Notes No. 81.

Johnson, K. 1973. "The Butterflies of Nebraska." J. Res. Lepid. 11:1–64

Karges. J. 1994. *Checklist of Butterflies of Tarrant County.* Fort Worth: Texas. Privately printed.

Klassen, P., Westwood, A.R., Preston, W.B., and McKillop, W.B. 1989. *The Butterflies of Manitoba.* Winnipeg: Manitoba. Museum of Man and Nature:

Klots, A. 1951. *Field Guide to the Butterflies of North America, East of the Great Plains.* Houghton-Mifflin.

Lambremont, E.N. 1954. "The Butterflies and Skippers of Louisiana." *Tulane Studies in Zoology* 1:127–164.

Leahy, C., Walton, R. and Cassie, B. (in preparation). *Butterflies of Massachusetts.* Concord: Massachusetts Audubon Society.

LeGrand, Jr., H. (in preparation). *The Butterflies of North Carolina.*

Majka, C. 1972. A Checklist of New Brunswick Rhopalocera. Sackville, New Brunswick: Montana. Mt. Allison University.

Marrone, G.M. 1994. "Checklist of South Dakota Butterflies." J. Lep. Soc. 48: 228–247.

Mather, B. and Mather, K. 1958. "The Butterflies of Mississippi." Tulane Studies in Zoology.6: 63–109.

Minno, M.C. and Emmel, T.C. 1993. *Butterflies of the Florida Keys.* Gainesville: Scientific Publishers.

Minno, M.C. 1995. "Definitive Destination: Ocala National Forest, Florida." *American Butterflies* Winter: 4–11.

Morris, R.F. 1980. "Butterflies and Moths of Newfoundland and Labrador." Agriculture Canada, Research Branch Publication No. 1691. p. 407.

Mueller, S. 1994. *Butterfly Field Checklist for Michigan.* Lansing: Michigan Audubon Society.

NABA 1995. *Checklist and English Names for North American Butterflies.* Morristown, New Jersey: North American Butterfly Association.

Neck, R. 1996. *A Field Guide to Butterflies of Texas.* Houston: Gulf Publishing Co.

Nekola, J.C. 1995. *County Distribution Maps of Iowa Butterflies and Skippers*. Green Bay: Privately printed.

Nelson, John. 1979. "A Preliminary Checklist of the Skippers and Butterflies of Oklahoma." Proceedings of the Oklahoma Academy of Sciences 59:41–46.

New, T.R. *Butterfly Conservation*. 1991. New York: Oxford University Press.

Nielsen, M.C. 1992. "Preliminary Checklist of Michigan Butterflies and Skippers." Newsletter of the Michigan Entomological Society 37:5–7.

Nijhout, H.F. 1991. *The Development and Evolution of Butterfly Wing Patterns*. Washington D.C.: Smithsonian Institution Press.

Norton, B.G. 1987. *Why Preserve Natural Variety?* Princeton: Princeton University Press.

Opler, P.A. 1983. *County Atlas of Eastern United States Butterflies (1840–1982)*. Privately printed.

Opler, P.A. 1992. *A Field Guide to Eastern Butterflies*. New York: Houghton-Mifflin

Opler, P.A. and Krizek, G.O. 1984. *Butterflies East of the Great Plains*. Baltimore: Johns Hopkins University Press.

Pavulaan, H. 1985. "Field Survey of the True Butterflies (*Papilionoidea*) of Rhode Island." J. Lepid. Soc. 39:19–25.

Pavulaan, H. 1990. "The Skippers of Rhode Island with recent records of the True Butterflies." *Atala* 16: 6–13.

Pavulaan, H. 1996. *Virginia Butterfly Atlas*. (Preliminary copy) Privately printed.

Pyle, R.M. 1981. *The Audubon Society Field Guide to North American Butterflies*. New York: Knopf.

Pyle, R.M. 1992. *Handbook for Butterfly Watchers*. New York: Houghton Mifflin.

Richard, A. and Richard, H. 1993. *Butterflies of the Hill Country* (Photocopy) Riverside Nature Center Association.

Royer, R.A. 1988. *Butterflies of North Dakota*. Minot: Minot State University.

Scudder. S.H. 1889. *The Butterflies of the Eastern United States and Canada with Special Reference to New England*. Privately printed.

Sedman, Y. and Hess, D.F. 1985. *The Butterflies of West Central Illinois.* Western Illinois University Ser. Biol. Sci. No. 11.

Shapiro, A.M. 1966. *Butterflies of the Delaware Valley.* Special Publication of the American Entomological Society.

Shapiro, A.M. 1974. "Butterflies and skippers of New York State." *Search* 4:1–60.

Shuey, J. 1997. "Definitive Destination: Northwest Indiana's Lakeshore Communities." *American Butterflies* Spring: 4–13.

Shull, E.M. 1987. *The Butterflies of Indiana.* Indiana Academy of Science.

Smith, D.S., Miller, L.D., and Miller, J.Y. 1994. *The Butterflies of the West Indies and South Florida.* New York: Oxford University Press.

Smith, R.H. 1993. *The Butterflies of Howard County, Maryland: A Biological Summary and Checklist.* Howard Co. Chapter of the Maryland Ornithological Society

Stamp, N.E. and Casey, T.M., eds. 1993. *Caterpillars: Ecological and Evolutionary Constraints on Foraging.* New York: Chapman and Hall.

Stanford, R.E. and Opler, P.A. 1993. Atlas of Western USA Butterflies. Denver and Fort Collins, Colorado: Privately printed.

Swengel, A.B. 1991. *Checklist of the Butterflies of Southwestern Wisconsin.* Madison: Madison Audubon Society

Swengel, A.B. 1993. "Regal Fritillary: Prairie Royalty." *American Butterflies* Feb.: 4–9.

Swengel, A.B. 1994. "Skipping Over the Prairie: Dakota and Ottoe Skippers Fly Free." *American Butterflies* May: 4–9.

Swengel, A.B. 1995. *Checklist of the Butterflies of Northwestern Wisconsin.* Madison: Madison Audubon Society.

Tekulsky. M. 1985. *The Butterfly Garden.* Boston: The Harvard Common Press.

Thomas, A.W. 1996. *A Preliminary Atlas of the Butterflies of New Brunswick.* New Brunswick: New Brunswick Museum.

Tveten, J. and Tveten, G. 1996. *Butterflies of Houston.* Austin: University of Texas Press.

Tyler, H., Brown, K.S. Jr., and Wilson, K. 1994. *Swallowtail Butterflies of the Americas.* Gainesville, Florida: Scientific Publishers.

Williams, C.B. 1930. *The Migration of Butterflies*. Oliver and Boyd.

Williams, Stephen G. 1990. *The Butterflies and Skippers of Southeast Texas*. Houston: Privately printed.

Woodbury, E.N. Butterflies of Delmarva. 1994. Centreville, MD: Tidewater Publishers.

Xerces Society/Smithsonian Institution. 1990. Butterfly Gardening. Sierra Club Books.

Photographic Credits

EXCEPT FOR THE 37 PHOTOGRAPHS noted below, all photographs were taken by the author. I used a Minolta 7000i automatic-focusing camera equipped with a 100-mm macro lens and a 1200AF ring flash. Film was Kodachrome ASA 64. Other photo credits are the following.

Plate 1 Polydamas Swallowtail above, Ron Boender
Plate 2 Short-tailed Swallowtail above and below, Bernard Jackson
Plate 3 Bahamian Swallowtail below, James L. Nation, Jr.
Bahamian Swallowtail above, Thomas C. Emmel
Plate 14 Purplish Copper ♀ above, David H. Ahrenholz
Dorcas Copper ♀ *claytoni* above, Harry Zirlin
Purplish Copper ♂ above, David H. Ahrenholz
Plate 17 'Southern' Southern Hairstreak, Rick Cech
Plate 21 Disguised Scrub-Hairstreak, Joe Spano
Plate 22 Miami Blue, Harry N. Darrow
Plate 25 Northern Blue ♀ above, Robert Dana
Plate 27 Diana Fritillary ♀ below, Rick Cech
Diana Fritillary ♀ above, Charles V. Covell, Jr.
Plate 29 Freija Fritillary below, David H. Ahrenholz
Frigga Fritillary below, David H. Ahrenholz
Plate 33 Question Mark, orange form below, Don Riepe
Eastern Comma, orange form below, Peter W. Post
Eastern Comma, orange form above, Chris Adams
Plate 34 Hoary Comma below, Rich Kelly
Hoary Comma above, Harry Zirlin
Plate 35 Small Tortoiseshell above, Don Riepe
California Tortoiseshell above, Jack N. Levy

Index

Page numbers in **boldface** refer to color plates.

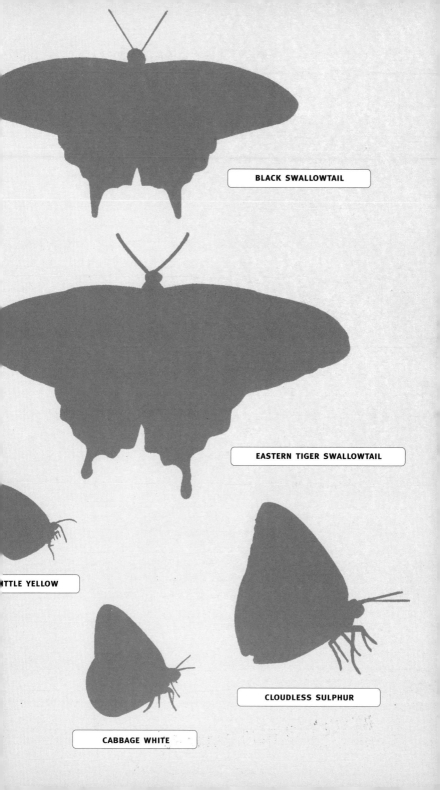

BLACK SWALLOWTAIL

EASTERN TIGER SWALLOWTAIL

NTTLE YELLOW

CLOUDLESS SULPHUR

CABBAGE WHITE

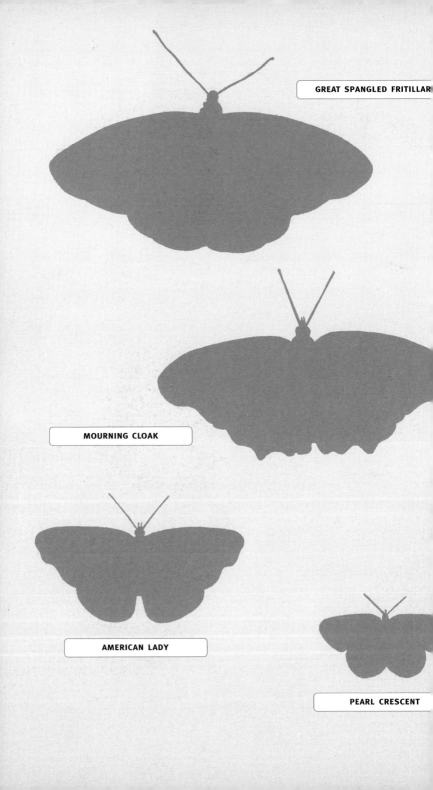

GREAT SPANGLED FRITILLARY

MOURNING CLOAK

AMERICAN LADY

PEARL CRESCENT